79

The UK Economy
A Manual of Applied Economics

The UK Economy
A Manual of
Applied Economics
Third Edition

Edited by
A. R. Prest M.A. Ph.D
Stanley Jevons Professor of Political Economy
and Cobden Lecturer, University of Manchester

Weidenfeld and Nicolson

5 Winsley Street London W1

First published 1966
Second impression 1967
Third impression 1968
Second edition 1968
Second impression 1969
Third edition 1970
Second impression 1971

PRINTED BY Unwin Brothers Limited
THE GRESHAM PRESS OLD WOKING SURREY ENGLAND

A member of the Staples Printing Group   (SO1894)

CONTRIBUTORS

Chapter 1

M. C. Kennedy, *B.Sc.(Econ.) (London)*
Lecturer in Economics, University of Manchester

Chapter 2

N. J. Gibson, *B.Sc.(Econ.), Ph.D.(Belfast)*
Professor of Economics, The New University of Ulster (formerly Senior Lecturer, University of Manchester)

Chapter 3

D. J. Coppock, *B.A.(Econ.) (Manchester)*
Professor of Economics, University of Manchester

Chapter 4

J. R. Cable, *B.A.(Nottingham) M.A.(Econ.) (Manchester)*
Lecturer in Economics, University of Warwick (formerly Lecturer, University of Manchester)

Chapter 5

I. Ll. Roberts, *M.A.(Liverpool)*
Lecturer in Economics, University of Manchester

Contents

TABLES

FIGURES

STATISTICAL APPENDIX

DECIMALISATION

Examples of equivalents between the old currency and the new one due to operate from February 1971 are as follows:

Old currency		New currency	
s d		*New Pence form*	*Decimal Form (£)*
6		2½p	0.02½
1 0		5p	0.05
2 0		10p	0.10
2 6		12½p	0.12½
5 0		25p	0.25
7 6		37½p	0.37½
10 0		50p	0.50
15 0		75p	0.75
19 6		97½p	0.97½
20 0		100p	1.00

Most, though not quite all, of the relevant figures in this edition are quoted in the new currency.

LIST OF ABBREVIATIONS

(1) Economic Terms

c.i.f.	Cost including Insurance and Freight
f.o.b.	Free on Board
GDP	Gross Domestic Product
GNP	Gross National Product
PAYE	Pay as you Earn
PDI	Personal Disposable Income
R and D	Research and Development
RPM	Resale Price Maintenance
SDRs	Special Drawing Rights
SIC	Standard Industrial Classification
SITC	Standard Industrial Trade Classification
TFE	Total Final Expenditure at market prices

(2) Organisations etc.

CBI	Confederation of British Industry
CIM	Commission on Industry and Manpower
CIR	Commission on Industrial Relations
CSO	Central Statistical Office (UK)
DEP	Department of Employment and Productivity
ECE	Economic Commission for Europe
ECSC	European Coal and Steel Community
EEC	European Economic Community
EFTA	European Free Trade Area
FAO	Food and Agricultural Organisation
GATT	General Agreement on Tariffs and Trade
IBRD	International Bank for Reconstruction and Development
IFC	International Finance Corporation
IMF	International Monetary Fund
IRC	Industrial Reorganisation Corporation
MC	Monopolies Commission
MHLG	Ministry of Housing and Local Government
NEDC	National Economic Development Council
NBPI	National Board for Prices and Incomes
NRDC	National Research Development Corporation
OECD	Organisation for Economic Co-operation and Development
SIB	Shipbuilding Industry Board
TUC	Trades Union Congress
UN	United Nations
UNCTAD	United Nations Commission for Trade and Development

(3) Journals etc.

AAS	*Annual Abstract of Statistics* (HMSO)
AER	*American Economic Review*
BEQB	*Bank of England Quarterly Bulletin*
BJIR	*British Journal of Industrial Relations*
BTJ	*Board of Trade Journal* (HMSO)

EJ	*Economic Journal*
EPG	*Employment and Productivity Gazette (HMSO)*
ET	*Economic Trends* (HMSO)
FES	*Ministry of Labour, Family Expenditure Survey* (HMSO)
FS	*Financial Statistics* (HMSO)
IFS	*International Financial Statistics*
ILRR	*Industrial and Labour Relations Review*
IR	*Industrial Relations*
JIE	*Journal of Industrial Economics*
JRSS	*Journal of Royal Statistical Society*
LBR	*Lloyds Bank Review*
LCEB	*London and Cambridge Economic Bulletin*
MDS	*Monthly Digest of Statistics* (HMSO)
MS	*The Manchester School of Economic and Social Studies*
NIBB	*National Income Blue Book* (HMSO)
NIER	*National Institute Economic Review*
PE	*Preliminary Estimates of National Income (HMSO)*
ROT	*Report on Overseas Trade* (HMSO)
SIPEP	*Statistics on Incomes, Prices, Employment and Production* (HMSO)
TBR	*Three Banks Review*
TER	*Treasury Economic Report* (HMSO)

Foreword to the Third Edition

The foreword to the first edition of this book, published in 1966, began as follows:

'The central idea behind this book is to give an account of the main features and problems
of the UK economy today. The hope is that it will fulfil two functions simultaneously,
in that it will be as up to date as possible and yet will not be simply a bare catalogue of
facts and figures. There are many sources of information, official and otherwise, about
the structure and progress of the UK economy. There are also many authors to whom
one can turn for subtle analyses of the problems before us. Our effort here is based on
the belief that there is both room and need for an attempt to combine the functions of
chronicler and analyst in the confines of a single book.

The contributors to these pages subscribe rather firmly to the belief that economists
should practise, as well as preach, the principle of the division of labour. The complexity of a modern economy is such that, whether one likes it or not, it is no longer possible for any single individual to be authoritative on all its aspects; so it is inevitable that
the burden of producing a work of this kind should be spread among a number of
people, each specialist in his or her particular field. Such a division carries with it the
obvious dangers of overlap and inconsistency. It is hoped that some of the worst pitfalls
of this kind have been avoided and there is a reasonable unity of purpose, treatment
and layout. At the same time, it was wholly undesirable to impose a monolithic structure and it is just as apparent to the authors that there are differences in outlook and
emphasis among them as it will be to the readers.

The general intention was to base exposition on the assumption that the reader
would have some elementary knowledge of economics—say, a student in the latter part
of a typical first year course in economics in a British University. At the same time, it
is hoped that most of the text will be intelligible to those without this degree of exper-
tise. We may not have succeeded in this; if not, we shall try to do better in future.'

We still regard this as an accurate description of our intentions. On this occasion, there
has again been a good deal of re-writing as well as updating of material, with the consequence that the 1970 edition differs quite a lot from those of 1966 and 1968.

Chapter 1, 'The Economy as a Whole', is primarily concerned with recent movements
of total output and total demand in the economy. A good deal of time is spent on the
short term movements in demand and output of the last few years and the measures for
dealing with them. Various problems of inflation and growth are also discussed. The chapter ends with a short section on the economic prospects in the near future. Chapter 2,
'Monetary, Credit and Fiscal Policies', starts with a brief discussion of the general theoretical background and then analyses in detail the theory and practices of monetary,
credit and fiscal policies in the UK in recent years. The final section discusses the various
trends in policy over the period. Chapter 3, 'Foreign Trade and the Balance of Payments',
deals with the importance of foreign trade and payments to the UK economy, concepts
of equilibrium in the balance of payments, an assessment of recent performance trends
in visible and invisible trade and problems of policy in the context of devaluation and international monetary developments. Chapter 4, 'Industry and Commerce', gives a brief
summary of various theories of firms' behaviour and then outlines the size structure of
industries and trades and recent trends in output growth. The public enterprise sector is
discussed at some length, together with government policy on monopolies and restrictive
practices, regions and agriculture. There is also a section on the forces determining industrial efficiency. We suffered a very severe blow from the death in 1969 of Dr Shirley
Lerner, the original author of Chapter 5, 'Social and Labour Problems'. However, we were
fortunate in being able to persuade Mr Ivor Roberts to bring it up to date. Various char-

acteristics of the UK population and labour force are outlined; this is followed by a discussion of collective bargaining, taking account of the recent spate of literature on that
subject; the last two sections are entitled 'Wealth and Poverty' and 'Housing'.

Each chapter is accompanied by a list of references and further reading. The Statistical
Appendix has twelve tables dealing with different aspects of the UK Economy. There is
an index as well as the detailed list of headings and sub-headings given in the Contents
pages. We also include a note on Decimalisation.

We acknowledge the great help given to us by Mr W. J. Tyson in preparing the
Statistical Appendix. We are also heavily indebted to the secretarial and computing staff
of the Faculty of Economics, and last, but not least, to those who have sent us comments
on our previous efforts.

A. R. PREST

University of Manchester
April 1970

Addendum

The body of the text was completed well before the outcome of the General Election of
18 June 1970 and so it has not been possible to take account of this except in various
footnotes.

July 1970   A. R. PREST

1

The economy as a whole

I INTRODUCTION

I.1 Methodological Approach

This chapter is intended as an introduction to applied macroeconomics. It provides a very brief description of the national accounts and then goes on to discuss the multiplier, the determination of aggregate demand and output in the short run, short-term employment policy, inflation and economic growth. It does not claim to provide all the answers to the problems it raises but aims, rather, to propose some tentative ideas which will provide the reader with a basis for further and deeper study.

In approaching applied economics it is a useful thing to bear in mind the general methodology of scientific enquiry, a methodology which applies in economics as well as in any other branch of study concerned with questions of causation. 'Economic Theory' in the sense of what is to be found in many elementary and advanced textbooks, is overtly logical or mathematical. Assumptions are made and inferences are drawn from them. The reader who has not progressed much beyond a textbook of theory may be tempted to expect the wrong kind of thing when he encounters applied work. He may, on the one hand, hope to find that it is essentially descriptive in nature, providing him with all the facts which are missing from what he has already studied. He may, on the other hand, expect applied economics to be what its name misleadingly implies—a direct application of economic theory in which all the facts of the economic universe are fitted neatly into the theoretical framework which he has already learned.

Neither interpretation of applied economics is correct. The view that it is essentially a descriptive procedure stems from an outmoded view of scientific enquiry[1] under which it was maintained that scientific laws were arrived at by a process (which happens to be logically invalid) of induction or generalisation from observed facts. This interpretation of scientific activity encourages the erroneous view that the collection and classification of data is all that matters and all that scientists do. It neglects that such activity, in so far as it is practised, is invariably preceded by an interest in some particular problem and by some, or perhaps several, ideas of how it may be solved. The data are needed not to provide generalisations but as tests of the hypothesis or hypotheses from which the scientist began. Seen in this way the collection of data has a very real and interesting point. Seen in the other way it is little more than a method of preparing a rather dull sort of encyclopedia. One suspects that an encyclopedia of economic observations would be more boring than most.

The other misconception of applied economics is not only wrong but positively danger-ous. If one is to start out with the view that the world behaves precisely like some text-book theory, the danger is that any experience which tends to contradict this view will be concealed from view or perhaps written off as an erroneous piece of observation. This can

---

[1] For a highly readable account of the issues of scientific method the reader is referred to P. B. Medawar, *Induction and Intuition in Scientific Thought,* Methuen, 1969. K. R. Popper, *The Poverty of Historicism,* 1961, and *Conjectures and Refutations,* 1963, Routledge, and Kegan Paul, are essential to the serious student. The distinction between 'normative' and 'positive' is set out in M. Friedman, *Essays in Positive Economics,* University of Chicago Press, 1953.

only encourage the development of an extremely rigid and unbending dogma. If economics were to be pursued in this way it would be in danger of becoming a creed, and would cease to be a developing subject.

A more acceptable interpretation of method in applied economics is that it is an attempt to answer problems of causation by the process of advancing hypotheses and confronting them with observations which are used to test them. The hypotheses may be sought in textbooks of economic theory, or they may come intuitively, or by luck. They will develop as the confrontation process goes on, changing form and covering more facts. The object throughout is to develop hypotheses that are true for all time and all places. The actuality is hypotheses of a limited but increasing applicability.

It is probably an oversimplification to regard the role of factual evidence as one of deciding, once and forever, whether a hypothesis is rejected or corroborated. Strictly speaking a fact which is not consistent with the logical implications (predictions) of a particular hypothesis does indicate that the hypothesis is faulty. But a faulty hypothesis can be anything from one which is plain wrong and worthy of no further consideration to one which is incomplete and lacking in sufficient generality. In the latter case the addition of some new variable to the hypothesis may modify it so as to cover the exceptions to the rule. This is an important point to remember because in reality we find ourselves working with hypotheses which do not fit all the facts and which (a) clearly need modification and (b) may even be utterly misconceived. In these circumstances it seems necessary to recall again the tentative nature of all economics and to proceed extremely critically.

The property possessed by hypotheses of being testable through their factual implications also earns them the right to be called 'positive'. 'Positive' here is meant not in the usual dictionary sense of being unquestionably correct, but in the philosophical sense of being independent of value judgments. One may have explanations of a phenomenon, and inflation is a good example here, which one may regret because they pose awkward social dilemmas. But if they are reasonably well tested by the evidence they become part of the 'reality' which one has to live with. It is still a hypothetical reality, but it forms the basis of one's thinking about the means of economic policy.

It is a little misleading to regard the discussion of economic policy, which also comes into this chapter, as a wholly normative (i.e. non-positive) subject. Its normative content consists in the evaluation of policy goals and priorities, but the means for attaining such goals derive from the positive hypotheses of economics. They involve questions of cause and effect, the hypothetical answers to which are appraisable by reference to evidence. In making recommendations for the achievement of policy goals, however, the economist treads on rather thin ice. This is partly because his positive knowledge is not inevitably correct but also because it is seldom possible for him to foresee all the side-effects of his recommendations, and these may themselves have implications for other policy goals. Try as he may to make himself aware of all the politicians' ethical preconceptions he can never be sure of knowing them all. The role of the economic adviser is a delicate one, and it is not helped by the fact that he is a mortal being with policy preconceptions of his own.

The reader of this chapter, therefore, is invited to take it with a pinch of salt. He must remain critical of the hypotheses that are suggested and be on his guard against the author's personal predilections.

I.2   Gross domestic product

Most of the topics discussed in this chapter require some knowledge of the national accounts statistics. A full explanation of what these are and of how they are put together would take up more space than can be afforded and is, in any case, available elsewhere.[1]

---

[1]   See, for example, R. and G. Stone, *National Income and Expenditure*, Bowes and Bowes, 1964; H. C. Edey and A. T. Peacock, *National Income and Social Accounting* (2nd edn), Hutchinson, 1959; or the official handbook, *National Accounts Statistics, Sources and Methods*, HMSO, 1968.

It may be useful, however, in the next few pages to remind the reader of the main national accounting categories in so far as they affect this chapter.

The most important concept of all is gross domestic product, or GDP for short. This is the total output of the whole economy. Its significance can be most easily visualised by imagining that the economy is like some simple productive enterprise, such as a farm. Suppose that such a farm produces only wheat, the amount being 100 bushels a year and the price being £1, then the value of toal production will be £100. This is also the sum which is divided between the various factors of production, since what is not paid in rent to the landowners or in wages to the labour force will be allocated to the farmer's own profit. Thus total output is equal to total incomes. Furthermore, total output will also be equal to total expenditure on the output. For any output that is not sold for immediate consumption will be left over as an addition to stocks, and, as such, will be regarded as investment. Thus the income, output and expenditure of the farm may be counted in such a way as to make them all identically equal to each other. The same is true of total domestic output, or GDP.

The gross domestic product of the UK, by analogy with the simple production unit, can also be added up in three different ways: from the sides of income, output and expenditure. The first of these, total income, measures the sum of all the incomes of the residents of the UK earned in the production of goods and services in the UK during a stated period. It divides into income from employment, income from self-employment and profit, and income from rent. These are factor incomes earned in the process of production, and are to be distinguished from transfer incomes, such as pensions and sickness benefits, which are not earned from production and which, therefore, are excluded from the total. The breakdown of factor incomes is illustrated for 1968 in table 1.1 (page 5).

As with the simple production unit the value of output accruing in the form of unsold stocks is included in total factor output. But a problem arises when the prices at which stocks are valued in the national accounts vary during the course of the accounting period. When this happens the value of stocks held at the beginning and end of the period will have been reported at two different prices, and it is then necessary to make a special valuation adjustment known as the 'adjustment for stock appreciation'. A firm holding stocks of lead, for example, may increase its holding from 100 tons on 1 January to 200 tons on 31 December. If the price of lead was £1.0 a ton at the beginning of the year and £1.1 at the end of the year the increase in the monetary value of stocks will show up as (£1.1 × 200)−(£1.0 × 100), which equals £120. This figure is inflated by the amount of the price increase and fails, therefore, to give an adequate record of what the CSO calls 'the value of the physical increase in stocks'. In order to rectify this the CSO tries to value physical changes in stocks by the average price level prevailing during the period. If, in the example, the price averaged £1.05 over the period then the amount of stock investment would be shown as £1.05 (200-100) which equals £105. The difference of £15 between this and the previous total is known as the 'adjustment for stock appreciation'. It must be deducted from the total reported value of factor incomes in order to reach an estimate of gross domestic income.

Gross domestic product is measured from the production side by adding up the value of production of the various firms and public enterprises in the country. This procedure presents two types of problem. First, the goods and services produced by one firm may also form part of the output of some other firm. Wheat produced on a farm, for example, is entered as farm output but it may also be used by a bakery to produce bread in which case it will be entered as bread output as well. Thus the addition of the farm's output to that of the bakery will result in some double-counting. This means that a distinction must be drawn in the production accounts between output sold to final buyers as total final output and intermediate output sold to other productive units. Intermediate output must be excluded before arriving at a firm's contribution to gross domestic product. Secondly, imports are not domestic output at all but are produced by foreign enterprises.

Their value, therefore, must be subtracted from the value of total final ouput in order to derive UK domestic output. In table 1.1 the various categories of output are all measured net of intermediate output and of the import content of final output.

Gross domestic product (GDP) can also be measured from the side of expenditure. Conceptually this total is identical to the income and output total; but in practice the statistics are collected from independent sources and do not lead to exactly the same figure. The difference between the two estimates is called the residual error and is sometimes quite large. In 1968 it was 0.4 per cent of GDP, which is also about the average for the last ten years. In some years, however, the residual error has been as high as 1.0 per cent of GDP, and in the quarterly estimates of GDP the residual error is often quite a lot larger. The fact that different estimates of GDP can diverge by fairly large amounts often makes it difficult to arrive at a clear assessment of the economic situation.

The breakdown of the expenditure total is especially important in the analysis of aggregate demand. Expenditures are undertaken by four types of spending unit: households, public authorities, firms and foreign residents. Purchases by households are described as consumers' expenditure, or, more loosely, as consumption. The latter description, however, may be slightly misleading when applied to expenditure on durable goods such as motorcars and refrigerators, the services of which are consumed over several years and not solely in the year in which they are purchased. We shall see later that the forces determining durable goods expenditure sales are not quite the same as those determining nondurable consumption. One form of personal expenditure, however, which is not classed as such, is the purchase of new houses. These are deemed to have been sold initially to 'firms' and included under the broad heading of domestic capital formation or gross investment. Fixed investment, other than housing, represents the purchases by firms of physical assets that are not completely used up in current production but which accrue as additions to the nation's capital stock. The preface 'gross', however, warns us that a year's gross investment does not measure the change in the size of the capital stock during the year because it does not allow for withdrawals from the capital stock due to wear and tear, or scrapping. The gross concept of capital formation is also carried through into the definition of domestic product itself. Net domestic product would include additions to the capital stock net of capital consumption.

The sum of exports, consumers' expenditure, government current consumption and gross investment is known as total final expenditure at market prices, or TFE for short. Each of the four components contains two elements which must be subtracted before arriving at GDP at factor cost. The first of these elements is the import content of the expenditure which must, of course, be classified as foreign rather than domestically produced output. The simplest way of dealing with imports is to take the import total as given by the balance of payments accounts and subtract it from TFE, and this is the usual method. Estimates do exist, however, for the import content of the separate components of final expenditure in the input-output tables,[1] but they are drawn up much less frequently than the national accounts. The second element of total final expenditure which must be excluded from GDP at factor cost is the indirect tax content (net of subsidies) of the various expenditures. This is present for the simple reason that the most readily available value for any commodity is the price at which it sells in the market. This price, however, will overstate the factor incomes earned from producing the commodity if it contains an element of purchase tax or other indirect tax; and it will understate factor income if the price is subsidised. Thus the sum of indirect taxes, net of subsidies, must be deducted from the market price total in order to arrive at GDP at factor cost. This deduction, which is known as the factor cost adjustment, is most conveniently made globally since it can be found from the government's records of tax proceeds and subsidy

---

[1] 'Provisional Summary Input-Output Tables for 1963', *ET*, August 1964, HMSO, table 8.

TABLE 1.1

Gross Domestic Product and Gross National Product at current prices, UK, 1968

FROM INCOME

	£ million	Per cent of domestic income
Income from employment	25,267	68.2
Income from self-employment	2,840	7.7
Income from rent	2,359	6.4
Gross trading profits of companies	5,117	13.8
Gross trading surplus of public corporations and other public enterprises	1,463	3.9
Total domestic income	37,046	100.0
less Stock appreciation	−650	
Residual error	−129	
Gross domestic product at factor cost	36,267	

FROM OUTPUT

	£ million	Per cent of domestic output
Agriculture, forestry & fishing	1,127	3.0
Mining and quarrying	687	1.9
Manufacturing	12,527	33.8
Construction	2,456	6.6
Services & distribution	20,249	54.7
Total domestic income	37,046	100.0
less Stock appreciation	−650	
Residual error	−129	
Gross domestic product at factor cost	36,267	

FROM EXPENDITURE

	£ million	Per cent of TFE
Consumers' expenditure	27,065	52.7
Public authorities' current expenditure	7,702	15.0
Gross fixed investment in dwellings	1,585	3.1
Gross fixed investment other than dwellings	6,213	12.1
Investment in stocks	204	0.4
Exports of goods and services	8,610	16.8
Total final expenditure at market prices	51,379	100.0
less Imports of goods & services	−9,038	
less Taxes on expenditure	−6,960	
plus Subsidies	886	
Gross domestic product at factor cost	36,267	
Net property income from abroad	419	
Gross national product at factor cost	36,686	

Source: NIBB, 1969, tables 1, 10 and 12. *ET,* October 1969.

payments. But estimates of its incidence on the components of TFE are available annually in the National Income *Blue Book.*[1]

Gross domestic product from the expenditure side is thus reached by adding up the components of TFE at market prices, and by subtracting imports of goods and services together with the factor cost adjustment. GDP is the concept of total output which we shall use throughout most of this chapter and it relates to the total production in the UK of the residents of the United Kingdom. It differs from the other aggregate concept, gross national product (GNP), in that it does not include interest, profits and dividends earned by UK residents from productive activity that is carried out overseas, and it does not exclude the profits of foreign-owned enterprises producing in the UK. The balance of these two amounts is known as net property income from abroad and must be added to GDP in order to obtain GNP. It is fairly small and does not fluctuate much from one year to another.

Gross domestic product at constant prices: Table 1.1 summarises the national accounts for 1968 at the prices obtaining in 1968. As such it is a useful source of information as to the way in which domestic income was divided in a particular year. If, however, we want to know something about how the volume of goods produced has varied from one year to another we must use a different set of figures. These are the estimates of GDP in constant prices, and they are presented in the Statistical Appendix, table A-2. They show the value of GDP for each year since 1950 in terms of the prices ruling in 1963, and are computed by the CSO for both the production and expenditure sides of GDP. They are derived almost entirely from movements in quantities, and the various quantities for each year are added together by means of the value weights obtaining for 1963. The result is three conceptually equal estimates of real domestic output but, as with the current price series, there is often a large residual error between them. For convenience we shall adhere in this chapter to the expenditure estimate.[2]

Gross domestic product is an important entity in its own right and changes in its real amount are the best estimates available of changes in UK production. Even so, it must be remembered that it leaves a good deal out of the picture by excluding practically all productive work which is not sold for money. The national income statistician neglects, for example, the activities of the housewife and the amateur gardener even though together they must add many millions of hours to the UK production of goods and services. It is also important to recognise that GDP does not stand for the total expenditure of UK residents. It is the total expenditure of all persons, resident or foreign, on the goods and services produced by the residents of the UK. This means that GDP cannot be interpreted as a measure of national welfare, with welfare equated to total spending. The total that is more appropriate for this purpose is GDP *plus* imports *minus* exports. This is sometimes called 'domestic absorption' and is equal to the UK's total use of resources, which is the sum of consumption, government expenditure and gross investment. It is a total which can diminish quite substantially when there is a sharp improvement in the balance of payments, such as might be expected from a devaluation of the exchange rate. But again, this estimate of the total use of resources will not include the enjoyment of unsold goods and services, such as the benefits received from housework and leisure.

1.3   National Accounts and the Multiplier Hypothesis

As an illustration of the way in which the national accounts can be useful in suggesting answers to questions of macroeconomic importance we may begin by asking what is the likely value of the multiplier in the UK economy. Here it is necessary to make a number

---

[1]   *NIBB*, 1969, table 12.

[2]   With the exception of the series graphed in figure 1.7 below.

of quantitative assumptions about the way in which domestic output is divided among income recipients, and the extent to which the income is saved, taxed or spent on new domestic output. The problem of making these assumptions is, as will become apparent, made very much easier by the existence of a well organised system of national income statistics.

At the outset it may be supposed that total final expenditure at market prices (TFE) rises by enough to raise GDP by £100 million. The increase in TFE needed for this result will depend upon its domestic output content. In the cases of fixed investment expenditure and exports of goods and services the increase in the market price amount would have to be of the order of £125 million since imports and indirect taxes are, together, likely to absorb about one-fifth of the expenditure increase.[1] Investment in stocks is thought to have a very large import content and might have to rise by as much as £200 million to secure an increase in GDP of £100 million (see section II.4 of this chapter). Public authorities expenditure, on the other hand, has a high domestic output content and would probably have to rise by only about £115 million in order to secure the assumed rise in GDP.

It must now be asked how the additional £100 million of domestic output and income is going to be distributed between income recipients. At this point one may consult the *Blue Book*[2] and its counterpart in table 1.1. It may be assumed that none of the new income is income from rent. Thus the £100 million will be divided between income from employment and self-employment, the trading surpluses of public enterprises, and company profits. From the *Blue Book* it may be seen that these three classes of income have remained in very close relationship to each other, and in particular that income from employment and self-employment has amounted to some 82 per cent of total domestic income excluding rent. Thus it may be assumed that £82 million out of the original £100 million enters directly into personal income (see figure 1.1). The remaining £18 million is of little importance since it is not likely to re-enter the income flow for a considerable period of time. Some of it, about £5 million, is likely to increase the trading surpluses of public enterprises. The other £13 million will constitute an addition to company profits, where it will be taxed, saved or distributed to persons as dividends. The dividends, which are not likely to amount to more than £3 million, will eventually re-enter the income flow but as their amount is so small and the time lag in the paying them rather long they can be neglected for the purpose of estimating the multiplier value. Similarly, the addition to business savings (i.e. undistributed profits) may eventually be spent upon investment goods, but here the lag between receipts and expenditures is likely to be even longer than in the case of dividends. Thus the only immediate increase in personal income is income from employment and self-employment.

The next step is to estimate how much of the additional £82 million will remain after the deduction of income tax and other income-related transfers. This sort of question is not easily answered without expert knowledge. An indication may be sought by examining year-to-year movements in disposable personal income and total personal income, and if this is done for the period 1964-8 the ratio of one to the other can be found to be about 70 per cent. Almost exactly the same result is obtained if it is assumed that the average income recipient pays the standard rate of income tax, which at 41.25 per cent of each £ (8/3d), less the earned income allowance of two-ninths, works out at 32 per cent. A leakage of this order between personal income and disposable income will imply a rise in the latter of £56 million.

At this stage it is necessary to make an assumption about the value of the marginal propensity to consume, i.e. the ratio of an increase in consumers' expenditure to an

---

[1] See table 8 of 'Provisional Summary Input-Output Tables for 1963', *ibid.*, and table 1.4 below.
[2] NIBB, 1969, table 1. The reader may find that it helps to read this section with the *Blue Book* alongside.

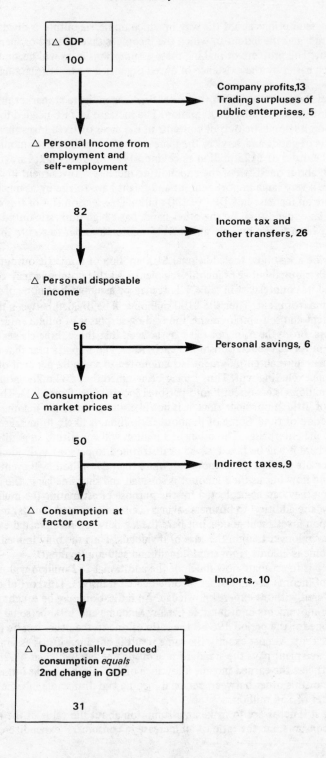

Figure 1.1   The Multiplier Round

increase in disposable income. As is shown in the next section of this chapter this ratio
has fluctuated quite a lot in recent years so that to assume that it takes its average value
of nine-tenths may be a somewhat hazardous procedure. Nevertheless, some such assumption must be made even though it is tentative. It means that an increase in disposable income of £56 million will be followed by a rise in consumption at market prices of £50
million, the difference between these two amounts being the increase in personal savings.

Two further leakages must now be considered. The first is the indirect tax content of
the new consumption, which the most recent *Blue Book* estimate puts at 18 per cent.
This means that consumption at factor cost rises by £41 million. The other leakage is the
import content of this amount, which comes to about 19 per cent of the market price
value, i.e. about £10 million. When this is subtracted from the previous total the rise in
what may be called domestically-produced consumption at factor cost is found to be
£31 million. Since this is all domestic output it constitutes an addition to GDP.

The conclusion is that an increase in GDP of £100 million is likely to generate a second
increase of about £31 million. The conclusion follows from a series of assumptions, some
of them more tentative than others, which have been made with the help of the national
accounts.

It is now only a short step from this conclusion to an estimate of the value of the multiplier. At the end of the first round of the income flow, GDP is higher than its original
level by its initial increase of £100 million, plus a secondary increase of £31 million. The
secondary increase is 31 per cent of the initial increase, and if we make the defen-
sible assumptions that the marginal propensities to divide domestic income, to consume,
pay taxes, etc. all remain unchanged during the multiplier process, then the secondary increase in GDP must lead in turn to a tertiary rise of 31 per cent of £31 million. Each successive rise in GDP leads to a new rise 31 per cent as large as the previous one so that the
full increase in GDP is given as the initial injection plus the sum of all round-to-round increases. This amount is represented by the following series:

i.e.   £100 $[1 + 0.31 + (0.31)^2 + (0.31)^3 \ldots \ldots + (0.31)^n]$ million, or approximately, as:

£100 + 31 + 9.6 + 2.8 + 0.9 + 0.3 + 0.1 = £145 million.

The successive spending of incomes, therefore, is likely to raise an initial increase in GDP
of £100 million into an eventual increase of about £145 million, so that the multiplier on
these calculations is 1.45. It should be appreciated that this is a hypothetical figure which
rests entirely on the assumptions that have been made. Of these, the marginal propensity
to consume is probably the least reliable. If this assumption is changed from 0.9 to 0.7,
and this latter figure is well within the range of possibilities, then the value of the multiplier will change too. The extent of the change, however, is not enormous. The reader
may like to check for himself that the value of the multiplier then becomes 1.32, which
is not so far off the value of 1.45 which has been taken as the more plausible figure. Thus
the multiplier value which has been derived above does not seem to be seriously sensitive
to changes in the assumptions upon which it is based.

One matter which has not been mentioned so far is the question of how the effects
of the multiplier will be felt over time. We have seen, however, that it represents the sum
of a series of increments in GDP, each increment following its predecessor after a time-
lag. The length of the time-lag is given by the time it takes between a receipt of personal
income and the spending of part of the proceeds. There is no simple way of determining
this lag but most of the work that has been done suggests, not implausibly, that it could
be in the region of three months. This means that an increment of GDP of £100 in the
first quarter of a year will generate an increase from the initial level of £131 in the second
quarter, £141 in the third and £143 by the last quarter. (It is assumed that the initial £100
of new GDP is sustained.) Thus the consequence of a time lag of only three months is that
the multiplier will almost completely work itself out within the course of a year.

Finally, it may be noted that this rather complicated multiplier hypothesis bears a completely analogous relationship to the simpler textbook case where national income (Y) is divided into consumption and investment (I) and the multiplier is expressed as the reciprocal of the marginal propensity to save, i.e.

$$\frac{\Delta Y}{\Delta I} = \frac{1}{1\text{-marginal propensity to consume}} = \frac{1}{\text{marginal propensity to save}}.$$

In the more complex case there are a number of other leakages in the system besides personal savings so that neither of the expressions above is adequate. Furthermore, the existence of the indirect tax and import contents of investment means that it is no longer possible to look upon a rise in investment expenditure as being equivalent to so much domestic output. Thus the equivalent expressions in the more complex case we have discussed are:

$$\frac{\Delta Y \text{ (final)}}{\Delta Y \text{ (initial)}} = \frac{1}{1 - \text{marginal propensity to} \atop \text{re-spend domestic output}} = \frac{1}{\text{marginal propensity to leak}}$$

$$= \frac{1}{1 - \dfrac{82}{100} \cdot \dfrac{56}{82} \cdot \dfrac{50}{56} \cdot \dfrac{41}{50} \cdot \dfrac{31}{41}} = \frac{1}{1 - 0.31} = 1.45$$

Here the simple marginal propensity to consume has been replaced by a more general coefficient which may be named 'the marginal propensity to re-spend upon domestic output'. This more general coefficient is 0.31, and it is determined as the multiple of the five coefficients representing the stages of the income flow (shown as proportions in the expression above). Similarly, the marginal propensity to save of the textbook becomes, in the more complex case, a 'marginal propensity to leak', i.e. a marginal propensity for output not to be re-spent upon itself. But in spite of these differences from the simpler case the basic principle of the multiplier, as a process generated by the successive spending of income, remains unchanged. And, as is always the case, the assumption must be made that the rise in domestic output is not restrained by shortages of capacity.

II   THE COMPONENTS OF AGGREGATE DEMAND

It is now widely accepted, within the limits set by full employment of productive resources, that the level of domestic output in the short run is determined along Keynesian lines by the level of aggregate demand. The relevant demand total is the sum of all demands for domestic output whether from consumers, business, the public authorities or foreigners. This total is an *ex ante* concept. It represents desired spending on all goods and services produced by the domestic economy and, as such, is only equal to actual spending, or GDP *ex post*, in a state of full demand equilibrium. This means that it may not always be correct to use recorded GDP as an estimate of aggregate demand because total demand and total expenditure may not be in equilibrium with each other. This difficulty, however, is generally ignored in practice since GDP is the only available approximation to total demand. Similarly, the components of GDP, such as consumers' expenditure and investment, are generally taken as indicating their own respective demand levels. In making such approximations, however, it is advisable to bear in mind the possibility that in periods of very intense use of resources the demand for some classes of commodity may well be in excess of actual expenditure. When this is the case one must hope that some independent statistics, such as large unfilled orders, will prevent misunderstanding.

Aggregate demand may now be divided into the main expenditure categories, and each discussed separately.

II.1 Consumers' Expenditure

Consumers' expenditure is the largest single element in aggregate demand. It accounts for half of TFE (see table 1.1) and, after the removal of its import and indirect tax content, for about the same proportion of GDP at factor cost.[1] It is generally regarded as one of the more stable elements in total demand and this is true in the sense that fluctuations in consumption are small when measured as percentages of its own total. The total itself, however, is so large in relation to GDP that even fairly small percentage variations can have important repercussions for output and employment. An understanding of consumption behaviour, therefore, as well as an ability to predict it, are important objectives for economic analysis. A great deal of attention has, in fact, been given to consumption, both in theory and statistically, although this work has been more heavily concentrated upon consumption in the US where the relevant statistical data is available for a longer period than in the UK.

The starting point for most studies of consumer behaviour is the well known hypothesis of Lord Keynes, whereby the level of spending is taken to be largely determined by the level of current personal income after tax. 'The fundamental psychological law', wrote Keynes,[2] 'upon which we are entitled to depend with great confidence both *a priori* from our knowledge of human nature and from the detailed facts of experience, is that men are disposed, as a rule and on the average, to increase their consumption as their income increases, but not by as much as the increase in their income.' Keynes believed that the marginal propensity to consume (i.e. the ratio of additional consumption to additional income) was positive, fractional, and reasonably stable over the short run. As it happens, two of these properties have not held true in practice. The marginal propensity to consume (MPC) has been fractional in most years, but in 1955 and again in 1958 it exceeded unity and in 1967 it was 1.0 exactly (see figure 1.2). As for stability, the value of the MPC has ranged quite widely with a maximum for the period 1955-69 of 1.22 and a minimum of 0.62. Its average value over the whole period was 0.90 (equalling the average propensity to consume), but its mean annual deviation from the average was 0.11. This latter figure implies that any attempt to predict consumption using the average value of the MPC would be prone to an average error equal to 11 per cent of the annual change in income. As the annual change in income was about £1,200 million the prediction error comes out at £130 million, i.e. 0.7 per cent of the total value of consumption. The conclusion is that any attempt to explain consumption solely in terms of a stable marginal propensity to consume out of current income is liable to a fairly appreciable degree of error.

Most of the theories of consumption since Keynes have emphasised the role of expected future income as well as current income, and Keynes himself was at pains to emphasise 'changes in expectations of the relation between the present and the future level of income'. One way of incorporating the distinction between expected income changes and actual changes is to postulate that the marginal propensity to consume will depart from its average value when the change in money income is sharply different from the average change in income. The hypothesis is that consumers expect income to increase each year by an amount which may be represented by the average change. When their expectations are fulfilled they consume a constant proportion of the rise in income,

---

[1] It is misleading, although not uncommon, to compare expenditures at market prices, inclusive of their import contents, with GDP at factor cost.

[2] J. M. Keynes, *The General Theory of Employment, Interest and Money*, Macmillan, 1936, p. 96.

but at other times they behave more cautiously. Thus when the actual change in income exceeds the average change the MPC will be small, and when it falls short of the average change the MPC will be large. Figure 1.2 presents some fairly strong evidence for this hypothesis although 1955 is an exception to what is otherwise a good correlation. One implication of this hypothesis is that a small decline in personal income would not necessarily be accompanied by a decline in consumption, in which case the marginal propensity to consume would be negative, thereby contradicting the last of the three properties mentioned above. But this implication cannot be put to the test as personal income in the UK has not declined on a year-to-year basis during the period when official figures have been compiled. In the United States, however, it has been found to be the case that small declines in income are not accompanied by declines in consumption.

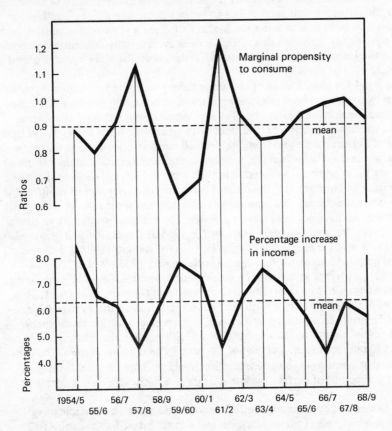

Figure 1.2   The Marginal Propensity to Consume and the Percentage Change in Personal Disposable Income, UK, 1955-69. (Note: each m.p.c. is measured as the ratio between the annual change in consumers' expenditure and personal disposable income, both at current prices.)

In focusing so exclusively upon the marginal propensity to consume there is a danger of losing sight of what seems to be a significant trend. This is the long-term decline in the average propensity to consume (APC) illustrated in figure 1.3. The essential features here are a very high propensity to consume (over 0.95) before 1955; followed by a period of six years of really sharp decline; followed in the period from 1962 to the present by a fairly steady APC in the region of 0.91 to 0.92.

The reasons behind this decline in the APC can probably be found in the high volume of savings accumulated during and for some time after the second world war and in the pent-up demand for durable and other goods which were rationed or in otherwise short supply at the same time. The timing of the really steep decline in the APC is, perhaps, a little later than those considerations may suggest, although it must be remembered that rationing was at its peak in 1948, three years after the end of the war, and that it was not totally eliminated until 1958 with the derationing of coal.[1] Nevertheless, this steep decline in the APC serves as a reminder that there are other factors besides income and income expectations in the explanation of aggregate consumption, notably accumulated wealth and unsatisfied demand. These factors are, perhaps, less important at times which are long removed from periods of major upheaval, but they should not be neglected altogether.

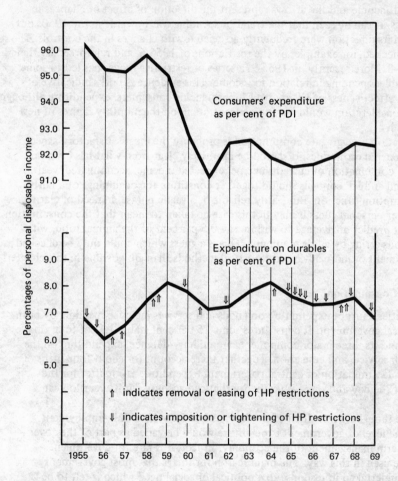

Figure 1.3   The Average Propensity to Consume and the Propensity to spend on Consumer Durables, UK, 1955-69, (total and durables as percentages of personal disposable income). (Note: arrows indicate direction of effect of HP restrictions.)

[1]   For further details, see J. C. R. Dow, *The Management of the British Economy 1945-1960*, Cambridge University Press, 1964, chapter VI.

Besides these factors, another important influence upon the course of consumers' expenditure is the availability of credit, and particularly the availability of credit for financing the purchase of durable goods.[1] The goods, which constitute 7-8 per cent of total consumption, are more of the nature of capital equipment than of consumption in that they yield a flow of income over time. It is natural where income is generally rising that such goods should be bought extensively on credit, and something like one-half of their total is financed by hire purchase. The availability of this form of finance is subject to government regulation in two main ways: by the stipulation of a minimum HP deposit, and by the specification of a maximum period of repayment. The regulations have been varied extensively in recent years, and their influence on durable goods expenditure may be gauged from figure 1.3. The lower graph of the figure charts durables' expenditure as a percentage of income and the arrows represent the direction of effect of changes in the HP controls. It can be seen that the trend of spending was upwards in the 1950s but that changes in its direction were frequently associated with changes in the controls. The uptrend was checked, for example, by the restrictions of 1955-6, and reinforced by their easing in 1957-8. More recently, in 1965-9, a series of restrictive moves has led to some decline in durables spending in relation to income. This evidence is fairly indicative of the short-term effectiveness of HP controls in influencing consumers' expenditure although any detailed consideration would have to concentrate upon the monthly figures of new credit extended.

The explanation of aggregate consumption is probably the most satisfactory aspect of aggregate demand economics. It should be intuitively clear from what has been said above that the combination of current income, expected income, accumulated wealth, pent-up demand and HP controls should together constitute the beginnings of a fairly reliable consumption function. But 'fairly reliable' is a vague phrase, in need of clarification. As a rather personal guess it may in this case be taken to mean that the consumption function might predict on average to within, say 0.5 per cent of the annual total, with some predictions erring by a larger amount. This is a guess which could only be checked by the employment of more advanced statistical methods than are possible in this chapter.

II.2   Public Consumption

Public authorities' current expenditure on goods and services includes spending by both central and local government. It constitutes some 15 per cent (table 1.1) of total final expenditure, and its three major components are military defence, expenditure on the national health service, and education. Together these account for about four-fifths of the total. The determination of central government expenditure is a matter for the government of the day and there is no theory that can account for its year-to-year variations.

It might be thought, in the light of the Keynesian approach to full employment policy, that the level of government expenditure would be varied as part of the government's short-term management of the economy. In fact, it is rare for government spending to be used in this way. The main reason for this is that most government activities are undertaken in response to a political or social need which is felt to be largely independent of the cyclical state of the economy. Expenditure on schools and health, for example, cannot be readily subjected to the whims of the business cycle. Another reason for not using government expenditure as a cyclical instrument is that the administrative machine is too sluggish to bring about rapid changes in its spending. Indeed there is some danger, when business cycles are short in duration, that anti-

---

[1]   It should be noted that the *Blue Book* definition of durable goods includes cars, motor cycles, furniture, carpets and electrical goods but, perhaps arbitrarily, does not include clothing, curtains, pots and pans, or books.

cyclical changes in government spending might be delayed so long as to be pro-
cyclical at the time that they become effective.

Occasions do arise, however, when substantial changes, generally cuts, are made in
government expenditure programmes. These tend to occur as results of longer-term
reassessments of the size of the public sector in relation to the whole economy. They
will occur, for example, if over-optimistic forecasts of the growth of GDP and therefore of government revenues, have misled ministers into believing that a certain level of
expenditure can be sustained without higher tax rates or unwanted inflationary pressure.
They will also occur if the government decides to put a higher priority than previously on
some aspect of private spending, such as exports or fixed investment. Some cuts in government expenditure announced in January 1968 were a case in point. The government's
programmes had been based on the overoptimistic GDP predictions of the 1965 National
Plan, and were clearly implying higher taxation or more inflation at lower and more
realistic levels of output. Moreover, the devaluation of the pound in November 1967
could not have been expected to work unless more resources were made available to the
industries producing exports and competing with imports. Thus, on both scores, it was
deemed necessary at the time to curtail government expenditure programmes over the
longer run.

II.3   Gross Fixed Investment

Fixed investment expenditure is a less homogeneous aggregate than is sometimes supposed.
Its division by sector and by type of asset purchased may be seen from table 1.2 (below).

TABLE 1.2

Gross fixed capital formation, UK, 1968.   (£ million at current prices.)

	Dwellings	Other building	Vehicles, ships, aircraft, plant and equipment	Total
Private sector	755	779	2,447	3,981
Public sector	830	1,659	1,328	3,817
Total	1,585	2,438	3,775	7,798

Source: *NIBB*, 1969, table 51

Investment in dwellings comprises something like one-fifth of gross fixed capital formation. Nearly half of it is undertaken by local authorities and is financed partly out of
local resources and partly from central government grants. The amount of public
authority house-building is determined largely by political and social considerations although there will be times when the public sector is competing with the private sector
for the capacity of the building industry as a whole. The amount of private house-
building depends on a number of factors, which include the size of the population and,
more particularly, the number of marriages and births. Most new houses are bought on
mortgages which have to be repaid out of future income. Thus the total expected future
income of the population is probably the most important single factor in the demand for
houses. Most building societies insist on a deposit and the ability to find money for this
is largely a function of accumulated past savings. The role of interest rates is rather complex. They will influence demand directly by determining the size of the monthly interest
payment. But they sometimes have an indirect effect on demand through the availability
of mortgage credit; for high interest rates tend to drive down the value of the securities
held by the building societies and, rather than raise rates to existing borrowers, the

societies may simply ration mortgage credit. Interest rates and credit availability also act
upon the supply side of the market where building materials and wages must necessarily
be paid out of borrowed funds. The capacity of the building industry as a whole can be
an important constraint on the total amount of housing as can the availability of
materials such as bricks and cement.

The other component of gross domestic fixed capital formation is *investment other
than dwellings*. It comprises expenditure on industrial buildings, new plant and
machinery, both by private companies and by public corporations. The essential features
of this form of investment are, first, that it either adds to the stock of productive assets,
or it is used to replace worn out or discarded equipment. Secondly, investment goods are
bought not for their own sake but for the sake of the goods and services they are used to
produce. Thirdly, their value to the purchaser depends heavily upon two matters of an
expectational character—the expected value of future sales and the expected costs of operating it. Finally, because investment goods must be bought in advance of the proceeds to
which they give rise the demand must be influenced, at least in some degree, by the availability of funds and the cost of borrowed money. Most of the hypotheses which have
been advanced to explain aggregate investment have relied upon one or other of these
features, but, as we shall see, none of them appears to have been outstandingly successful.

One of the oldest of these hypotheses is the acceleration principle, whereby the level
of net investment is assumed to be proportional to the change in output in the
period. This is the simple, unlagged form of the acceleration principle and it derives from
the notion of a fixed technical relationship between total output and the capital stock.
Thus to increase output the capital stock must be increased, and the amount of the increase is the amount of net investment. There are a number of serious limitations to this
hypothesis, some of which may be mentioned here. In the first place, the principle can only
apply when output is at full capacity, and this makes it of very little relevance to year-to-
year movements in the UK economy when the degree of resources utilisation is fluctuating.
Secondly, it makes no allowance for the possibility that changes in technology may alter
the relationship of capital to output thereby changing the acceleration coefficient. Thirdly,
it cannot be a complete theory of investment even at full capacity with unchanging
technology because it fails to take account of profitability factors. These are serious deficiencies, yet it may appear from table 1.3 that the facts are consistent with the acceleration principle. Investment, for example, was at very high levels in 1961 and 1964, both
years of rapid change in GDP. The more likely explanation for this kind of correlation,
however, is that the causation was the other way round, with an increase in investment
helping to cause the increase in output through its effect upon the general level of demand.

There is also a lagged form of the accleration principle whereby investment in one
period is proportionally related to the change in output in the preceding period. Clearly,
in this form, the principle is no longer a technical relationship, since the output change
precedes the addition to the capital stock. It may however be supported as a rather crude
expectational hypothesis whereby the last known change in total output is interpreted by
businessmen as an indication of future changes. Support for this hypothesis may be
sought in the experience of 1961 and 1962 (table 1.3) when investment was at very high
levels after two years of fast increases in GDP. The high level of investment in 1965 is,
perhaps, another case in point. But it is not difficult to find counter-examples such as
1968 when investment was at record levels despite a rise in output of less than 2 per cent
in the previous year. Thus the evidence for this hypothesis is not entirely convincing, and
this, perhaps, is not surprising in view of the rather simple theory of expectations that
lies behind it.

An alternative hypothesis to the acceleration principle is the profits theory, according
to which the level of business investment is assumed to be governed largely by the size
of business profits. This theory presupposes that investment is largely financed from internal funds and that the full amount of after-tax profits does not have to be distributed

as dividends. Both these propositions apply fairly well in the case of the UK. External sources of finance have been found to contribute only 10-30 per cent of company investment over the period 1954-63,[1] and dividends do not vary much in relation to the size of total profits. In these conditions it might be expected, so long as investment opportunities are plentiful, that the level of investment undertaken in one period will depend upon the level of undistributed profits in the previous period. Table 1.3 shows that investment declined in 1962 after a fall in undistributed profits in the previous year, and that it rose in 1964 after a rise in undistributed profits in 1963. On the other hand, it also shows counter-examples such as 1967 and 1968, so that it is not possible to give unqualified approval to this hypothesis either.

Interest, clearly, is a cost to the purchaser of the investment goods. It must be paid on all funds that are borrowed from outside the firm and it must be foregone on internal funds which could have been lent at interest but which, instead, are used to finance the firm's own investment projects. Table 1.3 shows the course of the industrial debenture rate, which is perhaps the most relevant interest rate from this point of view. It may be seen that this rate has not fluctuated a great deal, and possibly not enough, except in the case of 1969, for it to have exerted a significant effect upon decisions to invest. Taking the period from 1958 the declines in investment in 1962 and 1969 and the rise in 1964 probably fit the interest-rate hypothesis best, but there are also a number of years when investment varied considerably, whilst interest rates did not; the examples are 1960, 1965 and 1968. All that can be said is that the evidence is neither totally consistent nor totally inconsistent with the view that interest rates affect investment.

Table 1.3

Investment and related indicators, UK, 1958-69

	Fixed investment other than dwellings		Per cent change in real GDP	Undistributed profits of companies and corporations[a]		Yield on industrial debentures[b]
	Level (£m 1963 prices)	Per cent change from previous year	(expenditure estimate)	Level (£m 1963 prices)	Per cent change from previous year	Per cent
1958	3,093	–	–	2,375	–	6.2
1959	3,283	6.1	3.4	2,592	9.1	6.0
1960	3,584	9.2	4.9	2,768	6.8	6.3
1961	3,952	10.3	3.5	2,615	−5.5	7.1
1962	3,905	−1.2	1.1	2,727	4.3	7.0
1963	3,972	1.7	4.2	3,114	14.2	6.3 (est)
1964	4,542	14.4	5.2	3,367	8.1	6.7 (est)
1965	4,751	4.6	2.7	3,689	9.6	7.1
1966	4,899	3.1	1.9	2,807	−23.9	7.7
1967	5,204	6.2	1.7	2,865	2.1	7.6
1968	5,472	5.1	2.9	2,915	1.7	8.2
1969	5,387	−1.6	1.3	2,992	2.6	10.3

Sources: NIBB, 1969, PE, 1970, AAS
a   Undistributed profits at 1963 prices have been estimated by the author by deflating current price figures by the implicit price index for fixed investment other than dwellings; this method of deflation is not recommended for all purposes.
b   Figures for 1963 and 1964 are not given in the official source and have been estimated by the author from changes in the yield on industrial preference shares.

---

[1]   See 'Internal and external sources of company finance', reprinted from *ET,* February 1966, in *New Contributions to Economic Statistics,* Fourth Series, CSO, 1967.

This somewhat inconclusive result is typical of attempts to explain investment. It seems probable that both the profits and the interest-rate hypotheses have a part to play but the relative strengths of their influence is not easily established by simple methods. They both ignore the all-important factor of the expected state of future demand, and it is doubtful whether the lagged acceleration principle can cope effectively with this problem. The fact is that macroeconomics is, as yet, some way from being in a position to explain and predict fixed investment except within very large margins of error. The fact that the investment forecasts of the Treasury, National Institute and other bodies have relied much more upon the results of questionnaires to businessmen than on economic hypotheses bears testimony to this unsatisfactory state of affairs.

II.4   Stocks and Stockbuilding

Stockbuilding, or investment in stocks, is the addition to final expenditure brought about by a change in the level of stocks between the beginning and end of the period. To understand its nature one must examine the reasons for holding stocks.

Stocks consist of unsold finished goods, work in process of production, and stocks of materials and fuel for further processing. Of these, stocks of work in process are a technical necessity of production and can be assumed to bear a more or less proportionate relationship to it. Stocks of materials and fuels, and stocks of finished goods, are not immediately necessary for production. They are held because businessmen can never be completely sure that the current level of production will precisely coincide with sales of the product or deliveries of raw materials. On these grounds it is reasonable for businessmen to hold stocks in order to guard against the danger of running short of materials or of finished goods. This suggests that they might carry in their minds the notion of a certain desired ratio, k, of stocks to future output. Thus the desired level of stocks at the end of the period will be equal to k times the expected level of output in that period. If future output is known, or if it can be approximated by current output, then the desired level of stocks is determined, and desired investment in stocks is by definition the difference between desired stocks and current actual stocks. It follows from this hypothesis, which is known as the stock-adjustment principle, that the amount of stock investment is likely to be inversely related to the stock-output ratio,[1] so that when the ratio is high stock-building tends to be on the small side and when the ratio is low stock-building tends to be large. Some evidence for this view is given by the data for manufacturing stocks plotted in figure 1.4 below. It can be seen from the figure that the stock-building peaks in 1956, 1960 and 1964 all coincided with low values of the stock-output ratio; and the troughs of 1958 and 1962 with high values. Ideally, a theory of stock-building should also be able to explain why the desired stock-output ratio is not always attained in practice, but this would require a theory of why expectations of future sales and output are not always realised.

---

[1]   In symbols

$$S_{t+1}^* = k . Y_{t+1}^* \qquad \text{(by assumption)}$$
$$Y_{t+1}^* = Y_t \qquad \text{(by approximation)}$$
$$I_{t+1}^* = S_{t+1}^* - S_t \qquad \text{(by definition)}$$
$$\therefore \quad I_{t+1}^* = k . Y_t - S_t \qquad \text{(by substitution)}$$
$$= k . Y_t - r . Y_t$$

where S_{t+1}^* is the desired stock level; Y_{t+1}^* expected output; I_{t+1}^*, desired stock investment; and k, the desired stock-output ratio; and r is the actual stock-output ratio at the end of the previous period.

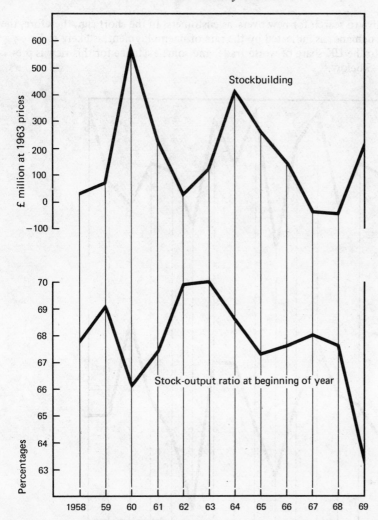

Figure 1.4   Stock Ratios and Stockbuilding in Manufacturing Industry, UK, 1958-69.

II.5   Exports of Goods and Services

The behaviour of exports is much more fully discussed in chapter 3. Their volume can be
expected to depend largely upon two factors: the state of overseas demand as indicated
by the volume of world trade, and export prices relative to those of competing commodities. In the short run we should not expect changes in relative prices to be sufficiently
large to bring about substantial changes in the export volume, although sharp changes
such as those arising from devaluation may be expected to have visible effects within a
year or two. Over the longer run, however, the rise in UK prices relative to other countries
was probably responsible for much of the decline in the UK share of world trade.

Besides these two factors there may also be room for a third influence in the form of
the pressure of demand upon UK resources. When domestic demand is high in relation to
capacity we should expect firms to experience difficulties in obtaining materials and in
meeting demand both at home and abroad. When domestic demand is lower, however,
the firm is likely to find it a lot easier to supply the export market, and there may well

be a direct incentive to search for new overseas customers. In the short run, therefore, the pressure of home demand, as indicated by the rate of unemployment, is likely to be inversely related to the UK share of world trade, and some evidence for this view is presented in figure 1.5 below.[1]

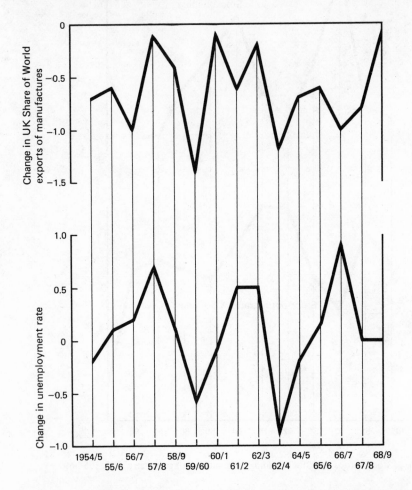

Figure 1.5   Changes in the Pressure of Demand and the UK Share of World Trade in Manufactures, 1954-69

As figure 1.5 shows, movements in the UK share of world trade have been downward in every year since 1955, and the extent of these declines has been loosely related to the change in the unemployment rate. In interpreting this result, however, it must be borne in mind that the demand for exports is one of the determinants of unemployment so that the causal relationship could run both ways. Nevertheless, changes in export demand have not been the predominant influence on the economy over this period so that it is probably safe to assume that most of the correlation shown is the result of the influence of the

[1]   See also R. J. Ball, J. R. Eaton and M. D. Steuer, 'The Relationship between United Kingdom Export Performance in Manufactures and the Internal Pressure of Demand', *EJ*, September 1966; and for a contrary view, W. Beckerman and associates, *The British Economy in 1975*, Cambridge University Press, 1965, pp. 60-4.

pressure of demand on exports, and not vice versa. But the question of whether exports in the long run thrive best in conditions of low demand pressure in the home market is another matter, and depends a good deal on the way in which the growth of productivity is influenced by home demand.

II.6   From TFE to GDP

The categories of final expenditure discussed above have all been valued at their market prices. If one is interested in the rewards of factors of production then one must, as explained in section I.2 of this chapter, subtract indirect taxes from the market price and add in subsidies. The 'factor-cost adjustment' is the net amount of these two elements and comes to about 12 per cent of TFE. Indirect taxes[1] are levied mainly on consumer goods such as cars, beer, cigarettes and household appliances and the subsidy element in market prices is relatively small. Hence the factor-cost adjustment is proportionately larger for consumers' expenditure than it is for the other categories of final expenditure. The proportions are set out in table 1.4.

TABLE 1.4

Domestic Output Content of Total Final Expenditure at Market Prices, UK, 1968.

Percentages of market price totals

	Consumers' expenditure	Government current expenditure	Gross domestic fixed investment	Exports of goods and services	Total final expenditure
Indirect taxes less subsidies	18	6	7	2	12
Imports of goods and services	19	8	15	17	16
Domestic output content	63	86	78	81	72

Source: *NIBB,* 1969, table 12. 'Provisional Summary Input-Output Tables for 1963', *ET,* August 1964.

Imports: Finally, to arrive at demand for domestic output we must subtract the imported component of each category of final expenditure. This is also illustrated in table 1.4, where it can be seen, for example, that the import content of consumers' expenditure is higher than for other categories of expenditure.

The ratio of imports to final expenditure was about 18 per cent in 1969. The ratio has shown a long-term tendency to rise, which may be explained by factors such as trade liberalisation and the tendency for the prices of UK manufactures to rise faster than those of foreign manufactures. These are discussed in chapter 3. But superimposed on the long-term upward trend are short, sharp, year-to-year variations. The ratio rose by 1 per cent in 1959-60, for example, and in 1963-4 it rose by about 0.5 per cent. Fluctuations as large as these have important repercussions on the balance of payments: a 1 per cent rise today would add over £400 million to the balance of payments deficit.

Short-term movements in the import ratio can be explained by movements in stocks, movements in the pressure of demand, or by a mixture of the two. The first is the more widely accepted explanation. Sharp movements in stock-building involve sharp increases in the rate at which raw materials and fuels are imported from abroad so that years of

---

[1]   For details see chapter 2.

high stock-building are likely to be years in which imports are high in relation to final expenditure. This has nearly always been the case, as can be seen from figure 1.6. Other things being equal, a change in stocks of £100 million is normally associated with a change in imports of about £50 million.[1] An implication of this estimate is that movements in stock-building will have a much less pronounced effect on domestic output than movements in other types of final expenditure. A rise in stock-building will be met as to only one-half by domestic production whilst increases in other expenditure will generate output increases of something more like three-quarters depending on the type of expenditure.

Changes in the import-ratio are also likely to be associated with changes in the pressure of demand. When pressure is high producers in the home market experience difficulties in meeting new orders because of shortages of particular types of labour and materials. Delays will occur and buyers are likely to look overseas for their supplies. This factor is not likely to be important in the case of raw materials since these are almost entirely imported. But in the case of finished and semi-finished manufactures imported articles are frequently close substitutes for home production. The fact that movements in the pressure of demand have tended to coincide with movements in stock-building makes it difficult in practice to distinguish the one influence from the other. But it may be misleading to think in terms of a stable and precise 'import-content of stock-building' even though this assumption fits the facts quite well.

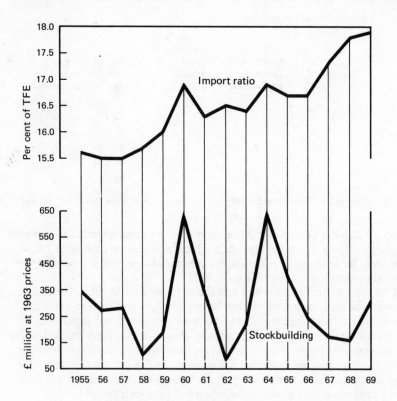

Figure 1.6   The Import Ratio in relation to Stockbuilding, UK, 1955-69

---

[1]   See the article *'Forecasting Imports'*, by W. A. H. Godley and J. R. Shepherd, *NIER*, August 1965.

III   ECONOMIC ACTIVITY AND ITS REGULATION

III.1   Fluctuations in Economic Activity

Cycles in national output and employment with a peak-to-peak duration of 7-10 years
were a regular feature of British economic history in the nineteenth century. Full employment, or something like it, obtained only at the cyclical peaks, and there was generally a
substantial amount of unemployment in the recession. This pattern changed after the end
of the first world war, when for two decades unemployment was massive not only during
the recession but also at the peak of each cycle. Economic activity fluctuated well short
of full employment, and unemployment did not fall below 9 per cent of the labour force
in any single year from 1921 to 1939. The worst year was 1932, when unemployment
reached 22 per cent (2.8 million people), and the rate was above 15 per cent from 1930 to
1935.

Large-scale unemployment has largely disappeared in the postwar period although it is
still a serious problem in some regions, most notably in Northern Ireland. The prewar
sequence of ups and downs in GDP has also gone, and since 1947 there has been only one
decline in GDP between two full years—a fall of less than 1 per cent between 1957 and
1958. This absence of declines in GDP makes it difficult to detect a cyclical pattern, but
if attention is focused upon the rates of change in output from one year to the next a
fairly regular sequence of slow and fast increases can be observed (see figure 1.7, page 24).
The numbers unemployed, moreover, still move up and down in cyclical fashion, and
these now serve as a fairly good indicator of cyclical performance in the postwar period
(see table 1.5).

TABLE 1.5

Unemployment Rates in Postwar Fluctuations

1951-5		1955-61		1961-5		1965-9	
1951	1.2	1955	1.1	1961	1.5	1965	1.4
1952	2.0	1956	1.2	1962	2.0	1966	1.5
1953	1.6	1957	1.4	1963	2.5	1967	2.4
1954	1.3	1958	2.1	1964	1.6	1968	2.4
1955	1.1	1959	2.2	1965	1.4	1969	2.4
		1960	1.6				
		1961	1.5				
Average	1.5	Average	1.6	Average	1.8	Average	2.0

Source: EPG (registered unemployment)

The table shows three complete cycles during the period from 1951 to 1965. It is
interesting to note that both the highest and the average rates of unemployment during
each complete cycle tended to increase from one cycle to the next. The last of the cycles
shown in the table is still uncompleted. It differs from the earlier pattern in having a more
extended period of stagnation during the trough (1966-9), a result which was entirely
attributable to government policy towards the pressure of demand.

Movements in unemployment have thus been accompanied by a succession of slow and
fast increases in GDP and the level of employment. More surprisingly, they have also been
accompanied by slow and fast movements in the ratio of GDP to employment, i.e. output-
per-employee or 'productivity' for short. This cyclical pattern of productivity change is
also illustrated in figure 1.7. It can be seen that the increases in productivity in boom
years were well above the average rise, whilst in periods of very slow expansion productivity rose hardly at all. For example, in the 1963-4 boom productivity increased by 4.6

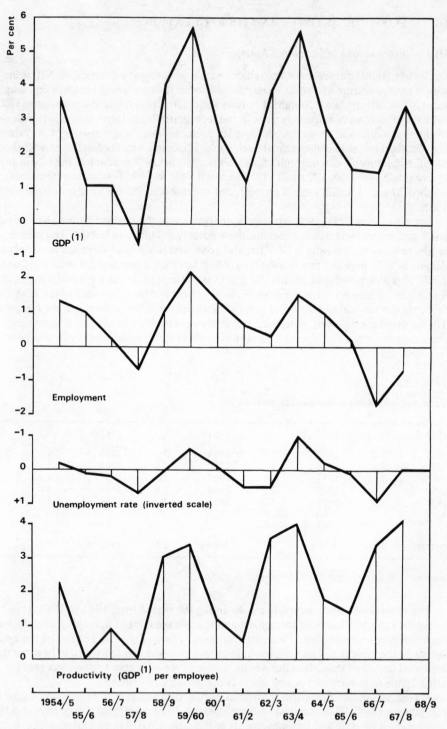

(1) Note: GDP changes are averages of the expenditure, income and output series, and
         productivity changes are derived from these.

Figure 1.7   Year-to-Year Movements in Real GDP, Employment, the Rate of Unemployment and
             GDP per man (per cent), UK, 1954-69.

per cent whilst in the slack period of 1961-2 it rose by only 0.4 per cent. The reasons for this pattern appear to be threefold. First, a rising pressure of demand on manpower resources leads to the working of more overtime and to some setback in the generally downwards trend of the average working week: thus employment-hours generally rise faster than employment, and output per man-hour goes up less rapidly than the crude productivity measure shown in the figure. A second reason is believed to be that employers hold on to skilled labour during recessions for fear of being caught short-staffed in the ensuing boom. The result is that the skilled men are shown as being in employment in the Ministry of Labour's statistics, although they are being paid for little or no work. This means that the figures of output per man will be depressed when there is substantial 'labour-hoarding', as it is called, but will rise again when the hoarded labour is given work to do. A third reason, which perhaps is more conjectural, is that the most efficient combination of capital and labour is one in which the machinery is being fully utilised at full capacity, so that when demand falls below the full capacity rate output per man will decline. The implication of these considerations is that short-term changes in productivity have to be interpreted as reflections of the way in which business employment policies react to cyclical change and not as indicators of productive efficiency at optimal levels of output. In particular, it is extremely hazardous to draw conclusions for the growth of productivity in the long run from changes between one year and the next.

Another relationship brought out by figure 1.7 is that between employment and unemployment. It will be noticed that the changes in unemployment as a percentage of the labour force are by no means large enough to match the changes in employment. In 1963-4, for example, employment rose by 1.3 per cent whilst the unemployment rate came down by rather less than this—by 0.9 per cent. The implication is that the labour force itself (i.e. employment plus unemployment) tends to fluctuate during the cycle. In the recovery phase of the cycle marginal workers, such as married women who have not previously been registered as unemployed, enter the labour force and remain in it whilst demand remains high. Similarly, workers who have reached retiring age are pressed to remain in their jobs during periods of high demand, whilst in periods of recession they are retired early. Thus, we can conclude that the phase of the cycle has an important influence on the size of the labour force and the level of output per man, as well as on the more obvious figures such as GDP itself, employment and unemployment.[1]

The causes of cyclical changes in total production and employment must be sought in the behaviour of aggregate demand as described in section II of this chapter. Theoretical models of the cycle, such as the multiplier-accelerator model, tend to emphasise the inter-relationships of consumption and investment behaviour. A theory of the postwar cycle, however, would have to take account of the other sectors of demand, such as exports and government expenditure, and also of the actions of the government in stimulating and retarding the level of consumers' expenditure. Some consideration of these actions is given in sections III.2 and III.3 of this chapter, but meanwhile it is useful to bear in mind the way in which the various demand categories have moved during recent cycles. These movements are set out for the period from 1955 to 1968 in figure 1.8 below. The object of this figure is to represent the importance to economic activity in general of movements in the various expenditure categories. For this reason the year-to-year changes in expenditure have been expressed as percentages of total final expenditure. Consumption has not shown a single decline during the period but its annual increases have varied from 0.5 per cent of TFE to 2.5 per cent, and this variation has exerted an important influence upon the rate of increase of GDP. Still more important is investment in stocks, which despite its relatively small total, has shown year-to-year

---

[1] For a fuller discussion, see W. A. H. Godley and J. R. Shepherd, 'Long-term growth and Short-term policy', *NIER*, August 1964.

movements which range from −0.9 per cent of TFE to +1.4 per cent. Fixed investment, which is much larger in total amount, has shown year-to-year movements ranging from −0.1 per cent to +2.2 per cent. In contrast to these rather unstable elements of final expenditure, changes in exports and public expenditure have been less important. Ignoring 1968 when the rise in exports reflected the dock strike at the end of the previous year the export changes have ranged from −0.3 to +1.0 per cent of TFE, and changes in public expenditure from −0.5 to +0.7 per cent.

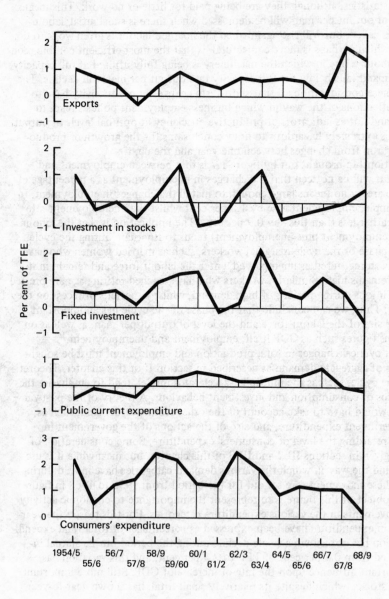

Figure 1.8   Year-to-Year Movements in Expenditure as percentages of TFE at constant prices, UK, 1954-69.

III.2   The Management of Aggregate Demand

It is a moot point whether, or not, the economic fluctuations we have just described should have been allowed to occur. For, since 1944, successive governments have accepted the responsibility, set out in the White Paper on Employment Policy,[1] of maintaining 'a high and stable level of employment'. The White Paper, however, did not attempt to define the target level of employment at all precisely, and individual governments have interpreted the wording according to their own particular wishes and priorities. There is, of course, no unique definition of full employment and few postwar governments have disclosed their intentions, in this respect, to Parliament or to the electorate. (The last Labour government was an exception since it made it fairly clear that it regarded unemployment rates of 2-2½ per cent as acceptable.) It must be presumed, however, that some given target level of employment, or, as seems more relevant, of unemployment was the aim of every Chancellor of the Exchequer, and that this target together with the forecasts of prospective GDP and employment determined the amount of the change in taxation at the time of each budget. Indeed, the activity of demand management can, on these lines, be divided into three main stages:

First, the normative stage of setting targets for employment, unemployment or GDP.
Second, a forecast of the prospective level of economic activity in the absence of
    government efforts to regulate it.
Third, governmental action to close the gap between the target and prospective
    levels of activity.

We shall discuss these stages in sequence.

The policy target: The first stage, then, is to select the target level of economic activity. On some considerations this would be taken to be the highest level of output and the lowest level of unemployment that was physically possible. This would not be an unemployment rate of zero because there is likely to be a number of workers, the so-called 'unemployables', who have little prospect of being taken on even in periods of acute labour shortage. Allowance must also be made for the fact that workers are not perfectly mobile between jobs, so that some unemployment will arise as a result of workers having to take time in moving from one job to another and in training for new kinds of work. Even aside from these considerations, however, there are reasons for doubting whether a physical minimum for the unemployment rate is likely to be accepted by any government as the optimum to which policy should be directed. The most potent reason for opting for something more than the minimum is the hypothesis that a low level of unemployment leads to a fast rate of inflation. This relationship between inflation and unemployment, which is discussed in section IV of this chapter, suggests that governments may feel obliged to make some compromise between the conflicting demands of full employment and price stability. Another consideration is that low levels of economic activity and low rates of inflation are both conducive to balance of payments equilibrium, and there have been periods, most obviously in the last three years, when the desired level of employment has been governed very largely by balance of payments considerations.

Having selected some target for the rate of employment or unemployment there is the further problem of translating it into a desired level of GDP. This has to be done by reference to the considerations set out in section III.1 of this chapter. The problem is at its simplest when the current level of unemployment and the desired level of unemployment in, say, eighteen months' time, are one and the same thing. When this is the case the desired increase in GDP will be equal to the demographic change in the labour

---

[1] Cmd 6527, HMSO, 1944.

force plus the so-called 'underlying increase in output per man'. The latter is determined
by changes in the amount and quality of productive factors (see section V) but for short
periods is generally taken as the trend increase over the last few years, which is currently
thought to be some 3 per cent per annum.[1] Therefore, if the labour force is growing by
0.2 per cent a year for purely demographic reasons, the desired rise in GDP with no
change in unemployment will be about 3.2 per cent a year.

More often, however, the current level of unemployment is different from the
desired level, and the required increase in GDP will not be equal to the sum of the underlying increases in productivity and employment. An example was the period between the
second quarter of 1963 and the second quarter of 1964. The main changes that took
place between these two periods were as follows:

change in unemployment rate	−0.8 per cent
change in employment	+1.4 per cent
change in productivity	+3.8 per cent
change in GDP	+5.2 per cent

The unemployment rate in the second quarter of 1963 was 2.4 per cent, seasonally adjusted, for the wholly unemployed. If the government's aim at the time was to reach an
unemployment rate of 1.6 per cent in twelve months' time (as in fact happened) then
it would have been necessary to translate this into a required rise in GDP of about 5 per cent.
With some knowledge[2] of the underlying trends in productivity and the labour force, and
of the way in which short-term changes can deviate from trend, it should have been possible to arrive at something like the correct figure. But it would be wrong to under-
estimate the difficulties of making such calculations in practice. The relationships between
output, employment and productivity changes are by no means stable; the statistics of
recent levels of GDP are often ambiguous; and the figures for employment are notoriously subject to revision.

Forecasts of national income: The second stage in the management of aggregate demand
is a forecast of the likely course of GDP over the next 12-18 months. The comparison of
the prospective and desired paths of GDP can then be used to decide upon the appropriate
magnitude and direction of government stabilising action.

National income forecasts are prepared in the Treasury three times a year. The timing
of the three main forecasts is geared to the budget which is normally in the first half of
April. A preliminary assessment of next year's prospects is generally made in late autumn,
and this is brought up to date and extended a further six months in February and March.
A third forecast is made in early summer.

From a policy point of view the most important forecast is the one made in February
and March. This extends from the last known figures for GDP (which relate to the third
quarter of the previous year) as far as the second quarter of the following year. This
period covers seven quarters altogether of which the last five quarters, from April of this
year to June of next, are genuinely in the future. The first two quarters, from last October
to March of the current year, represent a sort of no-man's land between the relatively
well-known past and the unknown future. The problem for this period is one of piecing
together bits of statistical information, such as the monthly figures of exports, imports,
retail sales and industrial production, into a reasonably coherent picture of the base period.
This is always difficult because there is very little monthly information about investment
or government expenditure, and the difficulties are sometimes made worse by apparent
contradictions between the available monthly figures of production and sales.

Once the base period for the forecast is established the forecast proper (i.e. the part

---

[1] *Financial Statement and Budget Report*, HMSO, 1970, page 11.
[2] Godley and Shepherd, 'Long-term growth and Short-term policy' *ibid.*

relating to the future) can be begun. The method by which this is done is difficult to describe in detail[1] but the general approach is to combine the maximum use of direct information from business firms and government departments with macroeconomic relationships of the simple type found in section II of this chapter. Government current expenditure and the government component of fixed investment, for example, can, or should, be quite easily predicted from information provided by the nationalised industries and the government departments. The forecast of business fixed investment (excluding housing) is made on the basis of the sample enquiries into investment intentions conducted by the Board of Trade. These enquiries have been regarded as being fairly reliable predictors of reality, although their value is limited by the fact that they relate only to annual periods, so that the forecaster still has the problem of spreading the total for a calendar year over its four constituent quarters. A related difficulty is that the enquiry extends only to the end of the calendar year, so that quite separate considerations are needed to predict the investment levels for the first half of the following year. There is little doubt, however, that these sample surveys are an invaluable aid to the national income forecaster. Forecasts of housing investment are derived largely from figures of housing starts and an assumption about the average period of house construction.

Exports present a difficult problem for the national income forecaster in that they depend predominantly upon the volume of world trade and production. It follows that a full set of assumptions has to be made about the world economy before a forecast of exports can be made. Recently, the problem of forecasting exports has been made particularly difficult by the sharp change in price competitiveness brought about by the devaluation of the pound.

Exports, fixed investment and government current expenditure are the main 'autonomous' parts of the national income forecast in the sense that they are not in the short run thought to depend much upon the level of GDP.[2] The dependent components are stock-building, consumers' expenditure, imports and the factor cost adjustment. In section II of this chapter we have suggested various hypotheses, such as the stock-adjustment principle, the propensity to consume, and the relationship of imports to GDP and stock-building, which might be used to forecast these categories. Some of these relationships, to judge from the published accounts, are indeed used by the government forecasters, albeit in somewhat modified forms. But the government has a rather more complicated and indirect method of forecasting consumers' expenditure, and on this the reader is referred to the official account of government forecasting.

The main upshot of the government forecasting work is a table in considerable detail of the course of GDP and its components, quarter by quarter, over a 12-18 month period. In the case of the pre-budget forecast it will extend to the middle of the calendar year after the budget.

The instruments of demand management: The final stage of short-term economic management is the action that is taken to close the gap between the prospective increase in GDP, as given by the national income forecast, and the required increase, as determined by government priorities. If the forecast increase over the next twelve months is 2 per cent, for example, and the increase required to achieve the employment objective is 3

---

[1] The reader who is interested in a fuller discussion is advised to read through one of the recent forecasts by the National Institute of Economic Research (any *NIER*) since the methods are probably similar to those used by the Treasury. Also useful is the official account 'Short-term economic forecasting in the United Kingdom', *ET,* August 1964, and the *Fourth Report of the Estimates Committee,* pp. 474-80, House of Commons, 1966. Some of the difficulties of forecasting are described in A. K. Cairncross, 'Economic Forecasts', *EJ,* December 1969.

[2] The distinction between exogenous and endogenous expenditures cannot be drawn too sharply. Exports, for example, may be partly determined by the pressure of home demand and stock-building by the rate of change in GDP—see section II of this chapter.

per cent, then the Chancellor of the Exchequer has to find ways and means of raising aggregate demand for GDP by 1 per cent more than it would otherwise be. His choice of instruments for achieving such a result ranges, in principle, over the whole paraphernalia of government expenditures, subsidies, grants, transfer payments, taxes and monetary instruments. In practice, however, his choice is more limited, since government expenditure, as we have already noted, is difficult to change quickly for both administrative and political reasons. Alterations in the scale of investment grants to the private sector are also unlikely to be changed for short-term purposes, chiefly, it seems, because investment plans are difficult to alter at short notice and the effect, therefore, is largely on company savings. The exclusion of these two instruments means, in effect, that the main brunt of short-term economic management must be borne by personal consumption. A variety of instruments are available for this purpose, of which the ones most commonly used have been income tax, the indirect tax regulator, and hire-purchase restrictions.

The effect of a rise in personal income tax is to bring an immediate decrease in personal disposable income, and this, via the marginal propensity to consume, leads to a fall in consumers' expenditure. The fall in consumption is accompanied by a fall in GDP, but this will be of a smaller amount, since indirect taxes and imports will form some part of the expenditure decline. All these effects, and their multiplier consequences, can be estimated quite simply using income-flow relationships of the type we have discussed above in section I.3. But the first step is to calculate the increase in income tax revenue at the prevailing level of personal incomes. This amount, which is almost equal[1] to the decline in disposable income, can be estimated by the Inland Revenue Department. The method of working out the further effects of the tax change can be illustrated using the relationships set out in figure 1.1. It was assumed there that a change of £56 in disposable income would lead to a change in GDP of £31. Therefore, if the tax increase leads to a fall in disposable income of £x, it will lead to a fall in GDP of 31/56ths of this amount, i.e.

$£\left(\frac{31}{56}\right)$ x. This is the initial change in GDP. The multiplied change is found by applying the

multiplier, which in section I was put at 1.45. In principle, however, the value of the multiplier will change as a result of the new tax rate. The new tax rate will alter the overall propensity to 're-spend domestic output' by affecting the relationship between changes in total personal income and changes in disposable personal income. Whereas previously this relationship was 56/82 (see figure 1.1) it will now be less than this by a fraction x/y in which x is the revenue change and y stands for total personal income. Thus the new

marginal response coefficient is $\left(\frac{56}{82} - \frac{x}{y}\right)$, and if this is substituted for the old coef-

ficient of 56/82 the new multiplier may be calculated. In practice, however, the calculation of the new multiplier is hardly worth the effort since the change implied by an alteration in income tax will be small in relation to the total propensity to leak.[2] Thus for most purposes the final change in GDP may be found by taking the old value of the multiplier (in this case 1.45) and multiplying it by the initial change in GDP. On this basis the change in GDP after a lapse of three or four quarters may be approximated in

this example as $£1.45\left(\frac{31}{56}\right)$ x.

The same principles are involved in calculating the effect of a rise in indirect taxes. If the change in the tax yield is denoted as before by £x, then the effect is to reduce the

---

[1]   Not exactly, because graduated National Insurance contributions are also related to gross income.

[2]   For example, a 2½ per cent change in the rate of income tax (6d in the £) alters the marginal propensity to leak from 0.31 to 0.31 x .975 = 0.302 and the new multiplier becomes

$$\frac{1}{1-0.302} = 1.41,$$ which is scarcely different from the old multiplier of 1.45.

factor cost value of consumers' expenditure by this amount. The change in GDP will then be this amount less the marginal import content, and may be seen from figure 1.1 to work out at £$\left(\frac{31}{41}\right)$ x. The final change in GDP is then found as before by multiplying this amount by 1.45.

Some estimates of the effects of tax changes are given in table 1.6. The most expedient tax instrument for short-term stabilisation purposes is the 'regulator', under which the government is empowered by Parliament to vary, by up to 10 per cent either way, the rates of purchase tax and the excise taxes on drink, betting, tobacco and petrol. The full use of this power is estimated to change GDP, after allowing for the multiplier, by about 0.7 per cent. The effect of 2½ per cent (6d) on the standard rate of income tax is rather less than this—only 0.4 per cent of GDP.

One interesting and important feature of these estimates is that what are regarded as quite severe changes in taxation appear to have quite small effects upon the economy. A Chancellor of the Exchequer who decided, for example, to use the regulator in combination with 6d on the income tax would be regarded as being exceptionally tough, yet the effects of this combination would be to reduce GDP by only 1.1 per cent from what it would otherwise have been. There have been circumstances, however, when the economic situation has called for much larger adjustments than this (in retrospect 1962 appears to be an example), and when it would have been necessary to supplement tax changes by other instruments of control.

One of the alternatives to tax measures is the control of hire purchase transactions. Alterations in the statutory minimum HP deposit and in the maximum repayment period have, as we saw in section II.1 of this chapter, been used frequently as stabilisation instruments over the last ten years. The effect of raising the down-payment is to choke off purchases until consumers have managed to save the increase in the deposit, whilst a shortening of the repayment period has the effect of deterring purchasers from buying until they are satisfied that their current income will cover the higher monthly payments. These restrictions cannot be expected to be effective if consumers have access to alternative sources of finance, but the presumption is that a good many of them have no such alternative and a tighter control over personal bank advances can always be arranged to take care of the few that do. The main objection to the use of HP controls is not so much that they are not effective (indeed figure 1.2 suggests the contrary) but rather that their effects are temporary. The estimate in table 1.6 of a 0.5 per cent decline in personal consumption as a result of changes in HP restrictions represents savings worth roughly £28 million a quarter (in 1963 prices), and it may take only a few months' savings out of rising incomes for consumers to be able to afford the increase in HP deposits. The effect of the restrictions, therefore, is to postpone rather than to reduce personal spending, and there is a possibility that the period of postponement may be too short for the purposes of government policy.

Monetary measures are discussed more fully in chapter 2. Alterations in interest rates of the small size normally encountered in postwar Britain are generally thought to have a somewhat feeble effect on fixed investment other than house-building, and even the effect on house-building is likely to be delayed. The restriction of bank advances and other direct reductions in the quantity of money may, however, have significant effects on fixed investment by small business, and possibly on the buying of consumer durables. Perhaps the main reason why so little use has been made of monetary policy, at least until quite recently, is that so little is known about its effects. With fiscal measures, as we have seen, it is possible to calculate, admittedly within fairly wide margins of error, the initial and multiplier effects of a tax change on disposable income, consumption and GDP. With monetary changes, however, there is much more uncertainty about the size, direction and timing of the effects. Correlations between the value of the national income and the quantity of money have been undertaken by a number of economists, and these may reasonably be interpreted as evidence of a fairly stable demand for money. If this is the case and the demand for money is stable in terms of money income it is possible to infer, as quantity theorists have for centuries, that for given levels of real income the equilibrium level of average prices will be determined by the stock of money. What is not clear is how money affects the economy when the level of real income is able to vary. Does an increase in the stock of money then lead to higher prices, higher real output or lower interest rates? And, even if this question can be answered in qualitative terms can it also be answered quantitatively? These are all difficult questions and the answers to them are anything but settled.

TABLE 1.6

Effect of Certain Tax and HP Changes on Consumption and GDP

	Percentage	changes	in:
	Consumption (initial)	GDP (initial)	GDP (final)
2½ per cent (i.e. 6d in the £) on the rates of income tax[a]	−0.6	−0.3	−0.4
Use of regulator (10 per cent on main indirect taxes)	−1.0	−0.5	−0.7
Tightening of HP restrictions (repayment term from 27 to 24 months on cars and 30 to 24 months on domestic appliances; minimum deposit $33\frac{1}{3}$ to 40 per cent on cars and 25 to 33½ per cent on domestic appliances)˙	−0.5	−0.3	−
Additional £0.25 per head on selective employment tax	−0.5	−0.2	−0.3

[a] Strictly speaking these results applied to the effect of across-the-board tax changes prior to the budget of 1970, but as far as can be estimated the effects are not likely to be very greatly different with the new structure of rates and personal allowances.

Source: the left hand column is taken from *NIER*, February 1968, table 5, p. 18, and the remaining columns are calculated from the multiplier relationships in figure 1.1 of this chapter.

III.3   The Pathology of Short-term Policy

In setting out the approach to economic management that has been adopted in the UK we may have glossed over the fact that the course of the economy over the last ten or fifteen years has been anything but smooth. GDP, as is shown in figure 1.7, has increased in a series of slow and fast phases, whilst unemployment fluctuated for much of the period in cycles of roughly constant duration. It must now be asked why it is that the government, with its equipment of forecasts and stabilisation instruments, has allowed the economy to pursue such an unstable course.

There have been various suggestions in answer to this question. One view[1] which seems to be mistaken is that 'Chancellors behaved like a simple Pavlovian dog responding to two main stimuli: one was *a run on the reserves* and the other was *500,000 unemployed.*' The fallacy here is that it conceives policy decisions as being no more than frantic re-

---

[1] The quotation is from S. Brittan, *Steering the Economy,* Secker and Warburg, 1969, pp. 266 *et seq.*

sponses to past economic indicators. It allows no role to the Treasury's system of econo-mic forecasting which has been in operation since the late 1940s and which seems more likely to have been the basis upon which decisions were actually taken.

In fact the failure of economic forecasts to provide a reliable background to the taking of policy decisions may well turn out to have been the best explanation of the course of the economy over the early 1960s. The evidence for this view has, unfortunately, to be rather indirect since the government did not publish its economic forecasts during this period. The forecasts of the National Institute, however, were prepared on rather similar lines and often by economists who had previously worked as government forecasters.

If the Treasury's forecasts can be assumed to have been similar to those of the National Institute then the ups and downs of the period from 1959 to 1963, which covers about one-and-a-half cycles, become much easier to understand. In the boom year of 1959, for example, the forecast annual change in GDP from the end of the previous year was for a rather slight increase—less than 1 per cent (see table 1.7). With unemployment still fairly high it was not surprising that the budget of that year was a generous one, stimulating the economy by about 1.4 per cent. Thus the pre-budget forecast plus budget effect implied an increase in GDP of 2.3 per cent, whereas the actual rise was 6.6 per cent. This meant that at the end of the year GDP was probably some 4 per cent higher than the government had intended at budget time. GDP was again higher than target at the end of 1960, when the pre-budget forecast seems to have been too low by 1.3 per cent. In 1961, however, the forecast turned out about right and unemployment rose to reach 1.8 per cent after the end of the year. This was probably about the level at which the government was aiming. But in 1962 the forecast was over-optimistic. GDP, instead of rising by 3.6 per cent as predicted, rose by 1.4 per cent. Although a neutral budget had seemed justified in view of the national income forecast it is clear in retrospect that expansionary measures were needed. By the end of the year unemployment had reached 2.3 per cent, and then in 1963 the speed of the recovery was underpredicted. An expansionary budget was introduced and GDP, in-stead of rising by 4.6 per cent as expected, rose, from end-year to end-year, by no less than 7.1 per cent.

TABLE 1.7

Economic Forecasts and Policies, 1959-63

					percentages
	1959	1960	1961	1962	1963
Unemployment rate, seasonally adjusted, in first quarter of each year	2.3	1.7	1.5	1.8	3.3
Forecast annual increase in GDP from fourth quarter of previous year	0.9	3.3	2.5	3.3	3.7
Estimated effect of measures taken at the time of the budget (later measures in brackets)	+1.4	−1.1	−0.1 (−0.6)	.0 (+0.3)	+0.9
Forecast increase after allowance for policy changes	2.3	2.2	1.8	3.6	4.6
Actual increase in GDP	6.6	3.5	2.0	1.4	7.1
Forecast error (forecast−actual), per cent of GDP	−4.3	−1.3	−0.2	+2.2	−2.5

Notes.   The forecasts are those of the National Institute of Economic and Social Research. The forecast errors were smaller in 1964 and after; for details see M. C. Kennedy, 'How well does the National Institute forecast?' *NIER*, November 1969.

The forecasts for this period seem to have produced a cyclical pattern of errors. The booms of 1959 and 1963 were both under-predicted, whereas the recession of 1962 was not foreseen until it was too late. These were, of course, National Institute forecasts, but on the credible assumption that the government's forecasts were similar, they go a long way to explain what has been labelled 'stop-go'.

The same is not true of the period from 1964 to 1969. The high pressure of demand in 1964 may be attributed to the forecasting errors of the previous year, whilst the fact that the budget of that year was not as deflationary as it might have been is probably attributable to the onset of a General Election. The electoral explanation of policy, which affects targets rather than forecasts, may also have held for 1965 and the early months of 1966, although it is fair to say that the government of the time was committed on intellectual grounds (in its own eyes, at least) to a belief that low unemployment was consistent with a fast rate of growth and that its inflationary consequences could be curbed by incomes policy.

The last phase of the period may be said to have begun with a package of severely deflationary measures in July 1966. Since then the target level of GDP was dominated by the balance of payments—in 1966 and 1967 by an attempt to correct the fundamental disequilibrium by the deflation of home demand, and after the devaluation of November 1967 by a continued deflation aimed at facilitating a switch of resources into exports and import-competing industries. During this period the government was clearly content with an unemployment rate somewhere between 2 and 2½ per cent, and was remarkably successful in keeping to this target.

There are two conclusions to this all too brief account of recent experience with short-term policy. The first conclusion is that there is no single, simple explanation of what happened, and it may be noted also that the attempt to blame successively forecasts, politics and the balance of payments for the three phases of the period may itself be something of an oversimplification. The second conclusion is that economic forecasts, although essential to any rational attempt to control the course of the economy, are subject to fairly wide margins of error. It is naive to suppose in the present state of economic knowledge that forecasts are reliable enough for the economy to be steered precisely on course.

IV   INFLATION

IV.1   Postwar Inflation

The postwar economy, whatever its limitations, has at least been free from heavy unemployment. But it has not been free from inflation. Prices, which in the interwar period were tending slowly downwards, have since 1940 shown a fairly continuous increase. The rate of price increase since the end of the second world war has been somewhat in excess of the rate of decline between the wars. The contrast between the two periods is illustrated in table 1.8.

TABLE 1.8

Average Annual Changes in Retail Prices, UK, 1919-69

	Per cent per annum
1919-29	−2.6
1929-39	−0.3
1939-47	+5.9
1947-55	+4.9
1955-65	+3.1
1965-69	+4.2

Sources: London and Cambridge Economic Service,
The British Economy, Key statistics, 1900-
1966, and *EPG*

The index of retail prices (or 'cost of living index') is but one of several indicators of the rate of inflation. It registers the prices of a collection of goods entering into a typical retail shopping basket. It is a 'true' price index in that it is collected directly from data of actual prices. In this respect it differs from an average value index, such as the index of consumer prices, in which the 'prices' are derived by the division of consumers' expenditure at constant prices into consumers' expenditure at current prices. The effect of doing this is to arrive at a current-weighted index, changes in which can be brought about by changes in the pattern of expenditure as well as by changes in actual prices. The consumer price index, along with similar indices for investment goods, exports, and goods and services bought by the public authorities, forms part of the average value index of final prices. The average rate of change in final prices over the last ten years is shown in table 1.9. Consumer prices have gone up by about 3½ per cent a year, whilst the prices of government-bought commodities have increased somewhat faster and those of investment goods and exports rather more slowly.

TABLE 1.9

Increases in Average Value Indices, UK, 1959-69

		Overall increase 1959-69, per cent.	Average annual increase, per cent.
1.	Consumer goods and services	39	3.4
2.	Government expenditure on goods and services	63	5.0
3.	Gross domestic capital formation	27	2.4
4.	Final goods sold on the home market (1 + 2 + 3)	41	3.5
5.	Exports of goods and services	26	2.3
6.	Total final expenditure (1 + 2 + 3 + 5)	38	3.3

Sources: *NIBB,* 1969, tables 12, 14, 16 and *PE,* 1970.

It must not be forgotten that inflation in the postwar period is not simply a UK problem. In the ten years since 1959 consumer prices in France and Italy have increased by 45 per cent and in Japan by 68 per cent. The UK increase of 39 per cent was smaller than in these countries though it exceeded those of Germany, Belgium, the US and Canada, which were all within the range of 26-30 per cent.[1]

IV.2   The Generation of Inflation

One widely accepted interpretation of the nature of inflation is that it originates in the form of an excess of demand over supply in the markets for labour and for goods. Excess demand is a state of disequilibrium, defined as a situation in which the demand for a commodity at the going price (or wage in the case of labour) exceeds the supply. Inflation, in the form of increases in prices and wages, is the process of correcting such disequilibria when they are widespread throughout the economy.

The origins of such disequilibria may be various. Excess demand may be created by some autonomous increase in final demand for goods and services such as an investment

---

[1]   These figures are taken from *NIER,* February 1970, table 18.

boom, an expansion of exports, or a war. It may be started by an increase in the supply
of money and credit beyond the amount that is wanted at current price and income
levels. It may also come from the side of supply in the form, for example, of an autonomous desire on the part of the labour force for higher wages at the prevailing level of
employment. It may arise from greater trade union militancy. Even a rise in import
prices will create excess demand. Higher prices of imported materials will lead producers
to ask a higher price than before at a given volume of sales, and this, by definition, is a
shift in supply which, with demand unchanged, involves a rise in excess demand.

Excess demand is so broad a concept that it is difficult to see how any type of inflationary impulse can escape its logical net.

The rate of wage and price inflation over time is likely to be a function of the amount
of excess demand. When excess demand is zero everywhere prices and wages will not
change, but as the amount by which demand exceeds supply increases so will the rate of
inflation.

The concept of excess demand is quite easily envisaged but not so easily identified in
practice. There are very few statistical series for unfilled orders in the UK economy so
that excess demand for goods is almost totally unmeasured. It may be approximated by
excess demand for labour but the accuracy of the approximation depends not only on
the strength of the link between excess demand in the labour and goods markets, but also
on the validity of the available indicators of excess demand in the labour market. These
are primarily the figures of unemployment and unfilled vacancies. The unemployment
figures register excess supply rather than excess demand. But they have the advantage over
the unfilled vacancy figures in that they are likely to be a much more complete record.
This is because unemployed workers have a direct pecuniary motive in the form of unemployment benefit for registering at the labour exchange. Employers, on the other hand,
receive no payment for registering vacancies, and many do not bother to report them.
Thus the unemployment figures rather than the vacancy figures are most widely used as a
single indicator of excess demand, although sometimes they are used in combination.

The use of the unemployment figures for this purpose is not without its limitations.
Unemployment might rise in one market and unfilled vacancies might fall in another by
an offsetting market, thus leaving total excess demand unchanged. But if the rise in unemployment is statistically recorded whilst the change in vacancies is not, it will be wrong-
ly inferred that aggregate excess demand has fallen. If unemployment was to be a wholly
reliable indicator of aggregate excess demand it would be necessary for all changes in
demand or supply to be felt equi-proportionately throughout the economy. But clearly
this sort of condition cannot hold in practice, although it may hold approximately.

There are other difficulties too. The unemployment rate cannot really be expected to
indicate those states of excess demand which, by definition, arise from changes in import
prices or changes in the supply curve of labour. If, for example, prices go up and unions,
in attempting to maintain their real incomes, ask for higher money wages for the same
hours of work as before, a situation of excess demand is created by the shift in the labour
supply, but there is no accompanying change in unemployment.

Because unemployment is an indicator, albeit an imperfect one, of excess demand in
the labour market, and because inflation is thought to be related to excess demand, one
may expect to observe a statistical relationship between the change in wage rates and the
rate of unemployment. But it cannot be expected to be a very precise relationship because
of the imperfections discussed above in the link between unemployment, on the one
hand, and excess demand, on the other. In dealing with such relationships it may help the
reader to bear in mind that there are two distinct hypotheses at work; one of them is
primarily *economic* and relates price or wage changes to excess demand; the other is primarily *observational* relating unseen excess demand to an observable indicator such as the
rate of unemployment. If the main causal variable is seen through a distorted lens the
hypothesis which we are testing may not come out as well as it should.

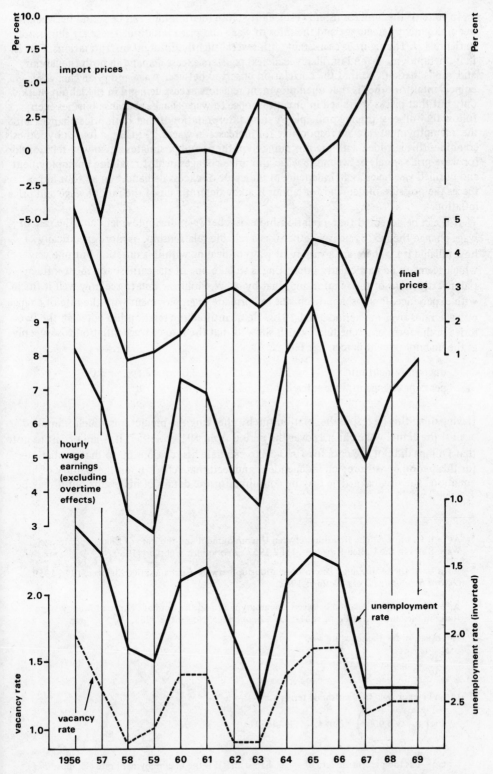

Figure 1.9   Unemployment and Vacancy Rates with yearly changes in Hourly Wage Earnings (to October, excluding overtime effects), Final Prices and Import Prices (to 4th quarter), UK, 1956-69.

In spite of the limitations, however, fairly close relationships can be found between the unemployment percentage and the rates of wage and price inflation. These are illustrated in figure 1.9. The figure is consistent with several slightly different interpretations. One is that unemployment (and unfilled vacancies) registers excess demand in both the labour and goods markets, so that the correlation observed between wage and price changes is coincidental. Another is that unemployment registers excess demand in the labour market only but that prices are raised in direct response to wage changes because businessmen follow the full-cost pricing principle. A third interpretation is that both price changes and the unemployment rate are responsible for increases in wages.[1] Finally, a fourth hypothesis combines this last idea with the preceding hypothesis and postulates a two-way relationship (or wage-price spiral) between the wage and price changes, whilst retaining unemployment and unfilled vacancies as an independent indicator of excess demand.[2] In all four hypotheses the pressure of demand for labour is a key determinant of the rate of wage and price inflation.

If it can be accepted that a relationship exists between unemployment and the rate of wage change the next issue is whether it is a reliable relationship, or more specifically of how reliable it is. There are a variety of ways of dealing with this question but one way which seems to be particularly interesting is to take one of the earliest and most influential investigations of the relationship, that by A. W. Phillips,[3] and to see how well it fits in with experience. Phillips' approach was to correlate unemployment with the rate of change of wage rates over the period 1861-1913. He quantified the relationship between the two series in the form of a schedule[4] which showed that the rate of wage inflation rose steeply as the unemployment percentage fell, *viz:*

unemployment rate	1.0	1.5	2.0	2.5	3.0
per cent change in wage rates	8.7	4.6	2.8	1.8	1.2

Having done this he tested the relationship by checking the predictions which it implied against the actual wage changes over the period from 1913 to 1957. It is important to note that Phillips did not use data for 1913-57 to estimate his relationship so that predictions for this period constituted an independent and legitimate check upon the validity of his equation. The original article may be consulted for the details of his results but it may be

---

[1] As in R.G. Lipsey, 'The Relation between Unemployment and the Rate of Change of Money Wage Rates in the United Kingdom, 1862-1957', *Economica,* February 1960.

[2] As in L. A. Dicks-Mireaux, 'The Inter-relationship between Cost and Price Changes, 1946-1959', *Oxford Economic Papers,* October 1961.

[3] A. W. Phillips, 'The Relation between Unemployment and the Rate of Change of Money Wage Rates in the United Kingdom, 1861-1957', *Economica,* November 1968.

[4] The equation for the schedule was:

$$\frac{\Delta W}{W} = -0.900 + 9.638\, U^{-1.394}$$

It can be expressed in logarithmic terms as:

$$\log\left(\frac{\Delta W}{W} + 0.900\right) = 0.984 - 1.394 \log U$$

where $\frac{\Delta W}{W}$ is the percentage rate of wage change and U is the unemployment rate (Phillips, *ibid.*).

noted here that the relationship, or Phillips Curve as it has been named, did exceptionally
well in the postwar period from 1948 to 1957.

This raises the interesting question of whether Phillips' Curve is still able to predict
wage changes in the period following the publication of this article. The evidence needed
to answer this question is provided in table 1.10 where the predictions implied by Phillips'
original relationship are set against the actual wage changes for 1958 to 1969. It may be
seen that until the last three or four years the predictions were not at all bad. Taking the
period from 1958 to 1965 the largest error was 2½ per cent and the mean absolute error
was 1.1 per cent. Furthermore, the results appear to have been fairly free from bias, the
positive errors tending to cancel out the negative errors. An implication of this last result
is that the relationship performs rather better over a run of years then for an individual
year. It would, for example, have been possible in 1958, when Phillips published his
article, to have predicted the wage level for end-1965 from unemployment figures for
1958-65 to within only 2½ per cent of what it actually turned out to be. This is a truly
remarkable result from a relationship based largely upon data from Victorian and
Edwardian times.

Table 1.10

The Accuracy of Predictions from the Phillips Curve, UK, 1958-69.

	Unemployment Rate	Change in Wage Rates predicted by Phillips' Equation	Actual Change in Wage Rates[1]	Error (prediction less actual)
	Per cent	Per cent	Per cent	Per cent
1958	2.1	2.5	3.6	−1.1
1959	2.2	2.3	1.1	+1.2
1960	1.6	4.1	4.1	.0
1961	1.5	4.6	3.4	+1.2
1962	2.0	2.8	4.4	−1.6
1963	2.5	1.8	4.3	−2.5
1964	1.6	4.1	3.8	+0.3
1965	1.4	5.2	4.6	+0.6
1966	1.5	4.6	3.3	+1.3
1967	2.4	1.9	5.9	−4.0
1968	2.4	1.9	7.1	−5.2
1969	2.4	1.9	5.7	−3.8

Mean absolute error	1958-65	1.1
Mean absolute error	1966-69	3.6
Mean algebraic error	1958-65	−0.3
Mean algebraic error	1966-69	−2.9

[1]   Change over 12 months in the index of weekly wage rates (as used by Phillips, *op. cit.*)
from December of the previous year.
Source: EPG, AAS

From 1965 onwards, however, the Phillips Curve appears to have led to some rather
poor predictions. On average from 1966 to 1969 the actual wage change has exceeded the
predicted figure by 3 per cent. It must be asked whether these results constitute a refuta-
tion of the relationship or whether the exceptions can be deemed to have 'proved the rule'.

The answer to this question can only be tentative but it looks as if the explanation lies
partly in a failure of the Phillips Curve and partly in factors of a new and exceptional kind.
In the first place it may be observed from table 1.10 that on three of the four occasions
prior to 1966 when unemployment was 2.0 per cent or more the predictions turned out to

be too low. The average error over these four years (1958, 1959, 1962 and 1963) was −1 per cent, so that a downward bias in the Phillips Curve at high unemployment rates can account for about one-third of the discrepancy that has to be explained. A second source of error seems to stem from a comparatively recent change in the relationship between unemployment and excess demand.[1] It can be seen from figure 1.9 that unfilled vacancies were much higher for a given amount of unemployment in 1967-9 than in the 1958-65 period. Rough calculations suggest that the vacancy rate for these three years was what used to be associated with an unemployment rate of 2.1 per cent (instead of 2.4). If this is the correct measure of excess demand then it is possible to claim that the wage increase should have been about ½-¾ per cent higher than predicted by the original Phillips Curve. A third factor is devaluation and the consequent rise in import prices. The latter, at 5.0 per cent a year since 1965, can probably account for an additional 1 per cent rise both in final prices and in wage rates. Taken together these three factors account for 2½-2¾ per cent out of the observed discrepancy of 2.9 per cent. It is interesting to note that a fourth new factor, prices and incomes policy, appears to have had no depressing effect upon the rate of change of wage rates other than in 1966 when, in the second half year, wages were held constant by law. But the analysis above does not suggest that incomes policy has been perverse.

IV.3   Inflation and Economic Policy

Avoiding inflation has been a goal of government policy for longer than the maintenance of full employment. The consequence of inflation which has been most feared by governments is its adverse effect on export prices and the balance of payments. These are results that can, strictly speaking, be neutralised by appropriate adjustments of the exchange rate. Internally, the most unfortunate consequence of inflation is the arbitrary and uncontrollable manner in which it redistributes real income and wealth. Under conditions of fast inflation the retired person living on a pension that is fixed in monetary terms faces a considerable erosion of his real standard of living. The fall in his real income is matched by a rise in that of the government or institution responsible for paying the pension. Inflation also redistributes income between borrowers and lenders, and between those who belong to strong trade unions and those who belong to weak ones. Such redistribution is extremely difficult to avert except by attempting to control the inflation itself.

The analysis of inflation suggested by the Phillips Curve and discussed above poses an awkward policy dilemma for governments. If the rate of price increase is inversely related to the rate of unemployment the policy-maker is forced to choose between two evils. On the one hand he may opt for a low level of unemployment and faster inflation; on the other he may have little or no inflation and large-scale unemployment. The exact form of the trade-off between the two goals depends on objective considerations, but the choice between the two is subjective, social or political. If the analysis of the preceding section is right and if output per man is rising at 3 per cent a year it may not be possible to avoid price inflation unless unemployment is in the region of 3 per cent,[2] that is about 750,000

---

[1]   The change in the way unemployment moves in relation to movements in unfilled vacancies may be attributable to three factors which have been present since 1966: the Selective Employment Tax, redundancy payments, and the introduction of earnings-related unemployment benefits. See *NIER*, February 1970, p. 34.

[2]   The association in the schedule on page 38 of a 1.2 per cent wage increase for 3.0 per cent unemployment must be adjusted upwards by 1 per cent on account of its downward bias at high unemployment rates and by ¾ per cent for the shift in the unemployment-excess demand relationship. This implies an increase in wage rates of roughly 3 per cent which is offset, in terms of labour costs per unit of output, by the gain of 3 per cent in output per man. Naturally these calculations are not meant to be precise. Phillips, 'The Relation Between Unemployment. . .', and F. W. Paish, in 'Incomes Policy', *Hobart Papers No. 29,* 1967 put the critical unemployment rate at about 2¼ per cent.

persons. Most people would agree that this is too high a price to pay for price stability. Not only is the unemployment most objectionable in itself, but the implied loss of national output between this and the recent unemployment rate of 2.4 per cent would be at least £200 million. In an economy where there is constant pressure to improve the provision of hospitals and schools and to increase the volume of private expenditure it is not difficult to see why governments have been reluctant to adhere to a policy of high unemployment in order to prevent inflation.

The search for alternative means of controlling inflation is nothing if not understand-able. In 1965 a great deal of hope was placed in the possibility that prices and incomes policy would be able to keep inflation in check quite independently of the pressure of demand. But the only period when this policy[1] appears to have had real effect was, not surprisingly, in the latter half of 1966 when wage rates were held down by statute. Since then the various attempts to impose guidelines for the rate of wage increase, to use delay-ing powers, and to insist on links between wage and productivity increases, have been of little or no avail. Wage rates have increased no less rapidly than might have been expected from past experience. It remains to be seen whether the new emphasis on a 'voluntary' in-comes policy is anything more than a face saver.

One other approach, which comes more under the heading of regional policy,[2] is to attempt to iron out the large variations in excess demand between the different labour markets in the economy. If only demand could be increased where there is already excess supply and if, at the same time, it could be reduced where there is excess demand, it would be possible to have less unemployment for a given amount of excess demand in the aggregate and a given wage increase. This result, which is equivalent to a shift in the Phillips relationship, is difficult to bring about. It means paying industry to move where it may not want to go or paying workers to do likewise, and it may be unrealistic to expect large effects from such a policy.

The conclusion is that there is no sure way of completely stopping inflation without creating more unemployment than is tenable on social grounds. Instead it may be necessary to accept a moderate rate of price increase as one of the costs of a high employ-ment policy.

V   ECONOMIC GROWTH

V.1   The Growth of Productive Potential

In section III of this chapter it was accepted that the current level of domestic output was something which could be determined by the prevailing level of aggregate demand. This is the underlying principle of Keynesian economics and it may be expected to hold whenever there are unused productive resources. It implies that so long as these are pre-sent the rate of increase in output will be determined by the rate of increase in demand.

The economics of growth is concerned with a different sort of problem. It asks what rate of growth of domestic output is sustainable at full employment or at some definable margin of unused resources. For this purpose it requires the concept of 'the growth of productive potential' and 'the underlying trend of productivity'. The first of these is defined as the rate at which GDP could grow without any change in either direction in the pressure of demand on productive resources. The underlying trend in productivity is similarly defined as the growth of output per man, or sometimes per man hour, between periods of identical demand pressure. Identical demand pressure can be generally[3] indicat-

---

[1]   See chapter 5.

[2]   See chapter 4.

[3]   Although not always precisely; see section IV of this chapter.

ed by equal or closely similar rates of unemployment. The periods 1900-13, 1922-38, 1950-7 and 1957-65 all began and ended with the same or similar unemployment rates, so that the growth rates of GDP and productivity in these periods should be in reasonable conformity with the definitions above. They are shown in table 1.11.

TABLE 1.11

Economic Growth, UK, 1900-65

Percentage increase per annum in:

	GDP	GDP per man	Civilian Labour Force	Capital Stock Excluding Dwellings
1900-13	0.9	−0.1	1.0	1.9
1922-38	2.2	1.0	1.2	1.1
1950-57	2.7	1.9	0.8	2.6
1957-65	3.1	2.3	0.8	3.4

Source: London and Cambridge Economic Service,
            The British Economy, Key Statistics, 1900-1966.

As the table shows both the growth rates of productive potential and the underlying trend in productivity seem to have increased fairly steadily since the beginning of this century.

The concept of the underlying growth rate is not without its limitations. In the first place it says little or nothing about the causes of growth but simply states a time-trend that has fitted closely with past data. An extrapolation of the growth of potential output for any period into the future could easily turn out wrong if the forces that determine full employment output are going to be present in different amounts or combinations from those of the past. As one knows so little about what these factors are or how to quantify them an extrapolation of the past growth rate is hazardous.

A second reservation concerns the interpretation of growth *rates* generally and their relation to *levels*. In calculating growth from 1957 to 1965, for example, one takes the compound rate of increase which will transform the level of GDP in 1957 into that of 1965. This says nothing about what happens in the intervening years and the growth rate so obtained is no guide to the average level of output over the intervening period.

TABLE 1.12

Annual Average Percentage Rates of Growth, 1955-65

	GNP	GNP per Employed Person
Belgium	3.5	3.0
Denmark	4.8	3.7
France	4.8	4.6
Germany	5.5	4.4
Italy	5.3	4.3
Netherlands	4.5	3.4
Norway	4.2	3.9
Sweden	3.6	NA
United Kingdom	3.0	2.4
Canada	4.4	1.9
United States	3.3	2.1

Source: OECD, *Economic Growth 1960-1970*, Paris, 1966.

So far as the calculation is concerned there could have been a huge increase or decre.
in output between 1957 and the middle of the period. In fact what happened was tha
there was a substantial shortfall from trend with consequently high unemployment in
1962 and the early part of 1963. An allied point is that the *level* of potential output in
this case was quite arbitrarily defined as being consistent with an unemployment rate of
1.6 per cent and does not necessarily represent the maximum attainable level. A whole
series of levels, each corresponding to a different unemployment rate, can be drawn
for any given growth rate.

One of the questions which the economics of growth must try to answer is why some
countries have grown so much faster than others and why, in particular, the growth of
the UK economy has been slower in the postwar period than that of most other industrial
countries (see table 1.12). The answer, if it is to be found at all, must be sought under
the more general heading of the causes of economic growth.

V.2   The Sources of Economic Growth

The causes of 'increasing opulence' have been discussed by economists since the time of
Adam Smith. Since growth is defined as the growth of productive potential it is clear
that it must depend, in the first instance, upon the rates of increase in the quantity and
quality of the factors of production and on the efficiency with which they are combined.
These rates of increase may be influenced, however, by factors on the side of demand
such as level and pressure of demand and the degree to which demand fluctuates.

The supply of labour depends on the evolution of the population of working age,
including net migration, the secular decline in hours worked, and the increase in the
length of annual and national holidays. Changes in the pressure of demand, however, exert
an influence on the size of the labour force and the number of hours worked. It is possible
that such tendencies, which we have observed during periods of cyclical change, also operate over longer periods and have an important effect upon migration.

The quality of labour must in large degree depend upon the facilities available for
education and training, the opportunities taken of them, and the degree to which they
match the changing demands for skill arising out of changes in technology and the structure of aggregate demand. Measurement of these influences, however, is difficult and there
is little evidence to show which way, if at all, they have affected the international comparison in table 1.12. The mobility of labour from job to job and from area to area is
probably an important factor in economic growth in so far as it reflects the degree to
which the labour force can adjust to economic change. It has been argued, not without
evidence, that much of the relatively fast growth of the German, Italian and French
economies can be attributed to the movement of labour from the agricultural to the
industrial sectors.[1] But it is still not clear how much of this mobility has been a cause
and how much a consequence of the disparity in growth rates between the agricultural
and industrial sectors.

One obvious influence on the growth of labour productivity is the rate of increases in
the nation's stock of capital, both in quantity and in quality. Some indications of the
growth of the UK capital stock are given in table 1.11, where it can be seen that the rate
of increase, like that of productivity, has tended to rise during the course of this century.
The stock of capital, however, is extremely difficult to measure. This is because the figures
of depreciation in the national accounts are based on data collected for tax purposes and
do not necessarily serve as an indication of the rates of scrapping and deterioration of
existing capital. Moreover, the economic value of a piece of capital equipment is an
inherently subjective concept, depending on expectations of future returns and modified

---

[1]   A. Maddison, *Economic Growth in the West,* Allen and Unwin, 1964.

by problems of evaluating risk. Estimates of the capital stock, therefore, must be treated with a good deal of reserve.

The quality of the capital stock is, perhaps, even more important and even more difficult to measure. According to one widely accepted view the quality of capital depends, by and large, upon its age structure. This view looks upon the capital stock as a series of vintages of gross investment, each new vintage containing machines of higher quality than the previous one. Scientific and technical progress are embodied in new machines, not old ones, so that the most recent capital equipment is likely to be the most efficient. This view is the basis of the 'catching up hypothesis' which has been advanced to explain the faster growth of some countries in the early postwar period. The argument is that those countries where the capital stock was seriously depleted by the war were in a position to replenish it with more efficient equipment, and were thus enabled to grow faster than those countries where the bombing and destruction had been less severe. The embodied view of technical progress, together with the difficulties of measuring the quantity of capital, has led a number of economists[1] to emphasise gross rather than net capital formation in a period as the better indicator of the extent to which capital resources have been enhanced. A high rate of gross investment, even if it is entirely for replacement purposes, will reduce the age of the capital stock and increase its quality.

Turning now to influences on the side of demand, two sides of the question need to be distinguished: the average pressure of demand and the size of fluctuations around the average. It can certainly be argued that a low average pressure of demand such as obtained (to choose an extreme example) in the early 1930s is inimical to innovation and investment. It hinders investment because capital equipment is under-utilised and because its continuation for any length of time is likely to set an unfavourable climate for expectations. High demand, on the other hand, will generally have the opposite effect. It has also been argued that high demand encourages managers and workers to devise new and better ways of working with existing equipment, thereby making technical progress of a variety which is not embodied in new types of machine. This effect has sometimes been described as 'learning by doing', and it fits in with the view that the scale of productive problems that have to be solved is itself a stimulus to their solution. Evidence has been produced to show how the time taken to assemble a prototype airframe has progressively diminished as the work force has gained experience by performing the same jobs over and over again. On the other hand, it has also to be borne in mind that high demand pressure may work the other way. The presence of a sellers' market with easy profits could also diminish the incentive to innovate and even lead to rather lazy attitudes to production. Again, extreme pressure can promote mental and physical exhaustion. Thus for any single firm there may be some optimum pressure of demand where technical progress is maximised, and beyond which the rate of progress tends to fall. For the economy as a whole the optimum pressure of demand is likely to be a rather complex average of the individual production units, and not something about which it is easy to make sweeping generalisations.

The other question is whether the amplitude of fluctuations tends to impede economic growth. It seems inevitable that the expectation of fluctuations will retard capital formation because profitability will be held down in periods of recession. It may also be the case that expectations of cycles lead to the installation of machinery which can be adapted to use in periods of both high and low output whereas the prospect of steady growth permits the introduction of machinery which can be specially designed to produce at a steadier level of sales. In this case it seems probable that the sacrifice of adaptability would mean a gain in the efficiency of capital, and growth would be faster. It may be no coincidence, therefore, that three countries with some of the lowest growth rates in the 1950s—the UK, US and Belgium—suffered sharper fluctuations in unemployment than

---

[1]   For example, Maddison *ibid.*

the others.[1] Japan is an exception to this rule but it may still be the case that a policy
that succeeds in keeping the economy at a steady pressure of demand could help to
increase the rate of economic growth.

V.3   Economic Growth as a Policy Objective

Economic growth has, in a limited sense, been an objective of economic policy since the
late 1940s. For so long as the productive capacity of an economy is increased each year
it is necessary for the sake of full employment to ensure that the level of total demand
rises by the same amount. Growth policy, in this sense, is part of the problem of short-
term economic management discussed in section III of this chapter.

Since the early 1960s, however, a growth policy has meant more than this. The objective changed from one of keeping demand more or less in line with a given growth of
capacity to one of raising capacity growth itself. The starting point was the establishment
by the Chancellor of the Exchequer, Mr Selwyn Lloyd, of the National Economic Development Office. This was in 1962. It set a target growth rate of 4.0 per cent for the period of
1961-6 but the actual growth rate in this period was 3.0 per cent and there was a recession
in 1962 and 1963. The NEDO, however, was a semi-official institution and its growth rate
did not receive a full official blessing until shortly before the election campaign of 1964.
By contrast the National Plan was prepared by a new Ministry (now extinct), the Department of Economic Affairs, with the prime function of raising the growth rate. Published
in the autumn of 1965 the National Plan looked to a growth rate of GDP of 3.8 per cent
per annum from 1964 to 1970, and to an annual productivity increase of 3.4 per cent.
The actual growth rate from 1964 to 1970 now looks like being only 2.4 per cent per
annum.[2] Whereas the planners had hoped for a 25 per cent increase in GDP over the six
years, the actual rise will have been 15 per cent.

These projections of economic growth have been wrong for several reasons. The first
mistake, which was made both by NEDO and the National Plan, was to pick a growth rate
as an assumption without properly examining the means of achieving it. The Plan's choice
of an overall increase in GDP of 25 per cent from 1964 to 1970 appears to have been
made without any attempt to relate the growth of output to the growth of productive
resources.[3] Its underlying productivity increase of 3.4 per cent per annum was substantially in excess of the 1960-4 increase of 2.7 per cent, yet very little justification was given
for it. It must be asked, however, whether enough is known about the causes of growth to
establish the conditions under which an increase of this order can be expected. The answer
is probably that not enough is yet known. Several economists have attempted to quantify
the effects of the various sources of economic growth, notably of additions to the labour
force, capital stock and technological knowledge.[4] But it is not unfair to say that the

---

[1] Maddison, *ibid,* pp. 43-56.

[2] Using the Treasury's latest forecast for 1970.

[3] 'In practice, given the comparatively short period we had to produce this document and do all this
very large amount of work, we decided to tackle it by taking as a starting assumption a growth of
the economy which was slightly higher than you would expect if past trends and policies had been
pursued, but not so much higher that it was unrealistic. This figure came out at around 25 per cent'.
(DEA witness, Minutes of Evidence taken before the sub-Committee on Economic Affairs, pp. 320-
1, *Fourth Report from the Estimates Committee,* Session 1966-7, House of Commons, 6 December
1966).

[4] For a survey of such work see R. R. Nelson, 'Aggregate Production Functions and Medium-Term
Growth Projections', *American Economic Review,* September 1964. For specific discussions of the
UK, see E. F. Denison's chapter in R. E. Caves, *Britain's Economic Prospects,* The Brookings
Instiution and Allen and Unwin, 1968, and the various contributions to D. Aldcroft and P. Fearon
(eds), *Economic Growth in 20th-Century Britain,* Macmillan, 1969.

assumptions that underlie such estimates are generally such as to demand an almost total surrender of one's natural scepticism. Although the National Plan and NEDO can hardly be blamed for having paid scant attention to such work, they do not appear, on the other hand, to have put anything else in its place. Thus the growth rates they proposed look now (as they did then to some observers) like little more than forlorn hopes. The fact is that rather less is known about the sources of economic growth than is necessary for the successful application of a growth policy. It may, indeed, be a very long time before governments are in a position to say that particular policies, such as a given rise in the ratio of investment to output, will be sufficient to raise the growth rate by so much per cent.

There is still, however, a widely held belief that the collapse of the National Plan can be wholly attributed to the deflationary and other measures that were introduced in order to rectify the balance of payments situation in 1966 and after. Of course it was a lamentable failure on the part of the planners not to foresee and forestall the serious balance of payments position that was developing. The deflationary measures raised unemployment to a higher level than had obtained at the beginning of the Plan period and this, in turn, meant that the rate of increase in actual output, measured from 1964, was less rapid than the underlying growth of capacity. But this interpretation of the failure of the Plan evades the issue of whether the growth of capacity could possibly have reached 3.8 per cent per annum even with a healthy balance of payments. There is nothing in the past experience of the UK economy to suggest that it could have reached this rate.

A faster rate of economic growth is a singularly enticing vision for the politician. It offers higher tax revenues at given tax rates and allows the government to choose between reducing taxes and increasing expenditures. It makes it easier to control inflation. But the means of implementing such a policy have yet to be elucidated in any but the most general terms.

VI THE ECONOMY FROM 1966 TO 1972

Economic policy in the three years from 1966 to 1969 was dictated by the need to correct a fundamental disequilibrium in the balance of payments. From mid-1966 until late 1967 the principal remedy adopted was one of deflating the level of domestic demand, the results of which have been observed in the rise in the rate of unemployment from 1.5 per cent in 1965 to 2.4 per cent in 1967 and the next two years. In November of 1967 it was at last officially recognised that deflation, by itself and in any tolerable degree, was inadequate for the size of the external problem, and the pound was devalued.

Although the balance of payments problem is essentially concerned with money values the remedy of devaluation cannot work unless it leads to a physical transfer of national output into the foreign balance. In terms of the national accounts this means that the physical volume of exports net of imports must rise. If GDP is not changing at the time this implies an actual decline in the domestic use of resources, which in expenditure terms comprises the consumption and investment of both the public and private sectors. Such a decline would constitute a fall in the national standard of living. With rising GDP, however, it is possible for the domestic use of total output to go on rising provided that it absorbs only part of the increase in output.

This change in the disposition of national output has been a central feature of the UK economy between 1967 and 1970. Its extent may be measured by comparing expenditures in real terms between the middle two quarters of 1967 and the second half of 1969.[1] During this whole period GDP rose at the slow average annual rate of 2.4 per cent,

---

[1]   This period of comparison, which was used by the Chancellor of the Exchequer in the Budget speech of April 1970, is less distorted than any other by the dock strikes of 1967.

but the domestic use of resources rose even more slowly, at only 1.2 per cent. The actual increase in GDP was some £800 million at 1963 prices but the domestic sector took only about £360 million of this rise (45 per cent) and the foreign balance took £445 million (55 per cent). The figures, which are set out in table 1.13, illustrate not only how devaluation operates by a switch in expenditures (see chapter 3) but also how the growth of the domestic enjoyment of total output is not always to be equated with the growth of GDP itself (as pointed out in section I.2 of this chapter).

TABLE 1.13

Changes in GDP and Domestic Use of Resources, 1967-9, and Official Forecast, 1969-71

£ million at 1963 prices, seasonally adjusted

		Level, 1967, 2nd and 3rd qtrs.	Actual Change[1] to 1969, 2nd half	Per cent of GDP Change	Forecast Change,[1] 1969, 2nd half to 1971, 1st half	Per cent of GDP Change
1.	Personal consumption	11,057	333 *(1.3)*		650 *(3.8)*	
2.	Gross investment and public expenditure	6,223	167 *(1.2)*		400 *(4.2)*	
3.	Indirect taxes less subsidies	−2,023	137		140	
4.	Domestic absorption of total output (1 + 2 + 3)	15,257	363 *(1.2)*	45%	910 *(3.9)*	115%
5.	Exports of goods and services	3,312	798 *(10.7)*		220 *(3.6)*	
6.	Imports of goods and services	3,537	353 *(4.4)*		340 *(5.8)*	
7.	Balance: net foreign absorption of total output (5 − 6)	−225	445	55%	−120	−15%
8.	GDP at factor cost (4 + 7)	15,032	808 *(2.4)*	100%	790 *(3.3)*	100%

1   Figures in brackets are percentage changes expressed at annual rates.
Sources: PE, 1970, *Financial Statement and Budget Report, 1970-71, HMSO, 1970.*

During this period of economic transition the balance of exports *less* imports of goods and services changed from an export deficit of £225 million in the two middle quarters of 1967 to an export surplus of £220 million in the second half of 1969. These figures are the physical counterpart of the balance of payments on current account (excluding the transfer element in invisible payments). The actual current account balance of payments, expressed in the more familiar and financially significant terms of money values, improved between the same two six-month periods from a deficit, seasonally adjusted, of £70 million to a surplus of £275 million.[1] In 1969 as a whole the current account balance was £370 million and the basic balance £390 million, a really notable achievement.

1   Unfortunately these current account figures include transfers but a completely comparable balance with the goods and services balances is not available at the time of writing and is never available in seasonally adjusted terms. The element of non-comparability is not serious.

The achievement of a balance of payments surplus was a physical sacrifice, not only in terms of the small size of the increase in output available for domestic use but also in the total loss of resources implicit in the policy of deflating domestic demand. The unemployment rate at 2.4 per cent for 1967-9 compared with an average rate for the earlier part of the 1960s of 1.7 per cent. There are some indications (see section IV of this chapter) that the rise in the unemployment rate did not mean an equivalent fall in the pressure of demand, but the fact still remains that in 1969, 560,000 people were registered as unemployed. Socially speaking, this is a deplorably large number.

Turning now to the economic future, part of the official forecast of April 1970 is given in table 1.13. It shows that GDP was expected to rise between the second half of 1969 and the first half of 1971 at an average annual rate of 3.3 per cent. This was a little faster, but not significantly different, from two other forecasts of the rate of change of output. The National Institute[1] in February was expecting GDP to rise at 2.2 per cent (annual rate) over this period, but with allowance for the effects of the April budget this increase probably becomes 2.7 per cent. The econometric forecast by R. J. Ball and T. Burns[2] gave a rise over the same 18-month period at the annual rate of 2.9 per cent. All three forecasts implied that the domestic sector would absorb most or all of the increase in output, and the official forecast (table 1.13) showed that it might be taking rather more than the total increase. The implication that the balance of payments, both in physical and monetary terms, would show some deterioration was not a cause for alarm given the very substantial surplus earned in 1969 and 1970.

The uncertainties in the economic forecasts were manifold. The most unpredicatable elements were the course of business fixed investment, where the possibility of a substantial revival of confidence could not be ruled out, and exports, where so much depended upon the future of world trade. These eventualities, as seen in May of 1970, were something which the reader will be better able to see for himself in late 1970 and 1971.

If the GDP-increase does stay within the range of 2¾ to 3½ per cent suggested by the forecasts there is no reason to expect much change in the rate of unemployment. Over the previous three years the government was committed to a high unemployment rate, and was highly successful in attaining it. In purely technical terms these were years of efficient economic management—much more efficient, it must be admitted, than in the unhappy period from 1959 to 1963 to which attention was drawn in section III. The budget of 1970 was very mildly expansionary, providing, in particular, for tax reliefs at the low end of the income scale. But in view of the economic prospect with which it was associated it could hardly have been accused of being wildly political, even though a General Election was to take place soon after. The government was still adhering to a policy of high unemployment relative to that of the earlier postwar period.

At the time this passage was written economic policy was, however, being questioned, and in some quarters attacked, for permitting too rapid an inflation. As has been emphasised in section IV of this chapter the control of inflation is a real dilemma. There is no doubt that the persistence with which the last government pursued its incomes policy was relaxed in early 1970. To those who are sceptical of the ability of incomes policy, short of a statutory wage freeze, to make any real impact this was no great loss. In the first edition of this chapter it was suggested that incomes policy might, regardless of whether it was formally approved by the *TUC*, merely antagonise the trade union movement. The partial abandonment of this form of nagging could, of course, be seen as part of an election campaign, but if its effects were only minimal, who cares?

Nevertheless, the 12-monthly increase in wages at the time of writing was in the region of 10 per cent, and as was pointed out at the time (rather obviously) a continuation

---

[1]   *NIER*, February 1970.

[2]   *Sunday Times*, 3 May 1970.

of such increases would be likely to undermine the balance of payments achievements of 1967-70. In section IV an attempt was made to explain the abnormalities of recent wage increases in terms of the aftermath of devaluation. The same sort of thing has happened in other countries, and it happened in the UK after the devaluation of 1949. This, and the other explanations of wage inflation, could prove wrong and there is also the possibility that the wage and price increases of early 1970 were the beginning of a hyper-inflation, where expectations of future increases lead to a loss of confidence in the currency and thus to actual price increases. This sort of inflation has never occurred in the UK but there have been times in the history of other countries when massive and disastrous hyper-inflations have been experienced.[1] In the opinion of the author nothing like this is going to happen in the UK between 1970 and 1972. The rate of wage increase will probably fall off. But it will be for the reader to follow the economy over this period and to check whether, or not, inflation becomes a real problem.

REFERENCES AND FURTHER READING

D. H. Aldcroft and P. Fearon (eds.), *Economic Growth in 20th Century Britain*, Macmillan, 1969.
W. Beckerman *et al.*, *The British Economy in 1975*, Cambridge University Press, 1965.
S. Brittan, *Steering the Economy*, Secker and Warburg, 1969, and *The Treasury under the Tories 1951-1964*, Penguin Books, 1964.
R. E. Caves (ed.), *Britain's Economic Prospects*, Brookings Institution and Allen and Unwin, 1968.
L. A. Dicks-Mireaux, 'The Interrelationship between Cost and Price Changes 1946-1959', *Oxford Economic Papers*, October 1961.
J. C. R. Dow, *The Management of the British Economy 1945-60*, Cambridge University Press, 1964.
M. K. Evans, *Macroeconomic Activity*, An Econometric Approach, Harper and Row, 1969.
W. A. H. Godley and J. R. Shepherd, 'Long-term growth and short-term policy', *NIER*, August 1964.
W. A. B. Hopkin and W. A. H. Godley, 'An analysis of tax changes', *NIER*, May 1965.
R. G. Lipsey, 'The Relation between Unemployment and the Rate of Change of Money Wage Rates in the United Kingdom 1862-1957', *Economica*, February 1960.
A. Maddison, *Economic Growth in the West*, Allen and Unwin, 1964.
National Institute *Economic Review*, February 1970 and earlier issues.
OECD, *Fiscal Policy for a Balanced Economy*, Paris, 1968.
F. W. Paish and J. Hennessy, 'Policy for Incomes?', *Hobart Papers (3rd edn.)*, 1967.
A. W. Phillips, 'The Relation between Unemployment and the Rate of Change of Money Wage Rates in the United Kingdom 1861-1957', *Economica*, November 1958.
D. C. Rowan, *Output, Inflation and Growth, An Introduction to Macro-economics*, Macmillan, 1968.
R. Stone, 'Private saving in Britain, Past, Present and Future', *MS*, May 1964.
'Short-term economic forecasting in the United Kingdom', *ET*, August 1964.

---

[1]   For a vivid account of one such inflation see F. Bresciani–Turroni, *The Economics of Inflation*, Allen and Unwin, 1937.

2

Monetary, credit and fiscal policies

I INTRODUCTION

The previous chapter attempts to convey an overall picture of the operation of the UK economy since the early 1950s, paying particular attention to fluctuations in economic activity, the behaviour of prices and economic growth. This chapter concentrates on a narrower area, the monetary, credit and fiscal policies of the authorities, that is, the UK government and the Bank of England.

The term policy implies the existence of both goals and a strategy or instruments to achieve them. The major policy goals most frequently cited in the UK since the second world war are full employment, price stability, economic growth, fixed exchange rates and a 'satisfactory' balance of payments position.[1]

Once a set of goals is chosen a host of questions arise. Are they mutually compatible within the particular economic system, given the usual policy instruments at the disposal of the authorities? If they are not, which goals should be sacrificed or modified? Are there alternative policy instruments that might be used to achieve one or more of the policy goals? Have the authorities, or for that matter has any one else, the necessary knowledge about the relationships between instruments and goals? Do they know exactly when and by how much to manipulate the policy instruments or even how many instruments they need?

Implicit in the foregoing discussion of goals and instruments are questions concerning both value judgments and how an economic system works. Both of these questions are recurring themes in this chapter. Section II looks briefly at the theoretical and empirical basis of monetary and fiscal policy. Section III discusses the structure of the banking and financial system and examines some money and credit theories. The taxation system is considered in section IV. Finally, the whole policy record since the early 1950s is described and assessed in section V.

II SOME THEORETICAL AND EMPIRICAL BACKGROUND

II.1 Extreme Keynesian and Quantity Theorist Positions

How do changes in the money supply or interest rates or changes in taxation and government expenditure affect the operation of an economic system? The use of monetary and fiscal policy implies some knowledge about the answers to these questions. However, the answers are highly controversial. One extreme viewpoint would argue that monetary policy is by and large ineffective and that, say, increases in the money supply and reductions in interest rates will have little or no effect as an encouragement to expenditure and hence will have little or no impact on economic activity. Another extreme view, but this time applied to fiscal policy, would argue that an increase in government expenditure will not stimulate an expansion of output and employment but will only substitute government

---

[1] See chapter 3 for an extensive explanation and discussion of the balance of payments concept.

expenditure for private expenditure. And, similarly, that a reduction in taxation will have no net expansionary effect on expenditure and hence output and employment.

Implicit in these contrasting statements are different models of the economic system. The first, which completely discounts the importance of monetary policy, is an extreme Keynesian viewpoint; and the second, which completely discounts the importance of fiscal policy, is an extreme Quantity Theorist position.

It has now been argued persuasively that the first viewpoint does far less than justice to Keynes himself.[1] Furthermore, there is accumulating evidence that it is untenable and that 'money does matter' and may even matter a great deal.[2]

At the same time neither the theoretical nor the empirical work supports an extreme Quantity Theorist position, one which has perhaps unkindly been paraphrased as 'money is all that matters'.[3]

II.2   Views of the British Authorities

For the authorities monetary policy has specifically *not* meant control and manipulation of the money supply as a policy instrument, but rather the control or influencing of 'the cost or availability of credit flows to the various sectors of the economy'.[4] Thus great reliance has been placed upon hire purchase controls, and control of bank lending through a proliferation of quantitative and qualitative restraints of varying degrees of effectiveness, including ceilings on advances, liquid asset ratios and special deposits. Moreover, 'credit controls have gradually become more specific and direct, in that the forms of credit to which restrictions are applied, the priorities to be observed and the exemptions to be allowed have been defined in more detail (though the authorities continue to have a strong aversion to making the banks' individual decisions for them)'.[5]

The growing emphasis on direct monetary controls followed on a period in the 1950s when monetary policy, as just defined, had been seen as largely permissive and subsidiary to fiscal policy, exchange control and the like. As the effectiveness of these latter policies became increasingly open to question the reliance on direct monetary controls grew. But it would seem that the position has now been reached where the authorities have, in turn, become somewhat disillusioned with the effectiveness of their brand of monetary controls and may be rather more sympathetic to the view that the money supply is after all of rather more significance for policy than had hitherto been accepted.

The economic model or models implicit in the policy of the authorities lean towards extreme Keynesianism, although this emphasis may have become rather less so over the years. But by and large the implicit emphasis is on an income-expenditure type of model, where fiscal policy can be expected to affect income and expenditure flows 'directly', and where monetary policy is conceived of as a supplement to fiscal policy and may be of some help when used in a 'direct' way to influence credit availability to particular sectors of the

[1]   Axel Leijonhufvud, *On Keynesian Economics and the Economics of Keynes: A Study in Monetary Theory, Oxford University Press,* 1968.

[2]   L. C. Andersen and J. Jordan, 'Monetary and Fiscal Actions: A Test of Their Relative Importance in Economic Stabilization', Federal Reserve Bank of St Louis *Review,* vol. 50, no. 11, November 1968; see also *Comment* by F. de Leeuw and J. Kalchbrenner, and *Rejoinder* by Andersen and Jordan, in Federal Reserve Bank of St Louis *Review,* vol. 51, no. 4, April 1969.

[3]   James Tobin, 'The Monetary Interpretation of History: A Review Article', *AER,* June 1965.

[4]   A recent explicit formulation may be seen in a paper 'prepared in the Bank of England in consultation with H. M. Treasury', and entitled 'The Operation of Monetary Policy since the Radcliffe Report', *BEQB,* vol. 9, no. 4, December 1969, pp. 448-60. The quotation is from p. 453.

[5]   *Ibid.,* p. 453.

economic system. Monetary policy in terms of manipulation of the money supply is generally ruled out, partly perhaps because it is felt to be too variable and unreliable in its impact, and partly because it would militate against government financing and debt management policies.

To those who have some sympathy with the new Quantity Theorist position (as does the author), and who believe that on the whole the evidence suggests that the demand for money is stable, and that changes in the stock of money do affect economic activity, the partial monetary approach is bound to fail.[1,2] For a partial plugging of credit loopholes must in time become less effective as new ones are discovered and evasion becomes more skilled. That precisely this has tended to happen will be seen as the policy record since the 1950s is examined in section V below.

II.3   Some Empirical Work

A great deal of the empirical work on the relative merits of monetary and fiscal policy as stabilisation instruments has been carried out in relation to the US economy.[3] The evidence is not conclusive but undoubtedly suggests that for the US economy monetary policy in terms of changes in the money supply are of the utmost importance for economic activity. Furthermore, some of the evidence also suggests that for stabilisation purposes monetary policy is more powerful than fiscal policy. However, it should be stressed that these conclusions are provisional and should be treated as such.[4] Nevertheless, there is no doubt that in the last five years or so there has been a major shift in professional opinion in the US on the importance of monetary policy as a stabilisation measure, which has frequently been coupled with a reduced emphasis on the significance of fiscal policy.

Unfortunately, as far as the UK is concerned there is rather less empirical evidence available about the relative merits of monetary and fiscal policy as stabilisation instruments. Moreover, the evidence that is available is to some extent conflicting.

One study, under the auspices of the National Institute of Economic and Social Research, tentatively suggested that fiscal policy might be more powerful and quicker

---

[1]   See, A. A. Walters, 'The Radcliffe Report—Ten Years After: A Survey of Empirical Evidence', in David R. Croome and Harry G. Johnson, *Money in Britain 1959-69*, Oxford University Press, 1970; David Laidler and Michael Parkin, 'The Demand for Money in the United Kingdom 1956-67: Preliminary Estimates', *Mimeographed Paper*, 1969. It should be stressed that to argue that the demand for money is stable is *not* to suppose that the income velocity of circulation of money, defined as income divided by the money stock, is *constant*. Velocity in this sense may and does vary in response to changes in interest rates and other variables. But this does not make velocity unstable. In principle and, indeed, in fact the variability of velocity can be explained to a substantial degree.

[2]   It can be argued that the use of the term 'Quantity Theorist' in this context is misleading and that the modern approach to the demand for money is more accurately described as an extension of the Keynesian theory of liquidity preference.

[3]   The term 'stabilisation' gives rise to problems of meaning and definition, particularly when a number of different policy goals are being pursued simultaneously. In the rest of this section it is assumed that the stabilisation objective is the rate of growth of gross domestic product. See also section V, pp 86-100. For further discussion, see G. D. N. Worswick, 'Fiscal Policy and Stabilisation in Britain', *Journal of Money, Credit and Banking*, vol. 1, no. 3, August 1969, pp. 474-95; and Karl Brunner, 'A Comment', *ibid.*, pp. 496-502.

[4]   In addition to references in footnote 2, p. 51 above, see Milton Friedman, *The Optimum Quantity of Money and Other Essays*, Aldine Publishing Company, Chicago; F. de Leeuw and E. Gramlich, 'The Federal Reserve—MIT Econometric Model', *Federal Reserve Bulletin*, January 1968; *ibid.*, 'The Channels of Monetary Policy', *Federal Reserve Bulletin*, June 1969; also R. G. Davis, 'How Much Does Money Matter?' Federal Reserve Bank of New York *Review*, June 1969; and M. W. Keran, 'Monetary and Fiscal Influences on Economic Activity—The Historical Evidence', Federal Reserve Bank of St Louis *Review*, vol. 51, no. 11, November 1969.

acting than monetary policy.[1] This conclusion is, of course, contrary to the analogous studies for the US. However, the authors of the National Institute study have major reservations about the econometric methods employed in these studies, including their own, and place little confidence in the conclusions of any of them.

Putting aside the fundamental questions relating to the methods used it would seem that the tentative conclusions of the National Institute study are extremely sensitive to the data employed, and perhaps to the time period used. For an alternative study, using different measures of economic activity and fiscal policy as well as a slightly different time period, produces conclusions about the relative effectiveness of monetary and fiscal policy that are consistent with studies for the United States.[2]

The absence of objectively convincing evidence about the merits of monetary and fiscal policy in the UK context makes it very difficult to give a confident assessment of the polices pursued by successive governments. However, it seems fair to say that professional opinion in the UK, whilst it may not have moved as much as in the US, is far less sceptical about the relevance of monetary policy, in terms of movements in the money supply, as an instrument for economic management than it was a very few years ago. This is not to say that professional opinion has seriously downgraded fiscal policy. Many British economists would still view it as much the more important instrument. But there is perhaps one thing on which professional opinion is now generally agreed and that is that neither monetary nor fiscal policy can, in the present state of knowledge, be used for 'fine tuning' or, alternatively, sensitive, short-run manipulation of the economic system.

III   THE BANKING AND FINANCIAL STRUCTURE AND MONEY AND CREDIT THEORIES

III.1   The Bank of England and the Cash Base Theory

The Bank of England is the central Bank of the UK; it has an overall responsibility for the management and control of the monetary and financial system and for its relations with the rest of the world. It acts as banker to the government and plays a basic role in smoothing government cash transactions and in administering and managing the national debt— broadly speaking the debt liabilities of the state to its nationals, to its own agencies, and to overseas holders. As agent of the government the Bank helps to regulate and control foreign exchange transactions and manages the Exchange Equalisation Account, which controls the official gold and foreign exchange reserves of the UK.[3]

The Bank is divided into two parts for accounting purposes; it produces two balance sheets, one for the Issue Department and one for the Banking Department. The origin of

---

[1]   M. J. Artis and A. R. Nobay, 'Two Aspects of the Monetary Debate', *National Institute Economic Review*, no. 49, August 1969. See also A. R. Prest, 'Sense and Nonsense in Budgetary Policy', *Economic Journal*, March 1968; J. A. Bristow, 'Taxation and Income Stabilisation', *Economic Journal*, June 1968; R. A. and P. B. Musgrave, 'Fiscal Policy', chapter 1 in *Britain's Economic Prospects*, R. Caves and Associates, A Brookings Institution Study, George Allen and Unwin, 1968.

[2]   M. W. Keran, 'Monetary and Fiscal Influences on Economic Activity: The Foreign Experience', Federal Reserve Bank of St Louis *Review*, vol. 52, no. 2, February 1970. See also A. A. Walters, *Money in Boom and Slump, Hobart Paper 44*, Institute of Economic Affairs, 1969; and Victor Argy, 'The Impact of Monetary Policy on Expenditure, with Particular Reference to the United Kingdom', *IMF Staff Papers*, vol. XVI, no. 3, November 1969.

[3]   See 'The Exchange Equalisation Account: Its Origins and Development', *BEQB*, vol. 8, no. 4, December 1968.

the double balance sheet system is to be found in monetary controversies during the first half of the nineteenth century. But the two balance sheets still retain a certain, if somewhat artifical, significance in that the Issue Department is classified in the national accounts of the UK as belonging to the public or government sector whilst the Banking Department is classified with the banking and financial sector. The position of the Issue Department on December 1969 is shown in table 2.1.

TABLE 2.1

Issue Department (Selected Items) December 1969. £ million

Liabilities			*Assets*	
Notes issued:				
	In circulation	3,371	Government	
	To Banking Dept	30	securities	3,375
		———		———
		3,401		3,375

Source:　BEQB

Note:　The balance sheet does not exactly balance because certain subsidiary items have been omitted. This is also true of other balance sheets summarised in this chapter.

The notes in circulation are necessarily held by persons, companies and financial institutions. Notes in the Banking Department would, of course, disappear from the accounts if the two balance sheets were amalgamated. The assets of the Issue Department are almost entirely government securities and any increase in the note issue implies an equal addition to holdings of government securities. In other words, when the Issue Department issues additional notes it obtains interest-earning government securities in exchange. Indeed the note issue may be looked upon as a gift to the government to help finance its expenditure.

The assets of the Issue Department are a means of helping the government to organise its finances in another way. The government is continuously concerned with the issue and redemption of its debt; it may need to borrow new funds or pay off maturing obligations. The government, and indeed the Bank of England also, is generally anxious to avoid large transactions, perhaps involving hundreds of millions of pounds, that might temporarily upset the securities market. They do this by arranging for the Issue Department to purchase new issues of securities that are not taken up by the public on the day of issue. Subsequently the Issue Department gradually sells to the public the stock it took up. Similarly, the Issue Department purchases stocks nearing redemption, avoiding large cash payments to the public when the actual redemption dates arrive. The Issue Department may in fact be in the market as a buyer or seller of government securities or both almost continuously. That is, it engages extensively in open market operations.

The balance sheet of the Banking Department is shown in Table 2.2.

TABLE 2.2

Banking Department (Selected Items) December 1969.　£ million

Liabilities			*Assets*	
Deposits:				
	Public	13	Government securities	461
	Bankers	221	Discounts & advances	70
	Other accounts	138	Other securities	51
	Special deposits	224	Notes and coin	32
		———		———
		596		614

Source:　BEQB

Public deposits are all government balances. They include those of the Exchequer, the Paymaster General, the Post Office and Trustee Savings Banks, the National Debt Commissioners, Dividend Accounts, and balances of the Revenue departments. The total amount involved is relatively small by comparison with bankers' deposits despite the enormous scale of government transactions. The main reason for this is that the government attempts to keep these balances as low as possible consistently with carrying out its operations. Any so-called surplus balances are used to retire government debt in an attempt to keep down costs. Net payments from the government to the community will have an immediate effect on bankers' deposits, increasing the cash holdings of the banking system. The reverse is, of course, also true and smoothing out movements of funds between public and bankers' deposits is a major preoccupation of the Bank day by day.

Bankers' deposits belong almost entirely to the clearing banks, though the total also includes deposits of the Scottish and Northern Ireland banks and deposits of accepting houses and the discount market. As bankers' deposits necessarily appear as assets in the balance sheets of these financial institutions and will therefore be discussed later, nothing more is said about them at this point.[1]

Other accounts include balances of overseas central banks and overseas governments and certain dividend accounts which are not *direct* obligations of the UK government. The accounts of the Bank's remaining private customers are also included here. These accounts are not without importance but they are not central to this chapter and so are not discussed further.

Special deposits are a relatively new category of deposit that the clearing banks and Scottish banks are from time to time obliged to transfer to the Bank as an aid to monetary policy. These deposits also necessarily appear in the balance sheets of the respective banks and for convenience their further discussion is postponed until later.[2]

Government securities introduce the assets of the Banking Department and include Treasury bills and longer dated government securities and Ways and Means Advances to the Exchequer.[3] These advances occur if the Exchequer finds itself short of funds at the end of the day and wishes to make up its balance; the advances are generally only overnight loans, being repaid the following day.

The Banking Department, through sales and purchases of government securities, affects the volume of bankers' deposits and hence the cash holdings of the banking system. In general, government securities in the Banking Department can be used in much the same way as those in the Issue Department to facilitate debt management and monetary policy. However, the assets at the disposal of the Banking Department are much smaller than those available to the Issue Department.

Discounts and advances are of two types, discounts and advances to the discount houses and to the remaining private customers of the Bank. The first are by far the most important to the operation of the monetary and financial system and attention is concentrated entirely on them. They are discussed in the next section dealing with the discount houses.

Other securities and notes and coin can be dealt with briefly. Other securities are non-government securities and include bills purchased by the Bank in order to keep a watch

---

[1] See below, p. 59.

[2] See below, pp. 61-4.

[3] A 'bill' in the sense used here is a piece of paper which is evidence of indebtedness on the part of the person or body on whom it is drawn. The bill is said to be 'discounted' when it is purchased at a price below its value on maturity. Hence Treasury bills are evidence of indebtedness of the Treasury. These bills have usually ninety days to run to maturity and might be acquired by the discount houses at, say, £98 10s. 0d. per £100 which would represent a discount of 6 per cent per annum on the value at maturity.

on the quality of bills circulating in the London market. The bank will not purchase bills of which they disapprove and this acts as a deterrent to their circulation. Other securities also include certain securities acquired by the Bank in the 1930s. Notes are the counterpart of the item in the Issue Department and some coin is held for ordinary business purposes.

Those notes and deposits of the Bank which are held by the commercial banks constitute, except for a small amount of coin, the cash base of the banking system. The London clearing banks which account for the greater part of commercial bank activity, maintain an essentially fixed proportion of 8 : 100 of Bank of England notes and deposits in relation to their own deposits. Now if the clearing banks were the only holders of Bank of England notes and deposits it would be very easy to see how a cash base theory of the volume of bank deposits might arise. For, given this fixed proportion or fixed cash ratio as it is generally called, all that the Bank of England would have to do to determine the volume of bank deposits would be to vary the amount of its own deposits and notes outstanding.[1] However, it is not so simple either in theory or practice.

For one thing Bank notes are held by the general public and other institutions besides the clearing banks. Thus if the Bank increases the cash base the non-clearing bank holders might absorb the whole increase and hence there would be no increase in clearing bank deposits. The simple cash base theory outlined above would no longer hold. But if the non-clearing bank holders also held Bank notes in a fixed proportion to their deposits with the clearing banks the cash base theory would hold once more, though in a slightly more complicated form. For every change in the cash base would be distributed between the clearing banks and other holders in such a way as to preserve a fixed ratio between the cash base and the money supply, defined to include clearing bank deposits and notes held by others.[2]

However, the facts also do not support this version of the cash base theory. The non-clearing bank holders of Bank of England notes do not hold them in a fixed proportion to their deposits with the clearing banks. Furthermore, it is not at all clear that the Bank of England determines the amount of its notes and deposits outstanding in the way required by the theory. Alternative theories, based on the clearing banks' liquid assets and their liquid assets ratio, have been much more in vogue in recent years. But before considering these it is useful to look at the activities of the discount houses.

III.2　The Discount Houses

The discount houses are a special type of financial institution which borrows a substantial proportion of its funds from the clearing banks and other institutional lenders such as accepting houses and overseas banks. Most of these funds are at call or short notice in the sense that these lenders may demand their repayment immediately or subject to very short notice. The discount houses use these borrowed funds to acquire assets such as short-dated British government securities, Treasury bills, commercial bills, local authority securities and certificates of deposit. If the clearing banks or other lenders demand repayment of their loans and the discount houses cannot borrow elsewhere or otherwise obtain funds, they turn to the Bank of England which makes funds available to them against

---

[1]　The Bank could do this in a number of ways, the most important being open market operations.

[2]　A little arithmetic may help to clarify this. Suppose deposits of the clearing banks equal 100 and they hold 8 Bank of England notes and deposits, whilst other holders have 2 Bank notes and the 100 clearing bank deposits. Thus the money supply, Bank notes and deposits held by other holders totals 102 and the cash base is 10. If the Bank increases the cash base to 15 the money supply must increase to 153, made up of 150 deposits and 3 Bank notes, with the clearing banks holding 12 of the cash base. The ratio 10 : 102 is the same as 15 : 153.

suitable collateral or by the purchase of bills. The discount houses are the only financial institutions which have automatic access to the Bank in this way.

The traditional practice was that the Bank acted as lender of last resort to the monetary and financial system, through the intermediation of the discount houses, by lending to them at or above a rate called Bank rate.[1] This rate is generally described as a penal rate as it is higher than 'market rates'—the rates ruling in the market for Treasury bills and prime commercial bills. The theory is that if the discount houses are borrowing at Bank rate they are therefore making losses and will hasten to pay off their debts to the Bank, with a consequential reduction in the cash base of the banking system. However, there have been periods when short-dated government securities of the kind held by the discount houses have yielded more than Bank rate. Thus the penal rate argument would not be valid for borrowings from the Bank against these securities. Moreover, it is conceivable that if the discount houses were expecting a reduction in interest rates they might be prepared to borrow for a time at the so-called penal rates to take advantage of capital appreciation and high running yields on some or all of their asset holdings. The Bank, of course, has the option, which it may or may not use, to charge more than Bank rate or to raise it. However, it is clear that the traditional penal rate argument is not totally convincing.

For many years, however, the Bank has helped to relieve cash shortages in the money market by purchasing bills from the discount houses at market rates, as well as providing funds at Bank rate or above, depending on which the Bank felt more appropriate in the light of monetary and economic conditions. But in June 1966 the Bank introduced an important modification in its method of lending. Previously *loans* to the discount houses had usually been for a minimum period of seven days and charged at Bank rate or occasionally above. But since then the Bank is prepared to lend overnight at below Bank rate and generally at market rates.

Thus the Bank may now exercise great flexibility in the terms on which it supplies funds to the discount houses. The Bank is also prepared to absorb by sales of bills to the discount houses surplus funds that they cannot otherwise conveniently employ. The Bank is therefore in a commanding position to influence day-to-day rates in this money market.[2]

The discount houses occupy a very special position in the market for Treasury bills. Each week as the Treasury issues new bills the discount houses tender as a syndicate at a single rate for the whole issue, except that individual houses may tender for some bills at rates above the syndicated rate. The joint bid of the discount houses is usually lower than outside bids. These higher bids are satisfied first and so the discount houses obtain the residual amount on offer.

The syndicated bid procedure has the merit from the point of view of the Treasury that it 'guarantees' them the funds they need and probably helps to stabilise Treasury bill and other short-term rates. However, from another point of view the procedure is an odd one. For in the final analysis the discount houses are able to tender for the whole issue of Treasury bills because, as already explained, the Bank stands ready to support them. Moreover, they would presumably become concerned if they could only cover the tender over a sustained period by borrowing at Bank rate. To avoid this the Bank may, as has been shown, supply the discount houses with funds at market rates. The discount houses then use the funds to acquire the new Treasury bills. But this is tantamount to the Bank

---

[1]   The significance of Bank rate as a key rate in the whole structure of interest rates in the UK may well be changing because of the more flexible lending and support policies of the Bank. These are described in the next paragraph. However, when Bank rate moves many other rates move. This is especially true of rates on bank deposits and rates in the discount market.

[2]   It is of interest that throughout 1968 and 1969 all assistance given to the discount houses was at market rates.

lending directly to the Treasury and so increasing the cash base of the banking system, as the Treasury spends the funds, unless the whole process is offset in some other way, such as by the Bank selling securities to the non-bank public.

There is, in fact, an element of charade about the whole procedure of the discount houses tendering for the full Treasury bill issue. The danger is that the charade hides what is really happening—the financing of the Treasury by borrowing from the central bank. This may tend to subordinate monetary policy to the exigencies of government financial needs and there is a lot of evidence suggesting that the consequences of this are likely to be inflationary.

III.3   The Clearing Banks

The London clearing banks are so named because they are all members of the London Bankers' Clearing House, the place where their representatives meet to settle interbank indebtedness. Up to 1968 there were eleven clearing banks, although not all of them were independent. But with the mergers of 1968 only eight clearing banks remain and these also are not all independent. The eight banks are dominated by the big four, Barclays, National Westminster, Lloyds and Midland, who between them control over 95 per cent of total deposits and have a network of some 12,600 branches. The clearing banks' primary function is the management of the payments system in England and Wales, although they necessarily carry out all the usual commercial banking functions.

For many years the clearing banks have acted as a cartel in fixing the interest rates they pay on deposits and charge on advances. These practices have recently come in for increasing criticism because of the encouragement they have given to uneconomic non-price competition, especially in the form of branch extension, and the general lack of dynamism in the system as a whole. It would, however, be false to argue that the banks have totally stood aside from competing in terms of price for deposits and in granting credit. For many of them have done so through subsidiaries and associated companies such as finance houses (described below) and other financial institutions. But this does not detract from the basic criticism.[1]

To be unduly critical of the banks, however, may be unjustified as it is highly likely that the authorities, with their predilection for short-run stability of nominal interest rates, would not have welcomed interest rate competition by the banks for deposits and advances. This preference of the authorities may well be changing and with the recent full disclosure of profits and reserves by the banks the time may not be far distant when they begin to compete directly in terms of price for deposits and advances.

Deposits are the main liabilities of the clearing banks and may be seen, together with other items of the balance sheet for December 1969 in table 2.3 (page 59). Gross deposits are made up of current, deposit and other accounts, and are practically all domestic liabilities. Current accounts or demand deposits are withdrawable on demand and transferable by cheque; they are the most important means of payment in the economy. Demand deposits do not generally earn an explicit rate of interest though the size of the credit balance may be taken into consideration in determining the charge for managing the account. Deposit accounts or time deposits do earn interest—at 2 per cent below Bank rate— and are subject to notice of withdrawal—at present seven days—and are not ordinarily transferable by cheque. However, these conditions can be waived, though usually

---

[1]   Monopolies Commission *Report* on the Proposed Merger of Barclays Bank Ltd, Lloyds Bank Ltd, and Martins Bank Ltd (HC 319), 1967-8.

with some loss of interest. Other accounts include credit items in course of transmission, contingency reserves and other internal accounts of the banks.[1]

Coin, notes and balances with the Bank of England have already been encountered. The notes and coin are used by the banks for their day-to-day business and balances with the Bank to settle interbank indebtedness and for making payments to the authorities.

TABLE 2.3

London Clearing Banks (Selected Items). 10 December 1969. £ million

(i)   *LIABILITIES*

Gross Deposits:		
Current accounts	5,350	
Deposit accounts	4,361	
Other accounts	1,013	10,724
TOTAL		10,724

(ii)   *ASSETS*

Liquid Assets:		
Coin, notes and balances with Bank of England	894	
Money at call and short notice	1,549	
Treasury bills	394	
Other bills	608	3,445
Investments		1,105
Advances to customers and other accounts		5,194
Special deposits with Bank of England		213
TOTAL		9,957

Source: BEQB

If for some reason a bank, or the banks as a whole, find that their cash holdings are tending to fall below 8 per cent of deposits something must be done to rectify the position. It may be possible for the individual bank to sell or exchange some of its assets for cash, perhaps by recalling some of its money at call and short notice from the discount market, which, as already explained may have to turn to the Bank of England. This will generally happen if the banks as a whole are short of cash. If the Bank does not wish to lend at Bank rate, perhaps because it is anxious to keep interest rates from rising, then it will normally enter the open market and purchase securities at market rates, paying for them with cheques drawn on the Bank and so relieving the cash shortage. However, if the Bank wishes to see some upward pressure on interest rates it will wait for the discount houses to come to the Bank and only make cash available at Bank rate or possibly even above.

Recalling money at call and short notice from the discount houses is not the only way the banks may attempt to restore their cash ratio. For one thing, as is explained below, some of the money at call and short notice is a liability of financial institutions other than the discount market. But apart from this the banks may attempt to sell some of their investments and negotiate repayment of advances that they themselves have made to their customers. However, unless there is an inflow of funds from abroad, the banks as a whole

---

[1]   Following the full disclosure of profits and reserves by the clearing banks changes are to be made in their accounting procedures. The mid-monthly statement of the clearing banks will use a different method of accounting for cheques in course of transmission and transit items and will also exclude hidden reserves from other accounts. The result will be to reduce substantially gross deposits, once and for all. The reduction is likely to be of the order of £750-£800 million.

can succeed in selling investments and having advances repaid only by engineering a reduction in their deposits. For if purchases by the authorities and an inflow of foreign funds
are ruled out, then the non-bank private sector can only acquire bank assets or reduce its
indebtedness to the banks by exchanging bank deposits for investments and advances.[1]
Once deposits are reduced the necessary cash holdings to satisfy the cash ratio are also
reduced. Thus the banks may restore their cash ratio in a variety of ways, the exact pattern of events depending to a large degree on the policy followed by the authorities. In the
end they are in a position to determine the ease or difficulty of the adjustment process.

Money at call and short notice is made up of two main parts. The most important is
loans to the discount houses, but of growing significance in recent years have been loans,
for periods up to one month, to other UK banks, to members of the stock exchange—with
easily marketable stocks and shares being used as collateral—and loans to bullion brokers,
and to money markets in other centres. Balances in sterling and in certain foreign currencies with other banks in the UK and overseas are also counted as money at call and short
notice.

The clearing banks buy their Treasury bills in the market and do not bid for bills at
the weekly tender, at least not for themselves, though they may do so on behalf of their
customers. Bills bought on their own account by the clearing banks are usually held to
maturity, though they are, on occasion, sold to the Bank if the latter is looking for
maturities that are no longer held by the discount houses. The purchase of bills by the
Bank from the clearing banks is one of the ways by which the Bank may relieve pressure
on the discount houses and obviate their need to borrow at Bank rate or above. This is
described as 'indirect help' to the discount houses as opposed to 'direct help' by means
of purchases from the houses themselves. From the point of view of monetary management the Treasury bill is the most important instrument in the London money market.

Other bills are a composite item that includes commercial bills drawn on UK residents,
various other bills such as Treasury bills of Commonwealth and foreign governments and,
beginning in February 1961, certain export credits which the banks may refinance or
obtain funds for from the Bank. These export credits arise from the banks' financing of
exports on a medium-term lending basis and, in the first instance, generally run for some
three to five years and are repayable by instalments. The Bank, as an encouragement to
the granting of finance for exports, is, subject in some cases to a ceiling, willing to refinance these credits when they have no more than eighteen months to go to final repayment. This clearly makes them a highly liquid asset from the point of view of the banks
and the Bank specifically gave them permission to include these refinanceable export
credits as part of their liquid assets. The significance of this will become clear shortly.

Investments consist of securities of the British government, Commonwealth governments, local authorities and mostly fixed interest securities of public companies. The
British government securities are the most important and are so arranged that some of
them mature each year and the major proportion of them within ten years. These
securities give the Banks additional flexibility in meeting demands for private credit
because they are highly marketable, and those close to maturity can generally be disposed
of without serious capital loss. The banks do not aim, at any rate in the short run, at a
specific ratio of investments to deposits and, in fact, over the years have greatly reduced
the ratio.[2]

Advances are of two main types, loans and overdrafts. With the loan the customer's
account is credited with the amount whereas the overdraft is literally an overdrawing of
a current account which is debited accordingly. Advances are generally assumed to be the

---

[1] Strictly speaking, the private sector could purchase bank assets with notes. But this possibility is
quantitatively unimportant and has been ignored in the text.
[2] In 1954 the ratio reached a postwar peak of almost 36 per cent and by 1969 it was just over 11
per cent.

most lucrative of the banks' assets. The rates payable are Bank rate, with a minimum of 4 per cent, for the nationalised industries, and for first-class commercial customers 1 per cent above Bank rate with a minimum of 5 per cent. Most other borrowers pay higher rates. As in the case of investments the banks do not maintain a fixed ratio of advances to deposits, though in ordinary circumstances there is probably some ratio, around 55 per cent, that they would not wish to exceed.[1]

As already mentioned, the authorities have shown a recurring interest in advances ever since the outbreak of the second world war and on numerous occasions have requested the banks to restrict or even reduce their advances in the interest of economic policy.[2] The authorities consider advances to be particularly inflationary as they put immediate purchasing power in the hands of potential spenders. This purchasing power would not be all that important if the authorities were prepared to restrain the growth of bank deposits and allowed interest rates to rise as the banks sold securities in order to enable them to make additional advances. For restriction of the growth of deposits and rising interest rates might be expected to have a dampening effect on expenditure. But, as indicated earlier, the authorities have generally been unwilling to restrict systematically the growth of deposits and were apparently anxious to avoid rising interest rates as a consequence of the balance sheet adjustments of the banks. Thus the authorities' concern about advances reflects, at least in part, a preference for particular interest rate structures and, implicitly, a rejection of the importance of bank deposit growth, or more generally the money supply, for economic policy. However, the whole problem has been complicated by the historically low percentage advances bore to deposits for most of the postwar period and the banks' evident desire to raise it.[3]

III.4   Liquid Asset Theories and Special Deposits

From the point of view of recent theories of the money supply the most important aspect of the clearing banks' activities is the behaviour of their liquid assets and the liquid assets ratio. Their liquid assets are defined to include currency (mainly Bank of England notes), balances or deposits with the Bank, money at call and short notice (mostly but not entirely to the discount houses), Treasury bills and other bills. At present the banks are expected to maintain a *minimum* liquid assets ratio equivalent to 28 per cent of their gross deposits. When the ratio first emerged in the early 1950s it was not fixed but in 1956 the Bank insisted on a minimum ratio of 30 per cent.[4]

By analogy with the cash base theory, if there were only one kind of liquid asset supplied by, say, the Treasury and held only by the clearing banks, it would be reasonable to postulate a liquid assets theory of deposit determination. These circumstances have never existed. But there was a period after the second world war when Treasury bills were far and away the most important component of the banks' liquid assets. It was then plausible to argue that the volume of deposits was determined by the supply of Treasury bills.

---

[1]   The ratio of the clearing banks for 1969 averaged 50.2 per cent and under present credit restrictions they are not free to approach a 55 per cent ratio.

[2]   See section V of this chapter.

[3]   In 1946 advances of the clearing banks were the equivalent of only 17 per cent of their deposits, and by 1954 the figure had only reached 27 per cent, perhaps about one-half of the long-run desired ratio.

[4]   In 1951 the Governor of the Bank of England indicated to the (clearing) banks that a liquidity ratio of from 32 per cent to 28 per cent would be regarded as normal but that it would be undesirable for the Ratio to be allowed to fall below 25 per cent as an extreme limit. From 'Bank Liquidity in the United Kingdom', *BEQB*, vol. II, no. 4, December 1962, p.252.

The argument never appeared in this precise form. At its simplest it assumed that *all* Treasury bills were held by the Bank of England, the clearing banks and the discount houses, with the latter financing their holdings by money at call and short notice from the clearing banks. The cash holdings of the clearing banks—the notes and deposits of the Bank of England—might be thought of as being covered by Treasury bills held by the Bank. Thus on this argument any change in the supply of Treasury bills would be reflected in the liquid asset holdings of the clearing banks and, given the liquid assets ratio, would permit a multiple change in the same direction in the volume of deposits.[1]

Another version of the theory, which owes much to Professor Sayers and the Radcliffe Committee, emphasises, in addition to the role of the Treasury bill, the importance the authorities attach to maintaining short-run stability of the Treasury bill rate.[2] Perhaps the most straightforward way to see some of the implications of this is to suppose that the authorities want to keep the rate completely stable but at the same time there occurs an increase in the supply of Treasury bills. If the discount houses buy these with additional money at call from the banks and the Treasury immediately spends the funds these will accrue as deposits to the customers of the banks. In other words the banks' deposits and their liquid assets will have increased but not, at this stage, their cash holdings. As far as liquid assets are concerned the banks are in a position to permit an expansion of their deposits. But if the 8 per cent cash ratio was exactly satisfied before the above transactions took place it will now no longer hold. The banks will have to take appropriate action. The traditional argument would be that the banks would attempt to obtain funds from the Bank via the discount houses. But if this happened interest rates would tend to rise. However, this suggestion does not make much sense as the banks are assumed above to have just extended additional call money to the discount houses. The point is that if the authorities are adamant in their determination to maintain stable rates they cannot stand idly by and allow the banks to experience any difficulties over their cash ratio. For any pressure on the cash ratios of the banks will tend to result in higher rates unless the situation is relieved by the Bank. The Bank, if it is to maintain rate stability, must provide the necessary cash, thus permitting the banks to exploit the addition to their liquid assets.[3]

In a simplified form this version of the liquid assets theory implies that if the authorities reduce the supply of Treasury bills, but at the same time keep their interest rate constant, the volume of deposits will decline. The reason is that with the interest rate held constant the non-bank public hold the same amount of bills, hence leaving less for the banks to hold, and so with a fixed liquid assets ratio the banks' deposits must decline. Alternatively, if the Treasury allows the interest rate to rise, but keeps the supply of bills constant, the non-bank public will demand more of the bills available, again leaving less for the banks, and once more leading to a reduction in the volume of deposits. Neither formulation of the liquid assets theory is supported by the facts, or at least not consistently so. The supply of Treasury bills has declined and the Treasury bill rate has increased without the volume of deposits decreasing.

If the volume of deposits can increase without any increase in the supply of Treasury bills and yet the banks maintain their liquid assets ratio then clearly the banks must be able to obtain other liquid assets besides Treasury bills and cash reserves. In fact, their

---

[1]   W. Manning Dacey, 'The Floating Debt Problem', *Lloyds Bank Review,* April 1956.

[2]   R. S. Sayers, 'The Determination of the Volume of Bank Deposits: England 1955-6', in his *Central Banking after Bagehot,* Oxford, 1957. Radcliffe Committee, *Committee on the Working of the Monetary System* (Chairman, Lord Radcliffe). See *Report,* Cmnd 827, paras 375 and 583-90.

[3]   For simplicity, the argument assumes that there are no inflows or outflows of funds from or to abroad.

commercial and other bill holdings and money at call and short notice have risen rapidly over the last five years or so.

Thus these original formulations of the liquid assets theory have been discredited.[1] However, the authorities, whilst recognising that controlling the supply of Treasury bills is not a sufficient condition for controlling the volume of deposits, still give great attention to the volume of liquid assets as a whole.[2] There appears to linger in the minds of the authorities the belief that if they could effectively control the supply of liquid assets to the clearing banks they would be able to control the volume of deposits and the granting of credit by the banks. However, it is unlikely that the authorities are prepared to accept the implications of maintaining tight control over the availability of liquid assets to the clearing banks. For one of the implications would be that interest rates would have to move more freely and this would tend to conflict with the management of the national debt, although the practice of the authorities in this matter may be undergoing some change.[3]

If these last statements are accepted then it follows that it is not the liquid assets ratio nor the cash ratio that have been of basic importance in relation to the volume of deposits, but the interest rate policy of the authorities and the factors that have influenced this policy. This in turn implies a much more complex approach to explaining the determination of the money supply than a simple cash base or liquid assets theory, though both ratios will necessarily appear in the explanation.[4]

Special deposits were defined earlier as a type of deposit that the clearing banks and Scottish banks are from time to time obliged to transfer to the Bank as an aid to monetary policy. The banks cannot draw cheques on special deposits or include them as part of their cash or liquid assets. The Bank first called for special deposits in April 1960. The calls are expressed as a percentage of total deposits with the calls from the Scottish banks being at one-half the rate of those from the clearing banks. The Bank ordinarily pays interest on special deposits at approximately the current rate on the latest issue of Treasury bills.[5] Special deposits were designed by the authorities to reduce the amount of liquid assets, such as Treasury bills, at the disposal of the banks. The authorities hoped that the introduction of special deposits would make it more difficult for the banks to expand their deposits and to grant additional credit to borrowers. The scheme is essentially an offspring of the liquid assets theory of deposit determination.

---

[1] Commenting on the period 1952-67 the Bank has stated that, 'During this period . . . neither the cash ratio, nor the liquid assets ratio, provided a really firm fulcrum for the authorities'. 'The UK Banking Sector 1952-67', *BEQB*, vol. 9, no. 2, June 1969, p. 177.

[2] 'Bank Liquidity in the United Kingdom', *BEQB*, vol. 1, no. 1, December 1960, pp. 248-55. See also the discussion of special deposits in the next paragraph but one.

[3] 'In the last years of the period [1959-69], as greater weight has been placed on monetary policy, there has been a greater flexibility in policy on interest rates and a greater willingness to allow upward pressures on rates in the market to take effect; and this has given more scope for flexible tactics in debt management'. *BEQB*, vol. 9, no. 4, December 1969, p.456.

[4] For a study along these lines, see W. E. Norton, *An Econometric Study of the United Kingdom Monetary Sector 1955-66*, unpublished Ph.D. thesis, University of Manchester, December 1967; and 'Debt Management and Monetary Policy in the United Kingdom', *Economic Journal*, September 1969.

[5] The Bank announced in May 1969 that, because the clearing banks had failed to comply with a quantitative restriction on their advances, the rate of interest payable on special deposits would be halved from 2 June. *BEQB*, vol. 9, no. 2, June 1969, p. 145.

From what was said above about these theories it will come as no surprise to find that it is concluded here that special deposits as originally envisaged are a rather ineffective policy instrument. This can perhaps be seen as follows. Special deposits are really a compulsory loan by the banks to the authorities, made in such a way that there is no reduction in the cash holdings of the banks. For if the loan reduced their cash holdings there would generally have to be a fall in the volume of deposits and an increase in interest rates. The authorities might accept the first but generally do not want the second, though there have been times when interest rates have risen simultaneously with, but not primarily because of, calls for special deposits. Thus when a call for special deposits is made the banks must—excluding the possibility of an inflow of foreign funds—find the cash for their payment by selling bills and/or securities directly or indirectly to the authorities. It will probably be in the banks' interest to sell securities and affect their liquid assets as little as possible. Insofar as they feel obliged to sell liquid assets they are highly skilled at replacing these fairly quickly or accumulating them in anticipation of calls. There is no reason to believe that special deposits which have little or no effect on the volume of the banks' deposits will reduce advances. On the contrary, special deposits may encourage an increase, if they earn less than the assets they replace and the banks are anxious to make good the difference by acquiring larger holdings of their most lucrative assets. The fact that the authorities have increasingly relied upon direct quantitative control of bank lending to the private sector in the form of bills and advances would seem to bear out the previous argument. This is not to argue that the authorities, through detailed control of the availability of liquid assets to the banks, could not make special deposits effective. But to do so would be to put in jeopardy their interest rate policy. In the event special deposits remain as a form of compulsory and apparently cheap form of borrowing for the authorities.[1]

III.5   Accepting Houses, Overseas Banks and Other Banks

The business of this group of banks varies substantially amongst themselves, although they have enough in common to allow them to be discussed together. Since about 1957-8, when exchange control restrictions were substantially relaxed and funds could begin to move more freely between international financial centres, the accepting houses, overseas banks and other banks have greatly expanded, and at a rate much more rapid than the clearing banks. Moreover, these non-clearing banks have been active participants in the development of new and important money markets, which are briefly described below.[2]

The term accepting house arose because of the important role the houses played and still play in 'accepting' bills of exchange, the commercial or financial bill already encountered in the discussion of the discount houses and the clearing banks. A bill is accepted by signing it and in so doing the acceptor becomes liable for payment of the bill on maturity. The accepting houses accept bills on behalf of clients and in this way earn commissions.

Accepting houses are also known as merchant banks. The name correctly implies that some of these houses carry on both a merchanting and banking business. Indeed the title suggests their origin, for the banking side of their activities generally emerged as a con-

---

[1] See below, p. 93. Norton, *Thesis,* p. 277, concludes that 'an increase in special deposits is expected to have no significant effect on advances, the money stock or expenditures'.

[2] For further information on these banks and money markets, see 'UK Banks' External Liabilities and Claims in Foreign Currencies', *BEQB,* vol. 4, no. 2, June 1964, pp. 100-8; 'Overseas and Foreign Banks in London: 1962-68', *BEQB,* vol. 8, no. 2, June 1968, pp. 156-65; 'London's New Markets for Money', *Midland Bank Review,* August 1966; and 'Recent Developments in London's Money Markets—II', *Midland Bank Review,* November 1969.

sequence of their business as merchants, particularly in overseas trade. Even today some merchant banks maintain both a merchanting and a banking business. One owns a refinery, others are concerned with the marketing and production of timber, trading in rubber and coffee and in the export trade. A number are active in the gold and silver bullion markets, the foreign exchange market, the foreign currency deposit business and engage in making new issues of both domestic and overseas securities, advise and manage investments on behalf of clinets and act as trustees. In fact, the activities of the merchant banks are excitingly diverse.

The overseas banks are banks which maintain offices in London but whose main business is overseas. There are now about 120 overseas banks compared with around 80 less than ten years ago and they play a major part in the movement of funds into and out of London and in the finance of international trade.

The remaining category, other banks, has only recently been separately distinguished in official statistics and, apart from some small merchant banks, mainly comprises subsidiaries of other British banks. It is largely through these subsidiaries that the clearing banks have come to participate, albeit indirectly, in the new money markets that are mentioned below.

In the twelve years since 1957 the total deposits of the accepting houses, overseas banks and other banks have grown from some £850 million to around £22,000 million. This is an extraordinary rate of growth, but it is to some extent misleading as the figures include a substantial amount of internal and inter-bank transactions. If these categories are deducted the £22,000 million is reduced to some £16,000 million, compared with around £10,000 million for the clearing banks. It should, however, be stressed that the deposits, and indeed the balance sheets generally, of this group of banks are in many respects very different from those of the clearing banks.

TABLE 2.4

Accepting Houses, Overseas Banks and Other Banks (Selected Items) December 1969

(i)   *LIABILITIES*

£ million

Current and Deposit Accounts:	Sterling	Other currencies	Total
UK banks	1,483	4,116	5,599
Other UK residents	2,103	397	2,500
Overseas residents	1,080	10,484	11,564
*Negotiable Certificates of Deposit	443	1,541	1,984
TOTALS	5,109	16,538	21,647

(ii)   *ASSETS*

	Sterling	Other currencies	Total
Coin, notes and balances with Bank of England	5		5
Balances with other UK banks	1,567	4,151	5,718
Money at call and short notice	249		249
Loans to UK local authorities	1,338		1,338
Sterling bills discounted	154		154
British government stocks	430		430
Advances:-			
UK residents	1,230	632	1,862
Overseas residents	236	11,373	11,609
Other assets	455	515	970
TOTALS	5,664	16,671	22,335

* These are denominated in only one foreign currency, US dollars.

Source: BEQB

The deposits of this group of banks are largely interest bearing and are deposited for periods of time varying from overnight to much longer periods. The sterling deposits with UK banks are the basis of an interbank money market that has developed rapidly in the last five years or so. Through this market the participating banks are able to satisfy their day-to-day liquidity needs with relatively little reliance on the discount market.

The foreign currency deposits of some £15,000 million consist mostly of euro-dollars, that is, dollar funds held outside the US.[1] It should be noted that the foreign currency deposits are roughly matched by foreign currency assets, a large proportion of which are in the form of advances to overseas residents. To the extent that the foreign currency transactions are matched they do not directly affect the UK gold and foreign currency reserves, other than through the commissions and fees earned by the banks.

The negotiable certificate of deposit was first introduced in London in May 1966. For the holder the certificate of deposit has the great advantage that, whilst it yields very little less than a fixed term deposit, it can be sold any time before maturity in the secondary market. The maturity dates may be up to a year or more and the discount houses have been active in creating a secondary market, that is, in dealing as principals in the certificates.

The banks hold a very small amount of funds with the Bank of England and mostly settle their interbank indebtedness through the clearing banks. The final item that needs to be mentioned is loans to local authorities. The demand for these emerged following a decision of the government in October 1955 to permit access to the Public Works Loan Board (under the Treasury) only if a local authority was unable to borrow elsewhere. Much of the loans are on a very short-term basis, being for seven days or less and often are for very large amounts.

The interest rates in the different markets, especially in the euro-dollar market that has grown so dramatically, are greatly influenced by international monetary and financial conditions. This development, in a world of fixed exchange rates, tends to unify international money markets and thereby to reduce the freedom of an individual country to pursue an 'independent' monetary policy.

This group of banks are not at the moment requested to maintain cash and liquid asset ratios, as are the clearing banks. To do so would be very difficult because of their diversity and because of their need for great flexibility in deploying their funds and taking advantage of interest rate differentials. However, in 1968 the Bank of England announced a 'cash deposits' scheme for these banks. It provides for the payment of cash deposits to the Bank, calculated as a percentage of certain of their deposits denominated in sterling.[2] The deposits would earn interest at a market rate, related to the Treasury bill rate.

The analogy with special deposits is clear. Furthermore, there is no apparent reason to expect cash deposits—they have not yet been implemented—to be any more effective than special deposits, unless the Bank is prepared to reduce the cash base of the total banking system. But if the Bank does this the brunt of the adjustment will fall on the clearing banks and not on the banks which are party to the new scheme. However, it is clearly not intended to work in this way. It is rather 'for use when moderate, rather than severe restraint is necessary'.[3]

---

[1] 'The Euro-Currency Business of Banks in London', *BEQB,* vol. 10, no. 1, March 1970, pp. 31-49.

[2] 'Control of Bank Lending: the Cash Deposits Scheme', *BEQB,* vol. 8, no. 2, June 1968, pp. 166-70.

[3] 'The Operation of Monetary Policy since the Radcliffe Report', *BEQB,* vol. 9, no. 4, December 1969 p. 457

III.6   Money and 'General Liquidity'

The extraordinary growth of the accepting houses, overseas banks and other banks, to a point where their deposits exceed those of the clearing banks, raises in acute form the question of the definition of money. What is it? How should it be defined?

There would seem to be two main approaches to these questions, one largely abstract and the other essentially pragmatic. The abstract approach tries to isolate unique attributes that may be attached to a particular group of assets. The well-known classical attributes are means of payment, store of value and unit of account. The Keynesian approach, whilst not repudiating the classical attributes, emphasised the motives for holding 'balances', transaction, precautionary and speculative.[1] Neither of these 'abstract' approaches is really satisfactory for in practice there is no group of assets that has a monopoly of either or both sets of attributes. Alternatively, many sets of assets have the attributes to varying degrees.

When faced with this dilemma, whereby it seemed plausible to extend the more traditional definition of money beyond currency and bank deposits, the Radcliffe Committee responded with the concept of 'liquidity'. 'It is the whole liquidity position that is relevant to spending decisions, and our interest in the supply of money is due to its significance in the whole liquidity picture'.[2] By 'liquidity picture' they appear to have had in mind a whole set of financial institutions, their assets and liabilities, trade and other types of credit and 'the ease or difficulty encountered by spenders in their efforts to raise money for the purpose of spending on goods and services'.[3] The Committee, in hearing evidence about the operations and activities of financial institutions and whilst recognising the great differences between these, was impressed 'not by these differences but by the fact that the market for credit is a single market'.[4] By this it meant that the same financial institution might supply both short- and longer-term finance and that borrowers were prepared, if one source of finance was curtailed or unavailable, to switch to another. It was thus the fact of highly developed money and capital markets and the way they operated that greatly influenced the Committee in emphasing the need to control 'the liquidity position of the system as a whole'.[5] It was highly sceptical about the emphasis and importance formerly attached to control of the traditional money supply.

The trouble with the 'liquidity' concept is that, if anything, it is even more difficult to relate to a specific group of assets. Thus the liquidity concept is not an improvement upon the earlier approaches and does not resolve the definition of money problems.

An alternative is to be somewhat more pragmatic and, starting with the primary function of money, namely means of payment, to see if there is a group of assets with this attribute, not necessarily to the same extent, for which a stable demand function exists and where there is a systematic relationship between the group of assets and economic activity. Furthermore, as far as monetary policy is concerned it is important that the authorities should be in a position to influence the behaviour and especially the rate of growth of the group of assets.[6]

---

[1] See Sir John Hicks, *Critical Essays in Monetary Theory,* Clarendon Press, 1967; also, N. J. Gibson, 'Foundations of Monetary Theory: A Review Article', *The Manchester School of Economic and Social Studies,* vol. XXXVII, no. 1, March 1969.

[2] *Report,* p. 132, para. 389.

[3] *Ibid.*

[4] *Ibid.,* p. 142, para. 125.

[5] *Ibid.*

[6] See D. Laidler and M. Parkin, 'The Demand for Money in The United Kingdom 1956-67: Preliminary Estimates' (to be published).

There is of course no guarantee that the same group of assets will be appropriate indefinitely. It would seem that this possibility must be accepted as a fact of life but need not be unduly disturbing so long as the appropriate group of assets does not change wildly and erratically. Moreover, past experience, despite the growth of non-bank financial intermediaries, is reassuring on this score.

If this approach is followed it seems probable that the appropriate group of assets in the context of the UK need not go beyond currency in circulation with the public, the net deposits of UK residents with the clearing, Scottish and Northern Ireland banks and deposits with the National Giro.[1] This, of course, excludes the deposits of the accepting houses, overseas banks and other banks, as well as those of non-bank financial intermediaries. It should be mentioned, however, that this suggestion is controversial and, in particular, conflicts with the official designation of the money supply in *Financial Statistics*, which also includes net deposits by UK residents with the discount market, accepting houses, overseas banks and other banks.[2]

The position taken above, which emphasises the importance of money as opposed to liquidity, should not be understood as implying that the activities of financial institutions other than the banks, whose liabilities are classified as money, are unimportant for monetary policy. Their importance must, in fact, be accepted. For they perform a crucial role in communicating the effects of monetary policy throughout the economic system. Furthermore, the evidence, incomplete though it may be, does not suggest that the activities of the non-monetary financial intermediaries are a serious offset to monetary policy, defined as effective control over a group of money assets, the manipulation of which affects economic activity.[3]

III.7   Finance Houses

A finance house is an institution which specialises in the financing of hire purchase and other instalment credit. There are hundreds of companies involved in this business but the bulk of it is carried on by about twenty of the large firms. Many of them are subsidiaries of the clearing and other banks. Hire purchase debt generally takes the form of a down-payment by the purchaser with the rest of the debt being paid off by instalments over a specified period. The period varies with the type of product and may be as little as six months for some household goods or as much as five years for industrial machinery; the period for cars—the most important type of hire purchase debt—may be up to three years. The finance houses attempt to organise their contracts so that the debt outstanding at any time on the hire purchase transaction is less than the value of the product being acquired; this gives them some security and indicates why they concentrate on financing the purchase of durable or semi-durable goods rather than perishable goods. In practice hire purchase debt is frequently paid-off well in advance of the terminal period. This is important in assessing the liquidity of finance houses' assets.

Deposits are the single most important liability of the finance houses. It is only since the early 1950s that they have come to rely on deposits as a major source of funds for their activities. They were forced in this direction by the recurrent restrictions on bank advances and the restraints imposed on capital issues.[4] Deposits are of two main kinds:

---

[1]   Walters, in *'The Radcliffe Report—Ten Years After'*, suggests that broadening the money concept does 'not appear critically to affect the demand function'. Thus there would seem to be little to be gained by broadening it and the principle of economy would indicate a preference for a less broad group of assets.

[2]   Cf. 'Money Supply and the Banks', *Midland Bank Review*, February 1969.

[3]   See, Walters, *'The Radcliffe Report—Ten Years After'*; also N. J. Gibson, *'Financial Intermediaries and Monetary Policy'*, Hobart Paper 39, 2nd edition, Institute of Economic Affairs, 1970.

[4]   See section V of this chapter.

fixed term deposits, usually for three or six months, and deposits subject to notice of withdrawal, again normally for three to six months. Deposits may, however, be for as long as twelve months. The deposits earn interest at rates which are greatly influenced by those ruling in the new money markets. Thus there is no inflexible link with Bank rate, as in the case of the clearing banks, and the rates paid are substantially in excess of those paid by the latter. The chief depositors are industrial and commercial companies, banks and other residents, as well as a small amount of funds from overseas residents. Current accounts are not unknown amongst the finance houses but do not appear to be a significant part of their business. Banks provide most of the remaining funds to the finance houses by means of discounting bills and by advances. Capital and reserves are also important.

Hire purchase outstanding usually accounts for some 80 per cent of their assets. Not all the hire purchase outstanding is owed directly to the finance houses; part of it arises from the purchase by the latter of debt from retailers and is known as 'block discounts'. Retailers do of course retain some hire purchase debt, but the finance houses own the bulk of it. Their next most important asset is advances and loans. These include loans to garages (to finance stocks of vehicles) and to property companies; and short-term loans to industrial and commercial companies. Very few assets are held in liquid form; the houses rely on their ability to attract additional deposits, on their borrowing powers and on the speedy repayment of their assets.

The finance houses, as already mentioned, have been subjected to severe restrictions in raising funds. But their activities have also been greatly affected by controls over the terms on which they are allowed to trade. The government has from time to time stipulated, as an instrument of economic policy, the minimum down-payments that must be made on different products and the maximum repayment periods.[1] There is evidence that controlling down-payments and repayment periods has, at least, a strong initial impact on hire purchase business and consequently on demand for consumer durables. The total effect on demand is less certain as consumers may transfer, at any rate, some part of their frustrated down-payments and instalments to the purchase of other goods and become increasingly successful at obtaining credit by other means. It is evident that hire purchase controls are highly discriminatory as regards the products affected. The consumer durables industries, especially the car industry, are seriously affected in organising their production and sales by the frequent changes in the controls.

The authorities are well aware of these criticisms of hire purchase and instalment credit controls and by the appointment of the Crowther Committee on Consumer Credit, headed by Lord Crowther, which is expected to report in 1970, have given official recognition to the whole problem. The large amount of attention given to the activities of the finance houses by the authorities is, of course, totally consistent with their approach to monetary policy. Doubts about the merits of this approach have already been expressed above.[2]

III.8   Building Societies

Building societies are mutual or non-profit making bodies which specialise in the provision of finance for the purchase of both new and second-hand houses. There are some five hundred building societies, about one-fifth of the number some seventy years ago, together with a network of branches. They cater for millions of customers, both as lenders and borrowers.

Over 90 per cent of the liabilities of building societies are shares and deposits. Both are essentially deposits, so that the term share is something of a misnomer. However, the shareholder is a member of the society whereas the depositor is not, and the latter has a

---

[1]   See section V of this chapter.
[2]   See also section V of this chapter.

prior right of liquidation over the shareholder. Deposits earn a slightly lower rate of interest than shares. Shares and deposits are subject to notice of withdrawal, though in practice both are paid on demand or on very short notice. The interest rates on shares and deposits are quoted net of income tax, which is paid by the societies at an average or composite rate and is less than the standard rate of tax. In May 1970 the interest rates recommended by the Building Societies Association were 5 per cent on paid-up shares and 4¾ per cent on deposits.

Mortgages usually account for over 80 per cent of the assets of building societies and are predominantly for private house purchase. Most mortgages are for between twenty and thirty years with continuous repayment by instalments. The average life is about ten years, making the assets of building societies much shorter than might appear. The recommended interest rate on mortgages was 8½ per cent in May 1970. But this is the gross rate as interest payments on housing are allowable against income tax assessments: if allowance is made for income tax relief at the full standard rate the interest rate is reduced to about 5¾ per cent net. For those who pay less than the standard rate of tax, or no tax at all, there is an option mortgage scheme, supported by the government, which reduces the cost.

All other assets, except such things as office premises, are classified as liquid assets by the societies. Both the type of asset and the maturity distribution are regulated by statute. At the end of 1969 the actual liquid assets ratio was 16.2 per cent of total assets; the ratio itself is not directly under statutory control. Cash holdings are relatively small and vary a lot seasonally.

The building societies dominate the market providing finance for house purchase. The finance they provide is therefore relevant, directly and indirectly, to the activity of the house building industry. The societies cannot for long expand the supply of finance to borrowers unless there is a corresponding net inflow of funds from new shares and deposits otherwise they would deplete their liquid assets and in time risk upsetting public confidence in their management. The interest rates the societies pay and the relationship they bear to competing rates would appear to be a major determinant of the net inflow of funds to the societies.

If Bank rate is taken as a rough measure of competing rates it is found that by and large the *smaller* the differential between Bank rate and the rates on society liabilities the larger the net inflow of funds, and vice versa. In fact, the societies do not change their rates with every change in Bank rate; they prefer relative stability in their rates. From the point of view of effectiveness of monetary policy this may be rather important. For instance, if Bank rate is raised as part of a restrictive policy measure and the societies do not raise their share and deposit rates they will probably soon have to curtail the supply of advances, which will presumably in time tend to depress house building activity, thereby supporting the generally restrictive measures of the authorities. Thus, given the behaviour of the building societies, the effectiveness of an increase in Bank rate in curtailing credit for house purchase depends crucially on its timing.[1] If, however, it is desired to insulate house purchase and house building from the effects of generally restrictive economic policy, then the reactions of the building societies are not, on the face of it, so helpful. The question of how this insulation might be achieved and the economic, political and social consequences of attempting it, have not received adequate attention.

III.9   Other Financial Institutions

The United Kingdom is particularly rich in the variety and number of its financial

---

[1]   If, as has already been suggested, the significance of Bank rate in relation to market rates may well be changing then the relationships described in the text may also be expected to change.

institutions. The term 'rich' is used advisedly. For financial institutions that are able to mediate freely between borrowers and lenders help to make the allocation of scarce resources more efficient. 'Improvements in their efficiency and the development of new financial intermediaries are analogous to productivity increases and innovations in industry'.[1] However, limitations on space prevent more than a brief mention of some of the remaining major financial institutions.

National Savings Bank and Trustee Savings Banks: The National Savings Bank, formerly the Post Office Savings Bank, and Trustee Savings banks offer a range of facilities, many of them similar, to depositors. Both of them accept ordinary deposits which earn interest at 2½ per cent per year; the first £15 of interest is free of income tax. Depositors with at least £50 in the 2½ per cent account may also hold deposits in investment type accounts on which higher rates of interest are paid. In 1965 the Trustee Savings banks were given power to provide current accounts with chequing facilities and the Post Office in October 1968 introduced a new system for transmitting payments, based on the continental giros and known as the National Giro. By December 1969 its deposits had reached £36 million.[2]

The funds on deposit at 2½ per cent are paid directly to the National Debt Commissioners, an official body with certain responsibilities for the national debt, who invest them in government securities. Both the National Savings Bank and the Trustee Savings banks have slightly more freedom in employing the funds obtained through their investment accounts. As well as investing directly in government securities they lend to local authorities. Thus the savings banks are channels by which funds flow directly to central and local government. However, in recent years the ordinary deposits at 2½ per cent have been declining as returns have risen on other forms of assets in the private sector.[3]

Insurance Companies: There are over five hundred insurance companies engaged in business in the UK, but by far the greater part of British business is carried on by those members of the British Insurance Association, which has some two hundred and ninety members. The discussion below concentrates on these.

Insurance falls into two main categories, life insurance, and a catch all, general insurance, which includes fire, marine, motor and other accident insurance. Life insurance for the most part gives rise to long-term liabilities which the companies must be in a position to meet. This gives them an interest in long-term investments and in assets that may be expected to increase in capital value over the years. General insurance, on the other hand, is carried on much more on a year-to-year basis, ideally with the premiums for the year being sufficient to cover the risks underwritten and to allow for expenses and the accumulation of limited reserves. So the disposition of funds arising from general insurance is largely governed by short-term considerations; assets must be quickly realisable without undue fear of capital loss.

The insurance companies, with total investments at the end of 1969 of around £14,000 million, are of great importance in the UK's capital markets. They are large holders of both government and company securities.

Investment Trusts: Investment trusts are limited companies which specialise in the investment of funds provided by their shareholders or borrowed from debenture holders

---

[1] Gibson, *Financial Intermediaries and Monetary Policy*, p.12.

[2] The National Giro does not itself make loans to account holders but it has an arrangement by which they can apply to a finance house, Mercantile Credit, for personal loans, with repayments through Giro accounts.

[3] In the April 1970 budget the Chancellor announced that he proposed to take powers to vary the interest rates payable on ordinary deposits.

or other lenders. Despite the term 'trust' they do not operate under trust deeds, which specify the terms and conditions governing the management of the investment funds.
In addition to investment trusts there are private investment companies and investment holding companies which often perform similar functions. But these are not considered to be investment trusts in the sense used here and are not discussed in this chapter. Attention is concentrated on the group of nearly three hundred investment trusts that currently make returns to the Bank of England.

Investment trusts expand by raising funds from new capital issues and by retaining some of the income and capital profits from previous investments. But once again it is the asset side of the balance sheets that is of chief interest. At the end of 1969 the total market value of assets of investment trusts making returns to the Bank of England were £5,060 million. Nearly all of this was invested in company securities, practically all ordinary shares. Over one-third of the company securities were those of overseas companies.

This extremely heavy concentration of investments in ordinary shares is a postwar phenomenon. Before the war investment trusts had substantial holdings of fixed interest securities. But the fear of inflation eroding the real value of fixed interest investments has encouraged the investment trusts to rearrange drastically the distribution of their assets. The size of the investment trusts make them important operators in the ordinary share market. They also fulfil an important function in helping to finance small companies by holding their unquoted securities. Their freedom to invest overseas has been seriously affected by government restrictions and tax measures.

Unit Trusts: Unit trusts perform a similar function to investment trusts. But unlike the latter they do operate under trust deeds and have trustees, often a bank or insurance company. The unit trusts are authorised by the Board of Trade and are run by managers who are quite distinct from the trustees. Two hundred and six unit trusts made returns to the Bank of England at the end of 1969 and the number continues to grow; in 1960 the figure was fifty-one.

Unit trusts do not issue share capital and are not limited companies but they issue units which give the owners the right to participate in the beneficial ownership of the trusts' assets. The units are highly marketable as they can always be bought from or sold to the managers at prices which reflect the market value of the underlying assets. As more units are demanded the managers provide more; for this reason they are sometimes called 'open-end' trusts, as opposed to 'closed-end' trusts such as the investment trusts which do not expand in this way.

Like the investment trusts the assets of the unit trusts are almost entirely company securities, made up of ordinary shares. But in contrast to the investment trusts some 90 per cent of the assets are domestic and about 10 per cent overseas. At the end of 1969 the total assets of the unit trusts were £1,340 million. Their rate of growth has been extremely rapid; in 1960 their total assets were only £190 million. There is little doubt that the rapidity of their growth is an attempt by small investors and others to protect themselves against inflation by participating indirectly in ordinary share investment.

The Stock Exchange: The Stock Exchange provides a market for variable price securities, both government and company securities. Without this market where securities may readily be bought and sold the whole business of raising funds through outside sources would tend to be more expensive and less efficient. The London Stock Exchange is by far the most important in the UK and is the one of primary interest here. However, most of the major cities have stock exchanges and currently a movement is afoot to integrate their activities more closely and ultimately to form a single UK stock exchange.

A feature of the stock exchange is the jobbing system. Jobbers are traders in securities; they act as principals, buying and selling on their own account and making their profits on the difference between their buying and selling prices, which they generally stand ready to quote for the securities in which they specialise. This function can be extremely important in giving stability to the market which might otherwise be much more volatile and possibly mislead investors.

Brokers generally act as agents for customers, buying and selling on their behalf, usually but not always through jobbers.

Speculation is a term frequently associated with the Stock Exchange and nearly always carries overtones of abuse and criticism. To a substantial degree this reflects ignorance of the functions of the Stock Exchange, though this is not to imply that speculation is always necessarily beneficial. However, when it is not the so-called harmful kind, speculation may reflect some other basic restrictions of one kind or another which inhibit the efficient operation of the market. But if the speculator is doing his job, and in the long run he will go out of business if he is not, he will be helping to keep the price of shares in touch with economic realities, damping down the effects of irrelevant rumours and false information; he will, in fact, be improving the communications of the economic system.

Traditionally the terms 'bulls' and 'bears' have been applied to particular types of speculation though they are now used more generally to refer respectively to markets tending to rise and fall in price. But traditionally a 'bull' was someone who bought securities on a rising market hoping he would be able to sell them at a profit before he had to pay for his purchase. The 'bear' sold shares that he had not got, on a falling market, in the hope that he would be able subsequently to buy and deliver them at a lower price.

An idea of the massive scale of stock exchange activities can be obtained from the figures on turnover, that is, sales and purchases. The total turnover during 1969 was about £30,000 million, a relatively poor year. Turnover of British government securities was some £19,000 million. Clearly, the stock exchange is of major importance to the financial activities of both the private and public sectors of the economy.[1]

IV   THE TAXATION SYSTEM

IV.1   Introduction

The Treasury, in its evidence to the Radcliffe Committee, made it clear that at least since 1948 it had relied primarily on fiscal measures 'for the regulation of the pattern and total of effective demand . . . monetary measures being regarded as having only a supporting role'.[2] Thus in the official mind fiscal measures were the dominant policy instrument. The importance the authorities attached to fiscal policy represents a victory for the Keynesian revolution.[3] For Keynesians the state, through its taxation and expenditure, can and should influence the level, forms and rate of growth of economic activity. Monetary policy is secondary, and by comparison relatively unimportant, at least for the extreme Keynesian.

The extreme Quantity Theorist view, as implied earlier, is in some ways precisely the opposite: monetary policy is of prime importance and fiscal policy is secondary, if of any significance at all.[4] This view had previously been stubbornly held by the Treasury between the wars and hence the use of the term 'victory' in referring to the equally stubbornly held extreme Keynesian views of the Treasury since the second world war. It will be evident that if the analysis and emphasis of this chapter is at all near the truth then there is

---

[1] The effects of taxation on the operation of the capital market are touched on below, pp. 80-1.

[2] *Report*, p. 184, para. 516.

[3] J. M. Keynes, *The General Theory of Employment, Interest and Money*, Macmillan, 1936, and *How to Pay for the War: A Judicial Plan for the Chancellor of the Exchequer*, Macmillan, 1940.

[4] See above, pp. 50-1.

an unmistakable irony in the official approach to policy over the last forty years. For, at the risk of oversimplification, between the wars the official approach neglected and perhaps misunderstood the role of fiscal policy and, since the second world war, monetary policy, although as already indicated the official attitude to monetary policy seems to be undergoing some change.[1]

IV.2   The Size of Government

It is well known that governments in this century have become, in terms of their own activities, far more important in relation to the economic life of the community. Nevertheless, it is by no means straightforward to measure the size of government economic activity relatively to the rest of the economic system. Perhaps the best that can be done is to take a number of different measures.[2]

One of these is the direct claims the government makes on the volume of goods and services available to the community in any time period. In this context 'government' includes central and local government, but excludes such things as the nationalised industries or more generally, public corporations. Table 2.5 shows that government expenditure has claimed around 20 per cent of the gross national product for most of the 1950s and 1960s. The figure was over 20 per cent in 1956, declined to around 19 per cent in 1958, and has gradually increased once more to around 23 per cent.

TABLE 2.5

Central and Local Government (Including National Insurance Funds) Current and Gross Capital Expenditure on Goods and Services as a Percentage of Gross National Product at Market Prices, 1956-69.

Year	1956	1957	1958	1959	1960	1961	1962
%	20.1	19.7	19.3	19.6	19.5	19.7	20.2

Year	1963	1964	1965	1966	1967	1968	1969
%	20.2	20.4	20.7	21.4	23.1	23.1	22.7

Source: NIBB, 1960 and 1969; and Preliminary Estimates of National Income and Balance of Payments 1964 to 1969, Cmnd 4328

Note: The figures exclude capital formation by public corporations. Its inclusion in 1969 would have increased the figure from 23 to 26 per cent.

It is arguable that the foregoing understates the 'size' of government. For instance, no account was taken of subsidies, grants and debt interest paid by the government and its net lending. The reason for this is that these are mainly classified as transfer payments. That is, the government raises the necessary funds by taxation and borrowing and transfers them back to the community and overseas. Thus the government does not buy goods and services directly as far as this type of expenditure is concerned. But there is no doubt that these transfers are extremely important, both in relation to taxation and government borrowing, and do influence the economic system. When they are included in government expenditure then the previous percentages are greatly increased. Table 2.6 shows that the 1956 percentage is raised to around 34 per cent of gross national product and that over the next ten years the trend has been upwards, with the 1968 figure some

---

[1]   For further discussion, see below, pp. 97-8.

[2]   See A. R. Prest, *Public Finance in Theory and Practice* (4th edn.), Weidenfeld and Nicolson 1970, for a discussion of some of the issues involved.

43 per cent. Clearly, grants, subsidies, debt interest and net lending have been increasingly important over the last ten years or so as a component of government expenditure.

TABLE 2.6

Central and Local Government Combined Current and Capital Expenditure as a Percentage of Gross National Product at Market Prices, 1956-69.

Year	1956	1957	1958	1959	1960	1961	1962
%	33.8	34.6	34.9	35.2	35.0	36.0	36.2

Year	1963	1964	1965	1966	1967	1968	1969
%	36.0	36.4	37.6	38.3	41.9	43.0	n.a.

Source: NIBB, Table 47, 1967 and Table 44, 1969

IV.3   The Budget

The budget is traditionally the annual financial statement which the Chancellor of the Exchequer makes in April in the House of Commons. The statement includes an account of the revenue and expenditure for the previous financial year and estimates for the year ahead. In the ordinary way there is only one budget, but in times of crisis a supplementary budget may be introduced to give the Chancellor the opportunity to modify his earlier policies by altering taxation and expenditure. Tables 2.7 to 2.9 bring together in an aggregated form the main features of the 1970-1 budget accounts.

TABLE 2.7

Central Government Revenue 1970-1 (estimated)   £ million

Inland revenue		
Income tax	5,653	
Surtax	277	
Death duties	371	
Stamps	119	
Corporation tax	1,900	
Capital gains tax	150	
Other	5	
Total Inland Revenue		8,475
Customs and excise		
Tobacco	1,160	
Purchase tax	1,260	
Oil	1,380	
Spirits, beer and wine	905	
Betting and gaming	120	
Other revenue duties	10	
Protective duties	230	
Import deposits and Export rebates	−430	
Total Customs and excise		4,635
Motor vehicle duties		430
Selective employment tax (gross)		2,042
Total taxation		15,582
Miscellaneous receipts		542
Grand total		16,124

Source: *Financial Statement and Budget Report 1970-1*

TABLE 2.8

Central Government Supply Services and Consolidated Fund Standing Services 1970-1 (estimated)
£ million

Supply services

Total defence budget			2,280

Civil supply

I	Government and finance	195	
II	Commonwealth and foreign	305	
III	Home and justice	291	
IV	Communications, trade and industry	2,899	
V	Agriculture	431	
VI	Local government, housing and social services	5,507	
VII	Education and science	485	
VIII	Museums, galleries and the arts	21	
IX	Public buildings, etc.	324	
X	Other public departments	26	
XI	Miscellaneous	28	
	Total Civil Supply		10,512
	Supplementary provision		141
	Total Supply services		12,933

Consolidated fund standing services

Payment to the National Loans Fund	288	
Northern Ireland – share of reserved taxes, etc.	272	
Other	33	
Total Consolidated fund standing services		593
Consolidated fund surplus		2,598
Grand total		16,124

Source: Financial Statement and Budget Report 1970-1

The receipts of the Exchequer shown in table 2.7 fall under five main headings: inland revenue, customs and excise, motor vehicle duties, selective employment tax, and miscellaneous receipts. The first two refer to the great revenue-collecting departments of state and the major taxes and duties collected by these are discussed extensively below. Motor vehicle duties are collected by the local authorities on behalf of the Exchequer. The selective employment tax is also discussed below. Miscellaneous receipts include interest and dividends, broadcast receiving licences and certain other receipts.

The two main categories of expenditure shown in table 2.8 are supply services and consolidated fund standing services. The first is voted annually by Parliament. The second is a standing charge against revenue.

The National Loans Fund is a newcomer to the budget accounts. Broadly speaking it is intended to carry further the separation of current and capital items in the accounts. Most of the domestic lending of the government and all of its borrowing transactions now appear in the National Loans Fund. Table 2.9 clearly shows just how important the central government is as a source of capital funds for the nationalised industries and local authorities. The government must raise these funds either through taxation or by borrowing. In these accounts there is a large estimated surplus from the consolidated fund so that the borrowing requirement turns out to be negative, allowing the government to pay off debt.

To explain adequately the financing of the borrowing requirement whenever it is positive would necessitate going far beyond the budget accounts and involve an extensive discussion of the financial transactions of the central government. However, it may be useful to indicate a few of the factors involved. For instance, an increase in the note issue as previously mentioned will help to finance it as will net purchases of government securities by the National Savings Bank and Trustee Savings banks. If these sources of funds are insufficient the government may have to borrow from the banking system, probably by issuing

TABLE 2.9

National Loans Fund 1970-1 (estimated)   £ million

(i) *Payments*		
Interest and expenses of national debt		1,423
Loans (net)		
To nationalised industries	536	
other public corporations	186	
local and harbour authorities	790	
private sector	−1	
within central government	33	
Total		1,544
Grand total		2,967
(ii) *Receipts*		
Interest on loans and profits of the Issue Department		
of the Bank of England	1,135	
Balance of interest met from the Consolidated fund	288	
Total		1,423
Consolidated fund surplus		2,598
Borrowing		−1,054
Grand total		2,967

Source: Financial Statement and Budget Report 1970-1

Treasury bills. The amount that must be borrowed will actually rise if there is an increase in the gold and foreign currency reserves. This is because the government must make sterling available to the Exchange Equalisation account to enable it to purchase an inflow of gold and foreign currency. Clearly, the budgetary system and monetary and financial system are highly interdependent and hence so are monetary, fiscal and credit policy.

The annual budget as an instrument of fiscal policy has frequently been criticised because of its inflexibility in the light of changing economic circumstances. This criticism needs to be examined from at least two points of view, taxation and expenditure.

The major taxes such as income tax and corporation tax are annual taxes and in the ordinary way cannot be varied between Finance Acts.[1] Thus though it might be thought desirable, because of changed economic conditions, to alter these taxes more frequently, this cannot be done without all the inconvenience of a supplementary budget. However, the authorities have more leeway over some other sources of revenue. From the point of view of flexibility one of the most important is the power, granted in the Finance Act 1961, to vary the rates of nearly all customs and excise duties and purchase tax by at most 10 per cent.[2] Thus there are now substantial powers to vary taxes between budgets. This, of course, leaves other problems, such as the timing and scale of tax changes. It is argued below that the authorities have been far from successful in these respects.

---

[1]   The Finance Act puts into law the budget proposals, subject to any amendments made by the House of Commons.

[2]   Thus if a current rate of duty is 20 per cent it may be varied between 18 and 22 per cent.

Government expenditure may be planned years in advance of its formal inclusion in the budget estimates. The plans can be and are modified, but this again gives rise to problems. Much of the expenditure is on a continuing basis and cannot be easily altered. Moreover, it may be extremely costly to slow down or postpone some kinds of expenditure, particularly investment expenditure. Hence variation of government expenditure is not an ideal instrument of fiscal policy.

The budget accounts, as already indicated, are incomplete in a number of ways. They deal, for example, only peripherally with local government finances and the national insurance funds.[1] Yet both of these 'tax' the community, the first mainly by levying rates and the second through insurance contributions. For the calendar year 1969 rates were some £1,676 million and national insurance contributions £2,011 million. Together they amount to the equivalent of some 58 per cent of the taxes on income in the same period.[2] The scale of taxation in the UK may be better appreciated when it is realised that taxes, rates, national insurance and minor other contributions totalled almost £16,500 million in 1969 or the equivalent of some 36 per cent of GNP at market prices.

IV.4   Income Tax and Surtax

Income tax is payable by individuals and, until April 1966, was paid by corporate bodies, when it was replaced by corporation tax on the latter. Surtax is legally an extension of the income tax as applied to individuals; it does not apply to corporate bodies.

In general, income tax is now chargeable on the income of individuals resident in the UK and on income originating there, even though the recipient may be resident elsewhere. If other countries operated their taxation systems similarly this might give rise to the same income being taxed twice. To obviate or ameliorate this the UK has a network of double taxation agreements. If, for instance, a resident of the UK is taxed in another country on income arising there he is allowed to offset this tax against his UK tax liability.

The amount of tax payable depends on the size of assessable income, and on various allowances and reliefs permitted. Income for tax purposes is classified under five schedules, B, C, D, E and F. Formerly there was also a Schedule A but this was abolished under the 1963 Finance Act. Schedule A had covered amongst other things the net income imputed to house ownership. This is no longer subject to tax, and various other items under Schedule A, including rents from land and buildings, were moved to Schedule D. Schedule B is of little interest and has also almost disappeared but covers income from woodlands that are not assessed under Schedule D. Schedule C refers to interest payments from some securities of the UK and overseas governments, where the payments take place in the UK. Schedule D covers the profits of trades, businesses and professions and it is under this schedule that short-term capital gains are chargeable, as are other items such as interest on loans and income from overseas. Schedule E refers to income from offices, employments or pensions. Schedule F is a new schedule introduced under the 1965 Finance Act and refers to taxes on dividends distributed by companies.

To arrive at taxable income it is necessary to take account of the allowances and reliefs given. For 1970-1 the earned income allowance—there is no allowance for investment income—is two-ninths of income up to £4,005 and one-ninth of the next £5,940, giving a maximum allowance of £1,550. The allowance for a single person is £325 and for a married couple £465. The allowance for children varies with age and takes into account taxable income of the child. The maximum allowance is £115 for children under eleven, £140 for those between eleven and less than sixteen, and £165 for those over sixteen,

---

[1]   National insurance is discussed further in chapter 5.

[2]   Figures from *Preliminary Estimates of National Income and Balance of Payments 1964-69*, Cmnd 4328.

except that these will be reduced by £42 for each child for whom family allowance is paid throughout the tax year. In addition, there is old age and small income relief, allowances for a dependent relative, housekeeper, widows with children, blind people, life insurance premiums, superannuation and mortgage interest.

Once taxable income has been determined it is all taxed at the 'standard' rate of 41.25 per cent. This rate corresponds to a marginal rate of tax on earned income, allowing for earned income relief, of 32 per cent.[1]

Surtax is chargeable in addition to income tax on incomes in excess of £2,500. However, allowances are also permitted in assessing the amount subject to surtax. On earned income the earned income relief against income tax is deductible for surtax purposes and there is also a special earnings allowance with a maximum of £2,000. A single person can earn about £5,500 before he has to pay surtax. The surtax rates vary from 20 per cent to 50 per cent. This makes a maximum combined marginal income and surtax rate of 91.25 per cent.

It is evident from the foregoing that one of the main features of income tax and surtax is their progressiveness. This is, of course, by design. It can be traced to notions of ability to pay. It is assumed that those with larger incomes are or should be able to pay proportionately more of them in taxation. In addition, progressive taxation lends itself to income redistribution to the extent that government expenditure benefits the less well-off in the community. Value judgments are implicit throughout the taxation system.

However praiseworthy or otherwise the particular value judgments, it would be a mistake to see them in isolation from other effects of a highly progressive taxation system. For with progressive tax rates the direct reward for extra work diminishes as income increases. It might be expected therefore that the system acts as a disincentive to additional effort. This, however, need not necessarily be true. It is possible to envisage circumstances where people might have fixed ideas about the amount of income after tax that they wanted and be prepared to work harder to achieve it if taxes were increased. But this possibility seems implausible if marginal tax rates become more and more progressive. The empirical evidence on the matter is not conclusive, at least so far as working harder in existing jobs is concerned. But this may reflect the inadequacy of the empirical methods as much as anything else.

Furthermore, it is suggested that there is evidence that steeply progressive taxation is a serious disincentive to movement from one job to another. It may be difficult to get a sufficiently large income after tax to compensate for the costs of upheaval and change. If this is correct then the tax system misallocates resources and is a drag on economic efficiency and growth. Following the ability-to-pay principle may be costly in these terms.

There is also no doubt that highly progressive taxation stimulates tax avoidance—the search for loopholes in the law permitting a reduced tax bill. If it is possible to spend less than a pound on advice to save a pound in tax then clearly this is a powerful incentive. The energies and resources of lawyers, accountants and tax experts generally are diverted into socially costly tasks.

---

[1]   The Inland Revenue recently sent a note to tax payers, referring to 1969-70, stating that, 'Few of us know our *average* rate for the year. But this is the sensible way of looking at tax and it is sometimes less than we think. . . . A married man with two young children earning a steady £20 a week pays 8 per cent of his income in tax. . . . If he earns £40 a week he pays about 20 per cent. Even the tax on the extra pound of earnings can rarely exceed one-third. For most people the highest rate they pay on overtime is just over 32 per cent. . .'. It seems to the author that the Inland Revenue with its assertion that the average rate is the 'sensible' way of looking at a tax is in total contradiction with the notion of optimal behaviour that lies at the heart of economics. That the Inland Revenue was aware of this is implicitly conceded in the second paragraph of the quotation which refers to the rate on marginal earnings and is consistent with the optimisation principle.

IV.5   Capital Gains Taxation

There are two capital gains taxes, the short-term and the long-term tax. The original
short-term tax was introduced under the Finance Act 1962 and has been modified by subsequent Finance Acts, especially that of 1965 which extended the range of assets on which
the tax is chargeable to bring it into conformity with the long-term tax introduced at that
time and which is described below. Both the short-term and long-term capital gains taxes
have also been modified by the introduction in 1967 of the betterment levy, under the
Land Commission Act 1967. The levy is 40 per cent on the realisation of the development
value of land. For the purposes of the Act the notion of development value has to be
distinguished from current use value. In fact, development value is the difference between
full market value and current use value, where the latter refers to its current value if it
were to go on indefinitely being used in its current use. It follows that changes in current
use value are *not* subject to the betterment levy. It is evident that this kind of tax law
must open up endless possibilities for litigation.[1]

Under the long-term tax gains are taxable on the disposal of assets that have been held
for more than twelve months; for lesser periods the short-term tax applies. Important
exemptions are a principal private residence, private motor cars, National Savings securities, most life insurance policies and betting winnings. In addition, the gains of individuals
if they do not exceed £50 a year are exempt, as are the disposal of British government and
government guaranteed securities. There are provisions generally allowing the offset of
losses against gains. The gains are taxed at a rate of 30 per cent except that an individual
with gains which do not exceed £5,000 is taxable at one-half his maximum rate of income
tax and surtax that would be chargeable if the gains were treated as unearned income. For
an individual liable at the standard rate the chargeable rate is approximately 20 per cent
instead of 30 per cent. For gains over £5,000 the full income and surtax rates become
operative unless the 30 per cent rate would lead to a smaller charge. The foregoing applies
to individuals, as gains realised by companies are ordinarily chargeable to corporation tax.
Special provisions relate to the taxing of unit trusts, investment trusts, superannuation
funds and other bodies.

The major justification put forward for the introduction of capital gains taxation is on
grounds of equity. The argument is roughly as follows. An individual may purchase
£100 worth of securities in 1970 and find that in 1971 they are worth £200. If he sells
the securities and if there were no capital gains tax he could maintain his capital intact
and still have £100 to spend, therefore this £100 is essentially income and should be
taxed as such. But is this really equitable with progressive income tax rates? It might be
that if the £100 were spread over a number of years a lower tax charge would arise. Does
this mean that gains should be averaged over a number of years or would a compromise
solution be to charge rates somewhat less than income tax rates? The UK long-term
gains tax seems to favour the latter.

In discussing the £100 gain above nothing was said about prices. But if prices have risen
by 5 per cent over the period then £105 would be required to maintain real capital intact
and the remaining £95 would be worth only some £90 in real terms. Is it legitimate to tax
nominal gains as opposed to real gains? The equity argument is by no means as straightforward as it might seem.

Capital gains taxation is, of course, important for other reasons besides those of
equity. It may affect investment and saving and the functioning of the capital markets,
and pose difficult problems of administration. To the extent that the return to investment
takes the form of capital gains—especially the return to risky investment—taxing them

---

[1]   It had been announced in the Queen's Speech (July 1970) that the Land Commission was to be
abolished.

may discourage such investment. This discouragement may, however, be mitigated to some extent, since the tax is postponable and payable only on realised capital gains. The allowance of losses as an offset to capital gains also works in the same direction. Nevertheless, the effect may well be to depress investment.

The effects on saving are perhaps even more problematical but may also be adverse, as may the effects on the operation of the capital markets. Since the tax is on realised gains this encourages the retention of the same securities as, of course, the holder has the income on the tax that would otherwise have to be paid if the securities were realised. There is therefore a discouragement to switching between securities which reduces the flexibility of the market and perhaps makes the raising of capital more costly. A possible offset to these effects is the realisation of capital losses since these are allowable for tax purposes against corresponding capital gains. .

The administrative problems are particularly great where problems of valuation arise. This is especially true of changes in the value of assets which do not ordinarily have a market value; an example is unquoted securities. The problems of valuation may become less acute as time proceeds and the community gets accustomed to the tax.[1]

IV.6   Corporation Tax

Corporation Tax was introduced under the Finance Act 1965 and came into full effect from 6 April 1966. Before that the profits of companies were subject to income tax and a profits tax of 15 per cent. Thus corporation tax is a part substitute for these. It is only a part substitute as in addition income tax has to be paid at the standard rate on dividends. To guard against evasion, companies are responsible for deducting tax on dividends and so the shareholder still receives his dividend net of tax as he did under the previous legislation. Special provisions relate to the incidence of corporation tax on unit trusts, investment trusts and insurance companies; provision is also made to permit double taxation relief against overseas taxes.

Corporation tax draws a forceful distinction between the company and the shareholder, taxing each as separate entities and in so doing discriminating between retained and distributed profits—for whereas the former is subject to corporation tax the latter is also subject to taxation on dividends. This distinction or bias is highly relevant to questions of equity, fiscal policy, investment and saving, and the operation of the capital markets.

Perhaps the simplest way to approach the equity argument is to contrast the tax position, if all profits were distributed and taxed as 'personal' income, with the current arrangements. The former would seem to be the more equitable. For the present system favours the retention of profits within the company, tending presumably to increase its value, and hence the value of the shareholder's stake in the company. But this increase in value to the shareholder is not subject to tax until it takes the form of increased dividends or realised capital gains. These may be postponed until far into the future and so are not comparable to taxation of profits as 'personal' income.

A basic argument used in favour of the corporation tax is the opportunity it gives the authorities to distinguish between the personal and the company sector for policy purposes. A good example under the present system is the encouragement given to profit retention in the belief that this stimulates investment and economic growth. The authorities may, for instance, wish to curtail consumption expenditure with as little adverse effect as possible on investment expenditure. An increase in income tax, leaving corporation tax unchanged, may tend to have the desired effect and may even encourage smaller dividend distributions, leaving more funds available to companies for investment purposes. The previous income tax-combination did not quite have this flexibility.

---

[1]   This section and the next rely heavily on Prest, *Public Finance In Theory and Practice, op. cit.*

The foregoing analysis begs, however, a number of important questions. Amongst these are the following. Should future consumption be preferred to present consumption, insofar as larger current investment makes possible a larger future income and so consumption? Are the companies with retained profits the ones which should grow? This is not at all self-evident. It means that companies avoid the discipline of having to raise funds in the market and probably favours the larger established company at the expense of the smaller or newer company. Furthermore, greater encouragement of profit retention tends to reduce the flow of funds through the capital market to the detriment of companies dependent on it. The corporation tax also tends to distort the operation of the capital market by encouraging firms to rely more on loan or debenture capital at the expense of ordinary or other forms of share capital, since the interest on the former is allowed as a cost in the calculation of profits and hence tax, whereas this is not true of the latter. It may be argued that the gains from introducing the corporation tax (and the capital gains taxes) outweigh the disadvantages. But there is little evidence to show that the pros and cons were weighed carefully in advance of their introduction.

IV. 7   Depreciation and Other Allowances

In assessing liability to corporation tax allowance is made, broadly speaking, for all the costs incurred by the company, including, as mentioned above, interest on loans and debentures but not dividends paid on shares. Depreciation allowances are also generally permitted on physical assets, but not all physical assets; there are no allowances on such things as retail shops, showrooms and offices. The allowance is at a rate of 4 per cent on the value or written down value of industrial buildings; 15 per cent is the standard rate for industrial machinery but for some it may be as high as or, exceptionally, higher than 25 per cent.

In addition to depreciation allowances for wear and tear successive governments have attempted to stimulate investment by various kinds of incentive. Three main kinds are or have been operative in the UK: initial allowances, investment allowances and investment grants. Initial allowances, introduced in 1945, are permitted in the first year in addition to the ordinary depreciation allowances. In other words the rate at which depreciation may be written off is accelerated; the total amount of depreciation permitted remains 100 per cent. Investment allowances on the other hand, introduced in 1954 and abolished in January 1966 with the advent of investment grants, did permit more than 100 per cent of the cost of the asset to be written off over its life. Thus if the investment allowance was 20 per cent—it was normally allowed in the year the investment took place—the total allowances would be 120 per cent.

Investment grants are cash grants to manufacturing, construction and extractive industries. The grants vary both regionally and to a limited extent according to the type of asset. The general rate is 20 per cent of the cost of *new* plant and machinery; expenditure on commercial vehicles and services do not qualify for grants. In the development areas— most of Scotland and Wales, Merseyside, large areas of northern England and southwestern England—the grants are 40 per cent of the cost of new expenditure on plant and machinery, including replacement expenditure. Investment in ships and computers receive special consideration. The grants themselves are not taxable but depreciation allowances are now calculated on the cost of the equipment less the cash grant. Initial allowances are still granted on those forms of capital expenditure, such as industrial buildings and second-hand machinery which do not qualify for investment grants.

This whole system of allowances and grants gives rise to many complicated issues, only a few of which can be touched on here. The first is whether depreciation allowances should be on an original or replacement cost basis. This question would be of little or no significance if prices were generally stable. But in periods of rising prices it would seem that, if the community is to preserve intact its physical stock of capital, allowances should be made on a replacement cost basis. However, if the problem is approached in a different way the argument is by no means as clearcut in favour of a replacement cost allowance. Suppose a firm purchases a piece of equipment and thereafter prices rise, including the price of the equipment. Thus the capital value of the old equipment rises, giving a capital gain to the firm. If allowances were permitted on a replacement cost basis the firm is, in fact, receiving untaxed capital gains. Is this equitable in relation to other sections of the community or is it a useful compromise to allow only original costs in calculating depreciation, so that the apparent capital gains are subject to corporation and income tax? The answer is far from obvious.[1]

Initial allowances, investment allowances and, more recently, investment grants should all act as a stimulus to investment. The first two may be regarded as reducing the amount of tax payable, and to that extent make investment more profitable. The third is, of course, a direct subsidy to investment and the benefits do not depend, as they do in the case of the first two, upon the availability of profits out of which to pay taxes. It is not at all self-evident that the subsidy is to be preferred as it may mean that investment takes place in forms of dubious profitability—there is therefore the likelihood of misallocation of resources.

A major feature of investment grants is the extent to which they are discriminatory. They make investment in certain places more profitable than in others and some types of investment more profitable than other types. This, of course, is by design and is intended to stimulate investment in the places and in the forms the government desires. The basis for this intervention hinges on the conviction that the market, reflecting the interacting decisions of consumers, savers and investors, if left to itself will lead to misallocation of investment and to underinvestment. But it can also be plausibly argued that personal and company taxation introduce a gap between the private and social return to investment, both material and human, and in so doing inhibit investment. Clearly, the issues that these questions raise are extremely complex and incapable of simple straightforward answers.

As far as the empirical evidence is concerned it would seem that investment incentives have not been very effective in stimulating capital growth, which has lagged behind that of the US and most western European countries.[2] Moreover, their use as stabilisation instruments depends crucially on the timing and actual variation in the grants and allowances. It may be doubted that government or anyone else has the knowledge to manipulate these successfully. Indeed, as far as the management of the UK economy is concerned, their use may well have been destabilising.[3]

IV.8   Selective Employment Tax

The selective employment tax was introduced in the May 1966 budget and came into effect in September 1966. The tax is paid by all employers in the public and private sectors and since July 1969 has been at a rate of £2.40 a week for men, £1.2 a week for women and for boys under eighteen, and 80 new pence a week for girls under eighteen.[4]

---

[1]   See Prest, *Public Finance In Theory and Practice, op. cit.* for further discussion.

[2]   See, R. A. and P. B. Musgrave, 'Fiscal Policy' in R. Caves (ed.) *Britain's Economic Prospects,* pp. 57-63.

[3]   See section V below.

[4]   In the April 1970 budget the Chancellor announced that from 1972 SET was to be transformed into a differential payroll tax and be charged as a percentage of the total payroll.

All employers pay the tax but employers in manufacturing industries outside the development areas have it refunded and such employers in these areas receive a premium.[1] Employers in transport, agriculture, the public service, nationalised industries, extractive industries and charities also have the tax refunded. Finally—apart from isolated cases such as hotel employers in certain parts of development areas who do get a refund—employers in the construction and the service industries, including wholesale and retail distribution, banking, insurance, finance and the like, receive no refund. Furthermore, to qualify for refunds more than half the persons employed in an establishment must come in the refund category, i.e. they must be engaged in manufacturing activities, transport, etc.

A number of arguments were put forward for the introduction of the selective employment tax. First, there was a wish to tax services which were supposed to be lightly taxed compared with certain manufactured products which are subject to excise duties and purchase tax. Secondly, there was a desire to release labour, broadly from the service industries, for employment in manufacturing industry so as to encourage economic growth and contribute to export earnings. Thirdly, there was an urgent need to raise additional revenue.

Since its inception the selective employment tax has caused a great deal of controversy and as yet there is little sign of its abatement. Of the arguments suggested for the introduction of the tax only the third commands widespread support. For SET has proved to be a substantial revenue raiser, bringing in some £527 million net in 1969-70, albeit at the cost of raising almost £1,900 million gross, and hence requiring repayments of over £1,300 million.

As far as the first argument is concerned, not all manufactured products, or even consumer goods, are subject to excise taxes or purchase tax. Thus in so far as these taxes distort relative prices there was no distortion to be corrected in the case of these goods. Furthermore, in so far as there is price distortion of some goods, the new tax could quantitatively only be described as the crudest form of correction, bearing little relationship to the relative weights of taxation on different kinds of product.

The second argument is perhaps the most controversial of all and raises some very complex issues about the economic system, how it *does* work and how it *should* work. The case for wanting to transfer labour from the service industries to manufacturing industry hinges on the theory that since overall growth of the economic system is usually associated with growth of the manufacturing sector, faster growth will be realised by transferring labour to that sector. Furthermore, since manufacturing industry is a major contributor to exports, growth of the manufacturing sector may be expected to strengthen the balance of payments position.

These arguments are by no means totally convincing. It is, for instance, not at all clear that shortage of labour has been a serious bottleneck to the expansion of manufacturing industry. Indeed, from what was mentioned above in the discussion of investment incentives, the fundamental problem may well be insufficient investment. Thus, even if the evidence of Reddaway and others—and even this is controversial—tends to support the effectiveness of SET in transferring labour from the services industries to the manufacturing sector it is not a foregone conclusion that this is really what is required in the interests of the community.[2]

IV.9 Customs and Excise Duties and Purchase Tax

The group of duties and taxes under this heading are generally called 'indirect' taxes

---

[1] The Conservative pre-election proposals indicated that the regional employment premium would be phased out.

[2] W. B. Reddaway, *Effects of the Selective Employment Tax: First Report, on the Distributive Trades*, HMSO, 1970. For a brief critical assessment of the Report see Margaret Hall, 'The Reddaway Report: Unsettled Business', *The Times*, 16 March 1970.

since they are not usually collected from the final purchaser but from the manufacturer, trader or wholesaler. The term customs duties refers to duties imposed on imports, whereas excise duties are imposed on domestically produced goods. Purchase tax is levied on both imports and domestically produced goods but does not apply to goods that bear excise duties: it is different from excise duties in that it is charged on broad ranges of goods rather than on a particular good or group of goods. Customs duties may be primarily for revenue-raising purposes, being levied on imported goods which are similar to the domestic goods that carry excise duties, or primarily for giving protection to British goods or preference to Commonwealth goods and, more recently, imports from the European Free Trade area.

As may be seen from table 2.7 the large revenue yielders are tobacco, oil, alcohol and purchase tax. Tobacco and oil together are estimated to yield £2,540 million in 1970-1, or almost 18 per cent of total revenue from taxation (allowing for SET refunds), alcohol and purchase tax a further 15 per cent. Purchase tax is currently charged at four different rates on the wholesale value, but is not chargeable on exports. Such things as clothes, footwear, kitchenware and wallpaper are charged at 13¾ per cent; confectionery, ice cream and soft drinks at 22 per cent; cars, gas and electrical appliances and drugs and medicines at 36⅔ per cent; and jewellery, gramophone records, watches, clocks and cameras at 55 per cent.

An outstanding feature of the duties and taxes on tobacco, oil and alcohol is their scale, the large proportion that they represent of the purchasing price. Ordinarily it might be expected that something which has the effect of substantially increasing the price of a product would lead to less of it, perhaps much less of it, being bought. By and large this does not seem to have happened with these three products—their demands are said to be inelastic with respect to price. However, some doubts are beginning to be expressed about the buoyancy of the revenue from tobacco, though this may be due to other causes besides the scale of taxation. The at any rate apparent inelasticity of demand with respect to price implies that these duties and taxes may have little direct effect on the allocation of resources. But there will be an indirect effect because the funds withdrawn by taxes from consumers will scarcely be spent by the state in the same way as if they had been left in the hands of the former.

It is often argued that indirect taxes are to be preferred because they are less of a disincentive to the supply of labour than direct taxes. This is an extremely difficult issue and depends on many factors, such as the scale of the duties and taxes to be substituted, say, for a reduction in direct taxes or for foregoing an increase, and the type and the extent of the goods involved. For an individual, in choosing between additional work or leisure, may well consider not only the direct tax on extra earnings but also the real value of goods and services that can be bought with additional income.

It is also arguable that on equity grounds indirect taxes are regressive in that they fall more heavily on the relatively low income groups. There would seem to be some truth in this as far as tobacco, beer and some purchase taxes are concerned, but possibly to a less extent for petrol, though bus fares are obviously affected by oil duties. On the other hand the relatively less well-off would seem to obtain substantial benefits from government welfare and other services. But if the community opts for extensive government expenditure on welfare services and education it seems unavoidable that one way or another a large proportion of the tax revenue must be raised from the mass of taxpayers. If at the same time the latter are important beneficiaries from government expenditure then they are indirectly paying for perhaps all of or a major part of these benefits. If this is correct then a substantial part of government revenue and expenditure is a process of taking funds from particular individuals and then handing them back either directly or in the form of services that the government thinks they ought to have.

IV.10   Death Duties

Estate duty is the only duty now payable on death, except for the application of the capital gains tax. Death counts as a realisation of assets, and gains in excess of £5,000 are subject to capital gains tax, but any tax payable is deductible in assessing the value of the estate subject to estate duty. The duty is charged on all property in Great Britain—Northern Ireland has separate provisions—that passes or is deemed to pass on death, irrespective of the domicile of the deceased. Property outside Great Britain is also chargeable if the deceased was domiciled in Great Britain. *Inter vivos* gifts are taxable if made within seven years of death, or one year in the case of charities, and gains arising on the making of *inter vivos* gifts, and indeed gifts generally, which total more than £100 in any year are liable to capital gains tax. Estates of less than £10,000 are exempt from estate duty. The first slice of estates greater than £10,000 but less than £17,500 is taxed at 25 per cent, the second slice up to £30,000 at 30 per cent, with successive slices being taxed more heavily up to a maximum of 80 per cent on estates greater than £750,000 provided that the estate is not taxed at a rate in excess of 80 per cent over all.

The main reason for estate duty is the belief that gross inequality in the distribution of wealth is undesirable. But experience in Great Britain would suggest that estate duty has not been very effective in reducing the inequality of wealth. However, it may be somewhat more effective in combination with the capital gains tax which in general taxes gains arising on wealth transfers both outside and within the *inter vivos* period. But whatever may be thought about extreme inequality of wealth distribution it is scarcely realistic to imagine a reasonably free society without some wealth inequality. This kind of judgement seems to be inseparable from this type of policy issue.

V.   POLICY SINCE THE EARLY 1950s

V.1   The Early Years: 1951-4

It was against a background of devaluation of the exchange rate in 1949 and renewed pressure on the balance of payments, accentuated by the outbreak of the Korean War, that what came to be called the 'new' monetary policy was introduced. In November 1951 Bank rate was raised to 2½ per cent, having been held at 2 per cent for almost twenty years except for a few weeks at the outbreak of the second world war. The Treasury bill rate rose from around ½ per cent to about 1 per cent and holders of Treasury bills were 'offered', up to a sum of £1,000 million, a longer dated security in exchange, called a serial funding stock and yielding 1¾ per cent interest.[1]

These were not the only monetary and credit policy measures taken about this time.[2] But those mentioned represented a 'new' departure in the sense that the previous commitment to essentially fixed low short-term rates and, particularly, a fixed Bank rate was abandoned. Monetary and credit policy were to be more flexible in future.

The 'new' monetary policy was introduced with large claims for its ability and power to influence and improve the functioning of the economic system.[3] The previous reliance

---

[1]   The word 'offered' is a euphemism as far as the banks are concerned. The Radcliffe Committee reports (p.140, para.406) that 'The banks were in effect instructed to take about £500 million out of the total'.

[2]   The banks issued a warning that requests for advances would be examined very critically and early in 1952 hire purchase controls were introduced, stipulating the minimum down-payment and maximum period for repayment on a range of consumer durable goods.

[3]   See the account in J. C. R. Dow, *The Management of the British Economy, 1945-60*, pp. 66-70. Cambridge University Press, 1964.

on physical controls and fiscal policy had fallen into disrepute amongst a wide range of commentators on economic affairs.

In spite of the claims made for monetary policy it was never relied on as the chief means of regulating economic activity, but was almost invariably combined with physical controls and fiscal measures, the whole action being called a 'package deal'.

The balance of payments improved during 1952 and, at least on the surface, remained satisfactory throughout 1953 and into 1954. The foreign exchange reserves which had fallen markedly between 1950 and 1952 rose substantially, though not by as much as the sterling balances, that is, the sterling holdings, mainly of overseas countries. At the same time production and output recovered, probably helped by an expansionary budget in 1953, the removal of some physical controls and a reduction in interest rates.

Thus in this period economic policy seemed to be working relatively well, though prices continued to rise. The Radcliffe Committee, 'looking back with the benefit of hindsight', argued that, 'the authorities went too far in the direction of stimulating demand, and. . .were too slow to change direction'.[1] Be that as it may, economic policy at the time seemed to be having a measure of success. But, clearly, this could not be attributed solely to monetary policy. However, for the time being monetary policy was back in favour.

V.2   Monetary Disillusion: 1954-7

In the second half of 1954 the balance of payments on current account was threatening to run into deficit and the authorities felt obliged late in 1954 to permit Treasury bill and other rates to rise. In January 1955 Bank rate was raised, followed by another increase in February, and hire purchase controls were reintroduced. But in the 1955 Budget the Chancellor of the Exchequer 'reduced taxation and planned for a larger overall deficit than in the preceding year', relying, in his own words, on 'the resources of a flexible monetary policy' to counter, if it should arise, an over-rapid expansion of demand and any associated balance of payments difficulties.[2]

Demand, however, continued to expand and the foreign trade balance remained adverse, 'Monetary policy was not operating as rapidly as had been expected'.[3] In July the clearing banks were requested by the Chancellor of the Exchequer to bring about a 'positive and significant reduction in their advances over the next few months'.[4] They had risen by some £290 million in the first six months, equivalent to an annual growth rate of about 30 per cent. At the same time hire purchase restrictions were made more severe and measures were announced to restrain public investment. But the balance of payments position continued to be unsatisfactory, partly because of an outflow of funds from London, encouraged by rumours that the official margins between which the exchange rate was held might be widened.[5] In October there followed a supplementary budget which raised both purchase tax on consumer goods and profits tax.

By the beginning of 1956 the balance of payments position had improved but the authorities remained apprehensive about internal demand and so additional measures were taken to restrict it. The banks were asked to continue to curtail their advances, Bank rate was again raised, hire purchase restrictions were strengthened, public investment was further reduced and investment allowances were suspended. Despite the re-

---

[1]   *Report*, p.142, para.413.

[2]   *Ibid*. p.144, para.418.

[3]   *Economic Survey, 1956*, Cmd 9728, p.35, para.68.

[4]   Quoted in *Radcliffe Report*, p.144, para.417.

[5]   The official margins were $2.78-$2.82 to £1.

quest to the banks, advances continued to rise until 'the Chancellor of the Exchequer took the unprecedented step of summoning the representatives of the clearing banks and the main banking associations to a meeting on 24th July, in order to ask that "the contraction of credit should be resolutely pursued".'[1]

Demand seemed to be under better control in the second half of 1956 though at the end of the year events were overshadowed by the nationalisation of the Suez canal and the crisis that ensued. Once this had subsided interest rates were permitted to decline, though the banks were still expected to curtail their lending.

Despite the latter, the 1957 budget contained widespread reductions in taxation. But by the summer of 1957 there was another balance of payments crisis, though the current account had a substantial surplus. In other words the capital account was reflecting the trouble and the foreign exchange reserves fell by almost £200 million between June and September. This fall in reserves is widely attributed to movements of short-term funds out of London and the delaying or hastening of payments as the case might be in antici-pation that the German mark was to be revalued.[2] On 19 September Bank rate was raised by 2 per cent to 7 per cent, its highest level since 1921. The banks once more were required to curtail advances and public investment programmes were again reduced.

Clearly, economic policy including monetary policy cannot be judged satisfactory over the three years briefly reviewed. Prices continued to rise, and though the exchange rate was held the balance of payments was a recurring problem, with the foreign exchange reserves being much too small to take care of movements on both current and capital account.[3] Economic growth had continued, but rather unevenly and at the relatively low rate of about 2 per cent per year.

There would therefore appear to be grounds for disillusion with economic policy as a whole in terms of its inability to achieve its various goals. Monetary policy was particular-ly suspect. Interest rates had risen to higher and higher levels, yet advances had continued their upward trend, so that the authorities felt forced to insist on their direct curtailment. Clearing bank deposits had actually declined between 1954 and 1956—they increased in 1957 but not quite back to the 1954 level—and yet monetary policy was evidently in-effective.

V.3   1957-61

It was mentioned above that in late 1957 the balance of payments on capital account was under severe pressure. The current account had continued in surplus and remained strongly so during the first quarter of 1958. Unemployment had for some time been gradually increasing; in 1955 it had averaged 1.2 per cent and in 1958 was to be over 2 per cent. There seemed from this and other evidence to be some basis for encouraging expansion, though prices and wages were still edging upwards.

Bank rate was reduced from 7 to 6 per cent in March 1958 and by the end of the year was down to 4 per cent. In July all restrictions were lifted on bank lending—the first time this had happened since the war—and later in the year hire purchase restrictions were removed. The 1958 budget was mildly expansionary: estimated expenditure increased slightly, initial allowances were raised and some reductions were made in purchase tax and other duties. Later in the year initial allowances were increased again.

---

[1]   *Radcliffe Report*, p.146, para. 422.

[2]   Importers fearing that sterling might be devalued *vis-à-vis* another currency have an incentive to hasten their payments. Exporters have the opposite incentive. This phenomenon is known as 'leads and lags' in payments. See Ch. 3, I. 5.

[3]   There is reason to believe that the authorities were not wholeheartedly committed to a fixed exchange rate throughout this period. See the account in Dow, *The Management of the British Economy, 1945-60*, pp.80-90.

This expansionary policy was carried substantially further by the 1959 budget with reductions in income tax, purchase tax and some customs and excise duties.[1] Monetary policy continued to be expansionary though there were no reductions in Bank rate in 1959. But the rates on short- and long-term government securities declined for about the first six months of the year.[2] Treasury bill rates, on the other hand, tended to rise. Between 1958 and 1959 clearing bank deposits increased by about 4½ per cent and their advances by some £600 million, or by about one-quarter. Over the same period their investments fell by about £300 million or 15 per cent. The banks, with their new found freedom, were engaged in a massive rearrangement of their assets towards a more preferred distribution.

Between 1958 and 1959, under the influence of these expansionary measures, output increased by around 4 per cent and unemployment declined. Prices and wages remained relatively stable. But the balance of payments was beginning to show signs of strain with a falling surplus on current account. By early 1960 the authorities were showing some concern about the situation. In January Bank rate was raised to 5 per cent and interest rates generally on government securities were tending to rise, though the authorities remained heavy net purchasers of gilt-edged securities.

Despite the more restrictive monetary policy the budget made only minor changes in taxation and government expenditure was planned to expand leaving a reduced budget surplus. Thus the budget was considered to be expansionary.

A few weeks after the April budget additional measures were taken in an attempt to reinforce monetary and credit restriction. The first call was made for special deposits and hire purchase controls were reintroduced. A second call for special deposits was made in June and at the same time Bank rate was raised to 6 per cent. Monetary and credit policy were to be restrictionary whilst fiscal policy continued to be expansionary.

The underlying balance of payments position remained disturbing. Imports were increasing rapidly and the balance of payments was in deficit on current and long-term capital account. Despite these deficits the foreign currency reserves increased, attributable in part to a marked inflow of funds to London, attracted by the relatively high interest rates.

Whilst the rate of growth of economic activity had slowed down in the first half of 1960, this gave no immediate relief to the balance of payments. The deficits on current account in the second half of the year were actually greater than in the first half. But once again the reserves increased, largely because of a large inflow of funds to London. This persistent inflow of funds, which might just as quickly be withdrawn, worried the authorities and prompted them to lower Bank rate in two moves between October and December from 6 to 5 per cent. The authorities were anxious that these reductions in Bank rate should not weaken credit restriction as they fully appreciated that the current and long-term capital accounts of the balance of payments did not justify it, nor did the be-

---

[1]   In this section it is assumed that budget changes are by and large expansionary or contractionary in so far as they, in the first case, lead to a reduction in the budget surplus or an increase in the deficit, and in the second case, lead to an increase in the budget surplus or a decrease in the deficit. This simplified way of proceeding is at best only an approximation since it makes no allowance for price changes and, furthermore, the effects of changes in the budgetary position will be highly dependent on other policy measures and, especially, the policies followed in relation to debt management and monetary policy. Cf section II of this chapter.

[2]   The authorities were heavy net purchasers of gilt-edged securities during the 4th quarter of 1958 and throughout 1959, acquiring £431 millions. These purchases helped to maintain the prices of government securities or, alternatively, helped to prevent or curtail a rise in interest rates. See E. Victor Morgan, 'Funding Policy and the Gilt-Edged Market', *Lloyds Bank Review,* October 1962, pp.40-53.

haviour of prices and wages which continued to move upwards.[1] Nevertheless they reduced hire purchase restrictions a month later in January 1961.

The crisis, which had been imminent for so long, finally broke at the end of February 1961 when funds began to leave London in anticipation of the revaluations of the deutschmark and the guilder. The authorities managed to mobilise substantial central bank support for sterling and it survived the immediate foreign exchange crisis. But the pressure on sterling persisted, with reserves continuing to fall even though the balance of payments on current and long-term capital accounts was showing signs of improvement. The crisis reached a new peak in July when the authorities were forced to introduce a battery of restrictive measures. Bank rate was raised from 5 to 7 per cent, a further call was made for special deposits, the 10 per cent surcharge on customs and excise duties and on purchase tax was used for the first time and government estimated expenditure for 1962-3 was to be substantially reduced.[2] And the Chancellor, Mr Selwyn Lloyd, called for 'a pause in the growth of wages, salaries and dividends'[3] —one of the early attempts at an incomes policy in the UK.

The four years from 1957-61 could not be described as years of achievement for the policy-makers. The expansion had barely got under way in 1958 and 1959 when balance of payments problems began to arise and domestic activity had, it seemed, to be slowed down if the exchange rate was to be held. But the balance of payments worsened during 1960 and the whole process culminated in the crisis of July 1961. Throughout the period wages and prices continued their upward movement. Perhaps it can be counted on the credit side that unemployment fell from just over 2 per cent in 1958 and 1959 to a little over 1½ per cent in 1960 and 1961.

The policy instruments which the authorities relied on were almost exclusively monetary, credit and fiscal. If, given a fixed exchange rate, a satisfactory balance of payments is given pride of place amongst the goals to be realised, then the authorities seriously overexpanded in 1958 and, perhaps even more so, in 1959. By their activities in the gilt-edged market in late 1959 and early 1960 they slowed down the rise in interest rates which would otherwise have taken place. They pursued essentially contradictory monetary credit and fiscal policies in the first half of 1960, the one restrictionary, the other expansionary. In late 1960 they reduced Bank rate to stem the inflow of funds whilst the underlying balance of payments was seriously in deficit and in January 1961 they relaxed hire purchase restrictions. And the April 1961 budget should have been much tougher given the flight of foreign funds from London in March. In retrospect economic policy seems to have been seriously at fault.

It may be asked if it is legitimate to assume the primacy of the balance of payments goal. The answer would seem to be yes. For in the final analysis the authorities were prepared to sacrifice both growth and employment and other subsidiary goals. Whether they should have done so is quite a different question and is touched on in the final section of the chapter.

---

[1]   *BEQB*, vol. 1, no.2, March 1961, p. 3.

[2]   The April 1961 budget had been deflationary in the sense that the Chancellor had budgeted for a substantially larger surplus than in the previous year. The surplus arose mainly because of the expected buoyancy of the revenue rather than because of increased taxation. Planned expenditure actually rose. But clearly the anticipated effects of the budget were going to be too long delayed to alleviate the current crisis.

[3]   *BEQB*, vol. 1, no. 4, September 1961, p. 5.

V.4   1961-4

In the second half of 1961 the balance of payments on both current and long-term capital accounts improved, though it would be a mistake to attribute the whole improvement to the July measures. Economic activity had been slowing down for months before these were introduced and from about the last quarter of 1960 the trend of imports had been downwards. Production was tending to decline and unemployment to increase. But despite the latter wages and prices continued to rise rapidly; many wage agreements had been negotiated in advance of the July measures. Nevertheless, by October 1961 the authorities felt able to reduce Bank rate from 7 to 6½ per cent and by April 1962, after four further reductions, it was down to 4½ per cent.

The 1962 budget was essentially a 'standstill' budget; the net changes in taxation were negligible, though many individual changes were made and, as already mentioned, the short-term capital gains tax was introduced. Government expenditure was planned to increase slightly and the budget surplus to remain much the same as for 1961-2.

Industrial production began to recover early in 1962 but unemployment remained relatively high. The authorities felt that the economy needed some additional stimulus and so they relaxed hire purchase restrictions and made the first repayments of special deposits. Later in the year the previous requests to the banks and other financial institutions to exercise credit restraint were withdrawn and the Chancellor of the Exchequer announced a further repayment of postwar credits and additional increases in investment in the public sector. In November he announced that in his next budget he proposed to introduce tax concessions to encourage investment in plant and machinery and industrial building and at the same time he reduced tax on cars from 45 to 25 per cent.

Many of these measures were taken in the light of continued slackness in the economy. But, despite the slackness, imports continued at a high level and the balance of payments remained barely satisfactory, whilst prices and wages maintained their upward trend. The economy was clearly very delicately balanced. Resources were not fully employed, yet wages and prices were rising, and any expansion of output might be expected to lead to balance of payments difficulties.[1]

The authorities, nevertheless, decided to stimulate the economy further. The top rate of purchase tax was reduced from 45 to 25 per cent and in January 1963 Bank rate was lowered from 4½ to 4 per cent. These measures were followed by what seemed to be a highly expansionary budget. Taxation was reduced and government expenditure increased, and for the first time for many years a deficit was planned. At the same time there was to be a borrowing requirement of almost £690 million.

Under the cumulative influence of this series of measures, combined with an increase in exports, activity grew rapidly and unemployment fell. Prices and wages went on rising. For the first half of 1963 the balance of payments on current and long-term capital account remained in surplus, but then ran into deficit. The foreign exchange reserves fell during the year.

Early in 1964 the authorities began to fear that the pace of economic activity could not be maintained, mainly because of the weakness of the balance of payments.[2] For some months Treasury bill and other rates had been rising and in February Bank rate was raised from 4 to 5 per cent. The budget increased taxation but government expenditure was planned to rise by almost 8½ per cent. A small budget surplus was anticipated,

---

[1]   'Imports may continue to rise as home demand increases', *BEQB*, vol. II, no. 4, December 1962, p. 242; and 'there is little sign of a substantial rise in exports', *BEQB*, vol. III, no. 1, March 1963, p.4.

[2]   *BEQB*, vol. IV, no. 1, March 1964, p. 3.

together with a large borrowing requirement of £790 million. The Chancellor was aware that he was taking a gamble, whether justifiably or not remains to be seen.[1]

Production continued to expand, though not as fast as in 1963, and unemployment declined substantially. Wages and prices rose rapidly. The authorities permitted some rise in interest rates but at the same time kept it in check by purchasing gilt-edged securities. Clearing bank deposits and advances grew quickly, at 7.3 per cent and 11.3 per cent respectively, over the twelve months from September 1963.

Meanwhile, the balance of payments deficits on both current and long-term capital account grew larger. The figures are shown in table 2.10. Between the 1st and 3rd quarters of 1964 the combined quarterly deficits increased from £144 million to £226 million. For a time the seriousness of the position did not show up in the foreign exchange reserves as funds continued to flow to London. But this precarious inflow changed to an outflow in the third quarter as sterling holders became aware of the balance of payments situation. Another crisis had almost matured.

TABLE 2.10

Balance of Payments Deficits—Current and Long-Term Capital Transactions   £ million

1963		July 1963–December 1964 1964				Cumulative
3rd qtr	4th qtr	1st qtr	2nd qtr	3rd qtr	4th qtr	Total
61	73	144	184	226	190	878

Source: *ET,* September 1969, Table 1C, p. XXVII

The new Labour government decided to take immediate action and in October announced a temporary surcharge of 15 per cent on most imports, except foods and raw materials, and a tax rebate on exports. These measures were followed by a special budget in November. The tax on petrol was raised and it was announced that from April next the standard rate of income tax would be increased by sixpence, a long-term capital gains tax would be introduced and corporation tax would be levied on companies instead of income tax and profits tax.

In the words of the Bank of England, 'Opinion abroad . . . was not reassured' by these measures and 'the gilt-edged and equity markets weakened sharply, mainly as a result of the uncertainty engendered by the proposals for a new capital gains tax and the corporation tax, and this weakness added to the difficulties in the foreign exchange markets'.[2] When two Thursdays elapsed without any increase in Bank rate—the usual day for changes— 'confidence weakened and there was renewed heavy selling [of sterling] in the market'. Sales on Friday were exceptionally large, and, as part of the government's policy to maintain sterling at its present parity, Bank rate was raised on Monday the 23rd November from 5 per cent to 7 per cent.[3] But confidence was still not restored and on the following

---

[1]   The Chancellor emphasised in his budget speech that the size of the increase in taxation required was a matter of judgment and that if circumstances altered further remedies might be required. Reported in *BEQB*, vol. IV, no. 2, June 1964, p. 87.

[2]   *BEQB*, vol. IV, no. 4, December 1964, p. 256.

[3]   *Ibid.*

two days heavy selling of sterling continued. The authorities quickly negotiated credit facilities of $3,000 million, helping to bring to an end the immediate crisis.[1]

The three years from 1961 to 1964 bring little credit to the policy makers; if anything they reflect in terms of the culminating crisis a worse performance than over the previous four years. Economic activity was slow to recover after 1961, the balance of payments was almost a continuous problem or threatened to become one, and prices and wages continued to rise throughout. The cumulative effects of monetary, credit and fiscal policy in late 1962 and during 1963 were over-expansionary and inconsistent with a satisfactory balance of payments position, price stability and sustainable economic growth. The failure to take adequate measures, during the first ten months of 1964 prior to the election, in face of a mounting balance of payments deficit, which in the third quarter of the year was running at an annual rate of £900 million, is one of the most irresponsible episodes in the history of economic policy in the postwar period.[2] The new Labour government also failed to come fully to terms with the extent of the crisis and some of their early measures accentuated the problem.

V.5   1964-8

Though the 1964 currency crisis may have passed its peak with the announcement of the large overseas credit facilities for the support of sterling, it was by no means over. The pound remained under pressure for the next couple of months as funds continued to leave London.

By the time of the April 1965 budget the balance of payments position had improved whilst unemployment remained low, but prices and wages continued to rise. There were few, if any, signs that the November measures were having a depressing effect on the economy. The budget was expected to increase both government expenditure and revenue by about 10 per cent, giving a slightly larger surplus than in the previous year. But government borrowing was to rise substantially and to absorb more than the expected surplus. Overall the budget could hardly be called deflationary.

Just after the budget the Bank of England became very concerned about the growth of advances and the commercial bill holdings of the banks. It called for special deposits, emphasising that the call should be allowed to affect the banks' lending activities and should be 'mitigated as little as possible by the sale of investments'.[3] The banks were also told that their lending to the private sector 'should not increase at an annual rate of more than 5 per cent during the twelve months to March 1966'.[4] Clearly, by this time the authorities had little confidence in their special deposits instrument which by now had essentially been superseded by direct control of advances.

In June Bank rate was reduced from 7 to 6 per cent and hire purchase restrictions were increased. The reduction in Bank rate with continued pressure on sterling seems surprising. The authorities, explaining it, emphasised that this was still a very high rate and that

---

[1]   It is extremely informative to contrast the content and emphasis of the Bank of England account of the crisis with that of the Treasury. A brief quotation from the Treasury's account will have to suffice here. 'In the second half of November a large-scale withdrawal of funds from London began to take place. Strong defensive measures were taken: first Bank rate was raised from 5 to 7 per cent; secondly, massive new credit facilities, totalling $3,000 million, were negotiated with Central Banks overseas.' *Economic Report on 1964*, HM Treasury, p. 4.

[2]   This statement takes for granted that the authorities were serious about maintaining the exchange rate.

[3]   *BEQB*, vol. 5, no. 2, June 1965, p. 111.

[4]   *Ibid.* Other financial institutions were similarly instructed.

it did not imply any relaxation in credit restriction.[1] The surprise is enhanced as the Chancellor announced a few weeks later—less than four months after the budget—new restrictions on public and private expenditure and further controls on foreign investment.

During 1965 production grew by about 3 per cent, unemployment remained low, but prices and wages continued to move upwards at rapid annual rates—retail prices by almost 5 per cent and average weekly earnings of manual workers by 8 per cent. The money supply grew by some 5.8 per cent, almost twice as fast as output, though this was supposed to have been a period of monetary and credit restraint.[2] The deficit on the balance of payments was less than half of that in 1964 but remained uncomfortably large.

Early in 1966, the Bank of England, still worried about the high level of activity in the economy and the state of the balance of payments, reinforced credit restrictions to the private sector by asking the banks not to increase their lending, until further notice, above the levels previously agreed for March 1966. Hire purchase restrictions were also further intensified. In the May 1966 budget expenditure was estimated to rise by 8.5 per cent and revenue by rather more, yielding a surplus of £1,047 million. But this was to be more than absorbed by lending, leaving a net borrowing requirement of £287 million. Once again this could scarcely be called an overall deflationary budget, though the Chancellor said he wanted to ease the pressure of demand.

Unemployment remained low, prices and wages went on rising and the balance of payments on current and long-term capital account continued in deficit. Heavy selling of sterling developed in June and worsened in July, perhaps accentuated by the seamen's strike, rising interest rates overseas, and measures taken by the United States authorities to strengthen their balance of payments position.

The renewed pressure on sterling stimulated the authorities to take additional measures. Bank rate was raised from 6 to 7 per cent; a further call was made for special deposits; hire purchase restrictions were made still more stringent; a surcharge of 10 per cent was imposed on purchase tax rates and on the duties on alcohol, oil and petrol; surtax rates were increased by 10 per cent for one year and postal charges were raised. 'A six-months standstill on prices and on wages, salaries and other types of income was imposed, to be followed by a further six months of severe restraint'.[3] And increased restrictions were placed on foreign expenditure, including the introduction of the £50 travel allowance for persons. Later in the year the Bank of England, attempting to strengthen the reserves, arranged increased credit facilities with other central banks.

In the second half of 1966 industrial production declined, unemployment increased, wages remained practically stable, the rise in prices slowed down and the balance of payments, whilst improving, still remained in overall deficit on current and long-term capital account. For the year as a whole, industrial production remained almost static, wages went up by about 3.5 per cent and prices by around 2.5 per cent. The money supply increased by over 4.6 per cent, rather less than in the previous year.

At the turn of the year the authorities were optimistic that a surplus would be achieved in the balance of payments in 1967. Bank rate was reduced from 7 to 6½ per cent in January; two further reductions brought it down to 5½ per cent by May. The Chancellor in the budget left the volume of taxation essentially unchanged. But estimated expendi-

---

[1]　This statement seems contradictory in that it is to be expected that as interest rates decline the demand for credit will increase. The authorities may have believed that they had so effectively controlled the supply of credit that a reduction in interest rates would not enable demanders of credit to get any more.

[2]　For convenience, the money supply is defined in the rest of this section as currency in circulation with the public plus net deposits of the clearing banks.

[3]　*Economic Report on 1966*, HM Treasury, p. 6.

ture went up by some £1,500 million, about 14 per cent, and revenue by slightly less, leaving an estimated surplus of £637 million. But loans to industry and others were planned at £1,580 million, leaving a net borrowing requirement of £943 million. The impact of this increased volume of government and government financed expenditure could in time only be expansionary and also inflationary, especially if the money supply was expanded to facilitate its financing. It makes little economic sense to say that the Chancellor 'did not propose to take any substantial action to influence demand'.[1]

The optimistic expectations about the balance of payments were not fulfilled. Notwithstanding this the authorities decided, as unemployment at over 2 per cent was thought to be uncomfortably high, to give some stimulus to domestic activity. Hire purchase restrictions were partly relaxed in June and August, and it was announced that increased social security benefits would be introduced from November, that the payment of investment grants would be speeded up and a new regional employment premium would be paid in the autumn to manufacturing establishments in the development areas. These measures led to increased sales of sterling.[2] The pressure on sterling was accentuated by the Middle East crisis and the closure of the Suez canal. In October the Bank raised Bank rate from 5½ to 6 per cent and early in November to 6½ per cent. But these measures were not enough to stem speculation against sterling and the reserves continued to fall even when buttressed with substantial credit from overseas central banks. The authorities realised 'that, without severe new measures, there would be another substantial deficit in the balance of payments next year; and the widespread conviction that the measures taken would include devaluation of sterling precipitated a further outflow of funds.

Devaluation took place on 18th November'.[3]

Additional measures were introduced or announced at the same time. Bank rate was raised to 8 per cent; bank lending to the private sector, except for exporters, was to be held at current levels; hire purchase terms on cars were tightened; *future* defence expenditure was to be reduced; the corporation tax was to go up from 40 to 42½ per cent in the next budget and selective employment tax premiums paid to manufacturers outside the development areas were withdrawn. New credits were negotiated with the IMF and overseas central banks to a total of almost $3,000 million and the rest of the Treasury's portfolio of dollar securities—£204 million at the new rate of exchange—was brought into the reserves.

The foreign exchange market soon took the view that the measures taken to curtail activity in the domestic economy were inadequate. The pound again came under pressure in December as funds were withdrawn from London. The whole position was further com-

---

[1] *BEQB*, vol. 7, no. 2, June 1967, p. 121.

[2] 'Following the announcement of further relaxations in hire purchase restrictions. . . there were fairly heavy sales of sterling.' *BEQB*, vol. 7, no. 4, December 1967, p. 339.

[3] *BEQB*, p. 336. It is again worth contrasting the description above with that given by the Treasury. 'By late autumn it was plain that the balance of payments was still in serious disequilibrium and likely to remain so in 1968, particularly if the Suez Canal remained closed. In the circumstances, and given the intensity of the speculative pressure which had built up against the pound, drastic corrective action was imperative. With unemployment exceptionally high and the recovery of output from the impact of the July 1966 measures barely established, renewed deflation was unacceptable to the government. Devaluation was therefore decided upon; and on the 18th November a new exchange partiy of £1 = $2.40 was declared.' *Economic Report on 1967*, HM Treasury, p. 7. Few observers would accept that the action was as deliberate as this account suggests. There is evidence that the government on taking office in 1964 had consciously rejected devaluation and were not converted to it until it was forced upon them by the balance of payments position and possibly the inability to continue massive foreign borrowing at the old exchange rate.

plicated by fears for the gold value of the dollar and the London market experienced very heavy demands for gold.

It need scarcely be said that 1967 was an appalling year for economic policy, though it should be added in mitigation that the problems were accentuated by a number of unpredictable factors, the Middle East war, closure of the Suez canal and the Liverpool and London dock strikes. However, the underlying economic situation, in terms of the failure to achieve the various policy goals, had been chronically unsatisfactory for years.

In the middle of January 1968 the Prime Minister announced cuts in the growth of public expenditure for 1968-9 and the following year. Slightly later the Chancellor of the Exchequer stated that he was bringing forward the budget from early April to 19 March. In the intervening two months there was a massive increase in consumers' expenditure in anticipation of increased taxation in the budget and the pound felt the effects of intensive speculation in the gold market in the expectation that the official dollar price of gold might be raised. This speculation subsided with the introduction of the dual market system for gold in March 1968.[1]

The 1968 budget brought the largest increases in taxation of any budget in the period under study. For the year 1968-9 they totalled £775 million. Income tax rates were unaltered but various changes were made in allowances; customs and excise duties and purchase tax were increased, as were motor vehicle duties and the selective employment tax, and for 1967-8 a special charge was levied on investment incomes in excess of £3,000. Total expenditure was to increase by over £600 million or by 5.6 per cent. Total revenue was expected to rise by £1,698 million or by over 15 per cent, which was calculated to leave a large surplus of £1,386 million. But this was to be more than absorbed by loans, leaving a borrowing requirement of £358 million.

The budget was generally welcomed as being what the economy needed, in terms of encouraging the release of resources for exports to take advantage of devaluation. However the budget remained in overall deficit, although to a lesser extent than in the previous year.

There was a short-lived improvement in the position of sterling after the budget and the Bank took the opportunity to reduce Bank rate from 8 per cent to 7½ per cent. But by April the position had again deteriorated. In May the authorities modified credit restrictions, bringing all bank lending in sterling, including that in connection with exports, under a ceiling that was not to exceed 104 per cent of the November 1967 level. Export lending was still to have priority and room for it was to be found by further restricting non-priority lending.

Throughout the first half of the year the balance of payments continued in deficit and the position of sterling remained precarious. By November it was felt that further restrictive measures were necessary. The Chancellor exercised his power to increase indirect taxation between budgets by use of the tax regulator and levied a 10 per cent surcharge on purchase tax and on the duties on alcohol, tobacco, petrol and oil. This measure was accompanied by an imports deposits scheme, covering about two-fifths of total UK imports, by which importers were required to deposit with H.M. Customs 50 per cent of the value of the imports. The deposits are repaid at the end of six months but bear no interest. In addition, credit was further restricted. The clearing banks were requested to reduce by mid-March 1969 their sterling lending, excluding fixed-rate lending, to the domestic private sector and to overseas borrowers, to 98 per cent of its mid-November 1967 level. Other banks and the finance houses were similarly restricted.

The period from 1964-8 was one of almost continuous crisis for sterling and the balance of payments. In the four years ending December 1968 the cumulative deficit on current and long-term capital account was over £1,200 million, massive foreign indebtedne

---

[1]   This issue is discussed further in chapter 3, III. 6.

was incurred, and the pound was devalued. Retail prices increased at some 4 per cent a year and unemployment rose from 1.4 per cent in 1965 to 2.4 per cent in 1968.[1] The money supply grew at about 5.1 per cent a year and output at only 2.4 per cent.

Economic policy over this period must be considered as having reached a kind of nadir. The major policy goals were consistently unrealised. Fiscal and monetary policy, interpreting the latter as control of the money supply, were generally over-expansionary as far as the balance of payments is concerned both before and after devaluation. If, however, exchange rate stability is given less priority relatively to other goals then the timing of devaluation must be questioned. For the postponement of the decision until 1967 adversely affected the attainment of other goals and especially economic growth and full employment.

V.6   1968-70

The year 1968 ended with the balance of payments still in a precarious position, and it remained so for the first quarter of 1969. The budget brought substantial increases in taxation; selective employment tax was raised, as was corporation tax and duties on petrol and wines. Total revenue was expected to rise by £1,645 million, or by over 12 per cent, and expenditure by £936 million, or 9 per cent, giving a large surplus of £2,457 million. Of this surplus loans were estimated to take £1,631 million leaving a *negative* borrowing requirement of £826 million. In other words the authorities were planning to be in a position to repay debt, a dramatic change of policy compared with earlier years and one that through its effects on the economy might be expected to strengthen the balance of payments.[2]

Shortly after the budget the Chancellor, in a letter to the IMF, emphasised the importance the government attached to monetary policy and, in particular, 'domestic credit expansion' (DCE); a new concept that requires some explanation.[3]

There are three main ways of considering DCE, each of which necessarily arrives at the same arithmetic total. The first stresses the credit expansion or lending approach and broadly defines DCE as bank lending to the public and private sectors, plus changes in notes and coin in circulation with the public, and overseas lending to the public sector. The second emphasises the borrowing approach and begins with the public sector borrowing requirement—already encountered earlier—deducts sales of public sector debt to the non-bank private sector and, subject to certain adjustments, includes bank lending to the private sector. The third is defined as the increase in the money supply plus, with some modifications, overseas lending to the public sector.

It is this third approach which finds most favour with the Bank as it directs attention to changes in the money supply, adjusted for an external deficit (or surplus) where the former covers the deficit on current account, plus the deficit on long-term and short-term private capital account, and official lending overseas.

The Bank's justification for the DCE concept hinges on the notion that for an open economy like the UK the money supply by itself is not an adequate indicator of monetary

---

[1]   The higher level of unemployment may be partly explained by the advent of redundancy payments and earnings related unemployment benefits encouraging some workers to remain voluntarily unemployed for longer periods. See ch. 1 IV. 2.

[2]   The effects on the economy would depend on many factors, including what forms the debt reduction might take and to what extent the money supply was affected.

[3]   See 'Money Supply and Domestic Credit: Some Recent Developments in Monetary Analysis', *E. T.*, no. 187, May 1969; Artis and Nobay, 'Two Aspects of the Monetary Debate'; and 'Domestic Credit Expansion', Supplement to the *BEQB*, September 1969.

conditions. The argument is that if, for instance, there is a deficit in the balance of payments the money supply will tend to decline as the community runs down its bank balances in financing it. But this essentially has the effect of understating the extent of domestic credit expansion, which can, however, be corrected by adding in the deficit and hence the DCE concept.

These arguments are scarcely persuasive. As already seen there are grounds for questioning the money supply concept employed by the authorities; these therefore also apply to the DCE concept.[1] Moreover, it seems extremely difficult to attach behavioural significance to this *broad* concept in relation to the operation of the economic system. Furthermore, if the credit aspects of the concept are stressed it is surprising that the definition employed excludes the credit and financial transactions of all financial intermediaries other than the banks, except in so far as the transactions are reflected in the money supply or external deficit. It comes therefore as something of a shock to find that the government for 1969-70 had committed itself to domestic credit expansion of not more than £400 million.

During the second quarter of 1969 the balance of payments showed distinct signs of improvement which were maintained and extended in the rest of the year. For the year as a whole the surplus—the first in any year since 1962—on current and long-term capital account amounted to £387 million. The recovery, helped by the growth of world trade as well as devaluation, was soundly based with a marked expansion of exports and a levelling out of imports.

Throughout the year the clearing banks had great difficulty in keeping their lending within the official ceiling. They failed to reduce it to 98 per cent of the November 1967 level by March and were even further away from it by May. As a penalty the rate of interest payable on special deposits was halved with the understanding that the full rate would be restored when the banks fulfilled the lending requirement. Despite the banks' difficulties, however, the money supply, on the definition already used, increased by only 1.5 per cent, the smallest increase for many years.

The strengthened balance of payments position persisted in the early months of 1970, giving a favourable external background for the 1970 budget, which made no major changes in the volume of taxation or expenditure. Certain alterations were made in income tax allowances and the rate at which surtax begins. The selective employment tax, instead of being levied per person employed, was from 1972 to become a differential payroll tax and expressed as a percentage of the total payroll. Import deposits were to be reduced from 1 May 1970. As a temporary stimulus to industrial building initial allowances were increased from 15 to 30 per cent on expenditure over the two years to 5 April 1972 and to 40 per cent in development and intermediate areas. Total revenue was estimated to increase by £858 million or 5.6 per cent and expenditure by £704 million or 5.5 per cent, leaving a large surplus of £2,598 million. Loans were anticipated to require £1,544 million thus allowing for the second year running a very large negative borrowing requirement.

The Chancellor also announced a reduction in Bank rate to 7 per cent and the abolition of the rigid ceiling on bank and finance house lending. However, he intimated that the restricted lending of the clearing and Scottish banks and finance houses should not increase by more than about 5 per cent by March 1971. But in contrast to these measures he announced a call for special deposits by ½ per cent for the clearing banks and ¼ per cent for the Scottish banks, in order to keep pressure on their liquidity position, which was relatively comfortable for this time of year. However, the rate payable on all special deposits was to be raised to its old level, the going average rate on Treasury bills.

---

[1]   See above, pp. 67-8.

The authorities are for the present in a very strong budgetary and monetary position. There is, of course, concern amongst the community at the relatively high level of unemployment, which reached 2.8 per cent in the early months of the year, at the rate of growth of prices and wages, and the sluggish rate of economic growth.

Since 1967 basic weekly wage rates and retail prices have risen on average by 5.9 per cent and 5.1 per cent a year respectively. Thus in this period wage rates have done little more than keep pace with the cost of living. However, substantial increases in wage rates are anticipated in the rest of 1970 and in part these can be expected to contribute to a further rise in prices. But there is no reason to believe that this price rise will be explosive provided that the authorities maintain their present budgetary and monetary stance. It is to be expected, in the light of past experience and policy, that prices and wage rates will continue for a time to rise in the face of restrictive fiscal and monetary conditions. In particular, a reduced rate of growth of the money supply may be expected to be offset to some extent by a rising velocity of circulation, accompanied by rising interest rates. However, if the restrictive policies are persisted in, price expectations will be revised downwards and eventually velocity and interest rates will tend to decline. Unfortunately, these adjustments are likely to coincide with relatively high unemployment and a slow rate of economic growth.

The authorities may well therefore be faced in the short run with a fundamental dilemma. If they wish to contain price and wage inflation and have some prospect of a continuing strong balance of payments position they may for a time have to sacrifice employment and economic growth. These are tough choices at any stage of the election cycle.

On the other hand if they substantially weaken their fiscal and monetary policies in the interests of short run employment and growth then rapidly rising prices, wages and nominal interest rates will continue and another balance of payments crisis will arise as the advantages of devaluation are undermined.

V.7   Policy In Retrospect

In terms of the goals set out in the introduction economic policy since the 1950s must be judged a failure. The pound has been devalued, balance of payments crises have followed each other with almost monotonous regularity, price stability has been the exception rather than the rule, and economic growth has been fitful, and low by recent if not historical international standards. The only goal achieved—at least until recently—more or less consistently has been full or nearly full employment.

It seems highly likely that the simultaneous achievement of the various goals over an extended period of time is impossible given the limitations on our state of knowledge and the policy instruments at the disposal of the authorities. Furthermore, it does not follow that if the authorities were given more instruments they would be able to achieve all the different goals. For enlarging the number of instruments increases the amount of knowledge required to operate them effectively. There is no reason to believe that this knowledge is available. If this is correct there is a plausible case for reducing the number of goals.

If the authorities were, in fact, attempting to pursue too many goals, what assessment can be made of their monetary, credit and fiscal policies? Did they implicitly attach more importance to the achievement of one goal rather than another? Did the degree of importance change through time? These are very difficult questions to answer.

However, in the preceding discussion of policy since the early 1950s it was assumed that major importance was throughout attached to maintenance of the exchange rate and a satisfactory balance of payments position, even at the expense of economic growth and to a lesser extent unemployment. The attainment of price stability seems on the whole to have had a relatively low priority despite its relevance to the exchange rate and the balance of payments.

If this ranking is more or less legitimate there remains justification for dissatisfaction with the policy record. For as far as the balance of payments is concerned—and the exchange rate—corrective measures were often delayed too long and expansionary measures taken too soon. To argue that the timing of policy measures was also dictated by the other policy goals such as the desire for economic growth and full employment is to beg the question whether, at any rate, economic growth might have been greater if the balance of payments position had been more stable and fewer reversals of policy had been necessary. This is not to say that economic growth and full employment should be sacrificed to the balance of payments and a fixed exchange rate. On the contrary, there would seem to be good grounds for taking the opposite view.

Finally, there remains the question of the actual policy instruments the authorities chose to use. It has already been emphasised that, except for a brief interlude in the mid-1950s and until very recently, control of the money supply as a policy measure had been almost totally neglected. Instead there had been increasing reliance on detailed quantitative restrictions, particularly on the banks and finance houses, with an almost total disregard for the competitive efficiency of the monetary and financial system.

On the fiscal side the criticisms need perhaps be less acute. However, there seems to have been a failure, perhaps because of the relative unimportance attached to the money supply, to appreciate the inflationary significance, and hence relevance for the balance of payments, of large net borrowing requirements, especially in conjunction with the continuing problem of debt management. Furthermore, there must remain a sense of astonishment at the introduction of a major new tax like the selective employment tax without extensive discussion and analysis of its quantitative implications for the economic system.

REFERENCES AND FURTHER READING

Bank of England Quarterly Bulletin

R. Caves and Associates, *Britain's Economic Prospects,* A Brookings Institution Study, George Allen and Unwin, 1968.

D. R. Croome and H. G. Johnson, (eds), *Money in Britain 1959-1969,* Oxford University Press, 1970.

J. C. R. Dow, *The Management of the British Economy, 1945-60,* Cambridge University Press, 1964.

Milton Friedman, *The Optimum Quantity of Money and Other Essays,* Aldine Publishing Company, Chicago, 1969.

N. J. Gibson, *Financial Intermediaries and Monetary Policy,* Hobart Paper 39, (2nd edn), Institute of Economic Affairs, 1970.

Bent Hansen, *Fiscal Policy in Seven Countries 1955-1965,* OECD, 1969.

E. Victor Morgan, *Monetary Policy for Stable Growth,* Hobart Paper 27 (3rd edn), Institute of Economic Affairs, 1969.

A. R. Prest, *Public Finance in Theory and Practice* (4th edn), Weidenfeld and Nicolson, 1970.

Report of the Committee on the Working of the Monetary System (Radcliffe Committee), Cmnd 827, HMSO, 1959 Principal Memoranda of Evidence (3 vols.) and Minutes of Evidence, HMSO, 1960.

R. S. Sayers, *Modern Banking* (7th edn), Oxford University Press, 1967.

A. A. Walters, *Money in Boom and Slump,* Hobart Paper 44, Institute of Economic Affairs, 1969.

3

Foreign trade and the balance of payments

I   THE UK BALANCE OF PAYMENTS

I.1   Foreign Trade and the UK Economy

The UK is an 'open' economy, by which is meant that the volume and structure of production and consumption of goods and services is dependent on international trade and division of labour. In the case of the UK this dependence is heavy. To maintain the present population at current standards of living it is necessary to import something like half of our total food requirements and the bulk of industrial raw materials. Broadly speaking, these are exchanged for manufactured goods which constitute the bulk of our exports of goods, though, as we shall see, the pattern of trade also involves the exchange of services, 'invisible' trade, on a massive scale. The monetary values of these and related international transactions are collected together in the Balance of Payments Account which forms an integral part of the general system of National Income Accounts of the country.

The importance of foreign trade and the balance of international payments for the prosperity and growth of the UK can scarcely be doubted by anyone who followed newspaper reports and discussions during the last few years, but this crisis period was only the latest demonstration of Britain's intimate dependence on foreign trade. In the nineteenth century the main trends in the growth of industrial production and real income have been shown to be closely connected with trends in our foreign trade, and major business fluctuations in the period were the result of a complex interaction of fluctuations in exports and residential building activity. The main cause of the heavy unemployment in the UK in the interwar period is also undoubtedly to be found in adverse trends in our export trade.

The second world war created a new set of foreign trade problems for the UK. Wartime destruction of merchant shipping, together with the forced liquidation of profitable overseas investments in the period before Lend-Lease, led to a marked decline in Britain's invisible receipts from abroad. On the payments side it was necessary to pay interest on a greatly increased level of indebtedness arising from the war, and to this was added a big increase in overseas expenditure by the government. In the early postwar years full employment and reconstruction were possible only as a result of massive economic aid from the US and Canada. In 1945 and 1946 the Anglo-American and Anglo-Canadian Financial Agreements provided the UK with long-term loans of $3.75 billion and $1.25 billion respectively. These loans were to be repaid in equal instalments over a fifty year period beginning December 1951 with interest at the very low rate of 2 per cent. Further aid from the US in the form of substantial grants was received under the European Recovery Programme during the years 1948-51. Ironically, it was the Anglo-American Loan Agreement that produced the first of Britain's postwar foreign exchange crises, the 'convertibility crisis' of 1947. This resulted from a premature attempt to make sterling freely convertible into gold or dollars on account of all current transactions. The policy, a requirement of the 1945 Agreement, had to be abandoned after five weeks because of the heavy drain on UK reserves. The second foreign exchange crisis came in 1949. In the course of an economic recovery, based on a huge expansion of exports and stringent control of imports, the country was forced by a speculative crisis to devalue the pound by 30 per cent in September 1949. Since 1949 there have been further foreign exchange crises, which have had powerful repercussions on general economic policy, the most important being the prolonged disturbance from 1964 to 1967 which led to the second UK post-war devaluation of 14.3 per cent in November 1967. The further crises in 1968 and 1969 were more the backwash effects of events abroad rather than effects of the over-valuation of sterling as had been the case before 1967.

Although Britain is often considered to be unusually dependent on foreign trade it is worth noting that our degree of dependence is actually less than that of some of our European competitors in international trade. For member countries of the OECD it is possible to compare the ratios of total exports or imports, inclusive of 'invisible' trans-actions, to national income on the basis of data which has been adjusted to allow for international comparisons. The UK export ratio for 1966 was 25 per cent or roughly the same as the average of European members of the OECD. It was considerably less than that of some members like the Netherlands (52 per cent), Belgium (44 per cent), the same as West Germany, and rather higher than Italy (22 per cent) and France (18 per cent).

TABLE 3.1

UK Imports, Exports and National Income for selected years

	1938		1955		1965		1969	
	£ million	per cent	£ million	per cent	£ million	per cent	£ million	per cent
Imports (Debits)								
Goods	835	82.3	3,386	70.2	5,054	68.3	7,214	69.8
Services	142	14.0	1,095	22.7	1,788	24.2	2,279	22.1
Property income net of tax	37	3.7	343	7.1	555	7.5	841	8.1
Total	1,014	100.0	4,824	100.0	7,397	100.0	10,334	100.0
Exports (Credits)								
Goods	533	56.0	3,073	65.5	4,817	64.0	7,056	64.4
Services	190	20.0	1,104	23.5	1,715	22.8	2,592	23.6
Property income net of tax	229	24.0	517	11.0	993	13.2	1,313	12.0
	952	100.0	4,694	100.0	7,525	100.0	10,961	100.0
Gross National Product (factor cost) £ million	5,175		16,983		31,333		38,617	
Total Imports % GNP	19.6		28.4		23.6		26.8	
Total Exports % GNP	18.4		27.6		24.0		28.4	

Source: NIBB, 1967 and 1969, PE, 1970, Cmnd. 4328

In table 3.1 the quantitative dependence of the UK on foreign trade is illustrated with figures for selected years and the broad structure of trade and payments is shown. Exports currently amount to some 28 per cent of the value of GNP and imports some 27 per cent. In each case the percentage has increased substantially as compared with 1938. The ratios of foreign trade to GNP reached very high levels in 1951, with total receipts at 32 per cent and payments at 35 per cent, the main influences being the abnormally high import prices following the 1949 devaluation and the Korean War and the success of the postwar export drive. Between 1951 and 1967 the prices of exports and imports have tended to rise more slowly than the prices of goods and services in general, whilst the volumes of imports and exports have grown faster than the volume of GNP. The net effect was to produce a decline in the ratios of exports and imports to GNP in current prices. The values shown for 1965 are about the average for the period 1964-6. Since the 1967 devaluation both ratios have shown a substantial increase to levels more or less typical of the period 1953-7.

From table 3.1 we see that the breakdown of total exports and imports into goods, services and property income shows relatively minor changes in structure between 1955 and 1969, but considerable changes as compared with 1938. On the export side the share of net property income in total receipts from abroad has fallen sharply since 1938, when such receipts constituted almost one-quarter of the total. Even so, more than one-third of total receipts are generated by the export of services and receipt of property income. On the import side the share of goods has fallen substantially since 1938, whilst payments for services, including expenditure overseas (excluding transfers) by the government, and property income, now account for about 28 per cent of total imports.[1] Some explanations of trends will be given later in section II.

I.2   The Concept of the Balance of Payments

Before we can proceed to examine the structure and behaviour of the UK balance of payments it is necessary to define this concept more rigorously. The balance of payments is, in principle, a record of all economic transactions, during a period of time, between residents of the UK and residents of the rest of the world. By residents of the UK we mean private individuals living permanently in the UK, the UK central and local authorities, and all business enterprises etc. located in the UK. The term includes agencies of the UK government which operate abroad but excludes any foreign branches or subsidiaries of UK firms.

The UK balance of payments is usually set out in terms of sterling though it is obvious that in principle every transaction involves some foreign currency. Where foreign trade transactions are invoiced in foreign currency, these values are converted into sterling values, for balance of payments records, at the appropriate exchange rate. In fact most UK exports and some 50 per cent of imports are invoiced directly in sterling since the pound sterling like the US dollar is regarded as a 'key' currency in international trade. This means that foreign trade may be carried on specifically in terms of these currencies which are internationally acceptable to a greater or lesser extent. The key currency principle is particularly important in relation to the collection of countries known as the *Sterling Area* or the *scheduled territories* as listed in official publications.[2] Imports into the UK from these countries lead to the creation of *Sterling Balances,* i.e. British bank deposits, Treasury bills and other UK government securities owned by non-residents of the UK. Normally such balances are temporary, being liquidated either by the purchase of exports

---

[1]   Note that the figures in table 3.1 exclude private and government transfers. These items are included in the current account of the balance of payments because of their recurrent nature but it is arguable that they belong more properly to the capital account. Until 1965 private transfers were of negligible net importance. Government transfers form a considerable part of current government expenditure overseas. In 1969 they accounted for 0.5 per cent of GNP and their inclusion in imports in table 3.1 would raise the figure given by 1.7 per cent.

[2]   Broadly consisting of the Commonwealth, except Canada and plus South Africa, Ireland, Iceland, Jordan, Kuwait and some others.

from the UK or by conversion into foreign exchange to settle payments with other countries. Sterling balances also arise when countries in the overseas sterling area sell goods to non-members and exchange the foreign currencies so acquired for UK bank deposits, and for many years it was the custom for members of the sterling area to keep the bulk of their international reserves in the form of sterling balances.[1] So sterling balances constitute a revolving fund with constant changes in the structure of ownership. Outstanding balances at any time represent short- or long-term lending to the UK government, not always voluntary, as the unfortunate owners of balances 'blocked' by the exchange control in the early postwar period would testify. Such lending is chiefly at the initiative of central banks or other official bodies, which acquire the sterling balances from their own residents in exchange for local currency and hold them as reserves. Sterling balances also arise when firms, etc. in non-sterling countries purchase UK money for use in normal trade and financial operations, and balances are also held by international organisations like the IMF and the International Bank.

Before the second world war the outstanding total of sterling balances was of the same order of magnitude as the UK official gold reserve, the exact values at the year-end 1939 being £517 million and £545 million respectively. During the war the outstanding total of sterling balances increased enormously to a level of £3,567 million at year-end 1945, of which some two-thirds was held by sterling area countries, whilst the gold reserve increased only to £610 million over the same period. The wartime increase in sterling balances occurred because the countries concerned supplied goods and services on credit to the UK government. Naturally, with the ending of hostilities the UK government was under pressure to release these balances for the purchase of essential goods and services since substantial sums were owned by relatively poor countries like India and Egypt. Despite the postwar balance of payments problems of the UK the volume of sterling balances was reduced by end-1949 to £3,143 million but the Korean War and its effect on primary product prices caused a subsequent increase in total to £3,577 million by the end of 1951.

Between 1951 and 1962 the outstanding total (excluding international organisations) fluctuated around an average of £3,500 million with no pronounced trend. From 1963 onwards the series for overseas sterling holdings was discontinued and a new series was published giving external liabilities and claims in sterling. Net liabilities on the new basis increased from £3,163 million from the end of 1962 (£3,501 on the old series) to £3,292 million at the end of 1969 (excluding international organisations). The figures for the later years are very much influenced by special aid to the UK from foreign central banks and do not reflect the true commercial and financial demand for non-resident sterling. Appendix A-8 gives summary data for both series.

I.3 The Structure of the UK Balance of Payments

In official statistical practice the UK balance of payments is divided into three main sections. These are:

1. The current account.
2. The long-term capital account.
3. Monetary movements.

In general economic analysis items (2) and (3) together are often referred to as the capital account. In addition to the three headings there is a separate item known as the *balancing item.* It represents the sum of errors and omissions in the various headings and

---

[1] In recent years this custom has been modified as members of the overseas sterling area have added to their own reserves of gold and non-sterling exchange. See A. R. Conan, 'Sterling: The Problem of Policy', *Westminster Bank Review,* November 1967.

has a value such that aggregate payments equal aggregate receipts for the balance of payments as a whole. A positive entry means (a) an unrecorded net export if the capital account is regarded as correct, or (b) an unrecorded net reduction in assets if the current account is regarded as correct, or (c) a combination of the two. Short-run changes in the item are almost certainly due to unrecorded capital movements but the item cannot be analysed with confidence in the longer run. It is often assumed, however, that the more volatile capital elements in the balancing item will cancel out when this is averaged over a number of years. Hence the term 'normal' balancing item, which is assumed to represent, mainly, the unrecorded flows of net exports. Now that an estimate has been made for net underrecording of exports for the period after 1963, the CSO takes the view that the remaining persistent errors should be roughly offsetting so that the normal balancing item will have a zero value.[1]

The current account is mainly concerned with items giving rise to income and expenditure flows in the national income accounts, i.e. exports (credits) and imports (debits) of goods (visible trade) and exports and imports of services (invisible trade). It also includes some items which ought to be classified as capital items, e.g. private transfers such as gifts and migrants' funds and government transfers such as grants to Commonwealth and other countries. Thus the true nature of the current account balance is blurred—not seriously in the case of private transfers, but government transfers represent a significant percentage of total government payments.

The two sides of the current account, debits and credits, or payments and receipts, need not balance in principle and rarely do so in practice. If total receipts exceed total payments we speak of a current account surplus, whilst an excess of payments over receipts is a deficit on current account.

An export or import surplus can only arise to the extent that offsetting or accommodating transactions arise in the two sectors of the capital account. This is because, for the balance of payments as a whole, every receipt of foreign exchange must be matched by a corresponding payment, since we are dealing with actual transactions recorded during a past accounting period. The country as a whole may be likened to an individual household or firm which cannot spend more than it receives without liquidating assets, including cash, or going into debt. As a first approximation we could say that the items in the two sectors of the capital account are *induced*, in an accounting sense, by the net outcome in the current account. A deficit in the current account may be financed either by long-term borrowing in the long-term capital account or by short-term borrowing or liquidation of foreign exchange reserves in the monetary movements account whilst a surplus in the current account implies the net acquisition of foreign assets. But this is too simple a view for any country and certainly for a key-currency country like the UK.

Capital account transactions may originate quite independently of the current account (though they may affect the current account) and such capital items may be termed *autonomous*. As an example, the UK government may decide to make a long-term loan to a Commonwealth government and may do this without knowing precisely what the state of the UK current account will be when the proceeds of the loan are spent or transferred. Or a firm or household in the UK may, with permission of the exchange control, purchase real or long-term financial assets abroad merely as an act of investment and will expect to be supplied with the necessary foreign exchange regardless of the state of the current account at the time of the transaction. In each of these cases it is possible that the autonomous act of lending abroad will alter the level of economic activity abroad and at home and cause the levels of UK exports and imports of goods and services to differ from the levels which would have occurred in the absence of the loans. Thus *autonomous* capital transactions have *induced* effects in the current account.

---

[1] See table 3.2 and *UK Balance of Payments 1969,* CSO, pp. 86-7.

TABLE 3.2

UK Summary Balance of Payments 1965-9   (£ million)

	1965	1966	1967	1968	1969
Current Account (credits +, debits −)					
Exports and re-exports (f.o.b.) (+)	4,777	5,122	5,042	6,143	7,013
Imports (f.o.b.) (−)	5,042	5,214	5,576	6,807	7,153
VISIBLE TRADE BALANCE	−265	−92	−534	−664	−140
Net under-recording of exports (+)	40	60	80	130	43
Payments for US military aircraft (−)	12	41	98	109	61
VISIBLE BALANCE	−237	−73	−552	−643	−158
INVISIBLES					
Government services and transfers (−)	447	470	464	462	457
Other invisibles and transfers (+)	603	583	694	796	981
INVISIBLE BALANCE	+156	+113	+230	+334	+524
CURRENT BALANCE	−81	+40	−322	−309	+366
Long-term capital account[1]					
Official capital (net)	−85	−80	−57	+21	−95
Private investment (net)	−112	−27	−82	−110	+116
BALANCE OF LONG-TERM CAPITAL	−197	−107	−139	−89	+21
Balance of current and long-term capital transactions (basic balance)	−278	−67	−461	−398	+387
Balancing Item	+31	−37	+227	−145	+182
MONETARY MOVEMENTS[1,2]					
EEA loss on forwards[3]	–	–	−105	−251	–
Miscellaneous capital (net)	+55	−110	−66	−17	+201
Change in liabilities in non-sterling currencies (net)	−125	−146	+213	+53	−109
Change in liabilities in overseas sterling area currencies (net)	+7	−45	+24	−46	+1
Change in external liabilities in sterling (net)	+57	+125	+167	+165	−603
Change in account with IMF	+499	−2	−318	+525	−15
Transfer from dollar portfolio to reserves	–	+316	+204	–	–
Change in gold and convertible currency reserves	−246	−34	+115	+114	−44
BALANCE OF MONETARY MOVEMENTS	+247	+104	+234	+543	−569

[1]   Assets: increase −/decrease +. Liabilities: increase +/decrease −.

[2]   Figures given in Monetary Movements for 1967 exclude revaluation adjustments arising from devaluation.

[3]   For explanation of this item see p. 108.

Source: ET, March 1970.

But what happens if the aggregate of such autonomous long-term transactions fails to be matched by an equivalent surplus of UK exports over imports, even allowing for any induced trade flows? Britain is then in the position of an individual who invests in long-term securities to an amount greater than the difference between his income and expenditure. The answer in both cases is that the difference must be made up out of cash balances or by borrowing short-term. We should say that the combined deficit on current and long-term capital account was met by accommodating or induced changes in the monetary movements sector. The sum of the balances on current account and long-term capital account is often referred to as the *basic balance* and this balance is assigned a key role in the assessment of performance. There is much to be said for this approach since it allows for interdependence between the current and capital accounts and reduces ambiguity which might be caused by arbitrary allocations of certain items to one account rather than the other.[1]

The upshot of all this is that the various sectors of the balance of payments are related by complex forces and government attempts to influence any sector in isolation may not be successful. If the government tries to reduce the size of the long-term capital outflow in order to increase its gold and foreign exchange reserves it may find that the net effect is a reduced surplus on current account with little change in reserves. We return to this problem in section III.

An outline picture of the UK balance of payments in recent years is given in table 3.2 and summary data for a longer period is given in appendix table A-7. The balance of visible trade is usually negative but is normally compensated by a surplus on invisible trade to give an overall surplus on current account; though since 1959 this has been true only in 1962, 1963, 1966 and 1969. Government net invisibles, i.e. net expenditure on military and diplomatic services plus transfers of economic aid, etc. are persistently negative but these are more than compensated by other net invisibles which will be shown in more detail later.

The balance of long-term capital is negative in most years, indicating that Britain was increasing her overseas assets. It also tends to be variable in size which is due since 1959 mainly to variations in net private investment. Net private investment is the outcome of substantial flows of investment in both directions by firms (direct investment) in overseas branches and portfolio investment (the purchase of foreign securities) and 'other' investment which includes substantial direct investment by oil companies. It is the inflow to the UK since 1959 which is the main cause of fluctuations in the net balance. The balance of current and long-term transactions or basic balance shows the overall amount of accommodating finance which has to be provided by monetary movements and the balancing item.

For a detailed description of the constituent items in the monetary movements account the reader must be referred to official sources, e.g. the *Balance of Payments Pink Book*, published each year around August. In general the account covers all identifiable changes in short-term assets and liabilities arising from the international transactions of individuals, firms, home and overseas banks and official organisations like the IMF and the Exchange Equalisation Account.[2] The account illustrates the fact that, for a country like the UK, a deficit or surplus on current and long-term capital account is not to be thought of simply as representing a net loss or accretion of reserves of foreign exchange.

---

[1] In some earlier discussions the 'normal' (positive) balancing item, estimated at about £50-60 million is included in the basic balance. In recent years the statisticians of the CSO have encountered problems arising from the interrelation between items in the long-term capital account and the monetary movements account. This may lead eventually to the need for a modified concept of the basic balance. See *ET*, March 1970, p xvii.

[2] The Exchange Equalisation Account is a department of the Treasury which acts as legal custodian of the UK reserves of gold and foreign exchange and has power to intervene in the foreign exchange market. Actual market operations are conducted for the Account by the Bank of England.

As an example of the way in which the balance of payments account is interpreted we may take the year 1965. From table 3.2 we see first that there was a visible trade deficit of £265 million. After allowing for payments for US military aircraft and the net under-recording of exports this was reduced to £237 million. The invisibles account showed a surplus of £156 million, since net receipts from interest, dividends and profits plus private services and transfers more than offset the net deficit on government account. The current account balance was, therefore, in deficit to the extent of £81 million. The long-term capital account also showed a deficit, of £197 million, indicating net accumulation of assets abroad. The basic deficit amounted to £278 million and this had to be financed by monetary movements of +£247 million after allowance for the balancing item of +£31 million. A positive sign in the monetary movements account signifies a decrease in assets or increase in liabilities yet we see that official reserves actually *increased* by £246 million since that entry is negative. The main explanation for this apparently odd result was the UK drawing on the IMF which made foreign exchange available to the UK. The counterpart of the IMF loans is shown as an increase in sterling balances owned by the IMF (£499 million). These aggregate entries for monetary movements in the period covered by table 3.2 conceal a great deal of assistance to the UK from overseas central banks. Reductions in non-official sterling balances caused by speculative effects were offset by increased sterling held by central banks as the counterpart of their assistance to the UK. It is impossible to disentangle such movements from the official tables since there are no separate entries to cover this type of central bank assistance. In 1966 and 1967 the reserves were temporarily increased by the sale of dollar securities owned by the UK government and previously treated as a second-line reserve, but given other financing needs in the two year period, the overall reserve still showed a net decline. The positive entries are needed to make the account balance and indicate a decrease of assets which is offset by the concealed negative entry in the change in reserves. The special items in 1967 and 1968, 'EEA loss on forwards', is again a balancing item. It arises from the intervention of the Exchange Equalisation Account in the forward exchange market in the period before devaluation. The Account was buying sterling for forward delivery at rates appropriate for the old parity and the change of parity involved losses on such transactions. The loss to the UK is really indicated by the concealed entries with a positive sign in the rest of the monetary movements account.

1.4   Equilibrium in the Balance of Payments

We have seen that the balance of payments as a whole must necessarily balance because of the way it is constructed. This does not mean that the balance of payments is always in a state of equilibrium. It is necessary, therefore, to consider the meaning of this concept and its importance for economic policy.

The following discussion takes for granted the fact that the UK is a member of the IMF and has, therefore, accepted the obligation to maintain the foreign exchange value of the pound within very narrow limits of a par value, the level of which can only be changed with the consent of the IMF, when necessary to correct a 'fundamental disequilibrium' in the balance of payments. If the foreign exchange rate was not 'fixed' in this way but was free to vary under the influence of forces of supply and demand in the foreign exchange market there would be no apparent problem of economic policy in regard to the balance of payments.[1] Any tendency for the level of imports, including purchases of foreign securities, to exceed the level of exports would imply an excess demand for foreign exchange and this would reduce the foreign exchange value of the

---

[1]   In the sense of preventing loss of reserves. But the consequences of this automatic balancing of the foreign market might raise awkward problems in other directions so that some short-term stabilisation would be regarded as necessary.

pound. This would raise the cost of imported goods in sterling and reduce the cost of British exports in terms of foreign exchange and, provided certain conditions were satisfied, the excess demand for imports and foreign exchange would be eliminated by market forces. The necessary conditions relate to the elasticities of demand and supply for imports and exports in the aggregate. The advantages and disadvantages of flexible rates are discussed in section III.6 of this chapter.

A system of fixed exchange rates necessarily implies that the authorities have access to a buffer stock of reserves of gold or foreign exchange or short-term borrowing facilities[2] so that a temporary excess demand for foreign exchange by its residents can be met. If such a temporary excess demand is quickly reversed by natural forces (i.e. the reversal of a mild inventory boom which first raises and then reduces the demand for imports relative to trend) and the reserves are adequate in size to meet the cumulative excess demand for foreign exchange, no problem exists. If the excess demand for foreign exchange is not quickly reversed, or reserves are inadequate to act as a buffer, a disequilibrium situation exists.

A country can run a persistent deficit on current account only if it has unlimited reserves of gold or foreign exchange to draw upon or if it can borrow persistently from the rest of the world to finance the deficit. No country has unlimited reserves and persistent short-term borrowing would be unwise, even if it were possible, since there is always a danger of cessation or reversal of the short-term capital inflow. In either case the immediate result must be that foreign exchange reserves are liquidated at a rate which may shatter confidence in the country's ability to maintain the external value of its currency, and a speculative foreign exchange crisis results. A persistent deficit matched by a long-term capital inflow is both possible and unobjectionable if the capital inflow is associated with policies to raise productive capacity and to stimulate the flow of exports or reduce dependence on imports. In the absence of such long-term loans, or grants of aid, the balance of payments may be said to be in disequilibrium if the value of imports persistently threatens to exceed the value of exports. A country faced with this situation must then introduce measures of economic policy to restore equilibrium in the balance of payments; indeed, such policy measures will be forced on the country by the threatened exhaustion of exchange reserves.

The previous argument needs to be qualified in a number of ways. For a given value of the exchange rate there will tend to be a positive correlation between the level of expenditure on imports and the level of employment or national income. The precise quantitative relationship may change through time as tastes and relative costs, etc. change, but some positive co-variation is highly probable. This means that if import values exceed export values at a given level of employment and income, a decline in employment and income will tend to restore the balance; indeed such a decline in incomes may arise automatically in certain cases owing to the operation of what is called the foreign trade multiplier process. Excess imports will not normally be eliminated completely by the automatic multiplier process unless the sum of expenditures on domestic investment and government purchase of goods and services falls more rapidly than levels of savings and tax collections, as income falls; but such a result may be contrived by economic policy.[2] The implication is that potential disequilibrium *may* be concealed if the country is operating at substantially

---

[1] The UK can borrow short-term by raising Bank Rate, and therefore other short-term interest rates, relative to levels in other financial centres. This induces an increase in sterling balances. This mechanism tends to fail, however, if foreigners fear an imminent devaluation.

[2] For a detailed discussion of this macroeconomic theory the reader must consult general texts. A good discussion is to be found in Kindleberger, *International Economics.* In a full analysis account must be taken of the 'feedback' effect of reduced imports on the level of exports, but this d alter the conclusion given in the text above.

less than full employment levels of output, an example of this being the UK situation in the 1920s. A corollary is that disequilibrium exists if an economy cannot pursue a policy of growth at full employment levels of output without being threatened with a persistent import surplus. Disequilibrium may also exist if a potential persistent import surplus is prevented by the imposition of abnormally severe restrictions on international trade: tariffs, import quotas and exchange control. The problem here is the definition of 'abnormal' and this can be settled only by reference to general aims and achievements in the field of international trade policy. Finally, for a relatively advanced and rich country like the UK the idea of equilibrium as a mere balance in the current account is too limited. UK governments have accepted the obligation to provide economic aid in the form of outright grants and long-term concessionary loans to underdeveloped countries, particularly those in the Commonwealth. There is also the fact that free mobility of capital from the UK to the rest of the sterling area is a traditional policy[1] and aside from the benefits of such lending to the receiving countries, the interest and dividends which result form an important part of our invisible earnings, whilst the capital export itself may benefit UK exports of goods or reduce the cost of imports. The UK government must also repay long-term loans from foreign governments, of which the chief are the Anglo-American and Anglo-Canadian loans of 1945-6 which jointly involve an annual capital repayment, at the new exchange rate, of some £36 million.[2] In addition to all this it is essential that the UK should build up her international reserves to a level adequate to meet a temporary disequilibrium in the balance of payments, allowing for temporary outflows of short-term capital.

1.5   A Formal Definition of Equilibrium and Disequilibrium

The preceding discussion leads to the following definition. The balance of payments is in long-term equilibrium when the average current account surplus over a period of good and bad years is sufficient to cover (i) the required level of net external investment including debt repayment and grants of aid, and (ii) the required trend increase in foreign exchange reserves, without recourse to less than full-employment levels of output and without recourse to trade and payments restrictions inconsistent with accepted international obligations. If these conditions are not satisfied the balance of payments may be said to be in a state of 'fundamental disequilibrium'.

The definition is meaningless unless there is an independent specification of target levels of external investment, full employment, etc. This is inevitable since such targets must, in principle, be subject to continuous political discussion and re-specification. Notice also that disequilibrium is a two-sided concept, a deficit disequilibrium for one country implying a surplus disequilibrium for at least one other country. In practice it is always difficult to get the governments of surplus countries to recognise this obvious truth, though recognition is likely to be rapid if the country switches from a state of persistent surplus to one of deficit.

Although reference is made to 'fundamental disequilibrium' the definition proposed is not taken explicitly from the Articles of Agreement of the IMF, which nowhere defines this critically important concept. Some writers have chosen to define 'fundamental disequilibrium', in the IMF context, as a persistent tendency to lose reserves or the

---

[1] The voluntary controls announced in the 1966 budget may well mark the beginning of the end of this policy. See section III of this chapter.

[2] Repayment of principal and interest on these North American loans may be deferred to the end of the century if the UK government considers it necessary. The right may be exercised only seven times and has been used in 1957, 1964, 1965 and 1968. Interest is payable at 2 per cent on the sums deferred.

acceptance of 'abnormal' policy measures to prevent this. In the case of the UK a persistent tendency to lose reserves is scarcely a relevant criterion since any serious loss of reserves in the postwar period has tended to provoke a speculative foreign exchange crisis which could annihilate the official reserves within a year in the absence of corrective policy measures. The secondary drain in reserves is partly a consequence of the liquidation of sterling balances, to avoid a decline in their foreign exchange value caused by the anticipated devaluation, and partly by the so-called 'leads and lags' effect, whereby foreign payments due to the UK are delayed and payments by UK importers accelerated, to avoid any windfall losses which devaluation would produce. The *Radcliffe Report* estimated that the size of the leads and lags effect could amount to hundreds of millions of pounds and the actual sum involved will inevitably increase as the current level of trade increases.[1]

1.6   The UK Balance of Payments since 1952—An Assessment

The formal definition of equilibrium will now be used to assess the performance of the UK balance of payments in recent years. We shall argue that the UK balance of payments, whilst never very strong before 1958, degenerated between 1959 and 1967 into a state of fundamental disequilibrium. Table 3.3 presents annual averages for the main items in the balance of payments for the periods 1952-5, 1956-60, 1961-4 and 1965-7. The first

TABLE 3.3

UK Balance of Payments, Annual Averages for Selected Periods (£ million) and Average Annual Growth Rates of GDP

	1952-5	1956-60	1961-4	1965-7
Visibles net	−260	−94	−213	−287
Invisibles net	+327	+227	+170	+166
(Government)	−99	−209	−337	−460
(Other invisibles)	+426	+436	+547	+626
Current balance	+67	+133	−43	−121
Long-term capital[1] (net)	−160	−187	−133	−148
Basic balance	−93	−54	−176	−269
Balancing item	+69	+93	−9	+74
Monetary movement[1]	+24	−39	+185	+195
(Change in gold etc. reserve)[1]	+19	−79	+82	−55
GDP (factor cost) average annual growth rate between selected years[2]	1951-55	1955-60	1960-64	1964-67
	2.8%	2.3%	3.3%	2.1%

[1]   Assets: increase−/decrease +. Liabilities: increase +/decrease−.
[2]   Calculated from mean of output and expenditure estimates at constant (1963) prices.

Sources: *UK Balance of Payments 1969,* CSO; *ET,* March 1970; *NIBB.* Detail may not add to totals because of rounding.

---

[1]   The leads and lags effect could also apply to payments between the overseas sterling area and non-sterling countries. Since many sterling area countries failed to follow the UK devaluation in 1967 this source of leads and lags should end but could be replaced by new leads and lags between the UK and such sterling area countries.

three periods cover complete short cycles of activity ending in a boom year with abnormally heavy imports and a serious deficit on current account. For 1965-7 the cycle is incomplete though the period again ends with a serious deficit year.[1]

In assessing the figures it is useful to have in mind the targets for achievement which have been set from time to time by the government. In the early postwar years the government was naturally preoccupied with the urgent problem of eliminating current account deficits and Britain's dependence on foreign aid, but by 1953 it was possible to take a longer view. The 1953 *Economic Survey* revealed that 'Over a period of years it is estimated that the annual surplus on current account needed to provide for commitments, and for some increase in gold reserves, might amount to something like £300-350 million'.[2] In 1959 the sights had been raised further and according to the *Radcliffe Report*[3] the rough order of achievement for the early 1960s was to be an average current account surplus of £450 million, the increase being mainly in the form of a higher long-term capital outflow.

From table 3.3 it is evident that the average current account surplus for the first cyclical period 1952-5 was well below the 1953 target level. To some extent this can be explained by revisions of the basic data which have reduced the size of the average surplus by some £60 million. The revisions, however, also reduced the net long-term capital outflow by a similar amount and left the basic balance more or less unchanged. It is clear from the negative basic balance of £93 million that the UK was not achieving a current account surplus big enough to cover the actual net long-term capital outflow, let alone a higher target level. Allowing for the positive balancing item, there was, during this period, a small cumulative worsening of the monetary movements account including a reduction of £76 million in the level of reserves.

The second cyclical period shows a distinct improvement in performance. The current account improved by an annual average of £66 million, which is explained by a pronounced improvement in the visibles account associated with a favourable movement in the net barter terms of trade.[4] The invisibles account worsened as a result of the substantial increase in the deficit on government account, with other invisibles showing only a small increase. The net outflow on long-term capital account increased but by less than the change in the current account so that the basic balance was reduced slightly to a level of −£54 million, which was easily offset by the favourable balancing item. As a result the monetary movements account showed a cumulative improvement of £195 million over the period, with gold and convertible currency reserves increased by the substantial total of £395 million.

One might say that the balance of payments was in a state of long-term equilibrium during the period 1956-60, despite the failure of the current balance to match the 1953 target, since the actual long-term outflow was covered and it was possible to improve the reserve-liability position. But this satisfactory performance was achieved only at the cost of a lower rate of economic growth as compared with the previous cyclical period. The

---

[1]   The dating of the cyclical periods is arbitrary and it could be argued that the third cyclical period should be dated 1961-5. We have chosen to end it in 1964 since the figures for 1965-7 should reflect the impact of the government's major policy aim of improving the balance of payments position.

[2]   P.44.

[3]   P.232.

[4]   This is the ratio of export prices to import prices. A rise in this ratio is conventionally described as an 'improvement' or 'favourable' and a fall in the ratio as a 'deterioration'. These terms may be misleading if the change in relative prices reduces or increases the purchasing power of foreign exporters to the UK and thus causes offsetting movements in the volume of UK exports.

UK unemployment ratio was allowed to increase from 1.2 per cent in 1955 to 2.3 per cent in 1959, though it fell to 1.7 per cent for the boom year of 1960. Between 1955 and 1958 real GDP increased only at the rate of 0.9 per cent per annum and the volume of imports of goods at about the same rate, so that, allowing for falling import prices, the value of goods imports (f.o.b.) in 1958 was roughly the same as that for 1955. Resumption of more rapid growth between 1958 and 1960 brought with it an adverse swing in the current account of £609 million and showed how precariously based had been the surpluses of 1956 and 1957.

The third cyclical period 1961-4 saw a striking deterioration in the UK balance of payments. The current account worsened by an annual rate of £176 million. This occurred partly because of the continued increase in the size of the government deficit, which more than offset the improvement in 'other' invisibles, and partly because of a deterioration in the visibles account, which resulted from accelerated growth of imports caused by the higher average growth rate of GDP. There was some decline in the average net long-term capital outflow, arising mainly from increased investment in the UK by foreigners, but the average basic balance deteriorated by £122 million per annum compared with 1956-60. The period saw two severe foreign exchange crises in 1961 and 1964, each involving massive drawings from the IMF and each connected with a complex of deflationary measures, including a 7 per cent Bank Rate. The cumulative adverse balance in the monetary movements account amounted to £740 million, of which £328 million was a decline in the level of the reserve of gold and convertible currencies.

Throughout the fourth period, 1965-7, the improvement of the UK balance of payments was a major concern of UK government policy. The policy measures used will be discussed in section III of this chapter but it is clear from table 3.3 that in spite of a marked decline in the rate of growth of GDP, the actual performance of the balance of payments for 1965-7 was worse than that for 1961-4. It is true that the years 1965 and 1966 showed a progressive improvement on 1964 and that relapse in the current account for 1967 was partly explained by factors outside the UK government's control, e.g. the deceleration of world demand and the closure of the Suez Canal with its adverse effects on the cost of UK imports of oil and shipping services. From table 3.3 we see that the average balance on current account worsened during 1965-7 by some £78 million as compared with 1961-4, whilst the long-term capital account showed a larger deficit of £148 million. The average basic balance worsened by £93 million compared with 1961-4 or £10 million per annum if calculated net of the large average balancing item. The monetary movements account showed a cumulative adverse balance of £585 million for the three-year period.

Averages for 1968-9 are not presented in table 3.3 since the contrast between the two years is too great and the period was one of transition. Although devaluation may have corrected a disequilibrium exchange rate, the lags in the operation of devaluation meant that the 1968 outturn for the balance of payments showed little improvement on 1967 and a further £543 million was added to the cumulative adverse balance of monetary movements. By 1969 one might describe the fundamental disequilibrium as ended even though the new target of £500 million for the basic surplus was not yet achieved. The causes of the improvement in 1969 are discussed in section III of this chapter.

As reference to table A-7 will show there were also sizeable deficits on monetary movements account for 1959 and 1960. There are grounds for regarding 1958-9 as a genuine turning point in the history of the UK balance of payments and as marking the onset of a state of fundamental disequilibrium.

Throughout the 1950s the UK had been removing the battery of restrictions on free international trade and payments which had served during the wartime and early postwar periods to protect her balance of payments. The trade controls had the effect of reducing the UK propensity to import with particular emphasis on imports from the dollar area so as to conserve current earnings and reserves of dollars. The payments controls were designed to restrict the convertibility of sterling acquired and held by various groups of non-residents for the same reason. In 1958 the pound was made freely convertible into gold or dollars for all nonresidents in respect of current transactions and in 1958 and 1959 most of those remaining import controls, which operated as foreign exchange saving rather than as strategic or protective devices, were eliminated. It is true that substantial reductions in import controls had been made in 1953 and 1954 and that preparations for the move to convertibility had been made in 1955 when the Exchange Equalisation Account had been instructed to support the rate for Transferable Account sterling within 1 per cent of the official exchange rate.[1] The main impact of these earlier relaxations had been concealed by the deflationary policy of the period 1955 to 1958. After 1958 the UK was operating under a relatively free trade and payments system (apart from the normal tariff structure which had been reduced somewhat in GATT negotiations) and any expansion of effective demand was bound to inflate the import bill. In fact the joint effect of the relaxations plus the stockbuilding boom of 1959-60 was to expand UK imports by 23 per cent between 1958 and 1960, and imports of manufactures, on which remaining controls before 1958 had been most severe, increased by 56 per cent in the two-year period.

In retrospect it is difficult to understand the optimism of the 1959 target. It seems probable that it had become obsolete long before the change of government in 1964. Official views may have been reflected in the NEDC targets which aimed to convert the 1961 current deficit into a surplus by 1966 of £300 million (with a positive balancing item of £100 million), which was later revised down to £225 million with a balancing item of +£50 million. Whether we measure achievement against any of these targets, or merely against the identified long-term capital balance, it seems impossible to evade the conclusion that between 1959 and 1964 the UK balance of payments was in a state of fundamental disequilibrium. The persistence of deficit between 1965 and 1968, in spite of corrective policy measures, supports the conclusion.

An implication of the persistent weakness of the basic balance in the period 1959-68 is that the monetary movements account for the period shows an adverse balance of £2,161 million, an amount roughly equal to twice the official reserves of gold and foreign exchange at the end of 1958. Even then the level of UK reserves was far too low for a major importing nation which was also a trading and reserve currency country. If we take the ratio of end-year reserves to imports for the same year the UK ratio for 1958 stood at 29 per cent. This compared with 154 per cent for the US and 48 per cent

---

[1] Transferable (Account) sterling was one of the four types of sterling after the consolidation of the exchange control system in 1954. Other types were: (1) balances held by residents of the sterling area which could be used freely within the area but not outside it; (2) American Account sterling which could be used anywhere and was fully convertible into dollars at the official exchange rate; (3) Security sterling which accrued to non-residents of the sterling area from the sale of assets in the UK and, in principle, could be used only for reinvestment in sterling assets. Transferable sterling could be used to make payments to any Transferable Account country or to the sterling area but in practice could be converted into dollars in unofficial free markets at a discount. Such conversions involved a loss of dollars to the UK since residents in the dollar area could make payments to the sterling area by acquiring Transferable sterling, at a discount, and the dollars accrued to the Transferable account countries instead of to the UK. In 1958 the Transferable and American accounts were consolidated. Security sterling remained for some years and was usually sold at a discount because of limitations on its use. In April 1967 it was abolished and non-residents were free to repatriate the proceeds from the sale of sterling securities at the official rate. It was hoped that this concession might encourage overseas investment in sterling securities.

for the average of the other main industrial nations.[1] By 1963 the corresponding ratios were 23 per cent for the UK, 91 per cent for the US and 47 per cent for the other main industrial nations.

The relatively poor reserve-import ratio of the UK and its deterioration over the five-year period is clearly indicated by these figures. In fact the UK ratio was inferior not only to the average of the industrial nations, but also to that of the less developed nations. It may be argued that relative figures prove little about the absolute adequacy of the reserves of the UK and that the rest of the world could profitably have learned from the UK how to economise on international reserves. This argument makes little sense in the light of the numerous foreign exchange crises which the UK has experienced in the post-war period. Even if we allow for the full exercise of drawing rights on the IMF (which, technically, are not available to deal with short-term capital outflows) the UK reserves have been too small to cover both the absorption of temporary deficits on the basic balance and the related speculative flight from sterling. The weakness of the UK reserve position is illustrated by events in the last quarter of 1964. At the end of September the resources immediately available to the UK consisted of first-line reserves of £907 million plus an IMF standby credit of $1,000 million and a further $1,000 million of short-term facilities with US and European central banks. In addition the UK could have mobilised, at relatively short notice, the dollar securities held by the Treasury and worth some £500 million, plus (on 1961 precedent) a further drawing on the IMF of some $1,400 million. In spite of the fact that the major part of the 1964 basic deficit had already been financed by the end of September these resources proved insufficient to maintain confidence in the external value of sterling. The UK was saved from a crisis devaluation only as a result of the potential support of the massive short-term loan of $3,000 million mounted in November by eleven central banks and the Bank for International Settlements.

Since May 1965 when the UK made a further drawing on the IMF of $1,400 the UK has been operating substantially on borrowed first-line reserves. In February 1966 and again in November 1967 the first-line reserves were raised by the transfer of the Treasury's dollar portfolio, the total transfer being valued at $1,375 million. This transfer should be taken into account when comparisons of reserves are made with periods before 1966. Periodic attacks on sterling have been met with the assistance of increased swap arrangements and other short-term assistance from central banks, the details of which are unimportant. By the end of December 1969 the total first-line reserves stood at £1,053 million (at the new rate of exchange) or some 13 per cent of imports (c.i.f.) for 1969. Of this total some £520 million was the result of the dollar portfolio transfer and the rest was more than accounted for by short- or medium-term borrowing from the IMF and other sources due for repayment at various dates at the new rate of exchange.

In section III of this chapter we shall discuss the policy implications of the fundamental disequilibrium in the UK balance of payments. In the next section we examine some trends in the constituent items of the current account and discuss the main causes of the decline in UK performance which led to a state of disequilibrium.

---

[1]   Reserve ratios quoted here are calculated from data given in IFS. The other main industrial nations are the EEC countries and Switzerland, Austria, Denmark, Norway, Sweden, Canada and Japan. Reserves include gold, foreign exchange, and the 'reserve position in the IMF', the last item being the amount which can be drawn more or less automatically from the IMF.

II   RECENT TRENDS IN UK FOREIGN TRADE

II.1   Merchandise Exports

We are primarily concerned in this section with trends in exports of manufactures which dominate our export trade.[1] This can be seen in table 3.4 where the percentage of exports (excluding re-exports) classified as manufactures has risen from 81 per cent in 1955 to 87 per cent in 1969. For the period 1935-8 the share was about 75 per cent. The growing importance of manufactures is partly accounted for by the steady elimination of exports of coal and coke which accounted for 8 per cent of total exports for the period 1935-8, but only about 2 per cent in 1955 and less than 0.5 per cent in 1969. To some extent coal exports have been replaced by exports (but not net exports) of petroleum products which increased from 1 per cent (1935-8) to 2.1 per cent in 1969. Since 1955 exports of all non-manufactured goods have grown at about one-half the average annual rate of exports of manufactures. Re-exports, which for 1935-8 amounted to 13.5 per cent of exports of home-produced goods, have declined greatly in significance in the postwar period. By 1955 they were only 3.9 per cent of home exports and 3.7 per cent in 1969.[2] Although the 1967 devaluation was followed by substantial increases in trade, both in volume and value, the broad area and commodity structure was little affected at the level of aggregation considered in this chapter, and differences between 1967 and 1969 are broadly in line with previous trends. Consequently tables 3.4 and 3.6 give data for 1969 rather than 1967 even though the main argument of this section is concerned with the causes of trends to 1967. As is explained in section III of this chapter devaluation may temporarily reverse the effects of adverse trends in trade flows but it does not, of itself, do anything to eliminate the underlying causes of any adverse trends.

TABLE 3.4

Commodity Structure of UK Merchandise Trade 1955 and 1969

SITC group	Description	Imports (c.i.f.) 1955 %	1969 %	Exports (f.o.b.) 1955(a) %	1969(a) %	1969(b) %
0, 1	Food, beverages, tobacco	36.2	23.2	5.8	5.9	6.2
2, 4	Basic materials	28.5	15.1	3.9	2.8	3.4
3	Mineral fuels, etc.	10.4	10.9	4.7	2.4	2.4
5, 6	Semi-manufactures	19.4	27.7	38.6	35.6	34.9
7, 8	Finished manufactures	5.2	22.0	42.3	51.0	50.3
9	Unclassified	0.3	1.1	4.7	2.3	2.8
	Total %	100	100	100	100	100
	Value £ million	3,936	8,323	2,957	7,039	7,338

Sources: AAS and *ROT.* (a) excluding re-exports, (b) including re-exports. 1969 (b) figures include some revisions.

---

[1]   The classification of manufactures is conventional and includes the SITC groups 5-8 viz. (5) Chemicals, (6) Classified by material, (7) Machinery and Transport Equipment, (8) Miscellaneous manufactures.

[2]   From March 1970 ROT has ceased to record re-exports separately and these are now merged with exports of home goods. The change came too late to permit all figures and calculations to be adjusted to the new basis, but separate figures for 1969 are given in tables 3.4 and 3.6. Because of late revisions to the 1969 data the difference between the 1969 export totals does not indicate the true value of re-exports.

The UK Share of Exports of Manufactures: In 1955 the UK share of exports of manufactures from the twelve main exporting nations[1] was 19.8 per cent. By 1967 it had fallen
to 11.9 per cent and by 1969, despite devaluation, to 11 per cent. This persistent decline
in the UK share of 'world' exports, so often quoted, was resumed after 1950. Between
1937-8 and 1950 the UK share of 'world' exports of manufactures actually increased against
the secular trend—from 21.3 per cent to 25.4 per cent according to one estimate—but
changes in the statistical basis make exact comparisons difficult. Britain's relative success
between 1945 and 1950 owed much to the successful export drive of the Labour government but this was helped by the postwar sellers' market, which resulted from the general
shortage of capacity relative to demand and the impaired productive and exporting abili-
ties of Germany and Japan, whose shares had fallen to less than half their prewar values.

Between 1950 and 1955 Germany made a rapid recovery in 'world' exports and
roughly doubled her share, largely at the expense of the UK. By 1967 she accounted for
19.7 per cent of the 'world' total as compared with 15.5 per cent in 1955. During the
same period the Japanese share increased from 5.1 per cent to 9.8 per cent. These gains
were achieved mainly at the expense of the UK and, after 1957, also the US.

Explanations of the Declining Share: Of itself the declining UK share of 'world' trade, or
its obverse, the relatively slower growth of UK trade by value and volume, is of no great
importance. There is no reason, in a world of nations with different rates of population
growth and economic growth per capita, why any one country should invariably match
the world growth rate. But taken in conjunction with the definite deterioration in the
UK performance on current account to 1967 the trend was significant, and explanatory
factors must be sought so that appropriate conclusions may be drawn regarding policy
measures to improve UK performance. It seems that there is no single explanation of the
poor performance of the UK. Various factors have operated jointly to produce the relative decline in share and these can be considered under three main headings.

Structural Factors: It has been suggested that the growth of UK exports has been retarded because of undue concentration on commodities or markets with a relatively
slow rate of growth of demand. The importance of this sort of factor depends on the
time-period chosen for analysis; before 1955 they may have been quite important but
since then their joint importance has been minimal. In 1957 the *Board of Trade Journal*[2]
showed that between 1951 and 1955 about one-quarter of Britain's loss of share of
exports of manufactures might be explained by the joint area-commodity structure. This
meant that if Britain had retained in 1955 the same relative share in exports of each commodity group to each market as in 1951, the differential growth rates of the various com-
modity-markets would nevertheless have reduced her share by one-quarter of the observed
reduction, leaving the remainder to be explained by other factors. In 1965, the *Board of
Trade Journal*[3] repeated the analysis, on a slightly different basis, for the period 1954-64.
The conclusion reached was that of the total loss of share of 6.46 percentage points between the two years only 0.36 points (5.5 per cent) could be explained by the joint area-
commodity pattern. Using the 1957 method of analysis the conclusion reached was that
no part of the loss of share could be explained by the area-commodity pattern.

---

[1]   These are the US, UK, EEC countries, Sweden, Switzerland, Canada and Japan. In 1967 they
     accounted for 86 per cent of world exports of manufactures (excluding Russia, China and Eastern
     Europe).

[2]   'Trends in Exports of United Kingdom Compared with other Countries', *BTJ*, 30 March 1957.

[3]   'Trends in UK and World Exports of Manufactures', *BTJ*, 3 December 1965.

Table 3.5 shows the distribution of UK and 'world' exports, for 1958 and 1968 by main markets and commodity groups, together with trend growth rates over the period. Over the decade the UK has become much less dependent on markets in primary producing countries whose total imports have grown only about half as fast as imports into industrial countries. Exports from the UK to Canada and the non-OECD sterling area are notable for their low growth, both absolutely and relative to 'world' exports. The UK has done well relative to others in exports to Japan and the Sino-Soviet bloc but absolute levels of exports are small. In terms of combined size of market and growth rate it is clear that the US and industrial Europe have been the most important destinations for UK exports. Similar conclusions would be drawn if the trends were taken from 1954 rather than 1958.

In the commodity analysis the table shows that by 1968 the structure of UK exports differed only slightly from that of the main exporters, which was also the case for several years before 1968. As compared with 1958, and earlier years, the UK has reduced her dependence on the slow-growing textiles group[1] and has succeeded in maintaining a relatively high share of the rapidly growing machinery group. The share of chemicals in UK exports has also increased and this is another group with an above-average growth rate in world trade.

Competitive Factors: If the UK relative decline in export performance cannot be explained by an adverse commodity-market structure we must seek explanations elsewhere, and a number of possible quantifiable and non-quantifiable explanations have been proposed. These cover prices, designs, delivery dates, after-sales service, salesmanship, etc.

It is clear that UK prices have risen faster, during the 1950s and 1960s than those of our chief competitors.[2] Over the 1954-67 period UK prices rose at 2.1 per cent per annum, compared with 1.3 per cent for the main manufacturing countries including the UK, implying that UK prices were rising about 1.0 per cent per annum faster than those of our competitors. This may seem a trivial difference, but cumulated over thirteen years, and assuming a price-elasticity of demand[3] for exports in the range of -2 to -2.5, it could explain some 40 per cent to 50 per cent of the UK loss of share between 1954 and 1967.

The exact quantitative significance of relative price movements for export volumes or values should be measured by econometric techniques, but technical problems make it difficult to get clear and unambiguous answers. Relative price changes often occur in conjunction with other changes which operate in the same direction on the level of exports, short-period and long-period reactions to changes in price and other variables may be different, and there are conceptual problems involved in the application of price theory to large aggregates like the volume of exports. A number of the earlier econometric studies suggested that relative price changes might be comparatively unimportant in causing changes in the level of exports. In recent years there has been a tendency to dispute the significance of these earlier results and to play down the so-called 'elasticity pessimism' which they generated. Experience of the effects of tariff changes and devaluations have made it clear that relative prices do matter for export performance in the field of manu-

---

[1] In 1954 the share of textiles in UK exports was 15.1 per cent.

[2] Indices of prices of exports of manufactures may be found in the statistical tables of *NIER*.

[3] This is an elasticity of UK export volume with respect to the ratio of UK prices to those of the rest of the world. The derivation of the result is too complex to present here; it assumes that the volume of UK exports is a constant proportion of the volume of exports from the rest of the world multiplied by the relative price to the power of $-e$ where $-e$ is the relevant elasticity.

factures and one recent econometric study[1] has indicated that longer-run price elasticities of demand may be as high as −3 to −5, though it must be admitted that these values
seem unduly optimistic in the light of responses to the UK devaluation of 1967. The NEDC
Report *Export Trends*[2] concluded that changes in UK relative costs and prices had been

TABLE 3.5

**Exports of Manufactures from UK and Main Manufacturing Countries ('World') by Market and
Commodity, 1958-68[1]**

	Pattern of exports 1958		Pattern of exports 1968		Growth rates 1958-68 (US $ Values)	
	UK %	'World' %	UK %	'World' %	UK %	'World' %
EXPORTS TO:						
OECD Europe	26.3	35.1	38.2	44.4	9.3	13.0
EFTA excluding UK	9.7	11.1	13.3	10.5	8.7	9.8
UK	–	3.7	–	4.4	–	12.4
EEC	13.1	18.1	19.1	26.8	9.3	14.9
United States	9.0	10.1	13.5	15.2	9.6	15.1
Canada	6.1	7.9	4.3	7.2	1.7	9.5
Japan	0.5	1.3	1.6	1.9	17.9	15.0
Industrial countries totals	41.8	54.4	57.6	68.6	8.7	13.1
Latin America	5.1	13.5	3.8	6.6	2.2	2.9
Non-OECD sterling area[3]	42.3	15.1	25.1	10.3	−0.1	6.3
Sino-Soviet bloc	2.1	2.9	4.4	3.5	13.2	12.6
Other primary producers	8.7	14.1	9.1	11.0	5.7	7.9
Primary producers totals	58.2	45.6	42.4	31.4	2.0	6.5
Totals	100	100	100	100	5.2	10.5
EXPORTS OF:						
Chemicals (5)	9.7	11.5	11.4	12.2	6.8	10.9
Textiles (65)	9.2	8.5	5.7	6.1	0.5	5.9
Metals and metal manufactures (67, 68, 69 excluding 681)	15.1	18.1	12.2	14.7	2.9	8.0
Machinery, non-electric (71)	20.1	19.3	24.0	20.2	6.8	11.2
Electric machinery, etc. (72)	8.4	7.3	7.8	8.9	4.8	13.1
Transport equipment (73)	21.5	16.3	17.2	18.0	3.3	11.4
Other manufactures (8 and rest of 6)	16.0	19.0	21.8	19.9	8.5	10.8
Total Manufactures (5-8)	100	100	100	100	5.3	10.4

Source: *BTJ*, 17 September 1969, p. 728, tables 2, 3, 4. Figures in brackets in commodity analysis
refer to the SITC Groups.

The growth rates in the lower part of the table are as computed by the Board of Trade and are
derived by fitting straight lines to the logarithms. Similar growth rates are not available for the upper
part of the table because of discontinuities in the data. The growth rates given here are computed
from terminal values and should be used only as a general indication of the trend.

[1] Main manufacturing countries are listed in footnote 1 of p. 117
[2] OECD Europe plus US, Canada and Japan
[3] Sterling area excluding UK, Iceland and Ireland. From 1966 Rhodesia is excluded from the
sterling area and included in 'Other primary producers'.

---

[1] H. B. Juntz and R. R. Rhomberg, 'Prices and Export Performance of Industrial Countries
1953-63', *Staff Papers,* IMF, July 1965.

[2] P. 16.

an important factor but not the *only* important factor responsible for our loss of share. It would seem prudent to make the elimination of further increases in relative costs and prices an urgent task of economic policy. Emphasis on costs may well be important since the process of competition may force exporters to limit their relative price increases at the expense of profit margins, with consequent adverse effects on investment, productivity and export promotion.

Export performance is not simply a matter of relative costs and prices. At a general level, behaviour in this field may be usefully interpreted in terms of the theory of monopolistic competition which stresses the importance of non-price factors where products are not homogenous. One might, therefore, expect to find the volume of exports of manufactures to be sensitive to factors like quality and design of products, the time period between orders and deliveries, including the degree to which promised delivery dates are fulfilled in practice, the size and effectiveness of after-sales services, the degree to which manufacturers are prepared to cater for local market conditions, and the effectiveness and scale of their market research, advertising and sales promotion activities. Complaints that UK exporters have been negligent under all these headings have been numerous and seem endemic in the history of UK export performance. Historical studies have revealed the same sort of complaints in the nineteenth century as those which have appeared regularly in the 1950s and 1960s.[1]

Unfortunately, it is not easy to quantify these various factors and test their influence by econometric methods, but expert studies have usually agreed that they carry considerable weight. In periods where the UK has lost market shares to important competitors in certain commodity groups, in the absence of significant price differentials, these factors must have been of overriding importance.[2]

Successful export performance depends upon supply conditions as well as demand, and it has been suggested that export opportunities have been lost by the UK because of inflationary pressures which diverted exportable goods to the prosperous home market. Acceptance of this view would lead to the policy conclusion that our export performance would improve if the economy were operated at lower levels of domestic demand and higher levels of unemployment. It is argued that this would also tend to reduce the rate of inflation and improve export demand via the cost-price factor. Opponents of this view have stressed the complementarity of export and home supplies and argue that reducing the level of demand will inhibit investment and productivity and thus the supply and quality of exportable goods. This is a complex problem which involves unsolved issues of economic theory and policy.

The problem has been discussed in chapter 1 and it is unnecessary to repeat the analysis here. The crude factual evidence seems to support the view that, in the short run, export performance is worsened by a high pressure of demand. It is true that the annual rate of increase of exports is highest during the domestic booms, when UK manufacturing production has grown most rapidly. But this is explainable by the fact that the volume of world exports has grown most rapidly during the same boom periods. What is significant is that the rate of decline in the UK share of world exports has been most rapid during the domestic booms.

Other Factors: Some part of our loss of share of trade has been caused by alterations in competitive advantage outside the control of UK exporters. The reduction of trade discrimination in our favour during the 1950s is an example which may have had serious con-

[1]   R. Hoffmann, *Great Britain and the German Trade Rivalry, 1875-1914*, University of Pennsylvania Press, 1933, pp. 21, 80.

[2]   See S. J. Wells, *British Export Performance*, Cambridge University Press, 1964, p. 61.

sequences for our exports to the sterling area. The major impact appears to have occurred as a result of the ending of severe import quotas against the US and Japan, which enabled these countries to capture substantial shares of these markets from the UK. This effect may have been reinforced by a small reduction in tariff preference margins enjoyed by the UK in the Commonwealth trading area.

Finally, there is the factor of export finance, the supply of which can be an important influence on the achieved level of exports, where a large and growing proportion of the trade consists of capital goods. In such conditions the exporter may find that the precondition for effecting a sale is the provision of a medium or long-term loan to the potential importer. Since the exporter himself will not normally be able to finance more than a fraction of such required loans, he must resort to a financial intermediary and this will only be possible if he can insure the transaction against any commercial, political or exchange risk. The *Radcliffe Report* referred to evidence of exports being lost to UK firms because the Export Credits Guarantee Department, the government department which provides virtually the whole of export insurance in the UK, was not prepared to offer insurance for a long enough period of time, the effective limit being some six to nine years from the date of contract regardless of the life of the capital asset exported. In 1960 it was announced that this limit would be abandoned where the longer-term credit was necessary to match that offered by competitors. Further improvements in the provision of insurance and credit were announced in 1961, 1962 and 1965-7, which broaden the coverage, reduce the cost and simplify procedure. Inadequate finance should no longer be a factor hindering the growth of UK exports. However, as the *Radcliffe Report* emphasised, such improvements represent in part an extension of international investment which may raise exports but not immediate receipts of foreign exchange. It is unlikely that recent improvements have had any substantial quantitative effect on the balance of payments position and they contrast oddly with the policy measures to reduce the outflow of capital abroad.

II.2   Merchandise Imports

In many discussions of the recent balance of payments crisis, attention was focused on the role of excessive imports, especially those of manufactures. Between 1963 and 1964 the value of total imports rose by some 15 per cent and manufactures rose by 27 per cent. Similar high increases were recorded in the periods 1958-60 and 1954-5. But these dramatic increases are inflated by stockbuilding in the booms[1] and exaggerate the trend growth rates of both classes of imports.

In the early postwar period the volume of imports was held down by various controls in order to limit the balance of payments problem. Taking the 1938 volume as 100 the volume of total imports was still only 95 in 1951[2] and did not exceed the 1938 level until the year 1955, when the index stood at 105 whilst industrial production had increased to some 156 per cent of the 1938 level. By 1951 the volume of exports had increased to 173 per cent of the 1938 level. Despite these disparate trends in merchandise trade volumes, the visible deficit in 1951 was £689 million compared with £302 million for 1938. The large relative increase in export volume was offset by a substantial deterioration in the net barter terms of trade which by 1951 had worsened by 28 per cent from the 1938 value. Import average values in 1951 were some 4.4 times their 1938 level compared with some 3.2 times for exports and a doubling of all prices entering into GDP. The net result was a ratio of imports (f.o.b.) to GDP in current values of 27 per cent for 1951, the highest

---

[1] Cf. chapter 1.

[2] Most of the index numbers used in this paragraph were taken from the series published in *The British Economy: Key Statistics 1900-1966*, London and Cambridge Economic Service.

level in the postwar period. Since 1951 the ratio has fallen, with minor cyclical fluctuations, to 16.5 per cent for 1967 as import prices fell absolutely on trend until 1962 and
relatively to prices of final output until 1967. The rise in import prices in sterling, following devaluation, and the continued growth of volume raised the ratio to 19 per cent by
1969. In 1938 the ratio of imports to GDP was 17 per cent.

Between 1952 and 1967 imports grew faster, in real terms, than either exports or GDP.
Taking average annual growth rates between the periods 1952-5 and 1965-7 as indicators
of trend the respective rates were 4.5 per cent for imports, 3.2 per cent for exports and
2.8 per cent for GDP. For the balance of payments outcome it is growth rates in current
values that matter and on this basis the trade differentials were less, with imports (f.o.b.)
growing at 4.3 per cent, and exports at 4.7 per cent, whilst GDP grew at 6.3 per cent. Over the
full period the growth of imports by value cannot be regarded as having been excessive
since the slightly greater growth rate of exports was sufficient at least to hold the average
visible deficit for 1965-7 at about the same level as that for 1952-5, though obviously a
smaller growth rate of imports would have been better. However, if trends are taken for
the period 1956-60 to 1965-7 the growth rate of imports, excluding US military aircraft,
by value was 4.9 per cent compared with 4.7 per cent for exports and, over this period,
the deterioration of the visibles account contributed significantly to the worsening of
the current account balance. The accelerating growth of imports between 1952 and 1967
was accounted for by the high and accelerating growth of imports of manufactures. Imports of non-manufactures grew at 2 per cent per annum, whether we take dates from
1952-5 or 1956-60 to 1965-7, but imports of manufactures increased their growth rate
from 9.6 per cent, between 1952 and 1967, to 10.6 per cent between 1956 and 1967. It
seems a reasonable inference that, insofar as UK imports were excessive before 1967, in
level and growth, it was the manufactured component which was to blame and which was
the appropriate target for policy measures.

The rapid growth of imported manufactures has resulted in substantial changes in the
commodity and area structure of UK imports since the early 1950s. Tables 3.4 and 3.6

TABLE 3.6

Area Structure of UK Merchandise Trade 1955 and 1969

	Imports	(c.i.f.)	Exports	(f.o.b.)	
	1955 %	1969 %	1955(a) %	1969(a) %	1969(b) %
Sterling Area	39.4	28.9	47.0	28.2	27.8
North America	19.5	19.7	11.8	16.6	16.6
US	(10.7)	(13.6)	(7.0)	(12.4)	(12.4)
Latin America	6.1	4.3	3.8	3.5	3.4
Western Europe	25.7	36.4	28.1	38.5	39.1
EEC	(12.6)	(19.4)	(14.0)	(20.0)	(20.8)
EFTA	(11.4)	(15.0)	(11.7)	(14.8)	(14.7)
Soviet Union and Eastern Europe	2.7	4.0	1.2	3.2	3.2
Rest of world	6.6	6.7	8.1	10.0	9.9
Total %	100.0	100.0	100.0	100.0	100.0
Value £ million	3,936	8,323	2,957	7,039	7,338

Sources: ROT, BTJ, 18 November 1966. Some figures for 1955 supplied by Board of Trade.
    Rhodesia is included in Sterling Area for 1955 and in rest of world for 1969. In 1965
    Rhodesia accounted for 0.5 per cent of UK imports and 0.7 per cent of UK exports.
    (a) excluding re-exports, (b) including re-exports. 1969(b) figures include some revisions.

show the percentage analysis for 1955 and 1969. The share of manufactures increased by a factor of 2 over the period whilst that of finished manufactures increased to 4.2 times the 1955 level. Compensating falls occurred in food, etc. and basic materials. Changes in statistical classification rule out exact comparisons with prewar levels but compared with the 1935-8 average the shares of manufactures and fuels have increased by a factor of 2.3, with compensating falls in other categories. Present proportions therefore represent a genuine structural change and not recovery from an abnormal postwar position. From table 3.6 we see that industrial regions have increased their share of UK imports as the share of manufactures in total imports has increased. Almost one-half of UK imports in 1969 came from EEC, EFTA and the US and some 68 per cent of these imports were manufactures. As primary products have declined in share, so the sterling area has declined in importance as a source of imports. On the export side the change in the area structure has been broadly similar, with increases in the shares of EEC and EFTA and a decline in the sterling area share. The share of exports to the US has increased substantially since 1955.

Causes of the Rising Share of Manufactures: The UK is not alone in taking a rising share of imports in the form of manufactured goods. In recent years this has been a trend in the main industrial and trading nations. In 1965 the NEDC Report *Imported Manufactures* gave figures for nine countries (EEC, US, Canada, Sweden and UK) showing, for the period 1957 to 1963, substantial increases in the share of manufactures, excluding non-ferrous metals, in total imports in each case. For 1963 the UK share was 28 per cent compared with an unweighted average of 51 per cent for the other countries. The rising trend continued after 1963 in every country, except Italy, and by 1967 the UK ratio was 38 per cent compared with an average for the rest of 56 per cent. These increasing shares are natural given the recent trend of increasing inter-trade between industrial nations, which is associated with the progressive removal of barriers to trade in manufactured goods and the development of regional free trade areas like the EEC and EFTA. Unlike the UK most of the countries have been able to increase their imports of manufactures without incurring any persistent balance of payments problem. In the case of the UK the rapid growth of imported manufactures and the loss of share of exports suggest that an overall lack of competitiveness in manufacturing production is reinforcing the effects of greater international specialisation and exchange. One might therefore expect to find the reasons for higher imports of manufactures similar to the reasons put forward to explain our loss of share of exports and this is indeed the case.

According to the NEDC Report 'there is no single dominant reason to account for rising imports that applies over the whole range of manufactures'. *Prices* and *costs* were found[1] to be a major factor in a wide range of semi-manufactures and finished consumer goods, the foreign prices being lower for a variety of reasons including economies of scale, lower labour costs, reductions in tariffs for EFTA countries, and price-cutting resulting from excess capacity abroad in the case of steel products. Relative prices were not considered important in the field of machinery where the main factor appeared to be superior *technical performance* and *design* or the absence of any effective British substitute. British deficiencies in *market research* and *marketing* generally were found to be important in the case of machinery and some consumer goods. *Shortage of capacity* has been a factor encouraging imports in the boom periods and it was suggested that there may be a 'ratchet effect' here

---

[1]   It should be noted that the findings of the Report were based not on econometric techniques but on evidence collected from various Economic Development Committees. Much of the evidence appears to reflect the views of trade and industrial users of imported commodities and should not be regarded as final.

which tends to raise the trend growth rate;[1] foreign suppliers capture markets in the boom and are not completely displaced subsequently when pressure is reduced in the UK home market. A final factor is the tendency for international companies to rationalise production of different products in different countries, which obviously leads to a greater degree of interchange, and should be compensated on the export side as long as the UK continues to attract a normal share of foreign enterprise. There seems to be some tendency for such companies to be less parochial than UK firms when it comes to the purchase of capital equipment; the so-called 'invisible tariff' of national preference does not apply.

II.3   Invisible Trade

The importance of invisible trade for the balance of payments of the UK is illustrated by tables 3.1 and 3.3. In 1938 invisible receipts accounted for 44 per cent of total export receipts and invisible payments were 18 per cent of total payments. By 1969 the proportions had altered to 36 per cent for receipts and 30 per cent for payments. Whilst the interconnection, through income-expenditure flows, between visibles and invisibles must not be forgotten, Table 3.3 shows that *proximately* the existence of a surplus on current account between 1952 and 1960 was dependent on a net surplus on invisible account and that the average deficit from 1961 onwards would have been much worse without the surplus on net invisibles. Despite the importance of invisible trade, this section of the UK foreign accounts has been comparatively neglected in professional studies of the UK balance of payments. It is well known that estimates of invisible receipts and payments are less accurately known than the corresponding figures for visible trade, and they exist exclusively in terms of current values, volume or average value series for the aggregate components being either non-existent or unpublished.[2] Until recently no attempt had been made to organise and analyse statistics of world trade in invisibles in the way that this had been done for visible trade. As a result of two pioneering studies[3] the veil of ignorance has been partially removed, but further basic research is needed if our understanding is to progress beyond the descriptive level.

From table 3.3 we have seen that the average annual surplus on invisibles declined from £327 million for 1952-5 to £170 million for 1961-4 and £166 million for 1965-7, and that this adverse trend reflected a rapid increase in the average deficit on the government sector of this account. Excluding the government sector, all other invisibles, net, showed an average surplus of £426 million for 1952-5 and £436 million for 1956-60 and this increased to £547 million for the period 1961-4, £626 million for 1965-7 and £889 million for 1968-9. Table 3.7 shows annual averages for debits, credits and the net balance by main subdivisions for each of the cyclical periods since 1951, as previously defined, together with the post-devaluation period 1968-9.

---

[1]   See F. Brechling and J. N. Wolfe, 'The End of Stop-Go', *LBR*, January 1965.

[2]   *NIBB* does give constant price estimates and 'price' (strictly average value) indexes for the aggregate of exports and imports of goods and services, but it is not easy to separate the sectors.

[3]   E. Devons, 'World Trade in Invisibles,' *LBR*, April 1961, and British National Export Council, *Britain's Invisible Earnings: The Report of the Committee on Invisible Exports*, BNEC, 1967.

TABLE 3.7

UK Trade in Invisibles, Annual Averages for Selected Periods (£ million)

		1952-5	1956-60	1961-4	1965-7	1968-9
Debits	Government	233	278	419	502	505
	Shipping	481	635	687	741	897
	Civil aviation	39	60	100	152	224
	Travel	99	156	228	287	300
	Other services	182	220	267	344	456
	Interests, profits, etc.	287	380	445	578	808
	Private transfers	69	104	124	182	230
	Total debits (−)	1,390	1,832	2,270	2,786	3,420
Credits	Government	134	69	42	41	45
	Shipping	538	632	658	745	942
	Civil aviation	39	68	125	180	260
	Travel	93	139	184	216	319
	Other services	327	422	526	661	930
	Interest, profits, etc.	513	632	788	974	1,205
	Private transfers	73	98	116	135	148
	Total credits (+)	1,717	2,059	2,440	2,952	3,849
Net	Government	−99	−209	−377	−460	−460
	Shipping	+57	−3	−29	+4	+45
	Civil aviation	0	+8	+25	+28	+36
	Travel	−6	−17	−44	−71	+19
	Other services	+145	+202	+259	+317	+474
	Interest, profits, etc.	+226	+252	+344	+396	+397
	Private transfers	+4	−6	−8	−48	−82
	Total invisibles *net*	+327	+227	+170	+166	+429
	Total less Government	+426	+436	+547	+626	+889

Source: *UK Balance of Payments. ET,* March 1970. Detail may not add to totals because
            of rounding

Table 3.7 shows that the average net deficit on government account just about doubled in successive periods to 1961-4, after which the rate of increase was checked. Between 1952-5 and 1956-60 the deterioration in the net balance owed more to a decline in defence aid (credits) from the US than to increases in government expenditure. Subsequently the main cause of the increased deficit was rising expenditure. For the period 1961-4 some 59 per cent of the average debit was accounted for by military expenditures, about 9 per cent by administrative and diplomatic expenditures and the remaining 32 per cent by transfers of economic aid, subscriptions to international organisations, and a small amount of military aid. These proportions altered for 1965-7 to 54 per cent, 10 per cent and 36 per cent respectively and to 55 per cent, 10 per cent and 35 per cent for 1968-9. For the period 1965-8 about 60 per cent of all net government expenditure was incurred in the overseas sterling area, but the proportion has fallen somewhat in recent years, the trend being reinforced by the devaluation.

The overall surplus on invisible trade owes its existence to two major sectors which generate very substantial flows of net credits. Before 1968 the biggest contributor was *interest, profits and dividends,* which was the net difference between considerable flows in each direction. On the credit side the major part of the income flow represents the return on private UK investment abroad which accumulated to some £4,600 million over the period 1952-67. Receipts from this item grew at 5.3 per cent per annum, on average, between 1952 and 1967. The growth of debit payments was more rapid at 5.8 per cent over the same period. The accelerating growth of debit payments is explained by several factors: the general increase in interest rates, the rapid increase in private investment in the UK after 1959, and, more recently, interest payments on official debts incurred as a consequence of the cumulative deficit on the overall balance of payments. Since 1960 the growth of debits has exceeded that of credits by a substantial margin. In principle, devaluation should have improved the net credit on this item, since receipts in foreign currencies would have a higher sterling value but this effect was obscured by other increases in the debit side. Continuance of government policy aimed at reducing the net outflow of long-term capital threatens to reduce the importance of this item in the invisibles account.

The other main contributor to the net surplus is the item *other services* which covers receipts and payments for education, films, royalties, commissions and banking services (excluding interest payments). Between 1952-5 and 1965-7 the average growth rate of credit items at 5.8 per cent exceeded that of debits at 5.2 per cent but more recently, between 1961-4 and 1965-7, the growth of debits was exceeding that of credits at rates of 7.5 per cent and 6.8 per cent respectively. Fortunately, this adverse trend was checked after 1967 and the net credit for 1968-9 averaged £474 million, more than enough to offset the heavy deficit on government overseas expenditure.

Payments for *civil aviation* show a rapid growth rate on each side of the account with a small but rising net surplus in recent years. The net balance on *shipping services* is the difference between very large payments each way, each of which is influenced by complex forces. The recent trend from net deficit to net surplus is useful and may have been partly the consequence of devaluation but it would be unwise to assume that it will continue. The UK has to contend with unfair competition in shipping from nations determined to maintain their own shipping industry, by discriminatory practices or subsidies, for military reasons or national prestige. Similar considerations limit the operation of comparative advantage in civil aviation and make prediction of trends difficult for both industries.

The two remaining sectors in the invisible account are *travel* and *private transfers*, both with rising adverse balances. The small exceptional net surplus for travel in 1968-9 would probably have disappeared in the absence of the exchange control restrictions on foreign travel for UK citizens, and the virtual abolition of this restraint in 1969 will probably result in a growth of debit payments in future years. However, it is thought that devaluation may have had a favourable effect on receipts from foreign tourists. *Private transfers* have shown a negligible net balance until 1964 but in the last few years this item has moved into a sizeable net deficit. A major factor seems to have been the growing volume of funds transferred by UK emigrants.

Excluding the government sector, trend growth rates in total UK invisible trade were similar to those of merchandise trade between 1956 and 1967. Between 1956-60 and 1965-7 private invisible credits grew at an average annual rate of 4.8 per cent compared with 4.9 per cent for private debits. The corresponding rates for visible exports and imports (excluding military aircraft) were 4.7 per cent and 4.9 per cent. Even in the absence of the growing net debit on government account these growth rates were unsatisfactory, since the slight excess growth of debits was enough to reduce the growth rate of the overall private surplus to about 1.6 per cent and without government debits the growth rate of exports would have been smaller. The growth of debits was also restrained by the policy measures taken in the period 1965-7. Invisible credits responded well to devaluation and the increase in world trade during 1968 and 1969, the average increase between 1965-7 and 1968-9 being almost as great as the increase in visible exports (by value) whilst invisible debits increased less than visible debits. Some reduction in growth rates after 1969 to levels more typical of the pre-1967 period must be expected, but with the growth of government overseas expenditure checked there seems a fair promise that the invisible balance should maintain its 1969 level and even exhibit some growth; this should ensure a modest overall surplus on current account, in the next few years, even if there is some deterioration in the visible balance.

III   ECONOMIC POLICY AND THE BALANCE OF PAYMENTS

III.1   Introduction

The 1967 devaluation was, without doubt, the major act of UK economic policy in recent years. It provided the necessary condition for a return to equilibrium in the balance of payments and, potentially, for the achievement of a more rapid rate of economic growth. It remains to be seen whether the new Conservative government will confirm the target for balance of payments performance as set by the Labour government in 1968, a basic surplus of £500 million per annum; but something of this order needs to be maintained for a number of years merely to complete the repayment of the substantial official debts incurred during the period 1964-8. We shall return to this topic in more detail later in this section, after a review of recent policy measures with particular reference to devaluation.

III.2   Policy Measures and the Current Account, 1964-9

Before the devaluation of 18 November 1967, there was little in the way of non-temporary policy measures which had any substantial impact on the longer-term improvement in the balance of payments. This was inevitable given the hostile rejection of devaluation by both major political parties and the virtual prohibition of drastic commercial policies or exchange control by our obligations under GATT and the IMF. As long as devaluation was an unmentionable word in official circles the UK was operating under a gold bullion standard and balance of payments policy had to be circumscribed by that fact, apart from judicious tinkering. The gold standard remedy for a disequilibrium is outright deflation of effective demand, output and the money stock which leads, in theory, to a fall in home costs and prices relative to those abroad, with consequential equilibrating changes in trade flows. The sterling crises of 1951, 1955 and 1961 were followed by deflationary measures strong enough to cause an increase in levels of unemployment and the facts indicate that such policies were effective in reversing the current account deficits until growth of demand was resumed. Such *absolute* deflation could, perhaps, be justified as a measure to deal with a temporary crisis caused by an inflationary boom leading to overfull employment. Given the downward rigidity of wages and prices in the UK economy the role of such policy in the correction of fundamental disequilibrium is obviously limited, unless the government is prepared to accept a trend increase in the percentage of unemployed resources.

The policy aim of recent governments therefore became a variant of the gold standard discipline, viz, *relative* deflation. The idea was that the growth of the UK price level should be restrained by various measures to a rate below that experienced by our competitors so that relative prices and trade flows could follow the gold standard rules. The relative deflation was to be achieved by a variety of policies including the control of the growth of demand and the money supply, an effective incomes policy and measure to promote the growth of efficiency and productivity which would also satisfy the other major policy aim, a higher rate of economic growth. The effectiveness of such an overall policy required not only that the domestic measures succeed but also that foreign governments cooperate by failing to restrain their own inflations. The major limitation of the policy is its inevitable slowness; a 3 per cent relative deflation needs to be maintained for five years to have the same impact as a 16 per cent devaluation. If foreign export prices grow more slowly than 3 per cent per annum—or decline—then some absolute fall in UK prices is necessary.

For the UK the disequilibrium was too severe and the reserve-liability position too weak for such a policy to succeed. The improvement in the current account from 1964 to 1966 was achieved mainly by the retardation of the annual rate of growth of real GDP to 2.2 per cent compared with the 3.3 per cent per annum growth between 1960 and 1964. The further improvement in the current account to the first quarter of 1967 was helped by a further dose of deflationary measures in July 1966 and the introduction of a statutory wage and price standstill. Unemployment grew rapidly and for four quarters the average value index for UK exports of manufactures was held constant at 118 per cent of the 1958 level. If this rigorous control of incomes, prices and demand could have been maintained for several years it might have made some impact on the balance of payments problem (though it would not have solved it), but the maintenance of such a policy for such a period would have been politically impossible. In the event it could not be held for more than a year. There is little doubt that the growing unpopularity of the government's policies, which was given practical demonstration in the election results in the first half of 1967, led to mild reflationary measures in June to August of that year designed to sustain the new 3 per cent growth target which had been announced in the 1967 budget speech. The relatively mild impetus to imports in conjunction with other adverse trends in the balance of payments in the second half of the year led to renewed doubts about the government's ability to maintain the sterling parity and, inevitably, to the fourth stage of the 1964-7 crisis and the final acceptance by the government that devaluation was unavoidable.

The other policy measures adopted during the period may be dealt with briefly. In October 1964 the government imposed a temporary import surcharge (i.e. tariff) of 15 per cent on most manufactures and semi-manufactures. This was reduced to 10 per cent in April 1965 and finally abandoned in November 1966. The surcharge was a technical violation of GATT and the EFTA agreement, though each of these agreements permits other kinds of negotiated import restrictions to meet temporary disequilibrium in the balance of payments. The surcharge was unlikely to contribute to the longer-run solution of the balance of payments problem, its purpose being as an emergency device to restrain the growth of imports that contributed so much to the 1964 deficit. Its effectiveness was obscured by other cyclical factors but estimates suggest that it may have reduced the level of imports, over the full period, by some £150-£350 million below the level that otherwise would have obtained.

In October 1964 the government also introduced a system of rebates of indirect taxes for exporters which was estimated to be worth, on average, about 2 per cent of the value of sales. This system of export subsidies was consistent with the rules of GATT, but the impact could only be slight. Withdrawal of the rebate was announced when the pound was devalued, though it had been intended as a permanent device. Judging by the reaction of exporters to the withdrawal the rebate was more important than its low percentage value might have indicated. The export rebate was later reinforced by improvements in the system of export finance and insurance, by measures to improve information services to exporters and to increase the degree of export promotion through overseas trade fairs, collective market research, etc. It was suggested that the Selective Employment Tax introduced in the 1966 budget would operate as a disguised export subsidy by virtue of the refund, with premiums, to manufacturers. The argument was doubtful in view of the smallness of the net subsidy after tax and the possible increase in the cost of services consumed by manufacturers. Any small favourable effect on visible exports had to be balanced against the adverse effects of the tax on substantial sectors of invisible exports. The refund of the SET premium to manufacturing industry in non-development areas was also withdrawn when the pound was devalued and in 1969 was withdrawn for development areas.

In November 1968 a system of import deposits was introduced. Importers were required to deposit 50 per cent of the value of imported goods before these could be cleared from Customs. The deposits were repayable after 180 days without interest and applied to about one-third of total imports as a result of the exclusion of such categories as foodstuffs, fuels and basic materials, imports for use in exports, and certain imports from under-developed countries. Assuming a perfect money market the policy would have been a variant of the import surcharge, since it would amount to a tariff of one-quarter of the annual interest rate payable by the importer on borrowed funds, or about 2 to 2.5 per cent. Since the money market is not perfect the scheme discriminated against importers without usable liquid assets or borrowing facilities. At first importers were allowed to borrow abroad to finance the deposits but this was later prohibited, though it is not clear how such prohibition could be policed. The policy effectively provided interest-free loans to the government. In November 1969 the scheme was renewed for a further year but the rate of deposit was reduced to 40 per cent and to 30 per cent in the 1970 Budget. Oddly enough, the policy was declared acceptable to EFTA although the previous import surcharge had been declared an infringement of the agreement. The effects on imports were probably slight.

From November 1966 restrictions were placed on the availability of foreign exchange for travel expenditure outside the sterling area, the maximum allowance being £50 per annum for each person, with higher allowances for business travel. These arrangements were effectively abolished in January 1970 when the allowance for private travel was raised to £300 per person, with increased allowances for business travel. The government has estimated that the restrictions improved the balance of payments by some £25 million per annum during the period of enforcement.

A major longer-term policy measure of the period was concerned with government expenditure overseas. We have seen in section II of this chapter that this item grew rapidly from 1952 to 1964. The average deterioration in the current account between 1956-60 and 1961-4 can be explained arithmetically, though not necessarily causally, by the increase in the level of such expenditure. In the National Plan of 1965 and other policy statements the government expressed an intention to reverse this trend and to bring about an absolute reduction in overseas capital and current expenditure (including aid) by 1970. The rate of increase of current net expenditure was, in fact, substantially reduced after 1965 so as to convert an average annual growth rate of 14.0 per cent for 1956-60 to 1961-4 into one of 5.9 per cent for 1961-4 to 1965-7. From 1966 to 1967 the level actually fell and by 1969 expenditure was only £22 million higher than in 1964. Had the trend from 1956-64 continued to 1968-9 the average net expenditure for the second period would have been £360 million higher than the actual average for that period. This does not measure the implied improvement to the balance of payments because a considerable part of UK aid has been 'tied' to UK exports and there is probably a substantial feedback effect on exports from military expenditures overseas. However, there can be no doubt that the current account has benefited substantially from the change in trend. With the change in government in 1970 it is impossible to predict the longer-term trend of government overseas spending, but in the short period, allowing for inertia, such increases may occur are unlikely to have much impact on the balance of payments position.

III.3   Devaluation

Devaluation of the pound by 14.3 per cent was announced on 18 November 1967, after seven months in which the prospects for the balance of payments had worsened dramatically and the spot rate for sterling against the dollar had declined from par in April to its effective lower limit. The final days before the announcement saw the development of a full scale foreign exchange crisis, with massive intervention in the foreign exchange market by the authorities, against a background of rumours that the government was seeking international loans of various sizes, some of which were supposed to be conditional on devaluation of the pound. At the time of the 1967 budget the Chancellor, Mr Callaghan, was still predicting a substantial improvement in the balance of payments with a prospective surplus for 1967 and a 'substantial' surplus for 1968. By early November it was clear that 1967 would show a massive deficit on current account and that this would continue into 1968 in the absence of remedial measures.

The main causes of this progressive deterioration during 1967 were the poor performance of exports after the first quarter as world exports of manufactures declined under the influence of recessions in Germany and the US, the failure of imports to decline following the anticipated rise in the first quarter after the removal of the import surcharge, the effects of the Arab-Israeli war and the closure of the Suez Canal which, for a time, added some £20 million per month to the UK import bill; and, later, the effects of the dock strikes in London and Liverpool which affected the flow of exports more than the flow of imports. To a great extent these adverse factors were of a temporary nature but this did not prevent them from influencing opinion in the foreign exchange market, where the initial decline in the spot rate for sterling in May 1967 had followed the UK decision to reopen negotiations for entry into the Common Market. Given the long-term weakness of the balance of payments, such a move was bound to revive discussion of devaluation and the easing of the prices and incomes policy after June 1967 led to further doubts regarding the government's ability to maintain the parity of sterling.

Whether the government was converted intellectually to the belief that devaluation was the appropriate policy, or had to accept devaluation as a result of *force majeure,* in the absence of a medium-term international credit, is a question best left to future historians. Contemporary accounts of behind-the-scenes activity differ. What is clear is that the size of the devaluation was discussed in advance with the major countries affected and seems to have been set at the upper limit of what was possible without provoking retaliation. The government was criticised for delaying the final decision to devalue and for delaying the announcement once the Cabinet had taken that decision. The delays were alleged to have involved a considerable loss to the reserves. The counter-argument of the government was that some cost to the reserves was justified as the price of consultation which precluded retaliatory exchange rate changes on the part of our main competitors in international trade. The UK devaluation was quickly followed by devaluations on the part of fourteen other IMF members, mostly countries in the sterling area or with strong trading or financial links with the UK. In aggregate these countries accounted for about one-sixth of UK exports in 1966 and their actions reduced the effective size of the UK parity change in proportion.

The Mechanism of Devaluation.   The essential purpose of devaluation is to produce rapid changes in relative costs and prices at home and abroad so that domestic expenditures are 'switched' away from imports to home-produced import substitutes, and expenditures by non-residents are switched in favour of UK exports, with a consequential increase in the devaluing country's net receipts of foreign exchange on current account. Under the IMF system an approved devaluation is effected by reducing the par value, in gold or the US gold dollar, of the pound sterling. If other countries leave their par values unchanged, or reduce them by less than the UK reduction, the immediate effect is to raise the existing foreign currency prices of UK imports and exports in terms of sterling.[1] The general effect of devaluation on trade flows is therefore analogous to that of the simultaneous introduction of a tariff on all import transactions and a subsidy on all exports, though without the fiscal implications of the tariff-subsidy system and without the possible welfare disadvantages of this method of trade intervention. On the import side the higher sterling prices will operate to reduce the demand for imports by reducing the total market demand and by making profitable an extension, or original production, of import substitutes. On the export side producers may reduce their prices in foreign exchange whilst retaining higher than original prices in sterling, so that additional quantities may be sold abroad and the needed extra resources may be profitably diverted from the home market. Both these effects will raise the level of demand for domestic resources so that, unless devaluation occurs when a country has unemployed resources, which may be absorbed into production, it is essential that it should be supported by measures to reduce the level of domestic demand. Otherwise, the resources needed to meet the new demand for exports and import substitutes will not be available, and the devaluation may achieve nothing more than the creation or aggravation of an inflationary situation.

The effects of devaluation may be viewed as producing a once-for-all reversal of previous losses of competitive advantage, for the devaluing country, caused by previous relative inflation, or other forces such as were discussed in section II of this chapter. But there is nothing in devaluation to eliminate a *trend* in the deterioration of the competitive position. If the trend forces are not eliminated by control of inflation or increases in productivity or export promotion, etc., the devaluation will merely provide a temporary respite which may be purchased at the cost of a worsening of the country's net barter terms of trade.[2]

For a devaluation to succeed there must be a net saving of foreign exchange spent on imports and/or a net increase in foreign exchange earnings from exports, the total improvement being sufficient in the light of targets for the balance of payments and the actual size of the devaluation. Alternatively, we may look for an improvement in the balance of payments expressed in the home currency but, in this case, a successful devaluation may be compatible with an increase in the home currency cost of total imports, provided that there is an even greater, and sufficient, increase in export receipts in home currency. The actual outcome is determined by a complex of supply and demand elasticities in the relevant markets and these will have different values depending on the time period allowed for adjustment. The precise nature of the elasticity conditions is a complex issue and reference should be made to general texts for a full discussion.

In the case of the UK devaluation of 1967 it was generally expected that the improvement in the balance of visible trade, expressed in sterling, would accrue from the export side, since the demand for visible imports was judged to be inelastic, so that expenditures on imports, in sterling, would increase even if government policy contrived to maintain an unchanged demand schedule for imports. Thus any volume decrease in imports would be more than offset by the increase in sterling prices of imports. A considerable increase in the volume of merchandise exports was expected since most analysts seemed prepared

---

[1]   The 14.3 per cent devaluation of the pound refers to the reduction in the value of the pound in terms of gold (or any foreign currency with an unchanged gold value). As a matter of arithmetic, the value of gold (or foreign currency) in terms of sterling is raised by 16.7 per cent so that this becomes the percentage increase in the sterling price of imports and exports, assuming that foreign currency prices remain unchanged.

[2]   It is sometimes overlooked that the worsened terms of trade occasioned by the act of devaluation may merely reverse a previous improvement in the terms of trade. Such a situation would arise if the devaluation was made necessary by a period of relative inflation. The full analysis of this point is too involved to present here but is worth some reflection by the student.

to accept a medium-term elasticity of around −2 with the possibility of a higher value after several years were allowed for complete adjustment to the price changes. It was not expected that UK exporters would reduce their foreign currency prices to the full extent allowed by devaluation. The ending of the export rebate and most of the SET premium refund, together with increases in costs arising from higher import prices and increases in indirect taxes in the 1968 budget, meant that the supply price of UK exports would be increased and it was expected that some exporters would exploit the export subsidy effect of devaluation to increase profit margins so as to finance export promotion and non-price competition. In the last edition of this book the figure of £850 million was suggested as the possible order of magnitude of the improvement in the merchandise trade balance over the 1967 level.[1] In addition it was expected that the invisible trade balance would improve by some £100 to £150 million but this prediction was subject to a wide range of error. In the event, the current account balance improved from 1967 to 1969 by less than £700 million. We shall now consider to what extent this improvement may be explained by the devaluation.

Has Devaluation Succeeded?: The analysis of devaluation is difficult enough when it is done under the normal simplifying assumptions of static economic theory, i.e. when considering the changes in trade flows from one pre-devaluation equilibrium state to a new post-devaluation equilibrium. When devaluation occurs in a real world situation any devaluation induced changes in trade flows are merged together with other changes which would have occurred anyway, in the absence of devaluation, such as those arising from the growth of world demand, the change in the real income of the devaluing country and any underlying trend change in the competitive position of the devaluing country. The basic methodological problem is that one needs to compare the post-devaluation situation with the situation which would have resulted in the absence of devaluation and this cannot be known, with any precision, in practice. As a result, the developments in 1968 and 1969 can be interpreted in radically different ways by proponents and opponents of devaluation as an instrument of balance of payments policy.

The short-period response of import and export prices was roughly in accordance with theoretical expectations. Export unit values, in sterling, rose by 5 per cent from the third quarter of 1967 to the first quarter of 1968. Over the same period import unit values rose by 11 per cent and the prices of exports, in foreign currency, fell by about 10.5 per cent. For the rest of 1968 and 1969 both export and import unit values drifted upwards but it becomes difficult to distinguish devaluation-induced increases from trend inflation.

The behaviour of the balance of visible trade and on current account during 1968 was viewed with pessimism at the time, particularly in the latter part of that year, and—predictably—the question began to be asked whether devaluation had failed. Much of the pessimism was misconceived, though it is undeniable that progress was slower than might have been hoped. It was predictable that the immediate effects of devaluation would worsen the visible trade balance, since the net barter terms of trade would worsen through the adverse differential rises in export and import prices, whilst any favourable volume changes from devaluation would take time to develop.

From 1967 to 1968 the value of total imports, f.o.b. (excluding US military aircraft) increased by 22 per cent, the volume increase being 9.1 per cent. Between 1968 and 1969 there were further increases of 5.1 per cent in value and 2.1 per cent in volume, giving a total volume increase over the two year period of roughly 11 per cent. This increase has to be judged against the average annual volume increase in imports, between 1963 and 1967, of 5.2 per cent and an expected once-for-all volume reduction, due to

---

[1]   On the basis of a more detailed estimate, R. N. Cooper suggested that the improvement might be about £800 million at the old exchange rate. See R. E. Caves and Associates, *Britain's Economic Prospects,* Brookings Institution and George Allen and Unwin, 1968, p. 192.

devaluation, of some 9.5 per cent. The inference is that devaluation either did not result in any contraction in the volume of imports or that any such contraction was completely swamped by forces leading to an abnormally high increase in imports. Some part of the increase in imports from 1967 to 1968 may be explained by special factors such as exceptional increases in imports of silver bullion and precious stones (which were largely for re-export), delayed recordings due to the 1967 dock strikes and, possibly, some unrecorded increase in stockbuilding, but there remains a substantial residual which cannot be explained except tautologically in terms of an unexpected increase in the propensity to import. It seems most likely that the short-period elasticity of demand for manufactured imports was greatly overestimated and that the volume response to devaluation was insignificant.

The behaviour of exports between 1967 and 1969 also poses problems of interpretation. From 1967 to 1968 the value of exports increased by 21.8 per cent (excluding allowance for net under-recording) and the volume increase was 14.3 per cent. From 1968 to 1969 the corresponding increases were 14.1 and 10.4 per cent respectively. Given the average annual increase by value and volume between 1963 and 1967[1] at about 5.6 per cent and 3.5 per cent there seems, at first sight, to have been a significant devaluation response. However, the volume increase from 1967 to 1968 was inflated by delayed shipments of exports resulting from the 1967 dock strikes and correction for this factor would reduce the increase to about 10 per cent. A further influence on exports during this period was the increased rate of growth of world demand, which was reflected in a volume growth rate of exports of manufactures, by the main manufacturing exporters, of almost 15 per cent per annum between 1967 and 1969 compared with an annual rate of about 10 per cent between 1963 and 1967. If we assume that the volume rate of growth of UK exports would have increased in the same proportion as that for 'world' exports, in the absence of devaluation, or at a rate of about 5.3 per cent per annum between 1967 and 1969, the excess growth rate for the two year period, which can be regarded as the devaluation response, is reduced to about 10 per cent. This compares with an effective reduction in (total) export prices, in foreign currency, by 1969 of some 8.5 per cent as compared with the extrapolated trend value from 1967 to 1969. Allowing for some upward drift in the export prices of competitors, which increases the relative price fall for the UK, the implied price-elasticity of demand is of the order of −1. A similar conclusion is reached if we assume that the UK *share* of 'world' exports of manufactures would, in the absence of devaluation, have declined between 1966 and 1969 at the same rate as the decline from 1963 to 1966, *viz.* at the proportionate annual rate of 5.7 per cent. This yields an estimated UK share for 1969 of 10.8 per cent and compares with an actual share of 11.0 per cent, indicating that any extra volume increase from devaluation had merely offset a decline in price.

These arguments do not necessarily lead to the conclusion that devaluation has failed; it is possible to take a more optimistic view of its effects. The assumption made above, that in the absence of devaluation UK exports would have maintained a volume growth rate proportionate to that of world exports between 1967 and 1969, is effectively an assumption of an unchanged competitive position during that period. There is no logical reason why this hypothesis should be given preferential treatment and devaluation responses allowed only as a residual effect. It is unfortunate that the statistical disturbance caused by the dock strikes of 1967 obscures the behaviour of exports in the period immediately after devaluation and thus conceals a possible increase, due to devaluation, in the

[1] These *trend* increases are taken from 'adjusted' data presented in *NIER* which eliminate the effects of the dock strikes in 1967. See, e.g. vol. 51, February 1970, table 14, p. 104.

UK share of 'world' exports of manufactures.[1] If figures for the fourth quarter of 1967 and the first quarter of 1968 are aggregated, the UK share of 'world' exports is 10.7 per cent. This may be compared with the hypothetical share on the assumption of a zero price-elasticity of demand for that period. The average decline in UK export prices for that period was about 8.5 per cent and if this is applied to the value of UK trade for the third quarter of 1967 the UK share for the subsequent six-month period should have been about 11.3 per cent. The difference between this and the actual 10.7 per cent represents an annual loss of UK exports at the rate of about £250 million and the recovery of the UK share in 1968 to 11 per cent of a higher value of 'world' exports could be regarded as an additional devaluation response. Whilst a calculation for such a short period should not bear too much weight, it is significant that the UK share of 'world' exports was virtually stable at 11 per cent for the whole of 1968 and 1969, the annual averages being 11.1 per cent and 11.0 per cent respectively, and the shares for the second quarter of 1968 and the fourth quarter of 1969 were identical at 11.1 per cent. In the context of a growth of 'world' exports of 34 per cent during the two year period, such stability of the UK share was unprecedented and suggests that the favourable devaluation response had simply been delayed more than was expected so that, instead of achieving an expected absolute increase in share, the UK had achieved only an increase relative to the trend decline. If the decline in the UK share continues to be retarded during 1970, as seems probable, the case for a successful devaluation response on the export side will become much stronger.

The balance of invisible trade also improved substantially between 1967 and 1969, from £230 million to £524 million, the increased surplus being substantially better than expectations at the end of 1967. Here again we must avoid the superficial judgment that devaluation was responsible for the whole of the improvement. The growth in world demand for merchandise exports is bound to have produced a similar growth in demand for invisible exports and the UK position has been improved unilaterally by the halt to the growth of government expenditure overseas and the restriction on tourist expenditures. There seems no reason to doubt that devaluation has helped, but further evidence and research will be needed before its contribution can be assessed.

Reference has been made to the crucial need for government policy to support a full employment devaluation by effecting the release of resources[2] from domestic use so that production of exports and import substitutes can be increased. Reductions in proposed government expenditures of some £400 million were announced with devaluation and further reductions of £300 million for the fiscal year 1968-9 and over £400 million for 1969-70 were announced in January 1968 after an 'agonising reappraisal' of public expenditures and commitments. In addition hire purchase terms were tightened and restrictions were imposed on bank lending. Further deflationary measures were taken with the 1968 budget which was designed to raise tax receipts by more than £900 million in a full year, though not all the proposed tax increases could have been expected to impinge on final expenditures, and thus release resources. Still further measures to restrict bank lending were announced in May and November 1968 and in the latter month there were increases in the severity of hire purchase controls together with increases in indirect taxes. There is no doubt that these measures, together with the effects of higher import prices due to the devaluation, constituted a formidable policy to divert resources, and it is significant that real consumer expenditures increased between 1967 and 1969 at an annual rate of only 1.3 per cent. It is unnecessary to raise the question of the adequacy of the policy complex since, whatever the actual devaluation response on exports, it

---

[1] The basic data for the following calculation are taken from *NIER*, no. 51, February 1970, table 20. The actual UK share fell from 12.4 per cent in the third quarter of 1967 to 10.1 per cent in the fourth quarter and recovered to 11.3 per cent in the first quarter of 1968. The increase of 1.2 per cent is a spurious result of the dock strikes.

[2] See Chap. 2, Section V. 5.

is quite clear that resources were released to allow a massive actual increase in the volume of exports, whilst the high levels of unemployment during 1968 and 1969 suggest that the overall pressure of effective demand on resources was not excessive.

Devaluation and Sterling Balances: One of the arguments used against devaluation before 1967, and which may have influenced official policy, was that it would be a breach of faith with owners of sterling balances since it would depreciate the foreign exchange value of such assets. This is a complex issue, which cannot be discussed adequately in a short space.[1] Holders of sterling are well aware of IMF rules, which permit devaluation in cases of fundamental disequilibrium, and on the whole they hold sterling because it suits them, and not out of motives of charity towards the UK. The interest received on such balances provides a sizeable compensation against the risk of devaluation when compared with the alternative of holding gold, and the excess of interest rates in the UK over rates abroad compensates for the risk of holding sterling rather than foreign currencies. The substantial losses taken by the Bank of England on forward contracts outstanding at the time of devaluation can be viewed as actual compensation for those who hedged in this market. But holdings of official balances suffered a reduction in foreign exchange value following devaluation and in 1968 there was some reduction in these balances. It was feared that this reduction might increase progressively, whilst some writers began to predict the disintegration of the sterling area system.

Following extensive discussions in 1968 the *Basle Facility* was announced in September, whereby twelve central banks plus the Bank for International Settlements agreed to extend aid to the UK to a maximum of $2,000 million, to offset the effect on UK reserves of any decline, below an agreed level, in official and private balances held by residents of the sterling area. Drawings on the facility were to be limited to a three-year period whilst any net use of the facility would be due for repayment between the sixth and tenth years. At the same time arrangements were made to terminate by 1971 an earlier facility, dating from 1966, to provide short-term finance to offset the effects on UK reserves of seasonal fluctuations in sterling balances.

In return for this assistance the UK had negotiated agreements with the sterling area countries whereby a dollar guarantee was provided for that part of each country's *official* sterling reserve (excluding equity holdings) which exceeded 10 per cent of the country's total reserves. The guarantee was conditional in each case on a commitment from each country to maintain a minimum proportion of its total reserve in sterling during the lifetime of the agreement, which in most cases was for three years, from September 1968, with a possible extension of two years. Private balances are excluded from the exchange guarantee.

Some use was made by the UK of this facility in 1968 but repayments were made in 1969 as sterling balances held by central monetary institutions rose after the third quarter of 1968. The increase in such sterling balances suggests that the agreements have been effective and beneficial for the UK reserves. But the arrangements are undoubtedly a costly form of short-term borrowing for the UK, since it might have been expected that exchange-guaranteed balances would carry a special and reduced rate of interest.

III.4   Policy Measures and the Long-Term Capital Account

The government may seek to correct a deficit on the basic balance of payments either by measures to improve the current account, or by measures to reduce the net long-term capital outflow, or by a combination of both. Under the IMF system exchange control

---

[1]   For an excellent pre-devaluation discussion, see F. Hirsch, *The Pound Sterling, A Polemic*, Gollancz, 1965, pp. 84-7.

over capital movements is permitted and throughout the postwar period the movement of capital by UK residents to non-sterling area countries has been subject to controls of varying severity. Following the severe basic deficit of 1964 a number of measures were taken in 1965 and 1966 to reduce UK private long-term investment abroad and to convert a net outflow into a net inflow. The 1965 budget introduced more stringent controls over direct investment outside the sterling area. Such investment would have to show substantial short-term and continuing benefits to the balance of payments (in the form of associated exports and flows of invisible receipts from dividends and profits) if exchange were to be made available at the official rate. Investment would still be allowed, however, if financed out of foreign borrowing or from investment currency, purchased at a premium, though measures were also introduced to reduce the potential supply of funds under the latter heading. In July 1965 it was announced that no official foreign exchange would be provided 'for the time being' for such direct investment. In January 1968 this restriction was partially lifted and it was announced that exchange would be made available, within limits and subject to stringent conditions regarding the prospective benefit to the balance of payments. Measures to reduce portfolio investment outside the sterling area were introduced in April and July 1965 by way of stricter exchange control. Investment currency represents balances accruing to sterling area residents from the sale of non-sterling assets. Prior to the new measures, such balances could be reinvested abroad and general exchange control on capital movements ensured that such balances could be sold at a premium in relation to the official exchange rate. The new measures effectively produced a partial repatriation of such foreign assets, first by requiring that certain assets which previously would have added to the overall stock of investment currency must be sold in the official exchange market at the official rate, and secondly by requiring that 25 per cent of proceeds of any sales of foreign assets must be surrendered for sterling at the official rate. Thus enforced repatriation was combined with an element of taxation. In addition to these measures various changes in the basis of company taxation, including the new corporation tax, were expected to operate eventually to reduce investment abroad and increase foreign investment in the UK, but the full impact of these measures was not expected for a number of years. In the 1966 budget the policy was extended by the introduction of 'voluntary' controls on investment in four developed sterling area countries (Australia, New Zealand, South Africa and Ireland).

These measures to control the long-term capital account gave rise to considerable controversy and the return to surplus in the current account will doubtless lead to pressure on the government for relaxation of control. The case for and against control is worth discussion in some detail.

The argument for control, as stated by the government in the 1965 National Plan, was that 'the extent of the capital outflow has not been commensurate with what the United Kingdom can afford, and a change in policy towards overseas investment. . . was essential. Much of the benefit of overseas investment accrues to the recipient countries, and the return from overseas investment is on average considerably less, from the point of view of the national economy, than the return on home investment. . . . The benefits of overseas investment to the balance of payments—in the form of interest and dividend income, and of increased exports of goods and services—are of course recognised, but in many cases these benefits accrue only over a longer period. And in a time of acute strain on the balance of payments short-term considerations must be given weight.'[1]

These arguments call for critical discussion. We begin with the concept of 'what we can afford' in the way of foreign investment. To suppose that this is determined by the actual surplus on current account would be erroneous, because of the causal linkage

---

[1]   Op. cit., p. 71.

between the capital and current accounts. Any foreign investment may involve repercussions on levels of exports and imports, insofar as it affects the level of activity at home and abroad, and this is particularly likely in the case of direct overseas investment. It is a mistake, therefore, to assume that the balance on current account will be invariant to a change in the level of capital exports. If exports of goods decline by substantially the same amount as the reduction in capital exports, what becomes of the concept of 'what we can afford'? It may be objected that such an outcome is improbable and that the basic balance will show *some* improvement when direct investment is reduced, even if the size of the improvement is uncertain. In this case the previous level of direct investment will have been partly financed, under a fixed exchange rate system, by drafts on UK reserves or by an increase in short-term liabilities abroad, so that the foreign investment will have involved a change of assets. But such an exchange of assets is not essential since a devaluation of the pound can increase the autonomous surplus on current account so as to finance the desired level of foreign investment without any worsening of the UK reserve-liability position. There may be good reasons for avoiding devaluation simply to maintain a level of foreign investment without loss to reserves but to argue that we cannot *afford* foreign investment because it would involve devaluation, without reference to the real costs and benefits of such a policy, is essentially question-begging and reduces to a straightforward defence of the existing exchange rate.

What then are the real costs and benefits of foreign investment? Suppose, first, that there is a complete linkage between the capital and current accounts so that, say, an extra £100 million of foreign investment leads automatically to an increase in net exports of the same magnitude, provided that the additional net exports can be made available. In this case there is clearly no risk of loss of reserves, nor is it necessary to adjust the exchange rate. If we are working in the context of a fully employed economy the real cost of the foreign investment is an opportunity cost, the cost of the foregone domestic consumption or investment which has to be reduced by market processes and/or by government intervention in order to free resources for the additional flow of net exports. To simplify the discussion we assume that monetary-fiscal policy is used to ensure that the whole impact falls on domestic investment. The problem then reduces to a comparison of the alternative yields of home and foreign investment. If the linkage between capital and current accounts is incomplete the analysis becomes more complicated and the real costs of overseas investment are more difficult to estimate. An extra £100 million of foreign investment will induce an extra flow of net exports of less than this amount. We again assume a devaluation sufficient to raise the increase in net exports to £100 million. Under conditions of full employment the extra flow of net exports induced by devaluation must involve a reduction in domestic expenditure, but, in this case, the opportunity cost of £100 million of foreign investment may be greater than £100 million of home investment if devaluation results in a worsening of the net barter terms of trade. The *volume* of net exports may need to increase by more than the increase in *value,* and the extra volume must be released from domestic use. The extra cost of foreign investment will be greater the *smaller* the degree of linkage between the capital and current accounts, the *greater* the deterioration in the terms of trade, and the smaller the improvement in the current account for a given percentage devaluation.[1] Assuming zero linkage the opportunity cost of £100 invested abroad will be £100 $(1 + x)$ of home investment foregone, where x is the ratio of the percentage worsening of the terms of trade to the improvement in the current account balance (taken as a percentage of the initial value of exports) both for a given (small) percentage devaluation. For the UK the value of x

---

[1] It is theoretically possible for the terms of trade to improve as a result of devaluation but this outcome is unlikely for a country like the UK.

might be taken in the range of 0.25 to 0.5 but could be higher if one takes a more pessimistic view of the effects of devaluation.[1]

The actual size of the degree of linkage between capital and current accounts is unkown and can only be estimated with difficulty and subject to a wide margin of error. Considerable interest was aroused by the conclusions of the *Reddaway Report* which was commissioned by the CBI to investigate such problems.[2] The Report estimated that an extra £100 invested in the overseas subsidiaries of British firms engaged in mining and manufacturing and plantations would raise the level of UK exports by only £9 as compared with the level obtaining in the absence of the investment. This degree of linkage was much lower than previous discussions had assumed. The estimate has to be used with caution since it reflects the average experience of a sample of firms in a range of industries over the period 1955-64. It was derived not on the basis of econometric study but through discussions with representatives of the firms involved and the margin of error is probably large. Apart from such considerations there are several reasons for believing that the *Reddaway Report* under estimates the feedback from investment to exports.

First, the £100 of investment relates to the increase in the overseas assets of the UK subsidiaries, not all of which need be financed from the UK. The *Final Report* makes it clear that the initial effect on UK exports of £100 invested by the UK depends on the proportion of the UK 'stake' to the total overseas net operating assets. For the period 1956-64 this proportion was about 63 per cent so that the figure of £9 can be grossed up to about £15, provided we assume the continuation of the relative shares of financing.[3] Secondly, the relationship is valid only if the theoretical model underlying the Report is valid and this assumes, *inter alia*, that an act of overseas investment proceeds regardless of whether it is financed by the UK or not. For reasons too complex to discuss here, the effect of the various assumptions of the model is to eliminate multiplier effects on trade flows and thus the feedback from investment to UK net exports.[4] Thirdly, the relationship is based on a period when it may be argued that UK exporters were increasingly trading with an overvalued exchange rate so that the competitiveness of UK exports was reduced. After the 1967 devaluation the pound should, for a time, no longer be overvalued and the degree of feedback from overseas investment to exports should increase. The degree of export feedback is likely to vary substantially with the type of country receiving the UK investment but, even allowing for the factors just mentioned, it might be wise to assume an average figure of less than 25 per cent. Thus an additional flow of investment would require a devaluation if it was to be effected without loss to the reserves.

We now consider the relative benefits of home versus foreign investment. The extra flow of foreign investment will raise productivity abroad and part of this additional output will accrue to the UK in the form of interest and profits. The reduction in home investment will reduce the level of national output as compared with the level it might otherwise have attained. Will the yield to the UK from foreign investment be less than that from home investment as argued in the National Plan?

---

[1] These values are based on guesses at the likely longer-run values of parameters in a theoretical formula. The terms of trade effect is very sensitive to the assumed elasticity of demand for imports and can be serious if the demand for imports is completely inelastic. The UK terms of trade deteriorated by about 4-5 per cent between 1967 and 1969, but for various reasons this cannot be assumed to be a typical proportionate change for future small devaluations, in the context of the present argument.

[2] W. B. Reddaway and others, *Effects of UK Direct Investment Overseas: An Interim Report*, Cambridge University Press, 1967; *Final Report*, Cambridge University Press, 1968.

[3] *Final Report*, pp. 233-5.

[4] This general point was recognised in the *Final Report*, chapter 19.

It is true that much of the benefit from overseas investment goes abroad, if only because profits accrue net of overseas taxes, but this is also true of foreign investment in the UK. Since UK net investment abroad has been the difference between substantial opposite flows, any attempt to prune the UK outflow runs the risk of retaliation and any net loss to the UK (but not necessarily to the world) involved in allowing a free flow of investment will be a very small percentage of GNP, of which some part is a beneficial transfer to countries with a lower income *per capita*. It is not easy to quantify the difference in marginal returns from home and foreign investment, though some data is available on average returns. The *Reddaway Report* estimated that the average rate of profit (net of overseas taxes) over the period 1956-64 was 8.7 per cent for the full sample of mining, manufacturing and plantations and 13 per cent for oil companies. For manufacturing alone the figure was 8.1 per cent.[1] These figures cover a large sample of companies and relate profits to the UK 'stake' in the net operating assets of overseas companies at book values. For mining and manufacturing there were wide variations in rates of return around the average in respect of different industries and different countries.

The average rate of return on capital invested at home (before tax) for a similar period was about 14 per cent for manufacturing industry,[2] which is considerably higher than the after-tax return on overseas investment. However, it is neither necessary nor probable that any marginal reduction in home investment will be in the manufacturing sector, since many companies regard home and foreign investment as complementary rather than competitive. So any policy-induced reduction in home investment is likely to fall in the non-industrial sector where the rate of return may be substantially less than 14 per cent.[3] There is thus no presumption that the rate of return per £100 invested will be lower for overseas investment. We have seen, though, that the opportunity cost of £100 worth of foreign investment will exceed £100. Does this tip the advantage in favour of home investment given, say, an equal rate of return? The answer is negative since the one rate of return is in terms of domestic output whilst the other is in terms of foreign exchange. The additional flow of income from the foreign investment will, in principle, allow for a partial reversal of the devaluation required to effect the original transfer of the foreign investment and this revaluation will improve the terms of trade and permit a release of resources to the value of $(1 + x)$ times the flow of overseas income, where x is defined as before. Thus the terms of trade factor cancels out since it relates both to the capital sum and the yield from the investment. There is a net balance of advantage to the overseas investment to the extent that the initial export feedback from the capital transfer does not involve a terms of trade effect.[4]

We are forced to conclude that there is no obvious case for a permanent restriction of foreign investment on the basis that this is less productive to the national economy. The case for not restricting such investment is that it leads *directly* to additional earnings of foreign exchange and, whilst it is possible that even greater earnings of foreign exchange might result from suitably directed home investment, there is absolutely no presumption that such greater earnings would result from the marginal extra investment which would result from a reduction in overseas investment. A further point is that it is

---

[1] Pp. 356-7.

[2] J. H. Dunning, 'Further Thoughts on Foreign Investment', *Moorgate and Wall Street Review*, Autumn 1966, pp. 12, 29. This article contains a useful discussion of the general problems involved.

[3] See Reddaway, *Interim Report*, pp. 93-5, *Final Report*, pp. 305, 336.

[4] We neglect the possible 'continuing' effect on net exports in view of the small size and uncertain accuracy of the Reddaway estimate. *Final Report*, pp. 344-5.

not necessary, in practice, to choose between the alternatives of foreign and home investment. The extra resources for foreign investment can be drawn from those released by reduced domestic consumption. It is far from obvious why the government should give free rein to the consumer's propensity to import, whilst restricting the propensity of firms to import titles to real assets which bring in a return in foreign exchange.

Is there a case for temporary restrictions on foreign investment? Our argument so far has assumed the willingness of the government to devalue so that foreign investment need not involve a drain on reserves. A reserve currency country like the UK might well reject a trivial devaluation designed purely to enable an increased flow of foreign investment even if the theoretical case for the policy were judged to be sound.[1] But this was not the case in 1965 and 1966 when a major devaluation was required and even the total elimination of foreign investment would not have saved the situation. In this sort of situation temporary controls on direct investment will only serve to postpone the day of reckoning and the ultimate crisis will probably be more severe than it need have been. Temporary control of portfolio investment may be justified in such circumstances to prevent what may amount to a flight from the currency but this leaves the underlying cause of the flight untreated. A case for temporary control might exist if a high level of foreign investment was causing an undue loss of reserves at a time when the balance of payments could not be regarded as being in fundamental disequilibrium. Given the volatility of international capital flows some periodic loss of reserves is inevitable and the ideal remedy is a sufficiently large volume of international reserves to act as a buffer. If this is not the case it would be preferable for the country to borrow abroad short-term as long as this could be done at a rate of interest less than the yield on outward investment. If short-term borrowing abroad is impossible there might be a case for restricting the outflow of portfolio investment rather than of direct investment, since the rate of return is appreciably lower on the former and interruptions to the latter flow will probably involve long-term damage to the operations of UK firms abroad and to the flow of exports.

Since foreign investment is a two-way process the extent to which permanent control of the outflow is required will depend on the size of the desired outflow relative to the inflow. Undue preoccupation with events in 1964 has tended to obscure the fact that the average annual rate of net private foreign investment had fallen substantially during the period 1961-4 as compared with 1956-60. It is true that between 1961 and 1964 the balance of private investment abroad swung from an inflow of £113 million to an outflow of £247 million. But capital movements are bound to be volatile and it was incorrect to regard this swing as evidence of a longer-term trend. Table 3.8 shows annual averages for the main headings in the long-term capital account for the various cyclical periods. It is not the case that private investment abroad by the UK had been growing at an excessive rate before 1964. In fact, the averages for 1956-60 and 1961-4 show only a slight upward trend and reference to annual data in table A-7 will show that the annual total had been relatively stable at about £300 million since 1957, the exceptions being 1962 when the total dropped to £242 million and 1964 when it increased to almost £400 million. Government long-term investment (net) has increased substantially, on average, until 1961-4, but the annual growth rate of combined government and private investment abroad was about 3.4 per cent between 1956-60 and 1961-4, which would have presented no problems given a satisfactory current account balance and normal growth of trade. The inadequacy of the current account during 1961-4 was obscured by a large increase in the flow of long-term capital to the UK from abroad, and it was the combination of a relatively low

---

[1]   This is effectively the line taken in the *Reddaway Report* and explains the substantially different approach to the assessment of costs and benefits from overseas investment as compared with the treatment in this chapter.

inflow and a relatively high outflow that produced the large net outflow in 1964. The rate of increase of foreign investment in the UK has been very high since 1952-3. Between 1958 and 1967 some 79 per cent of the direct component of this investment was from North America, mainly from the US.

An important influence on future levels of US investment in the UK will be the state of the balance of payments of the US, where restraint of private investment abroad has been used in an attempt to reduce the persistent outflow of gold in recent years. There were indications of a relaxation of this policy during 1969 following the change of President, but it remains to be seen whether this relaxation can survive the apparently intractable US balance of payments problem. American firms have also sought to maintain their investment programmes overseas by borrowing locally, which reduces the short-term balance of payments advantage of such investment in the receiving country.

TABLE 3.8

UK Long-term Capital Account, Annual Averages for Selected Periods (£ million)

	1952-5	1956-60	1961-4	1965-7	1968-9
Government (net)	−40	−56	−92	−74	−37
Private investment abroad	−180	−298	−319	−374	−663
Direct	n.a.	n.a.	−234	−288	−455
Portfolio	n.a.	n.a.	+15	+39	−118
Other	n.a.	n.a.	−100	−124	−90
Private investment in UK	+60	+167	+278	+300	+666
Direct	n.a.	n.a.	+172	+187	+276
Portfolio	n.a.	n.a.	+39	−31	+137
Other	n.a.	n.a.	+67	+144	+253
Private investment (net)	−120	−131	−41	−74	+3
Balance of long-term capital	−160	−187	−133	−148	−34

n.a. not available
Assets: increase −/decrease +. Liabilities increase +/decrease −.

Source: UK Balance of Payments 1969, PE, 1970

It is evident from table 3.8 that the UK controls did not prevent an actual increase in the average gross flow of private investment abroad after 1964, but the increase in the *net* outflow was small for 1965-7 and negative for 1968-9. Developments in detail in the long-term capital account have been too numerous, in recent years, for easy summary here and readers should refer to official publications, especially *Economic Trends,* for information. Substantial proportions of outward and inward direct investment are financed out of reinvested profits and, in accordance with government policy, a part of outward investment is financed by direct borrowing abroad and is recorded as inward investment, whilst some is financed by borrowing in foreign currencies from banks in London operating in the euro-dollar market, and this flow is recorded in the monetary movements account. In 1969 £55 million of inward portfolio investment resulted from public sector issues abroad following a government announcement in early 1969 that nationalised industries were to be encouraged to borrow abroad, with the government underwriting any exchange risk involved. Outward portfolio investment has been erratic in recent years for a variety of reasons.

III.5 Further Outlook

From the viewpoint of early 1970 the outlook for the UK balance of payments in the next few years was more hopeful than at any other time in the last decade. Yet our problems are still far from completely solved and it remains true that several years of careful management are needed if the transition to full equilibrium is to be made effective. The potential fruits of recent improvements could be lost by internal mismanagement even if the UK is not beset by further external hazards beyond the govenment's control.

The basic surplus for 1969 marked the end of an overvalued pound sterling but only the beginning of the means for repayment of the massive official debts which had accrued during the previous five years. The cumulative deficit on monetary movements during 1964-8 understated the need for accommodating finance since, inside that account, there were substantial items needing to be offset by official transactions, of which the most important was the reduction of some £1,200 million in privately held sterling balances. A part of the required official finance came from the sale of the Treasury dollar portfolio but most was provided by drawings on the IMF and by the short-term assistance to the UK from various central banks, referred to elsewhere in this chapter. In his 1970 budget speech, the Chancellor revealed that the total amount of such debts outstanding at the end of 1968 was £3,363 million. By the end of March 1970 this sum had been reduced by some £1,700 million and official reserves had increased by £120 million from their end-1968 level. Several factors contributed to this massive reduction in debt. Apart from the basic surplus, the UK was able to credit the reserves with the £171 million of Special Drawing Rights allocated to the UK on 1 January 1970. Substantial amounts of foreign exchange were also gained through the demand for sterling generated by revived confidence as the balance of payments improved and by relatively high short-term interest rates in the UK. By the end of March 1970 outstanding short- and medium-term debts stood at £1,650 million, of which the main items were the IMF drawing of 1968 (£583 million), due for repayment between 1971 and 1973, and the drawing of 1969-70 (£417 million), due for repayment between 1972 and 1975.

The full repayment of these debts requires the achievement of the target surplus for the period 1970-2 or a declining surplus for a longer period. Apart from this the UK needs to increase her official reserve which is absurdly low in relation to needs. It is true that further SDR allocations are due in 1971 and 1972, at least, and that there may be further gains to reserves from short-term capital inflows. The repayment of IMF drawings and other debts will also reconstitute facilities. But short-term capital flows are, by nature, reversible at short notice and it would be dangerous to ignore the possibility of new troubles arising from this quarter.

In the short period we must expect some worsening of the current account balance, *ceteris paribus*, as a result of the relaxation of restrictions on overseas travel expenditure, the probable phasing out of import deposits, and an increase in the growth of imports resulting from attempts to raise the growth of GNP, which may lead to an increase in stock-building. Such negative effects may be partly offset by delayed devaluation response and by a marginal advantage to the UK from the net effects of the French and German parity changes in 1969. In the longer run we must expect the beneficial effects of devaluation to erode if there is a return to the trend decline in UK competitiveness such as was evident before 1964 or 1967. The major threat to continued surplus will arise from failure to contain the accelerating wage-price spiral. The virtual breakdown of the Prices and Incomes Policy in late 1969 and 1970 and the substantial increases in wage and price levels could, if continued for long, present a serious threat to the balance of payments. This threat should not be exaggerated since export prices at the end of 1969 were still some 11-12 per cent below the level they might have achieved in the absence of devaluation or 9 per cent down, relative to those of our main competitors, as compared with the pre-devaluation quarter of 1967; and some of Britain's competitors are also having trouble in containing their inflations.

Perhaps the major threat to continued surplus stems from the renewed application, in 1967, for UK membership in the EEC. The full effects of this are difficult to judge until the terms of entry are known through negotiations but it is significant that even proponents of entry admit that the UK would incur serious immediate damage to the balance of payments and can promise, in return, only vague and 'unquantifiable' *general* economic gains.[1]

III.6   International Monetary Developments

Recent years have seen extensive discussion of the need to reform the international monetary system. Numerous plans have been suggested to this end but progress towards a solution acceptable to all interested parties has been slow. However, in 1969 a major step was taken on one aspect of the problem, an adequate growth of world reserves, with the final approval and activation of the scheme for Special Drawing Rights in the IMF (SDRs). The other main aspect of the problem, the adjustment mechanism, remains to be solved though some progress has been made towards a solution.

Although there has been a steady decline in the ratio of world reserves to trade during the postwar period there has never been general agreement that reserves were inadequate in total, nor is there any objective test by which this question could be decided. Between 1951 and 1969 the ratio of world official reserves and foreign exchange (including reserve positions in the Fund) declined from about 65 per cent to about 30 per cent, the latter figure being well below the equivalent ratio for the depressed 1930s and less than the ratio for 1928. Throughout the postwar period conditional reserves have been available in the form of drawing rights on the IMF in excess of the reserve positions. These amounted to about 7 per cent of world trade for 1969 and will increase in 1970 when quotas are increased by 33 per cent in the aggregate to a total of $29 billion. But access to drawing rights in excess of the reserve positions involves a country in consultation with the IMF and the obligation to accept a certain measure of IMF supervision over its general policies. Whilst good reasons exist for this surveillance, countries inevitably have a preference for owned over conditional reserves. Since October 1962 the IMF resources have had the potential support of the General Arrangements to Borrow by which it can mobilise reserves up to some $6 billion from the Group of Ten countries (EEC, UK, US, Sweden and Japan) so as to reduce the possible need to invoke the 'scarce currency' provisions of Article 7 of the IMF Agreement. Apart from this there has been the development of *ad hoc* measures of inter-central bank cooperation such as the short-term *swap* agreements between the US and other countries, whereby each agrees to lend balances to the other for a specified time, or to accumulate balances of the other's currency to an agreed limit for a given time period.

The UK has benefited greatly during the last few years from this sort of agreement, the size of which has been increased periodically. From a modest level of $50 million in 1962 the UK-US swap facility increased to $750 million in November 1964 and $2,000 million in March 1968. Other examples are the Basle credits of 1961, when several European central banks agreed to hold excess balances of sterling up to £300 million for three months, and the very large credits extended by central banks to the UK in the November 1964 crisis and at the time of devaluation.

Many contributers to the debate took the view that these *ad hoc* measures were themselves proof of the need for more formal and permanent measures to raise reserves. Opponents took the view that the actual growth of world trade and inflation indicated that world reserves were not inadequate and that faster growth of reserves would merely aggravate world inflation. However, it was agreed that recent trends in trade and reserves

---

[1]   The White Paper, *Britain and the European Communities*, Cmnd 4829 (Feb. 1970), gives a recent economic assessment. Douglas Jay's *After the Common Market*, Penguin, 1968, can be recommended as a corrective to much of the pro-Market wishful thinking published in recent years.

could, if continued, lead sooner or later to a dangerous pressure on reserves. An additional aspect of the problem, sometimes called the 'confidence' problem, was the degree of dependence of world reserves on foreign exchange in the form of dollar and sterling balances, the former representing a substantial part of the actual growth of reserves. With the persistent weakness of sterling before the 1967 devaluation and the persistent loss of gold by the US, after 1958 there was the ever-present risk of a severe liquidity crisis involving conversions of reserve assets into gold which would destroy a substantial part of world reserves as dollar and sterling assets were liquidated whilst gold reserves were merely redistributed between countries. The fact that pressure on world reserves has coincided with problems of balance of payments adjustment for the two main currencies has complicated reform and made for delay.

From the standpoint of the IMF system the remedy for the three interrelated problems of reserves, adjustment and confidence was simple. The pound and the dollar should have been devalued sufficiently relatively to the other main currencies to solve the adjustment problem whilst all currencies should have been devalued in terms of gold to an extent which would have ensured an adequate value and growth rate of the stock of world monetary gold. This solution came near to achievement in March 1968 when speculative buying of gold in Europe threatened such a drain on US gold stocks that their ability to maintain the gold price at $35 per ounce was in doubt. The crisis was halted by the adoption of a two-tier gold price, with the central banks committed to transact between themselves at $35 per ounce, and also to the policy of refraining from adding further to stocks of monetary gold, whilst the price of gold for industrial use and for private hoarding was to be determined by market forces. The problem of insulating the two markets from each other made this seem, at the time, to be a short-term expedient, essentially a delaying operation until the new SDR scheme could be activated and gold progressively reduced in importance as a means of international settlement. In the event the central bankers succeeded in preventing leakages of official gold into the private market. There followed a period of psychological warfare in which the leading producer of gold, South Africa, refrained from selling in the free market in the hope of driving up the price and breaking the insulation between the two markets, whilst the central bankers did their best to convey the idea that gold had already been demonetised. For a time it looked as if South Africa would win, and the free market price rose to a substantial premium, but in late 1969 a number of factors, including the high opportunity cost of holding gold and the prospects of an SDR issue, induced the gold speculators to lose heart and they began to liquidate their positions. The free market price fell rapidly after October 1969 and by December the premium over the official price had vanished. The prospect of a free price below the official price disturbed some central bankers, with its threat to the value of their gold stocks and at this stage a somewhat involved arrangement was concocted whereby the IMF would buy gold from South Africa when the free market price was at or below the official price. The outcome was a victory for the central bankers over the gold speculators, which was clinched by the first allocation of SDRs on 1 January 1970.

Special Drawing Rights: This new reserve asset was the result of several years of detailed discussion and negotiation and the final administrative stages necessary to make the scheme effective were taken by August 1969. Even then the actual operation of the scheme could not be taken for granted since the first allocation of SDRs depended on a proposal from the Managing Director of the Fund, with the concurrence of the Executive Directors, which had to be approved by the Board of Governors. Before making his proposal the Managing Director had to be satisfied that there was a collective judgment on the need to supplement existing reserves and 'broad support among participants to begin allocations'.[1] The required

---

[1] Article 24. The revised Articles of Agreement may be found in the IMF Annual Report for 1968 or in the book by F. Machlup listed in *References and Further Reading* at the end of this chapter.

proposal was made and approved at the 1969 annual meeting of the IMF Governors who also approved allocations, for the first 'basic period' of three years, of some $9.5 billion, with $3.5 billion to accrue on 1 January 1970 and the remainder in equal instalments on 1 January 1971 and 1972. Future allocations beyond 1972 are not automatic but depend on further proposals by the Managing Director under the terms of Article 24.

Allocations of SDRs to countries will be made on the basis of IMF quotas at the date of each allocation and will form part of the official reserves of each country. Although they will constitute reserve assets they will not be freely usable, at the discretion of the country, in the same way as are gold and foreign exchange reserves. SDRs may be used only in accordance with the terms of Article 25 to meet legitimate balance of payments needs and may not be used to change the composition of a country's reserves. A country in deficit will use SDRs by effecting their transfer, through the IMF, to another participant (or participants) in a strong balance of payments position and will receive convertible currency in exchange. Participants will be expected to accept a transfer of SDRs, in exchange for currency, up to a limit set at twice their net cumulative allocation.[1] When a country's balance of payments position improves again it will be expected to reverse the above procedure by itself accepting a transfer of SDRs from other participants in exchange for convertible currency, a process called 'reconstitution'. The incentive to hold SDRs is provided by the fact that they will be gold guaranteed and will carry an interest payment, provisionally 1.5 per cent per annum, provision for which will be made by imposing a similar charge on those countries which have made net use of their allocations. Charges payable and receivable will be denominated in SDRs so that the mechanism is self-balancing. The rules relating to reconstitution require that five years after the first allocation, and at the end of each calendar quarter thereafter, the average daily holdings of SDRs of a country over the most recent five-year period should not be less than 30 per cent of its net daily cumulative holdings over the same five-year period. In rough terms this means that 70 per cent of each allocation can be used up permanently or a greater percentage can be used for temporary financing of deficits provided the appropriate proportion is reconstituted within the five-year period. It must be emphasised that although the regulations do not prohibit the permanent use of SDRs such use would conflict with the spirit of the new facility since SDRs are intended to function in the longer period as money to hold in reserves rather than as money to spend.

Although at first sight the rules covering the new facility seem complex the basic principles are really quite simple and extremely ingenious. In essence, participating members of the IMF agree to extend credits to each other for indefinite periods in exchange for the right to receive credit in due course as it is needed. The system is multilateral since country A may transfer SDRs to country B and reconstitute them later by accepting a transfer from country C which has in the meantime accepted an equivalent transfer from country B. The system might be compared to a long-period multilateral version of the inter-central bank swap agreements. As a method of raising world reserves the SDR system is superior to a rise in the gold price since it avoids the waste of resources involved in the mining and storage of gold and the alleged political undesirability of a subsidy to South Africa and Russia. Also the reserve increases will not be allocated on the arbitrary basis of existing gold stocks and the size of the reserve increase can be controlled by the IMF in the light of 'agreed' needs, whereas an increase in the official gold price would need to be substantial to eliminate speculation on further rises unless one of the fancier schemes were adopted whereby the price would increase by a small percentage each month

---

[1] This is the total of SDRs allocated to a participant, less its share of any SDRs cancelled under Article 24, Section 2(a).

so as to raise the value of the existing stock of gold at an agreed rate. At a rate of creation of $3 billion per year the increase in world reserves would be about twice the absolute rate of reserve growth through monetary gold and foreign exchange which obtained in the period 1958-64. The way has been paved for the eventual demonetisation of gold and the creation of international reserves by book entries in an international central bank.

The Adjustment Mechanism: The introduction of SDRs may provide a long-term solution to the problem of adequate growth of world reserves but it will not solve the other main problem, that of correcting disequilibrium in the balance of payments of the major trading nations, i.e. the adjustment mechanism. Nothing could be more dangerous for the SDR system than the emergence of persistent debtor countries seeking to transfer their SDR holdings to a limited group of persistent creditor countries. At the time of writing the problem of adjustment had been solved, for the time being, for the UK, France and Germany, by the orthodox IMF method of parity changes,[1] though not without severe speculative crises in each case, but the persistent deficit in the US balance of payments remained to be corrected. The practical solution for the US problem has been indicated but this is impossible as long as the gold value of the dollar remains a sacred cow to the monetary authorities of the US. It has been said (as was said of sterling before 1967) that a devaluation of the dollar in terms of gold would be a breach of faith with non-resident official holders of dollar balances. But since March 1968 it has been clear that the US obligation to convert dollars into gold (for central banks) could be maintained only as long as the demand for such conversions was negligible! No gold is apparently to be preferred to some gold. The problem is made more confused by arguments that the world is now on a dollar standard and that there is no reason why the US deficit should be corrected or, indeed, that such action might be positively harmful. These arguments overlook the fact that, as long as separate national currencies remain, the non-residents of the US will only be prepared to hold the current stock of non-resident dollars at the right (i.e. equilibrium) prices in terms of their own currencies. Thus, if the non-dollar world considers that the US deficit should be corrected and the rate of growth of non-resident dollar holdings checked, without an increase in the official price of gold, the remedy is an upward revaluation of their currencies in terms of the dollar. But countries are notoriously reluctant to revalue their currencies and the orderly achievement of such a general parity change presents serious technical problems. Consequently there has been a growing weight of opinion in favour of the introduction of more flexibility into the exchange rate system in the hope, perhaps misguided, that national states will be prepared to accept a change in their exchange rate stemming from an automatic market mechanism that they would not be prepared to introduce by means of their own discretionary policy.

Freely Flexible Exchange Rates: The most extreme suggestion is that the IMF system of fixed rates should be abandoned in favour of a system of completely flexible rates in which the value of every currency should be determined, in terms of every other currency, by the operation of market forces, without intervention by the monetary authorities. Three major advantages are claimed for such a system. The *first* is that the need for official reserves is abolished[2] since supply and demand are equated in the foreign exchange market by price changes, it being assumed that markets are stable in the sense that an excess demand for a particular currency will be eliminated by an increase in its price in terms

---

[1] In the German case the unorthodox touch of preceding the change in par value by a period of managed flexibility was essentially the result of domestic political considerations.

[2] Actually reserves are still needed in so far as speculators intervene to stabilise the market, but these are privately owned.

of other currencies. The *second* claimed advantage is that adjustment to disequilibrium is gradual, and not sudden, since the exchange rate can respond slowly to the operation of trend forces, provided that the disequilibrium is generated in such a way. *Thirdly,* that such a system would eliminate the massive foreign exchange crises that arise under the present system when currencies become clearly overvalued, or undervalued, by a substantial amount, so that speculators can make substantial profits by anticipating the currency change and by the resulting 'hot-money' flows can justify their own speculative expectations in the absence of inter-central bank cooperation. In addition, a number of other technical advantages are claimed, e.g. that a country can insulate itself from world inflation by allowing its currency to appreciate and that flexible rates may be *de facto* alternatives to import restrictions and exchange controls when countries with weak currencies are reluctant to devalue.

The case for and against flexible rates depends essentially on the view which is taken of the effects of speculators in the operation of free markets. If these markets are to be cleared continuously, with narrow fluctuations, it is essential that speculators take over the role of the monetary authorities and operate in a stabilising manner. This follows, in part, because daily imbalances in foreign exchange demand and supply will result from seasonal and random factors even if the balance of payments is basically in equilibrium over a longer time span, and also from the fact that short-period trading adjustments to relative price changes are likely to be inelastic. The proponents of flexible exchange rates take the view that the role of speculators will be stabilising and that a body of professional speculators will emerge who will be able to predict the trend value of the exchange rate and will act so as to ensure minimal variations in the actual rate around the trend value. Opponents fear that this will not be the case, that trends in equilibrium exchange rates are not so easily predicted and that the foreign exchange market will imitate the behaviour so often seen in stock or commodity markets, where alternating moods of optimism and pessimism lead to substantial price variations in the short period, and a decline in prices is taken as a signal to sell rather than buy, with destabilising consequences. When one considers a worldwide system of flexible exchange rates the opportunities for errors of prediction and the potential for disturbances seem very great.

The view taken of the effects of speculation determines the importance of the remaining objections to a system of flexible rates. The *first* of these is that such a system would inhibit trade and investment by introducing uncertainties about future levels of exchange rates. Defenders of the system reply that narrow fluctuations are unimportant for trade and that speculative risks can be eliminated if traders operate in the forward exchange market, whilst investment risks cannot be eliminated even under fixed exchange rates. Opponents believe that fluctuations will not be narrow and that they will hinder the efficiency of international trade, especially if rates fluctuate with no pronounced upward or downward trend, as they may well do in the medium-period. They also believe that destabilising speculation may make facilities in the forward market either unavailable or too costly. The *second* argument against flexible rates is that if they fluctuate substantially there is a serious risk of a 'ratchet effect' which increases the rate of inflation. A depreciation of the home currency raises import and export prices in the home currency, with secondary effects. The following appreciation ought to reverse the price effects of the initial depreciation, but will not do so because of downward wage and price rigidity. Thus a series of fluctuations around the trend value will create an extra discontinuous upward pressure on prices. The *third* argument against is that substantial actual fluctuations in rates will require continuously variable monetary/fiscal policy to offset the effects of successive depreciation and appreciation on the absorption and release of resources. Present skills are unlikely to be equal to such a task. Naturally, this offsetting policy is not required if the short-term response of trade flows to rate changes is negligible, but in this case the flexible exchange rate system serves no useful purpose and the stability of such a system in the sense of narrow fluctuations around the average rate is dependent entirely on the correct response by speculators.

Managed Flexibility: It is extremely improbable that the governments of the leading nations in international trade would ever agree to a system of completely free and flexible exchange rates. Even if they were prepared to abandon fixed parities they would wish to intervene in foreign exchange markets to smooth out short-period variations, whilst allowing longer-run trends to be established. One snag with this policy aim is that there is no official handbook which explains how to distinguish between a short-term and a long-term influence. The second snag is that whilst this system of *managed flexibility* is possible for individual countries in a world of mainly fixed rates it is impossible as a generalised system. Suppose there are forty countries. Then the law of combinations tells us that there are 780 exchange rates between pairs of countries, but of these only thirty-nine are independent (in the sense that they cannot be deduced from other rates) and there are forty countries trying to stabilise thirty-nine rates. The system is overdetermined and, unless the monetary authorities cooperate closely and pursue consistent policies, it might easily become a paradise for the arbitrageur and speculator. Such a system might work if every nation, except the US, operated on the rate between itself and the US, leaving cross-exchange rates to take care of themselves, but it would be necessary for the US to stand aside and make no attempt to influence these rates. Consequently the US could depreciate only if the rest of the world was prepared to appreciate—which brings us back to the previous impasse, not surprisingly, because the system described would differ from the IMF arrangements essentially only by the abolition of the formal parity and the 1 per cent limits around that parity.

Sliding Parities: A third type of approach to greater flexibility is provided by various schemes for what are called 'sliding parities'[1]. These schemes require that parities should change not by sudden jumps of 10 per cent, 20 per cent, etc. but at a slow rate of, say, one-sixth per cent per month, or 2 per cent per annum. In the Williamson version countries would still specify a par value for their currency and the procedure for a change would resemble that under the present IMF arrangements except that the parity change once approved by the IMF would be effected over a number of years, at 2 per cent per annum. Such a scheme would make it possible to discuss devaluation as a policy without precipitating a speculative crisis since the potential gains to speculators would be drastically reduced. The great demerit of the system is that the parity change does not begin until fundamental disequilibrium is recognised and by then the overvaluation of the currency may be so great that a slow depreciation is really pointless. Another version of the sliding parity would abandon the fixed parity altogether and make the actual parity a trailing moving average of the actual values during a given previous period, with the monetary authorities required to stabilise exchange rates within a small percentage range of the sliding parity. Thus every day on which the currency stood below its moving average value in foreign exchange would cause a further reduction in the par value itself and permit a further slight reduction in the actual exchange rate, etc. etc. This method would allow modest year-to-year changes in exchange rates and continuous adjustment to disequilibrium at a modest rate whilst eliminating the possibility of serious speculation of a destabilising nature. The system would be very complicated to administer unless all par values were defined in terms of gold or in a central currency like the US dollar, in which case, as with managed flexibility, the dollar could only depreciate in terms of other cur-

---

[1] See J. H. Williamson, *The Crawling Peg,* Essays in International Finance, no. 50, Princeton University Press, 1965; J. Black, 'A Proposal for the Reform of Exchange Rates', *E. J.,* June 1966; J. E. Meade, 'Exchange Rate Flexibility', *Three Banks Review,* no. 70, June 1966.

rencies if they appreciated in terms of the dollar unless a sliding depreciation of the dollar in terms of gold were permitted.

The chief advantage of the sliding parity schemes is that they promise to avoid the major speculative crises that arise under the present IMF system when gross parity changes are anticipated. They also allow smooth adjustment to disequilibrium in the balance of payments. But the schemes are not without disadvantages. An implication of slow adjustment is that considerable emphasis is placed on the need for reserves to buffer the transition from disequilibrium to equilibrium and this may imply the need for a considerable degree of continuing cooperation between central banks. Also, whilst admirably suited to deal with a slowly developing disequilibrium such as that generated by a small upward trend in relative prices, they could easily break down if a country developed a sudden and substantial change in its competitive position such as might be caused by a wage and price explosion. It has been suggested that the knowledge that, under such a system, accommodating finance would have to be provided from other countries, might induce governments to be less concerned with the task of controlling inflation. The major disadvantage of such schemes would arise in relation to short-term capital movements. If it were known or expected that a particular country was to depreciate at, say, 2 per cent per annum it would be necessary to raise short-term interest rates in that country by 2 per cent in order to prevent an outflow of short-term capital. Alternatively, and having the same effect, owners of non-resident balances would need to be given some gold or foreign exchange guarantee to prevent capital losses. But once the principle of compensation is accepted there is no reason why this should not be adopted under the present international monetary system and then the case for change is much less strong. Changes in par values would be freed from the taint of 'immorality' and could be decided purely on the basis of commercial factors, and even a reserve currency country could contemplate small parity changes at more frequent intervals. The problem of speculation would not be eliminated completely since leads and lags might create difficulties and the prospect of upward changes in parities could still lead to speculation but the problems would be reduced in magnitude for smaller parity changes and, in any case, could be mitigated by various administrative devices. The whole question is now under official discussion in the IMF and elsewhere and it will be interesting to see what proposals emerge in due course.

REFERENCES AND FURTHER READING

R. E. Caves, and Associates, *Britain's Economic Prospects,* Brookings Institution and George Allen and Unwin, 1968.

C. P. Kindleberger, *International Economics,* Irwin, 1968.

F. Machlup, *Remaking the International Monetary System,* Committee for Economic Development and Johns Hopkins, 1968.

C. McMahon, *Sterling in the Sixties,* Oxford University Press, 1964.

W. B. Reddaway, *Effects of UK Direct Investment Overseas: An Interim Report,* Cambridge, 1967, *Final Report,* Cambridge University Press, 1968.

W. M. Scammell, *International Monetary Policy,* Macmillan, 1964.

S. J. Wells, *British Export Performance,* Cambridge University Press, 1964.

G. D. N. Worswick and P. H. Ady, *The British Economy in the 1950s,* Oxford University Press, 1962.

Official Publications
Bank of England Quarterly Bulletin.
Board of Trade Journal (weekly).

Economic Trends (regular analyses of balance of payments in March, June, September and December issues).

IMF Annual Report.

NEDC Reports, especially *Export Trends* (1963) and *Imported Manufactures* (1965).

Report of Committee on the Working of the Monetary System, Radcliffe Report, Cmnd 827, 1959.

Report on Overseas Trade (Board of Trade, monthly trade statistics).

UK Balance of Payments Pink Book (CSO, annually).

4

Industry and commerce

I   INTRODUCTION: SOME THEORETICAL BACKGROUND

This chapter is concerned with the behaviour of firms and industries. The orthodox micro-economic theory, incorporating the hypothesis that firms act as if maximising profit (net revenue),[1] can give us many insights in this area and lead to important conclusions over various government policy issues that are involved. However, the theory does not answer all the questions which arise. For instance, it is silent on the optimum conditions for tech-nological advance, and also on the way in which firms arrive at various equilibrium out-comes (as distinct from what these outcomes will be). The first is a vital contemporary issue in micro-economics, and the second can also be very important, especially in the con-text of government policy seeking to influence firms' behaviour in particular areas, e.g. in choosing locations.

Currently, there are a number of alternative theories of firms' behaviour. Among them is a group of 'managerial' models, whose origin is a recognition of the current divorce of ownership (by shareholders) and control (by top management) in large UK and US firms.[2] It is recognised that at least a survival level of profit must be earned (i.e. enough to satisfy existing and potential shareholders) and also that profit may be important to managers for other reasons (e.g. stock option schemes, profits-linked bonuses, etc.). But it is argued that where top management exercises the degree of control over policy that it appears to do in practice, firms are most likely to be made to behave in such a way as to maximise the value of variables yielding utility or satisfaction to managers, subject to some over-riding profit or other financial constraint. The variables regarded as giving rise to managerial utility vary from model to model. In Baumol's the firm is assumed to maximise sales re-venue, subject to a profit constraint.[3] Marris has developed an alternative, growth-maxi-mising model, subject to a security (stock market valuation) constraint.[4] Williamson has put forward a more general model of managerial utility, in which the objective function (i.e. the array of variables by which the firm is motivated) incorporates salary, the num-ber and quality of subordinates, control over discretionary investment, and expenditure on managerial perquisites of one kind or another.[5]

Firms pursuing such objectives would usually arrive at equilibrium outcomes which differ from those of a conventional profit-maximiser, e.g. in terms of price and output. They would often also respond differently to changes in the business environment, e.g. tax rates. Hence, in analysing firms' behaviour and in assessing the effects of government policy, we should generally reach different conclusions depending on the theoretical

[1]   See, e.g. R. G. Lipsey, *An Introduction to Positive Economics* (2nd edn.) Weidenfeld and Nicolson, 1966.

[2]   For details see A. A. Berle and G. C. Means, *The Modern Corporation and Private Property* (revised edn.), Harcourt Brace & World, 1968; and P. Sargant Florence, *Ownership, Control and Success of Large Companies,* Sweet & Maxwell, 1961.

[3]   W. J. Baumol, 'On the Theory of Oligopoly', *Economica,* August 1958, and *Business Behaviour, Value and Growth,* Macmillan, 1959.

[4]   R. Marris, 'A Model of the Managerial Enterprise', *Quarterly Journal of Economics,* May 1963, and *The Economic Theory of Managerial Capitalism,* Macmillan, 1964.

[5]   O. E. Williamson, 'Managerial Discretion and Business Behaviour', *American Economic Review,* December 1963, and *The Economics of Discretionary Behaviour: Business Objectives in a Theory of the Firm,* Prentice Hall, 1964.

model of behaviour. Unfortunately, there is no clear way of telling, at the moment, which model should be adopted. Empirical testing of the hypotheses has produced some evidence in support of each, but none of the theories—including profit maximisation— has yet been accepted as demonstrably superior. In this situation the most we can do when looking at the behaviour of firms and industries is to be very clear on the theoretical assumptions we make and, especially when appraising public policy issues, consider the various responses which might be expected under different models of the firm.

Alongside the managerial theories is another, somewhat more radical new theoretical departure. The 'behavioural' theory emphasises the organisational aspects of firms, and the limited amount of knowledge available in decision-making.[1] In the behavioural theory the firm is seen to pursue a number of goals in the form of independent, aspiration-level constraints—e.g. a particular sum of profits or level of sales or a target rate of return on capital—which firms attempt to 'satisfy'. Goals are imperfectly rationalised, may conflict, and receive sequential rather than simultaneous attention. Over time, aspiration levels for a particular goal will change in the light of past achievements in relation to past attainment. The firm is seen as an adaptive organism, solving pressing problems rather than attempting to apply plans leading to optimal, equilibrium values or growth paths of decision variables, as in more conventional approaches. In a situation of imperfect knowledge, search (the acquisition of information) is neither continuous nor determined optimally as an investment decision. Rather, search is 'problemistic', requiring to be motivated, for example, by adverse feedback on goal fulfilment or by some external event or evidence of failure. Search is 'limited' or 'narrow'; solutions are sought at first in the neighbourhood of problem symptoms and current alternatives and search widens only as satisfactory solutions fail to be found. In choosing among alternative strategies 'satisficing' procedures are adopted, the first acceptable strategy being selected. The firm's behaviour is constrained by standard procedural rules governing search, choice, etc., and these are abandoned only under duress. However, in the long haul the firm 'learns' from experience, and this 'learning' takes the form of search and choice rules being adapted. Typically, firms exhibit organisational slack in the form of excess resources within the organisation.

In order to derive quantitative predictions of firms' behaviour from the behavioural model it is necessary to develop specific models. However, the theory does permit of some general, qualitative analysis without this. One distinguishing feature of the behavioural model is that it specifically sets out to embody the decision process. Thus, unlike all the other models so far mentioned, the behavioural model *does* tell us how various outcomes are arrived at as well as what the outcomes will be.

The theoretical approaches to firms' behaviour so far discussed have generally been conceived with the private sector of the economy in mind and, especially, 'secondary' manufacturing industry rather than the 'primary' sector (agriculture and the extractive industries) and the 'tertiary' sector (transport, distributive trades, professional and other services, government administration, etc.). Nevertheless, there are some insights which they can give in all areas of industry and commerce, whether public or private. And the scope of this chapter is by no means limited to the private manufacturing sector only. Some of the issues we shall consider do mainly concern the private sector and manufacturing in particular (e.g. the question of monopoly control). But in another section we also consider the public sector issue of pricing and investment criteria for nationalised industries. And a number of the issues considered are common to both the public and private sectors and all industry and commerce, e.g. price control and the whole question of efficiency, productivity and technical progress.

---

[1]   H. A. Simon, 'A Behavioural Model of Rational Choice', *Quarterly Journal of Economics,* February 1955. R. M. Cyert and J. G. March, *A Behavioural Theory of the Firm,* Prentice-Hall, 1963. See also H. A. Simon 'Theories of Decision-Making in Economics and Behavioural Science', *American Economic Review,* June 1959.

II   THE GROWTH OF OUTPUT BY INDUSTRY 1950-69 AND THE SIZE STRUCTURE OF INDUSTRIES AND TRADES

II.1   Factors Determining Industry Growth Rates

Whatever our model of firms' behaviour, it is helpful to discuss the factors causing industries to expand or decline as they do in relation to industry demand and supply schedules such as we meet in orthodox theory.[1] Assuming, initially, that each industry produces a single homogeneous product, its growth may be conceived of as the movement to the right of the point of intersection between its demand and supply curves as time passes. Since such movements will occur only as a result of shifts in either the demand or supply curve, or both, any factor which can bring about such shifts will be a contributory determinant of the industry's rate of growth. From micro-economic theory we might expect the main factors on the demand side to be: changes in consumer taste, which could be purely autonomous or, for example, induced by advertising campaigns; changes in the relative prices of the outputs of different industries, since these will lead consumers to substitute the now cheaper for the now more expensive goods; and changes in consumer incomes, which will increase the demand for all except 'inferior' goods. On the supply side, the factors we seek are those affecting firms' production costs, since it is these which ultimately determine supply schedules. One obvious example will be technical progress in the form of process innovation—new techniques of production—the effect of which will be to shift cost curves downwards and hence supply curves to the right. The other main factor will be changes in the prices of the various inputs, due to changes in the equilibrium levels of price and output in factor and raw materials markets and, in some cases, to autonomous influences on the supply of primary inputs, for example population growth or shifts in relative income/leisure preferences and in the supply of labour.

The factors listed so far undoubtedly are important in the real world, but there are others. We can begin to see this when we qualify the preceding analysis to make it more realistic. First, we have so far thought of an industry's growth as occurring only via a movement from one equilibrium point to another. If in practice there are factors making for disequilibrium (e.g. temporary shortages of inputs or administered prices giving rise to excess demand or supply) an industry's growth may include movements towards or away from equilibrium outputs (as these factors appear or disappear) as well as or instead of equilibrium changes. Secondly, no industry really produces a single, homogeneous product. The industries in table 4.1, for instance, group together the outputs of different establishments whose principal products (i.e. products accounting for the largest proportion of total output) are not identical, but nevertheless do have some similarities mainly in terms of physical or technical properties.[2] Taking this into account we must think of an industry as facing not a single demand and supply curve, but rather sets of demand and supply curves for each product. We can expect the factors so far discussed to be at

---

[1]   If profit-maximising behaviour is not assumed, the demand curve is perhaps best thought of as an 'ideal' or 'boundary' curve, indicating what could be achieved, and firms may be at points on or below it. The supply curve is not so easily treated, for in given circumstances non-profit-maximising firms might supply *more or less* than a profit maximiser, depending upon its mode of behaviour. But a supply schedule of some sort must exist under any model of firms' behaviour.

[2]   The industries in table 4.1 are those of the official Standard Industrial Classification (SIC) on which nearly all government statistics are based. An 'establishment' is '. . . the whole of the premises under the same ownership or management at particular address', i.e. a 'factory' or 'plant' rather than a 'firm' or 'enterprise', which are units of ownership and control. The SIC divides economic activity into twenty-four *Orders,* which are broad groupings and are subdivided into *Minimum List Headings* and, in some cases, even finer subdivisions. In table 4.1 all except vehicles, shipbuilding, textiles and clothing are *Orders.*

work in each sub-market, and so the analysis still applies, with the simple qualification that growth for the group as a whole is the algebraic sum of developments in each individual sector. However, by introducing heterogeneity of industry output we also introduce a new factor affecting industry growth, namely the addition of successful new products to the existing range, or product innovation. Where such new products are intermediate goods—raw materials or other inputs for industrial users—rather than final consumption goods, their introduction clearly may have secondary affects on the growth of the user industry via the changes they induce in production methods, input costs or character of final product.

Recognition that the output of most industries is partly for final use and partly for intermediate use by other industries suggests a further factor affecting an industry's growth, i.e. changes in the fortunes of important user industries. But it should be remembered that these in turn would be ultimately attributable to the effects of basic factors of the sort already discussed, and would include, *inter alia,* changes in the supply prices and product specifications of the supplying industry, whose growth we are considering. Other additional modifications to our analysis might include bringing the role of the government into account. The government may influence growth rates by direct administrative intervention, or by participating in consumption, investment and production, or via fiscal and monetary policy, all of which generally have differential effects on different industries. Also, we should include the degree to which an industry participates in external trade as a factor affecting its growth record, since this determines how far it will be affected by developments in the world economy and by devaluation, etc. Finally, the question of firms' motivation and behaviour must be raised again. The various models discussed in the previous section suggest different behaviour patterns over things like R & D activity and response to cost increases and demand opportunities, etc. Such behavioural differences would result in the selection of different growth rates in given circumstances. Thus any inter-industry differences in the extent to which firms followed one pattern of behaviour or another would affect relative industry growth rates, and any changes in behaviour within an industry over time would affect that industry's growth.

It is not too difficult to find examples of the influence of many of the factors discussed above in UK industries over the past two decades. Before seeking to do this it will be helpful to set out a bare statistical outline of the growth of output by industry over the period.

II.2   The Growth of Output by Industry 1950-69: A Statistical Outline

The first column of figures in table 4.1 shows annual growth rates of eighteen major UK industry groups, manufacturing as a whole and GDP for the period 1950-69. The underlying growth trend is shown in each case, year-to-year fluctuations having been eliminated by statistical means.[1] Growth of net output (GDP by industrial origin) is measured in real terms (i.e. after allowing for price increases).

Table 4.1 shows that individual industry growth rates have diverged markedly from the overall average of around 2.7 per cent per annum over the period. At one extreme the chemicals industries, the public utilities, engineering, vehicles, and insurance, banking, etc. have experienced very rapid growth, chemicals at more than double the rate for the economy as a whole. At the other extreme two industries show an overall decline, namely shipbuilding and mining. In both cases, however, the overall trend conceals markedly different growth trends in the subperiods 1950-6 and 1956-69. Up to 1956 mining output

---

[1]   The annual growth rate was estimated as λ such that $L_t = L_0 e^{\lambda t}$, where L_t is the current level of output, L_0 the base year level of output.

was maintained at a roughly constant level, while shipbuilding output actually grew at an underlying rate of around 3.4 per cent per annum. Thus it is in the second subperiod that the real decline occurred.[1] In only one other industry (as defined in table 4.1) has there been very little growth and that is textiles. Here virtually all of the expansion in output was concentrated in the second half of the 1960s, the growth then being sufficient (around 3.5 per cent per annum from 1964-9) to produce a small overall increase for the period as a whole.[2]

In two broad areas of activity it is useful to supplement table 4.1 with other information. The first is transport. Table 4.1 understates the growth of transport services alone, at least on the passenger side, because the output series there includes some other activities but takes no account of private motoring. Table 4.2. shows that this is the major explanation of the very rapid increase in passenger mileages travelled, at a rate of 4.8 per cent per annum from 1953-69. The full impact of private motoring on the public road and rail services cannot be measured. Certainly the whole of the *actual* declines shown in table 4.2 can fairly safely be attributed to this cause, but how much public passenger traffic might have risen had there been no dramatic increase in private motoring is unknown. Road services felt the effects of rising car ownership first, with an especially rapid fall in the mid 1950s and a further sharp reduction between 1964 and 1966, and it is mostly stage services that have been affected, as there has been some increase in contract work. On the railways, passenger traffic rose slowly to a plateau in the late 1950s, but fell off rapidly thereafter. Despite very rapid growth (a more than threefold rise in ten years to 1968) inland air traffic is still of only slight importance except on certain particular routes. In the inland freight transport sector, however, table 4.3 shows that the growth rate for transport in table 4.1 (2.43 per cent per annum) is much more nearly in line with the overall increase in freight services measured in ton-miles. Table 4.3 also reveals that there has been a major reallocation of freight traffic between rail and road services, just as there has in passenger traffic.

The second broad area where it is useful to consider additional growth data is fuel. Growth trends in the various energy-producing industries become more meaningful when we consider what has been happening to direct consumption of the primary fuels. Between 1952 and 1968 UK fuel consumption increased much less rapidly than GDP, growth in one being 32.5 per cent compared with nearly 57 per cent for the other.[3] Over the period the direct use of coal fell markedly in both absolute and percentage terms, while there were quite dramatic increases for both oil and electricity (table 4.4). Quantities of gas consumed fell slightly up to 1961, recovered sharply in 1963-4 to the 1950 level, and have since continued to rise strongly, the turnround in the industry's fortunes being due

---

1   In the late 1960s shipbuilding staged a substantial recovery in terms of work on order and in hand, but by end 1969 this had yet to be reflected in output figures. See below p. 162.

2   The growth in this later period was far from steady, however. After regaining the 1950 level of output in 1964, the level then remained fairly stable until 1967 followed by a very sharp increase in 1968 and some further advance in 1969.

3   Although the difference between these two figures is perhaps surprising at first sight, too close a degree of correspondence is not to be expected. An 'energy coefficient' (i.e. percentage growth of fuel consumption per 1 per cent of growth of GDP) of less than one may be expected in industrial fuel consumption (around 60 per cent of total consumption) as a result of technical economies in fuel use and also of structural changes in the economy if, for instance, faster growing industries are not intensive fuel users. Domestic consumption is presumably a function of the price of fuel (as a whole) and of household incomes. Their precise effects are not immediately clear, but for whatever reason, consumers' expenditure on fuel and light has in fact grown more or less in line with total personal consumption expenditure, and hence slightly more slowly than GDP.

TABLE 4.1

UK Growth of Output 1950-69 and GDP by Industrial Origin, 1968

	Annual Rate of Growth (% p.a. 1950 -69 cumula- tive)[1]	Mean Residual Variance around Trend (%)[2]	Output in 1968	
			£ million	% of GDP
Agriculture, forestry and fishing	2.48[3]	1.6	1,127	3.1
Mining and quarrying	−1.44	3.4	687	1.9
Manufacturing				
Food, drink and tobacco	2.49	0.8	1,405	3.9
Chemicals and allied industries	5.65	2.6	1,187	3.3
Metal manufacturing	1.78	4.0	1,003	2.8
Engineering and allied industries	3.62	1.9	5,235	14.4
Shipbuilding and marine engineering	−1.79	6.6[4]	(251)	(0.7)
Vehicles and aircraft	3.96	5.7	(1,355)	(3.7)
Textiles	0.69	5.4	937	2.6
Clothing	1.80	3.5	452	1.2
Other manufacturing	3.53	3.2	2,308	6.4
Total manufacturing	3.15	2.2	12,527	34.5
Construction	3.23	2.5	2,456	6.8
Gas, electricity and water	5.05	1.4	1,288	3.6
Transport and communications	2.43[3]	2.0	3,065	8.5
Distributive trades	2.80[3]	1.6	4,082	11.3
Insurance, banking and finance	3.98[3]	2.1	1,206	3.3
Professional and scientific services	2.97[3]	0.9	4,731	13.0
Miscellaneous services	2.28[3]	2.1		
GDP[5]	2.69	1.2	36,267	100.0

Source: Derived from *NIER* and *NIBB* data.
Notes: [1] See p. 154.
[2] See p. 157.
[3] 1950-1968 only.
[4] See footnote 1, p. 157.
[5] Includes public services and administration, defence, ownership of dwellings, stock appreciation and residual error.

initially to the use of cheaper, imported, natural gas supplies and reformed refinery gas, and more recently to the use of North Sea gas.[1]

The impact of these trends on direct fuel consumption can be related to the output trends of the relevant industries in table 4.1 in the following way. The very rapid increase in petroleum is concealed within, and contributes to, the high rate of growth of chemical and allied industries. The growth rate of the public utilities as a whole understates that of electricity at least up to 1964, since gas was virtually stagnant. In mining and quarrying (in which coal represents over nine-tenths of output) the overall decline in output has been

---

[1] North Sea gas made its first measurable contribution to UK fuel supplies only in 1968, when it provided some 82 million therms out of a total of 55,110 million therms from all sources. By 1969 North Sea gas was supplying 8-9 per cent of energy supplies. At 1.2p per therm, the cost of North Sea gas compares with around 2.9-3.3p per therm for imported and refinery gas, and 5.4p per therm for gas produced by the traditional carbonisation process.

much smaller than the fall in direct consumption of coal and up to 1954 output was in fact rising. The main reason for this is that although electricity competes with coal in *direct* fuel consumption, the industry is itself a very large coal consumer. Thus the decline in direct coal consumption has been to some extent offset by rising sales to the electricity industry, whose share in total coal sales has risen over the period from less than 20 per cent to some 44.5 per cent.

Turning to table 4.1 once more, we can also see that there is a good deal of inter-industry difference in the steadiness with which expansion takes place. The second column of figures conveys an impression of the extent to which there were year to year oscillations around the underlying growth trend for each industry.[1] The figures may be meaningfully compared between industries—for example we can say that the output series for metal manufacturing was twice as volatile as that for transport and communications. The figures also have an absolute significance, which is that we can say that taking all the years to-gether the susceptibility of, for example, the chemicals industry to fluctuations in output was of the same magnitude as if output had been successively just over 2½ per cent above trend in one year and 2½ per cent below trend the next. In practice, the actual pattern of

TABLE 4.2

UK Inland Passenger Mileage 1953-68[1]   ('000m passenger miles)

Year	Air	Rail	Road Public service vehicles	Road Private transport	Total
1953	0.2 (0.2%)	24.1 (20.6%)	50.7 (43.3%)	42.1 (35.9%)	117.1 (100%)
1960	0.5 (0.3%)	24.8 (15.6%)	43.9 (27.7%)	89.4 (56.4%)	158.6 (100%)
1968	1.2 (0.5%)	21.1 (8.9%)	36.7 (15.5%)	177.7 (75.1%)	236.7 (100%)
% change 1953-68	+500%	−12.4%	−27.6%	+322.1%	+102.1% (=4.8% p.a.)

Source: AAS

[1] Percentage figures in parenthesis show respective contributions to the total in any one year.

year-to-year fluctuations would invariably be much more erratic than this. And the maxi-mum year-to-year changes in actual output would usually be much more than twice the figure shown in table 4.1. For instance, the largest year-to-year change of all was in tex-tiles, 1951-2, and amounted to 18 per cent of the industry's output in 1951.

The third column in table 4.1 does bring out the fact that, in general, it is the manu-facturing sector which contains most of the industries most susceptible to fluctuations in output. The service trades in particular exhibit output series which are fairly stable. Generally speaking, an industry will tend to be more prone to fluctuations in output if its products are mainly industrial inputs, for example raw materials for intermediate use (as in much of chemicals and in metal manufacturing), rather than consumer goods, expecially those which are basic necessities (e.g. food). And industries producing invest-ment goods (like machine tools, construction and commercial vehicles) are particularly

---

[1] The figure for shipbuilding is exaggerated, on account of purely statistical reasons; in fact year-to-year fluctuations in output have not been excessively large. The figure for mining in table 4.1 may also be a slight exaggeration. Other figures may be taken as they stand.

TABLE 4.3

UK Inland Freight Transport 1952-68[1]   ('000m ton-miles)

Year	Road	Rail	Coastal Shipping	Inland Waterways	Pipelines[2]	Total
1952	18.8 (37.2%)	22.4 (44.4%)	9.0 (17.8%)	0.2 (0.4%)	0.1 (0.2%)	50.5 (100%)
1960	30.1 (51.3%)	18.7 (31.9%)	9.5 (16.2%)	0.2 (0.3%)	0.2 (0.3%)	58.7 (100%)
1968	44.0 (58.3%)	14.7 (19.5%)	15.3 (20.3%)[3]	0.1 (0.1%)	1.4 (1.9%)	75.5 (100%)
% increase 1952-68	+134.0%	−34.4%	+70%	−50%	+1,300%	+49.5% (=2.5% per annum)

Source: AAS

[1] Percentage figures in parenthesis show respective contributions to the total in any one year.

[2] Excludes movements of gases by pipeline.

[3] New series begun in 1967 on basis of statute miles at sea (previously equivalent inland mileage). 1967 on old basis was 10.8 compared with 15.5 on new basis. Taking this into account the 'true' increase in coastal shipping 1952-68 would be +18.9 per cent; the true increase in total freight transport would be 40.4 per cent (=2.1 per cent per annum); and the share of coastal shipping in the total in 1968 would be 15.1 per cent.

TABLE 4.4

UK Fuel Consumption 1952-68[1]   (Tons of coal or coal equivalent, direct use)

Year	Coal	Electricity	Petroleum	Gas	Total Fuel[2]
1952	114.8 (49.7%)	38.0 (16.5%)	24.8 (10.7%)	20.0 (8.7%)	230.8 (100%)
1960	91.1 (34.5%)	64.5 (24.5%)	54.4 (20.6%)	18.7 (7.1%)	263.7 (100%)
1968[3]	52.2 (17.1%)	99.5 (32.5%)	103.3 (33.8%)	26.0 (8.5%)	305.8 (100%)
% Change 1952-68	−54.5%	+161.8%	+316.5%	+30.0%	+32.5% (=2.0% per annum)

Source: AAS

[1] Percentage figures in parenthesis show respective contributions to the total in any one year.

[2] Includes coke, breeze and other solid fuels, liquid fuel derived from coal and methane used at collieries.

[3] 1968 figures converted from therms.

susceptible to fluctuating demand conditions, due to such things as acceleration effects and also changes in fiscal and monetary policy. Of course, government policy also produces short-run demand fluctuations in some sections of personal consumption and investment, with direct implications for particular industries like vehicles (again) and housebuilding. In some industries, for instance aircraft and shipbuilding, a part of the observed fluctuations in output is due simply to the fact that output is 'lumpy', that is in units which are individually large relative to industry supply.

Table 4.1 also brings out that fluctuations in GDP as a whole, after allowing for the growth trend, are less than for individual industries, even service trades. Only two of the industries in table 4.1 show mean residual variances less than that for GDP, namely food, drink and tobacco, and professional and scientific services. This means that the ups and downs in the various industries must cancel each other out to a quite substantial extent. Such a thing is altogether to be expected when we note the considerable time that it will take for the effects of final demand changes to work through the economy and that the main impact of government restrictive measures does not fall simultaneously in all sectors.

II.3   Factors in the Growth of UK Industries 1950-69

Examples of the effect of rising incomes on the composition of demand as a factor influencing industry growth rates are fairly easily found. Thus, this is probably the main factor underlying the comparatively slow growth trend in food, drink and tobacco, on the one hand, and on the other hand it is almost certainly the main explanation of the rapid extension of car ownership and consequent very fast growth of vehicle production.[1] However, the effects of autonomous changes in taste and of the role of advertising, etc. as determinants of growth are not directly observable. An area where relative price move-ments have probably exerted at least a reinforcing effect is in the pattern of development of passenger transport services. Both rail and bus fares have risen very much faster over the period than have private motoring costs, with the main increases in both cases coming when traffic falls were greatest. However, it is not entirely clear how far these price move-ments have been the result rather than the cause of changes in traffic, and this problem of distinguishing cause and effect is invariably encountered when attempting to explore the effects of relative price movements. There are at least two other important areas where substantial relative price movements have occurred. These are chemical production and fuel use—in particular consumption of oil as against coal. In 1969 the price index of out-put of the chemical and allied industries was only about 11 per cent above its level in 1952, compared with a rise for all manufacturing industry of some 40 per cent.[2] In the other case, oil prices fell some 14 per cent in 1958 with the emergence of a world oil surplus and, despite the imposition of taxes on fuel oil to protect coal,[3] fuel oil prices have risen much less markedly than coal since the 1950s. Comparatively speaking, these are fairly clearcut cases, where there is a strong *prima facie* case for thinking that the price move-ments mentioned have been important causes of the changes in consumption of the pro-ducts concerned.

Unravelling the various factors affecting industries' costs and supply prices—input prices changes, innovation, etc.—is, again, a difficult business which really requires fairly sophisticated statistical methods. In the absence of this, a little can be said about one factor at work—process innovation—if we are prepared to accept that the 'residual' ele-ment in the growth of industries' output (i.e. the amount of the increase in output which is not accounted for by increases in the quantity of resources employed, but represents *more effective use of resources*) is a proxy measure of the rate of technical progress (ex-

---

[1]   The number of private cars currently licensed in Great Britain rose from 2.8 million in 1953 to 10.8 million in 1968.

[2]   *NIER*, February 1970, p.53, notes a general tendency *within* chemicals over the period 1963-8 for an inverse relationship between the rates of growth of various branches and their rates of increase in prices. In particular, the industries whose output rose fastest (synthetic resins and plastics, pharmaceuticals, organic chemicals) were also those actually reducing prices. The ex-planation offered is that 'rapidly expanding output helped to keep prices down and the relatively low prices generated further demand'. The link between expanding output and keeping prices down would presumably be scale economies.

[3]   In 1961 a 0.83p per gallon duty on fuel oils was imposed (equivalent to a £1. 15 per ton subsidy on coal). Fuel oil duty has subsequently been further increased.

cluding product innovation) in the industry. The residuals for nineteen UK industries over the period 1948-62 are set out in the final column of table 4.5. Careful comparison of the ranking of the industries in table 4.5 in terms of output growth and size of residual will suggest that there is a definite correspondence between the two, although with noteworthy exceptions, for example textiles (ranking 19 in terms of output growth and 8 in terms of residual), transport, etc. (15 and 7), distribution (9 and 17), agriculture (12 and 4), and chemicals (2 and 10). A simple statistical test confirms that industries' output growth and rate of process innovation (as measured) are not independent of each other, but that the degree of association is not strong.[1] In view of all the other factors which have been suggested as influences on growth, this is what we should expect.

One industry whose growth is probably rarely, if ever, from one equilibrium point to another is housing and construction. Thus in the 1950s almost all private development was held in check by government controls and shortages of materials up to 1952. There then followed a period of five years of very rapid expansion of private housebuilding and other private construction work, while public housing expenditure fell by half from its previous high level.[2] And later on in the period 1950-69 the slumps and booms in building and construction activity which have occurred have probably contained a substantial element of oscillation around equilibrium levels.

An example of product innovation contributing substantially to output growth would be in chemicals, and within chemicals there is the particularly striking example of plastics materials, where physical quantities produced have increased more than sevenfold from 1950-68. Electronics would be a second example, and man-made fibres a third. Since 1958 output of synthetic materials (by weight) has nearly tripled, and this expansion has been a major contributory factor in the previously mentioned recovery of output in the textile group as a whole. On the other side of the coin, two industries where output has suffered from the emergence of competitive new products are leather and steel.

The interdependence of one industry's growth rate with another's, on account of flows of intermediate products, is apparent in many examples. Thus, the decline of a substantial steel-using sector—defence, railways, shipbuilding and coal—has been a factor in the slow growth of steel production. The fast growth of vehicles and some other engineering industries has given rise to rapidly growing demand for chemicals and rubber products (including in 'other manufacturing'). Rapidly rising electricity consumption (at some 6¾ per cent, per annum) has required rapid expansion in production of generating, switching and transmission gear for the national grid, and of insulated wire and cables.[3] Modest growth or decline in a number of mechanical engineering industries can be attributed to their supplying specialised plant and equipment to industries where neither growth prospects nor the level of investment have been high, for example textiles and agriculture (apart from vehicles). Finally, the comparatively slow growth of inland freight transport has had much to do with the decline in coal and coke production and slow growth in the steel industry (and a reduction of traffic movements per ton produced), since these industries are two heavy transport users. These two factors are also important in accounting for the declining share of rail which, being particularly suited to long-haul, large-bulk work, has always been heavily dependent on carrying coal and coke and crude materials.

---

[1]   The rank correlation coefficient is 0.4414, and is significantly different from zero at the 5 per cent level.

[2]   It is difficult to say how much of the change in public sector spending was due to a shift in the effective demand in that sector occasioned by the change in government.

[3]   In 1969, however, there was a cutback in CEGB investment orders, after it was found that the estimated margin of spare capacity in 1973 is now 30 per cent compared with a desired level of 17 per cent.

TABLE 4.5

UK Industrial Input and Output 1948-62: Rates of Growth by Industry

	Output	Employment	Capital	Total Factor Input[2]	Unexplained Residual
Agriculture	2.6	−1.8	2.5	−0.2	2.8
Mining	−0.1	−1.5	2.9	−1.0	0.9
Manufacturing					
Food, drink and tobacco	2.5	1.8	3.9	2.8	−0.3
Chemicals	5.7	1.5	6.5	4.0	1.7
Iron and steel[1]	3.1	0.7	4.6	2.2	0.9
Electrical engineering[1]	6.2	4.0	3.8	3.9	2.3
Non-electrical engineering[1]	2.0	1.1	4.0	1.8	0.2
Vehicles	5.6	1.9	3.8	2.2	3.4
Other metal manufacture[1]	2.1	1.1	3.2	1.7	0.4
Textiles	0.5	−1.1	−3.1	−1.6	2.1
Clothing	2.2	0.2	1.1	0.4	1.8
Bricks, pottery, glass	3.2	0.8	5.4	2.1	1.1
Timber and furniture	2.8	0.2	2.8	0.5	2.3
Paper and printing	5.3	2.3	2.7	2.4	2.9
Other manufacturing	3.1	1.2	2.9	1.6	1.5
Total Manufacturing	3.4	1.1	3.1	1.7	1.7
Construction	2.7	0.9	9.4	2.0	0.7
Gas, electricity and water	5.5	1.4	3.6	2.5	3.0
Transport and communications	2.1	−0.4	1.0	−0.1	2.2
Distribution	2.8	1.7	4.2	2.4	0.4
Total Services	1.7	0.3	2.4	0.9	0.8

Source: R. C. O. Matthews, 'Some Aspects of Postwar Growth in the British Economy in Relation to Historical Experience', *Manchester Statistical Society*, 1964.

[1] 1951-60, not 1948-62.

[2] Total factor input in year t is given by $\frac{F_t}{F_b} = (1 - a)\frac{L_t}{L_b} + a\frac{K_t}{K_b}$, where L is labour input, K is capital input, and a and $(1 - a)$ are the shares of capital and labour respectively in the base year b (1956).

Alongside these examples of the external effects of an industry's growth rate, we may put some other external effects, namely, those resulting from technological change, for example the effects on the steel industry of technical economies in steel use secured in user industries; and the replacement of coal by other fuels in many uses (e.g. the transfer to electricity in the iron and steel industry; to diesel fuel and electricity in rail transport; to oil and nuclear fuels in power generation subject to government protection of coal); and to oil, electricity and gas in industrial and domestic space heating.

The effects of government action on one industrial sector—building and construction—have already been mentioned. Another example here would be vehicles, where protection of the home market by import controls as well as tariffs was an important contributory factor to an especially high rate of growth between 1952 and 1960 (6.5 per cent per annum) and where short-term output movements, in particular, have been much affected by alterations in purchase tax and hire purchase regulations. The effects of government policy on output and output growth are perhaps most marked in a third industry, agriculture, and the agricultural support policy is discussed in section VI of this chapter. Shipbuilding is a fourth important example, and an industry whose recent recovery of the prospect of a more hopeful future is at least partly due to government assistance in various ways. Once a major UK industry, its decline since 1956 in a situation of surplus world capacity has lef it in 1969 with only a minor share of engineering output. However, orders and work in hand had risen to their highest level for ten years at end-1968, and rose still further in 1969. Of the four main factors responsible for this improvement, three are directly at-tributable to the government.[1] First, the government has since 1963 provided for the ex-tension of cheap credit to shipowners placing orders. Initially for a total of £75 million for foreign shipowners, the scheme has subsequently been extended to £400 million and to include UK shipowners as well; a further extension to £600 million is proposed at the time of writing. Secondly, the *1967 Shipbuilding Industry Act,* following the Geddes Report of 1966,[2] established a Shipbuilding Industry Board to promote and administer some £37. 5 million in grants and loans for a massive restructuring of the industry, in-volving greater specialisation between shipbuilding and marine engineering and in the con-struction of different types of ships. This restructuring exercise is now more or less com-plete. Thirdly, shipbuilding gained a considerable cost advantage in world competition fro the UK devaluation of 1967, which gave rise to an estimated 7-8 per cent cut in UK ship prices abroad.

Mention of the shipbuilding industry takes us into the final group of factors affecting industry growth rates, i.e. those concerned with external trade. The other once-important UK industry whose postwar growth has been most affected by foreign competition is textiles. Competition has come mainly from low-cost countries like Japan, eastern Europe Italy and Portugal. The main burden has fallen on cotton and low priced woollen textiles and goods (footwear has also been affected). Production for export (some 25 per cent of total output for the textiles leather and clothing group as a whole in the early 1950s) was affected first, and home sales as well in later years.[3]

ll.4   The Size Structure of Industries and Trades

Table 4.1 gives a breakdown by industry group of total national output in 1968.[4] Engineering (including vehicles and shipbuilding) and distribution are clearly the two

---

[1] The fourth has been the lengthening of delivery dates among foreign competitors, especially Japanese yards, from which foreign competition has previously been most acute.

[2] *Shipbuilding Industry Committee 1965-66 Report,* Cmnd 2937, HMSO, 1966.

[3] The government has also come to the aid of the textiles industry. The *1959 Cotton Industry Act* provided compensation for scrapped equipment and grants for modernisation. Later, import quota provided a measure of protection for the industry (from the mid-1960s onwards) and the Govern-ment has now accepted a recommendation for more permanent protection by a 15 per cent tariff on cotton imports, probably with effect from the beginning of 1972. Unlike shipbuilding, however the main structural change in textiles is probably still to come. W. S. Atkins and Partners, *The Strategic Future for The Wool Textile Industry,* NEDO, (for The Wool Textile EDC) HMSO 1969 envisages that the number of producers in the woollen industry will fall from 1,000 to 600 by 1975, and employment from 144,000 to 121,000. A Textiles Council Report *(Cotton and Allied Textiles: A Report on Present Performance and Future Prospects,* Manchester, The Council, 1969) suggests that in cotton, the number of producing units will fall from 715 to 300, and employment from 101,000 to 55,000. Both sets of figures assume an unchanged level of output. As stated earlier, the recovery in output in the textiles group (table 4.1) is due to man-made fibres rather than a recovery in traditional textiles production.

[4] GDP by industrial origin represents the value added [total sales *less* the value of goods and services currently used up in production (inputs from other industries and imports)] and is perhap the nearest approximation in value terms to the concept of work actually done by an industry.

largest individual groups, followed by transport and communications and construction. All the remaining sectors (excluding the two miscellaneous groups—other manufacturing and other services) accounted for less than 4 per cent of GDP. Of course it must be remembered that some of these groups (notably engineering) are really composed of a very large number of quite disparate sub-trades.

Changes over time in the size-ranking of different industries come about because of inter-industry differences in the rate of growth of real output and of output prices. Ignoring the latter, there have been only minor changes in the size-ranking of UK industries in terms of real output over the period 1950-68, despite the inter-industry differences in growth rates recorded in section II.2. Between these two dates gas, electricity and water rose from thirteenth largest position to eighth, chemicals, etc. from fourteenth to tenth, and insurance, banking and finance from twelfth to ninth, while mining fell from eighth to fourteenth, and textiles from ninth to thirteenth. But in all other cases movements have been of not more than one place in either direction, and six industries retained exactly the same rank. Similarly, since 1950 there have been only minor changes in the proportion of GDP originating in the main broad sectors of the economy. The share of manufacturing has increased somewhat—from under 32 per cent in 1950 to just over 34½ per cent in 1968—but the shares of other industrial production (i.e. agriculture, mining and quarrying, construction and the public utilities) and of commerce (i.e. those activities concerned with the distribution and exchange of goods between the points of production and final use, namely the distributive trades, transport and communications, and insurance, banking and finance) have remained almost unchanged at around 15½ per cent and 23 per cent respectively. It is in the remaining sector, miscellaneous services, public administration and defence, etc. that one finds the decline offsetting the enlarged share of manufacturing.

Rapid alteration in the shares of output originating in these broad sectors of the economy is not to be expected. Over the very long term, as economies develop from relatively primitive states, there appears to be a general tendency for the bulk of economic activity to shift from the primary to secondary and tertiary sectors. Some consistency with this trend may be seen in the UK over the 1950s and 1960s insofar as there has been growth of secondary activities at the expense of primary ones (tertiary activities, however, retaining much the same share). But in a country like the UK which has already developed to a fairly high level, drastic changes are not to be expected over a period of this length. At the same time it should be remembered that a 1 per cent shift in resources between sectors will be large in absolute terms—say, approximately, £1,000 million worth of assets or 250,000 workers.

Because of differing capital/labour, capital/output and labour/output ratios, the size rankings of industries in terms of output, capital stock and employment need not coincide. Thus, for instance, in 1958 chemical and allied industries accounted for some 16 per cent of total capital employed in manufacturing and construction (excluding textiles) but only 6 per cent of manpower and 9 per cent of output. In the same way the rate of growth of an industry need not be the same or even similar in all three dimensions. A striking example here is agriculture, where total employment has fallen although both output and the value of capital stock have increased, and table 4.5 records the various growth rates for other industries for the period 1948-62. It is clear that while it may be perfectly valid and indeed most appropriate for some purposes to measure the relative size or growth of industries in terms of employment or capital rather than output, the measures need in no sense be substitutes for each other.

III   THE PUBLIC ENTERPRISE SECTOR

III.1   The Extent of the Public Sector

Public enterprise may be defined as where there is an undertaking which is publicly owned
and directed by a branch of the government or a body especially set up for the purpose by
the government. It is worth noting the immense size of the activities involved. First, our
definition would clearly include public administration (all central and local government
activities) and defence (6.2 per cent of GDP in 1968) and the public health and education
services (5.0 per cent). Secondly, there is the large group of nationalised industries—the
Post Office, the coal, gas and electricity industries, the two British airlines and airports
authority, the railways and other nationalised sections of transport (London Transport,
British Transport, the Docks Board, British Waterways, The National Freight Corporation
and The National Bus Holding Company), and the major part of the steel industry.[1]
Together these industries account for approximately 11 per cent of GDP, bringing the total
for all public enterprise to some 22 per cent. Annual gross fixed capital formation by the
nationalised industries is around £1. 7 billion per annum, somewhat larger than that of all
private manufacturing combined. Thirdly, there are a number of government agencies such
as the British Tourist Authority, the Forestry Commission, the Herring Industry Board,
etc.[2] *Total* public fixed capital formation over the past two or three years amounted to
some 49 per cent of the overall total for the economy. This figure compares with one of
around 33 per cent just prior to the second world war.

III.2   Price and Investment Policies for the National Industries: Theory

Price Policy: Unlike some other sections of the public sector, such as defence, education,
health, etc. the nationalised industries make charges for the goods and services they supply
which are not purely nominal. Various criteria could be used to govern the setting of these
charges. Whatever these are, the prices selected will affect the allocation of resources between different uses in the economy. For, in general, determining price simultaneously
determines output and this, with a given technology, determines the amounts of resource
used up by the nationalised undertakings involved.[3] Maximising social welfare requires
that an optimal allocation of resources is reached as between any one public enterprise
undertaking and the rest of the economy.[4] It is for this reason that economists have argued
that resource allocation should be the criterion used in determining nationalised industry
prices, and the specific recommendation is that for any good or service supplied price
should be set equal to marginal cost.

---

[1] A Bill introduced into Parliament in late 1969 would have added to the public sector all ports
handling more than 5 million tons per annum, which would be taken over by a National Ports
Authority. The Bill gave effect to the proposals set out in a White Paper, *The Reorganisation of
the Ports*, Cmnd 3903, but subsequently fell casualty to the 1970 Election.

[2] See R. Maurice (ed.), *National Income Statistics: Sources and Methods* Central Statistical Office,
HMSO, 1968.

[3] That is, taking any price we can read off the quantity which will be purchased from the relevant
demand curve, and, knowing output, we can solve for factor input requirements via the relevant
production function.

[4] Throughout this discussion the concept of optimality is the usual one—that a welfare maximum is
reached when no further redistribution of resources between uses, and outputs between consumers
can increase the utility of any one individual without reducing the utility of at least one other
(Pareto optimality).

A simple rationale can be given for the marginal cost pricing rule. On the one hand the demand curve tells us how much consumers will pay per unit for different quantities supplied, and so we interpret the demand curve as consumers' evaluation of the public undertaking's product as output is varied. On the other hand, the marginal cost curve tells us the incremental cost of producing each unit, and, if we can equate the money costs actually incurred by the undertaking with the true opportunity cost of diverting extra resources from alternative uses, we can construe the marginal cost curve as recording consumers' evaluation of the foregone alternative product. If consumers value the public enterprise's good more than the alternative (demand price exceeds marginal cost) then consumers' welfare can be increased by diverting more resources to the public enterprise, so increasing output, and *vice versa*. Hence, for an optimum level, price should equal marginal cost.[1]

On closer inspection, however, the marginal cost pricing rule raises a number of difficulties. First, marginal cost pricing in one sector or industry will maximise welfare only if a number of other conditions are met: e.g. if price is everywhere else equal to marginal cost; there are no taxes and subsidies which create differences in the relative prices between commodities as paid by consumers and as received by producers; producers and consumers have perfect knowledge; and others. Generally these conditions will not all be met, and where this is so the 'second best' solution would very likely be one in which price is not equal to marginal cost.[2] Hence, application of the marginal cost pricing rule in a particular case, regardless of what is happening elsewhere, cannot be relied on for an optimum.[3]

Secondly, demand for the public enterprise good depends, among other things, on the way income is distributed among consumers. Even if all other conditions were met, a top welfare maximum could be said to exist only if the existing distribution of income were accepted as ideal. If this were not so, it would be perfectly justifiable for the government to modify some or all nationalised industry prices in the name of social justice.[4]

A third difficulty arises from the divergence between social and private costs and returns. Where, for instance, increased output in one industry confers external benefits by reducing production costs in other industries, marginal *private* costs in that industry will exceed marginal *social* costs, and *vice versa* for an industry imposing net external costs. Thus, even if all other necessary conditions for maximum welfare were met, a nationalised

---

[1]   See also S. K. Nath, *A Reappraisal of Welfare Economics,* Routledge & Kegan Paul, London, 1969, chapter 7; R. Turvey (ed), *Public Enterprise,* Penguin Books Ltd, 1968; E. H. Phelps Brown and J. Wiseman, *A Course in Applied Economics* (2nd edn), Pitman, London, 1964; and First Report from the Select Committee on the Nationalised Industries, *Ministerial Control of the Nationalised Industries,* HC 371-I, II, III, 1968.

[2]   See R. G. Lipsey and K. Lancaster, 'On the General Theory of Second Best', *RES* vol. XXIV, 1956-7, pp.11-32. Specifically, '. . . . it is *not* true that a situation in which more, but not all of the optimum conditions are fulfilled is necessarily, or is even likely to be, superior to the situation in which fewer are fulfilled.'

[3]   A modification of the marginal cost pricing rule which takes some of this into account is to set price equi-proportional to marginal cost. Thus, if price is on average, say, 10 per cent above marginal cost in the economy, this same margin should be included in public enterprise prices. So long as we are concerned only with the relative output levels in commodity markets this has some merit. But it will not produce an *overall* optimum, since income-leisure preferences will be affected and the supply of labour (and hence also total output) will be less than is consistent with an ideal, i.e. optimum conditions might be fulfilled in commodity markets but not in factor markets.

[4]   It can be argued that this is precisely what the government does do in not charging or making only token charges for some public sector goods and services, e.g. health, education.

industry equating price with marginal private cost would be producing too much, from the community standpoint, if it gave rise to net external costs and too little if it conferred net external economies. In general, for maximum welfare external effects of this sort must be taken into account *in both the nationalised sector and elsewhere.*

A fourth difficulty with marginal cost pricing is in deciding whether price should be equated with short-run marginal cost (the rate of change of total costs in the short run, i.e. when some factor or factors are fixed) or with long-run marginal cost (the rate of change of total costs in the long run, when there are no fixed factors). The arguments in favour of each are somewhat complex, and it is sufficient here simply to note that economists are divided over this choice.

Finally, neither short-run nor long-run marginal cost pricing will automatically ensure that total costs will be recovered from revenue, i.e. that average revenue (price) equals average cost. Since marginal and average costs are equal only at that output at which average costs are at a minimum, marginal cost pricing will exactly equate total costs and revenues only if, by chance, the output level which results happens to be this one.[1] Otherwise, either a deficit (marginal cost is less than average cost) or a surplus (marginal cost exceeds average cost) will result. In practice, most of the nationalised industries are thought to be ones where average costs decline continuously over the relevant range of outputs, so that marginal cost is less than average cost and a deficit is likely to result. Again, economists are divided as to whether such deficits (or surpluses) should be tolerated. Some argue that they should, on the grounds that the only permissible pricing criterion is the marginal cost rule, if optimal resource allocation is the objective, and that to make consumers cover total outlays will prevent the optimum being reached. Others contend that if, for example, a deficit is tolerated there must be some subsidisation of current consumers of the good by the community via taxation, and this *may* have the effect of diverting income from poorer to richer sections of the community.

Investment Policy: There are two main requirements to be met for a correct investment policy for public enterprise. The first is that the costs and benefits of any project over its life be correctly evaluated. Secondly, estimates of future costs and benefits must be correctly related to the present decision-making period. In evaluating costs and benefits, due account must be taken of external effects on other producers and consumers. Moreover, since market determined prices in a 'second-best' world may be imperfect indicators of the worth of inputs and outputs to the community, it will usually be necessary to adjust these on to a socially desired basis.[2] The method of relating together costs and benefits in different periods that is generally thought best is to express the returns to an investment project in terms of net discounted present value.[3] Generally speaking, the

---

[1] This difficulty would not arise in the case of long-run marginal cost pricing under conditions of constant returns, for then the average and marginal cost curves are horizontal straight lines, and marginal and average costs are equal for all outputs.

[2] A difficult task. For an extended discussion of cost benefit analysis see A. R. Prest and R. Turvey, 'Cost Benefit Analysis: A Survey', *EJ*, December 1965.

[3] Net discounted present value (R) for any project with a life of n years is given by

$$R = \sum_{t=1}^{n} \frac{B_t - C_t}{(1 + r)^t} - I$$

where B_t, C_t are benefits and costs respectively in year t, r is the rate of discount and I is the initial cost. The main merits of this method over its chief rival (internal rate of return or marginal efficiency of capital) are that it always gives a unique solution and always ranks projects correctly. See W. J. Baumol, *Economic Theory and Operations Analysis,* Prentice Hall, 1965, pp. 434-77.

rate of time discount used in evaluating public sector projects should be the same as is used elsewhere (and any allowance made for the same degree of uncertainty should also be the same). Otherwise, the relative merits of private and public sector projects will be distorted. In practice, the private rate may not be easy to discover. Moreover, it does not follow that the public sector must inevitably take its cue from the private sector, since the private sector rate may not be at a socially desired level.

Even if public sector projects were appraised scrupulously, the maximum benefit would not be derived from the total of funds available for investment in the economy unless private projects were treated in exactly the same way. Ideally, all projects need to be evaluated identically, ranked in descending order of discounted net present value, and implemented in that order to the limit of available funds. In practice, private sector investments will almost invariably be evaluated with no explicit regard for external effects,[1] and in terms of market prices which may be distorted; various ways of treating uncertainty are likely to be used; and a substantial amount of decision-making will be by rule of thumb methods.[2] All this will distort the order in which projects are ranked and thus, at the margin, affect which projects are implemented. Insofar as the government is unable to regulate all private sector investment appraisal appropriately, the best that can be hoped for is a form of sub-optimisation, the correct principles being applied in the public sector only.[3]

III.3   Price and Investment Policies for the Nationalised Industries: Practice

The original nationalisation Acts laid down a minimum financial requirement that revenue should be not less than sufficient to meet outgoings properly chargeable to revenue account, taking one year with another.[4] In addition, the industries were generally explicitly required to operate an efficient system of supply and there was also some confirmation in the statutes that they should serve the national interest in some wider, social sense. Thus, for instance, in the 1947 Electricity Act the industry was required not only to meet its financial requirements and operate an efficient, coordinated and economical system of electrical supply, but also so far as practicable extend electricity supply to rural areas and promote the welfare, health and safety of its employees.

A White Paper in 1961 considerably tightened the financial requirements placed upon the industries. The previously indefinite period over which financial performance was to be measured was replaced by precise five-year ones; outgoings to be set against revenue were extended to include provision for depreciation at full replacement (rather than historic) cost, a contribution towards future capital development and a reserve for contingencies; and, most important, specific financial targets were introduced, usually expressed as a rate of return on assets employed, in place of the general obligation to break even. The targets varied between industries and in setting them some notional allowance was made for, *inter alia*, non-commercial operations undertaken by way of social services.

---

[1]   However, private investments *may* be subject to taxes or subsidies imposed by the government to ensure that external effects are taken into account.

[2]   See, e.g., NEDO, *Investment Appraisal*, HMSO, 1967.

[3]   A way of overcoming this difficulty has been suggested, but is itself likely to lead only to sub-optimal results in practice. For an account see Nath, *A Reappraisal of Welfare Economics*, pp. 184-5.

[4]   Surpluses of nationalised industries are not exactly comparable with profits in the private sector. Since interest, depreciation, redemption of capital and provision of reserves are chargeable against revenue some items are excluded which would be met from private sector profits.

Current price and investment policy for the nationalised industries was contained in a White Paper published in 1967.[1] The declared starting point for pricing policy was that accounting costs should be covered by revenue.[2] But the White Paper went on to lay down a long-run marginal-cost pricing rule, with the proviso that where there is excess capacity or demand prices should be lowered 'if necessary to the level where the escapable costs of particular services are just covered' (short-run marginal cost). The need to distinguish social obligations carefully from strictly commercial operations was stressed, and the government accepted financial responsibility for the former, for example by specific subsidies where current costs were involved. Two- or multi-part tariffs or unit prices proportional to marginal cost were recommended for the apportionment of fixed costs, etc. among consumers where necessary to cover total costs.

Social cost-benefit analysis was proposed for investment appraisal, and it was stated that the returns on investment projects would need to be presented in terms of discounted net present value. A test discount rate of 8 per cent was laid down for project appraisal, avowedly the equivalent of the 15-16 per cent looked for by private industry on marginal, low-risk investment.

Financial targets were retained. It was recognised that if appropriate price and investment procedures are applied the financial outturn, expressed as a rate of return on assets, is predetermined. But it was claimed that setting up a target shows the management what is expected of it, and provides a measure of expected performance to compare with actual achievements. Thus, rather than being the starting point of operating criteria, the financial objectives became a derived instrument of management control. Finally, we may note that the White Paper specifically retained for the government the right to bring national economic considerations to bear on the nationalised industries, by rephasing and retiming investment, etc.

One feature in the period up to 1967 was that there was no explicit pricing policy. In the absence of this a variety of rule of thumb techniques was apparently used. Thus, for instance, both passenger and freight rail charges were mainly based on a standard charge per mile—i.e. a uniform contribution per mile to the total cost of all the operations of the undertaking—rather than on the opportunity cost of providing the particular service used. As a result there was much cross-subsidisation among rail users, for example between consumers of well-loaded express journeys and of local, stopping services, especially those in remote areas. It was this sort of cross-subsidisation which the 1967 White Paper was attempting to eliminate by recommending marginal cost pricing *for each good or service supplied.*

There was also much subsidisation of non-commercial services by commercial ones. This can be regarded as undesirable on two counts. Firstly, if 'social services' of the kind under consideration are to be provided it is more just that they should be financed from general revenue than by other customers of the undertaking supplying them. Secondly, by raising the prices of purely commercial services, financing social services in this way will give rise to distortions in supply as between the undertakings involved and their competitors. It is true that after 1961 some notional allowance was made for social obligations in setting financial targets, and also that some costs were occasionally transferred to the

---

[1] *Nationalised Industries: A Review of Economic and Financial Objectives,* Cmnd 3437, HMSO, November 1967.

[2] However, since the White Paper also stated that subsidies might be made for some services and that 'the application of wider economic and social factors may involve overall losses' for some industries, this so-called 'starting point' of the policy takes on a rather special meaning.

axpayer.[1] But such methods were clearly very crude ways of allowing for the 'social service' element in the activities of nationalised industries, and there was very little attempt to identify and measure the cost of these unprofitable operations that were required on social grounds.

In addition to all this, the prices charged by nationalised industries tended to be subject to ministerial interference on political grounds. This was especially true before 1961. As a result prices tended to be too low (a fact which may well have contributed to the very rapid rapid rise in public sector investment, especially in the 1950s). Almost certainly, too, the nationalised industries have always been made to be more responsive to general government policy than have private sector industries, for example in observing price and wage restraint, in avoiding placing large overseas orders at times of balance of payments crisis, and in holding back investment programmes. A specific example here would be the requirement placed on the electricity industry to slow down the transfer from production from coal to production from oil, in order to moderate the run-down of the coal industry.

However, there were also some factors tending to favour the nationalised industries in this period. Perhaps the most important was the supply of capital. The industries obtained finance not from the capital market in the same way as private industry, but from the Treasury at rates which reflected the government's own borrowing power. In some cases, notably electricity and more recently gas supply, the difference between the actual capital charges and the terms on which capital would have been available from the market may not have been very great, since the borrowing strength of these growth industries in their own right would be considerable. However, the arrangements involved a substantial element of subsidy in other cases, notably coal and rail.

The 1967 White Paper obviously did introduce an explicit price and investment policy, which had previously been lacking. If properly applied, the proposals would undoubtedly lead to much less cross-subsidisation among the individual goods and services supplied, and a much clearer distinction between purely commercial and other activities, with an appropriate allocation of responsibilities in this area.[2] In choosing long-run marginal cost, and in requiring that total revenues cover total costs (including an appropriate return on capital invested), the White Paper entered a very controversial area.[3] There would not be universal acceptance that the policies advocated would lead to optimal resource allocation (ignoring all other difficulties) but, on the other hand, no policy could have been proposed that would have secured such universal acceptance.

The White Paper avoided certain problem areas. For instance, it took no account of the fact that in practice price will not equal marginal cost elsewhere in the economy, and of the second-best problem this raises. Similarly there was no recognition that in investment

---

As when some £400 million of accumulated deficit of British Railways was written off in 1962. A further £800 million was at the same time transferred into 'suspense account', carrying neither fixed interest nor fixed repayment obligations. Effectively, the railways were thereby relieved of exactly three-quarters of a total £1,600 million deficit. (See *Reorganisation of the Nationalised Transport Undertakings,* Cmnd 1248, HMSO, 1960.) Later, the 1968 Transport Act extinguished the £705 million deficit on suspended account remaining at end 1968, and also wrote off a further £557 million of interest bearing debt, reducing this to £365 million.

Subsequently, the 1968 Transport Act provided for grants for unremunerative rail services required for social or economic reasons, and these totalled some £60 million in 1969. (Grants were also provided for to relieve British Railways of financial responsibility for surplus track and signalling equipment. These amounted to some £15 million in 1969.) Also, the electricity industry has received some financial assistance to compensate for its lack of free choice of fuel for generation. See Electricity Council *Annual Report and Accounts* 1968-9 and *Coal Industry Bill* 1970.

The White Paper's recommendation of two- or multi-part tariffs would probably receive wide acceptance, given the requirement to cover total cost.

appraisal social costs and returns will not be taken into account in the private sector or, indeed, that much private sector appraisal of projects would not be undertaken according to the accepted principles laid down for public enterprise. Thus, some sort of sub-optimisation is the very best that could be hoped for. Moreover, some of the things which *were* in the White Paper could be criticised. For instance, in following the private sector rate of discount the White Paper gave tacit government acceptance that this satisfied all requirements, which is a highly doubtful proposition. In general, however, it would be true to say that publication of the White Paper marked a significant new step in official thinking, and a step which was remarkable for its attention to the kind of things thought important by economists.

It is not easy to assess what practical effects have so far flowed from this new development in policy. Some progress in separating off commercial and 'social' activities, and allocating financial responsibilities accordingly, has already been mentioned. So far as the general application of marginal cost pricing is concerned, however, official sources are not very revealing.[1] Thus, at the time of writing, subsequently published annual reports of four of the main industries involved contain only very scanty references to the White Paper and its implementation. The Electricity Council Reports for 1967-8 and 1968-9 do not mention the subject. The Gas Council Report for 1967-8 refers to the publication of the White Paper and gives some details of the investment provisions but does not mention marginal cost pricing.[2] The National Coal Board Report for 1967-8, however, indicates that procedures for review of investment proposals were being re-examined in the light of the White Paper.[3] And the British Railways Board's 1968 Report notes that the year w marked by a significant departure in passenger operations from the traditional policy of charging by mileage to a system of pricing 'according to market conditions'. The first stage of the new policy was introduced in September 1968, when traffic flows yielding some £70 million were repriced.[4] Clearly some changes have taken place, and doubtless others may have occurred or be in progress which have not been reported in these sources but it is very difficult to judge precisely what progress has been made.

One thing which is certain is that those responsible for the practical application of marginal cost pricing face many difficulties.[5] For instance, it is frequently difficult to specify the individual outputs (goods or services) to be separately priced; for example electricity may be regarded as a different commodity depending on the voltage level, area supplied, time of day and degree of security from breakdown, voltage drop, etc. and it is difficult to say where divisions should be drawn in the tariff structure. Then, simply estimating marginal cost for a given output involves difficulties of methodology and data availability and collection. Indeed, outputs may be impossible to cost separately

---

[1] But see R. Turvey (formerly economist to the Electricity Council), *Optimal Pricing and Investment in Electricity Supply*, Allen and Unwin, 1968; 'Peak Load Pricing', *JPE*, 1968, p. 101; 'Marginal Cost', *EJ*, 1969, p. 282.

[2] The Gas Council, *Annual Report and Accounts 1967-68*, HC 415, 1968, p. 28, para 120.

[3] National Coal Board, *Report and Accounts 1967-68*, HC, 401, 1968, p. 4, para 16.

[4] British Railways Board, *Annual Report and Accounts 1968*, H of C, 257, 1969, paras 5-8. The programme was accelerated as a result of the decision by the NBPI not to allow the railways a proposed general increase over the transitional period (except for the London area). The NBPI's recommendation was that prices should be adjusted according to the circumstances in individual markets

[5] See R. Turvey, 'Practical Problems of Marginal-Cost Pricing in Public Enterprise: England', in A. Phillips and O. E. Williamson (eds), *Prices: Issues in Theory, Practice, and Public Policy*, University of Pennsylvania Press, 1967. Also J. R. Nelson, *Marginal Cost Pricing in Practice*, Prentice Hall, 1964.

especially if their provision involves the joint use of some factors of production with other outputs (e.g. the use of railway track in both passenger and freight transport), for there is no known non-arbitrary way of allocating joint costs. Surprisingly often marginal cost turns out to be approximately zero over wide ranges of output, due to the presence of indivisible factors of production (e.g. the marginal cost of carrying one more passenger on a not-fully-loaded train). Marginal cost is then not uniquely defined, and a decision must be taken over what marginal unit average costs of supply must be taken as the measure of 'marginal cost'. Finally, perhaps the greatest difficulties of all would be met in evaluating the social costs and benefits, for example in placing a value on time lost by users of transport services as a result of congestion, in order to arrive at some estimate of congestion costs increased or decreased by a given investment project in the transport sector. The 1967 White Paper referred to such practical difficulties at various points, but gave very little practical advice on their treatment. It is difficult to escape the conclusion that marginal cost pricing in practice is likely to be either administratively costly, or very rough.[1]

Further difficulties in implementing the White Paper arise from the requirement that total costs be recouped from revenue, and that nonprofitable services which are required for social reasons be separately treated. Where marginal cost pricing would result in a deficit, but total costs must also be recouped, ways must then be found of raising average cost to the consumer without affecting marginal cost, and this is not easy.[2] The practical difficulty with social services is merely in identifying and costing them, and determining how they be financed and by whom. Thus, these two extra considerations may be expected to get in the way of marginal cost pricing.

The retention of financial objectives is likely to do the same, whatever their merits may be as a spur to managerial efficiency. Specifically, if strictly applied, financial objectives might tempt aberration from correct pricing policy in order to meet the targets laid down, especially in the latter years of a quinquennium when results had been poor in early years. If, on the other hand, financial objectives were not strictly applied (and the White Paper stresses their 'flexibility' and the possibility of revision in 'changed circumstances') their usefulness as an instrument of control may be doubted. More generally, the retention of financial objectives may have the effect of impeding the changeover in managerial thinking and accounting procedures from the old orthodoxy—in which satisfying financial obligations was the first requirement—to the newer emphasis on economic considerations, and resource allocation. That is, the mere fact of retaining financial objectives, for whatever reason, could promote a tendency for management of the nationalised industries to think of financial results first and marginal cost second, rather than the reverse.

III.4 Productive Efficiency in the Nationalised Industries

Many of the problems involved in securing efficiency in the nationalised industries, whether of a technical or organisational nature, will be of the same kind as are met in private enterprise undertakings. Because of the extremely large scale of the operations under one administrative control, however, it is certainly true that the organisational problems of the nationalised industries will undoubtedly exceed those of at least all but a

---

[1] R. Turvey, *ibid.*

[2] The method generally recommended is a two- or multi-part tariff involving a fixed payment plus a payment for individual units as, for example, in the system of rentals plus call charges for telephones. The difficulty is that if the fixed payment has to be at all high it may deter some marginal consumers altogether, thus interfering with resource allocation.

few, giant, private firms. Similarly, in view of the size of the real resources controlled by any one nationalised industry, the social consequences of a wrong decision or any short-fall in efficiency will be much more severe than those arising from similar shortcomings in individual firms in the private sector. The whole question of productive efficiency is discussed in general terms in section VII of this chapter. The purpose of this brief section is to consider some particular problems which are alleged to arise for the nationalised industries.

It is sometimes suggested that the nationalised industries tend to be inefficient because of their monopoly positions. But while it may be true that there is no direct competition with other 'firms' making the same produce, it is not true (with the possible exception of the Post Office) that the nationalised industries are entirely free from *market* competition, for example competition from close substitute products, as the present situation of the coal industry clearly shows. Moreover reliance on competition as a spur to efficiency is perhaps more hazardous than is thought.[1] Evidence that the nationalised industries *are* inefficient, for whatever cause, is sometimes found in the tendency of at least some of them regularly to incur deficits. However, failure to make 'profits' is by no means con-clusive evidence of inefficiency. A nationalised industry might be perfectly efficient and yet incur a deficit, this deficit being an inevitable outcome of the policy imposed upon the industry, and the activities required to be undertaken.

Thus, criticisms levied against public sector enterprises may not always be justified. In large measure they may be attributable to the conspicuousness of the industries, and the amount of information about them made available to the public. However, public owner-ship and control may genuinely have given rise to some losses in efficiency up to the present.

The need to reconcile operating efficiency with public accountability may, for instance, have created problems, the one perhaps requiring maximum autonomy and powers of dele-gation and decentralisation in nationalised industries, the other inhibiting this.[2] Secondly, weakness in government policy—the lack of clear financial objectives, especially before 1961, and the confusion and intermingling of commercially viable and other activities, etc.—may well have reduced managerial efficiency and general morale and productivity. Thirdly, a recent NBPI report indicates that an inadequate salary structure for top and middle management may have reduced the nationalised industries' ability to recruit, retain and suitably motivate high-calibre management.[3] Evidence such as this does serve to show that the efficiency of public enterprise is capable of improvement. Of course, it does nothing to prove whether, taking all factors into account, efficiency is any greater or less than in the private sector.

Recent developments in policy, and clarifications, may help to remove some of the existing impediments to efficiency. In addition, the 1967 White Paper discussed in the preceding section made some explicit references to general efficiency. There was a general exhortation to internal efficiency, and the point was made that the government's general

---

[1] See p. 181.

[2] One major conclusion of the Select Committee on the Nationalised Industries was that ministers have tended to do the opposite of what Parliament intended. Whereas they were supposed to lay down policies, but not intervene in management, they have in practice, until recently, given very little policy guidance, but been closely involved with many aspects of management.

[3] NBPI *Report* No. 107, *Top Salaries in the Private Sector and Nationalised Industries*, Cmnd 3970, March 1969. The report found that top salaries and retirement pensions were substantially lower in nationalised industries than in private industry, and that the difference was not due to differences in responsibilities. As a result there was undue compression of the salary structure for middle and upper management levels. To give headroom for a proper structure increases were proposed in salaries for chairmen of the main undertakings, from £12,500 or £11,000 to £20,000 and £17,000 per annum, respectively. The increases were to take place in three stages.

policies for increased productivity applied to the public no less than the private sector. Some specific items were mentioned in connection with internal efficiency, including the efficient use of qualified and skilled manpower and the need for labour saving; for flexibility on both sides of the industries towards manning practices; for the abandonment of restrictive practices, etc. In addition the heavy emphasis on correct methods of investment appraisal may, of course, be regarded as specific guidance on an important aspect of efficiency. A sanction on the efficiency of the industries was the involvement of the NBPI charged with both a general task of carrying out efficiency audits, and a specific duty of examining the underlying justification for price increases, their timing, and the extent to which costs could be reduced by increased efficiency.[1]

On the organisational side there have been a number of important recent developments. Several were embodied in the 1968 Transport Act which, *inter alia,* eliminated the regional divisions of British Rail; set up a National Freight Corporation and Freight Integration Council; created Passenger Transport Authorities for four major conurbations, and transferred the London Transport Board to the GLC making, effectively, a fifth; and established a National Bus Company for England and Wales, and a Scottish Transport Group. Then, from October 1969 the Post Office, previously a government department, became a public corporation, to be run on more commercial lines. Next, there was legislation pending prior to the 1970 Election to reorganise the gas and electricity industries. In the case of gas, the Gas Council would have been given powers to deal with supply, distribution, marketing, tariffs and technical developments for the industry as a whole. In electricity, similarly, an Electricity Authority (previously the Electricity Council) would have been given wide powers to plan and control policy for the industry as a whole. Whether the Conservative government will carry through similar measures is not clear at the time of writing. Finally, one recommendation of the Select Committee on the Nationalised Industries[2] was that a new Ministry be set up to oversee the commercial operations of fourteen nationalised industries, current responsibility being split between the Ministries of Transport and Power, the Board of Trade and the Scottish Office.

One recurring theme in these organisational changes is clearly to provide for better coordination and planning throughout the whole of the particular industries concerned or, in the case of the Select Committee recommendation, a large group of the industries taken together. In the case of gas the introduction of North Sea gas supplies has made such a change all the more desirable. The change in status of the Post Office removes a longstanding anachronism. Finally, the creation of the Passenger Transport Authorities and arrangements for London may be construed as measures to provide for local public decision-making and control over the particular social and economic problems arising in the provision of transport services in and around the major cities.

IV   CONTROL OF MONOPOLY, MERGER AND RESTRICTIVE PRACTICES[3]

IV.1   The Policy Targets

Laws regulating competition in the UK now have four principal targets: dominant firm monopoly, merger, restrictive trade practices, and resale price maintenance (RPM). Let us

[1] The decision to refer nationalised industry price increases to the NBPI was first announced in October 1967. The 1967 White Paper made all nationalised industries' applications *automatically* a matter for the NBPI. See p. 198, footnote 4 for the likely procedure after 1970.

[2] *Ministerial Control of The Nationalised Industries,* HC 371-I, II, III, 1968.

[3] See also Alex Hunter, *Competition and the Law,* Allen and Unwin, 1966, and *Monopoly and Competition,* Penguin, 1969; R. B. Stevens and B. S. Yamey, *The Restrictive Practices Court,* Weidenfeld and Nicolson, 1965; C. Brock, *The Control of Restrictive Practices since 1956,* McGraw-Hill, 1966; C. K. Rowley, *The British Monopolies Commission,* Allen and Unwin, 1966; and symposia on restrictive practices in *EJ,* September 1960, and *OEP,* November 1965.

examine the need for such laws in the light of the theories of the firm outlined in section I.

Under profit maximising assumptions the main criticisms of monopoly are that price exceeds marginal cost, with consequential resource misallocation and reduced consumers' welfare;[1] that supernormal profits are earned (price also exceeds *average* cost), so distorting income distribution in favour of producers; and that possession of market power permits practices such as price discrimination among consumers and cross-subsidisation among activities, which can also reduce welfare and, further, be used to protect a monopoly position. A fourth argument is that monopolists will tend to be inefficient—costs being higher than they need—because the presence of excess profits blunts the desire to seek out and apply cost-minimising techniques and factor combinations. This may well be true, but it is not consistent with profit maximisation, since it implies pursuit of some other objective, e.g. leisure, at some point.

The main significance of monopoly under the managerial theories is that the existence of market power is likely to increase the tendency for firms to pursue managerial objectives other than profit. The criticisms of monopoly derived from the profit maximising model may not apply, but managerial behaviour may well not lead to genuine cost minimisation (e.g. in Williamson's model organisational slack is typically present)[2] and, in general, a part of the stream of resources being generated by the firm is diverted for the satisfaction of managerial aims (sales, growth, discretionary investment, staff, slack, etc.) and away from consumers' welfare. The behavioural principle of 'satisficing' behaviour perhaps suggests that even if monopoly potential exists it will not necessarily be exploited. Whether the type of market structure will affect efficiency, under the behavioural theory, would depend on the effect on search and decision procedures, and little is known about this at present. In general, if the behavioural theory is adopted, the whole basis for discussing monopoly in terms of resource allocation and supernormal profit is lost.

Exactly why firms merge has never been explained satisfactorily in theoretical models. But clearly one *effect* may be to create monopoly situations (though this need not be the sole *objective*), with consequences as outlined above under the different theories. Current official thinking on mergers[3] emphasises the potentially anti-competitive effects of both horizontal and vertical mergers, but recognises that there may be substantial efficiency gains from scale economies, rationalisation of production, etc.[4] Conglomerate mergers are seen as a special category. Both the anti-competitive effects and potential for increased efficiency are considered likely to be smaller than for horizontal and vertical mergers, but there is concern that many may be taking place for purely financial reasons, and yield very little benefit in terms of increased efficiency, but some anti-competitive risk. More-

---

[1]   See section III of this chapter. Many of the difficulties concerning marginal cost and welfare are common to the public enterprise pricing and monopoly issues.

[2]   See above, p. 151.

[3]   See *Annex* to Monopolies Commission, *The Rank Organisation Limited and De La Rue Company Limited*, HC 298, 1968-9, and Board of Trade, *Mergers: A Guide to Board of Trade Practice*, HMSO, 1969.

[4]   Horizontal mergers are between competitors in the same market, vertical mergers are between customer and supplier. The first will, other things being equal, increase market concentration (the share of supply in the hands of a few large suppliers). Vertical mergers threaten competition where, for instance, a manufacturer takes over the firm supplying raw material both to himself and to his competitors, and would be able to charge disadvantageous prices to them; or where a manufacturer secures control over the sales outlets for both his own and his competitors' products.

over it is argued that conglomerate mergers could lead to substantial *losses* in operating efficiency.[1]

Under profit maximisation the argument against restrictive trade practices is, broadly, that by concerted action a group of firms may achieve the same result as a single firm monopolist. Thus, the formal model explaining joint profit maximisation by two or more firms turns out to be identical with the one that explains multi-plant monopolist behaviour.[2] Moving away from the formal model, it is also argued that if prices are set at a level which allows the least efficient to survive, many firms will earn abnormal profits without difficulty, the inefficient will not be eliminated, and the general competitive spur to efficiency will be lost; and that restrictive agreements may also provide a base for collusive action to forestall the entry of new competition, suppress new techniques and developments, etc. How the managerial theories might qualify these arguments has yet to be shown. In a behavioural analysis we should probably be much less suspicious of the motives underlying restrictive practices than if we assume profit maximisation. Assuming profit maximisation, restrictive practices would not exist unless profits were thereby raised; under behavioural analysis this need not be so. Moreover, restrictive practices fit fairly easily into the behavioural concept of the 'negotiated environment', the implication being that they are primarily uncertainty-reducing phenomena, perhaps with advantages in facilitating forward planning etc.

Under RPM manufacturers stipulate the prices at which their goods are to be resold and one certain effect is clearly to preclude price competition between retailers.[3] Opponents of the practice have argued, on broadly profit-maximising assumptions, that the prices set are likely to be at a level remunerative for the least efficient retailers, or those providing most services, and that RPM tends to increase the amount of services provided. As a result, prices are higher than if price competition prevailed and consumers were allowed a free choice between price and service. Such prices, it is claimed, prolong the life of too large a number of inefficient retailing units, and inhibit the introduction of new trading methods like supermarkets and discount houses, which rely on low-cost, low-margin, high-turnover trading.

Clearly the criticisms of monopoly and monopolistic practices do vary somewhat according to our choice of theoretical model. Moreover, whichever model we take, monopoly or monopolistic practices may confer advantages as well as disadvantages. For instance, against the adverse effects on resource allocation and income distribution under the profit maximisation hypothesis is the fact that, if scale economies are to be exploited, there may be room for only one firm of minimum optimum scale in some markets. Moreover, it has been vigorously argued that the security and profitability of monopoly is an

---

[1] Conglomerate mergers are those where there has previously been neither vertical nor horizontal links between the parties. Efficiency gains would probably be mainly financial or managerial; efficiency losses might arise because of the complexity of operations under one control. Competition might be harmed if the conglomerate firm, by virtue of its size, became accepted as a price leader in a particular market, or fought its way to a monopoly position in a market via a price war, accepting temporary losses in that market, compensated for by profits earned elsewhere.

[2] See, e.g., K. J. Cohen and R. M. Cyert, *Theory of the Firm*, Prentice Hall, 1965, p. 235. In practice, the degree of coordination of activities required is greater than would normally occur under a restrictive agreement between firms.

[3] There has been considerable controversy over the effects of RPM. See, e.g., B. S. Yamey, *Resale Price Maintenance and Shoppers' Choice*, Hobart Paper 1, 1960; and P. W. S. Andrews and F. A. Friday, *Fair Trade*, Macmillan, 1960. See also J. F. Pickering, *Resale Price Maintenance in Practice*, Allen and Unwin, 1966; and B. S. Yamey, *Resale Price Maintenance*, Weidenfeld and Nicolson, 1966.

important enabling condition for technical progress.[1] Both the uncertainty over the effects
of monopoly, etc. and also the need to allow for the possible advantages, are problems
facing any government legislating in this field.

A second problem, though one arising only if profit maximising assumptions are retained, concerns the 'second best'. Where competition does not prevail in every other market,
removal of an individual monopoly or monopolistic practice cannot be relied upon to
increase welfare (as a result of the ensuing change in resource *allocation*), and may indeed
reduce it.[2]

IV.2   Policy Measures 1948-70

The 1948 Monopolies and Restrictive Practices Act defined a monopoly situation as
where one-third of the supply of goods is controlled by a single firm or group of linked
firms. Apart from monopolies created by Act of Parliament, such situations were to be
investigated at the request of the Board of Trade by a Monopolies Commission (MC).
This was an independent, administrative tribunal, initially of ten members. Its powers
were of enquiry and recommendation only, and it was required to decide whether, considering 'all matters that appear to be relevant', the monopoly is contrary to the public
interest. This the 1948 Act defined as 'among other things. . . the production treatment
and distribution by the most efficient and economical means of goods of such types and
qualities in such volume and at such prices as will best suit the requirements of home and
overseas markets'. Elaborating this, the Act specifically mentioned organisation to secure
progressive increases in efficiency; the encouragement of new enterprise; the 'fullest and
best' distribution of men, materials and industrial capacity; technical improvements; and
the expansion of existing markets and the opening up of new markets. Hearings were to
be private, and majority and minority findings and views could be given in the report.
Responsibility for implementing recommendations remained with the Board of Trade
which, however, was not bound to accept the findings of the Commission.

In 1953 the Commission's size was increased from ten to twenty-five members and its
operations were speeded up by its being enabled to sit in divisions. In 1956, however,
when its responsibilities for restrictive practices were transferred to the newly created
Restrictive Practices Court, it returned to its original size and arrangements. Then, in
1965, the Monopolies and Mergers Act restored the size and organisation of the Commission, with minor modifications, to what they had been between 1953 and 1956. The
1965 Act also provided for control of mergers: previously, while monopolies were subject
to control, mergers which would result in a one-third market share were not liable as such.
Since the 1965 Act such mergers, whether actual or intended, or those involving assets
exceeding £5 million in value, may be referred by the Board of Trade[3] to the (enlarged)
Monopolies Commission. In addition, special treatment is provided for in the case of newspaper mergers, presumably on account of the political as well as economic implications.
The 1965 Act also reinforced and extended the powers of the Board of Trade, specifically
including the publication of price lists, the regulation of prices, outright prohibition of
(or the imposing of conditions on) acquisitions and the power to dissolve existing mono-

---

[1]   See J. Schumpeter, *Capitalism, Socialism and Democracy,* Allen and Unwin, London, 1943; J. K.
     Galbraith, *American Capitalism* (revised edn.), Hamish Hamilton, 1956 chapter 7; J. Jewkes,
     D. Sawer and R. Stillerman, *The Sources of Invention,* MacMillan, 1962; and C. F. Carter and
     B. R. Williams, *Industry and Technical Progress,* Oxford University Press, 1957, chapter 11.

[2]   See above, p. 165.

[3]   In 1969 responsibility for monopolies and restrictive practices was transferred to the Secretary of
     State for Employment and Productivity. Conservative policy has yet to emerge, but early indications
     are that this responsibility may revert to The Board of Trade.

polies. A further provision was to extend the legislation to cover the supply of services as well as goods, and monopoly situations incompatible with UK international obligations.[1]

Prior to the 1970 Election, new measures were proposed for the future control of monopolies and mergers. The 1970 Commission for Industry and Manpower Bill would have dissolved the Monopolies Commission, and most of the existing powers and procedures for monopoly control would have been transferred to a newly created CIM. This would also have taken over responsibilities from the NBPI,[2] which would have disappeared. In the monopoly control area, the CIM would have had a wider scope than the MC. References for investigation would have been possible not only where one firm had a one-third market share, but also where a firm merely exceeded a size limit of £10 million assets, or where two or more firms with a one-third joint market share were conducting their respective affairs so as to 'prevent, distort, or restrict competition', or to restrict exports. The bill listed a number of specific questions to be considered by the CIM: prices, charges or profits; salaries, wages and other incomes; the prevention, restriction or distortion of competition; and questions relating to the use of a dominant position. The job of the CIM would have been to find out matters of fact, assess the effect on the public interest, and make recommendations. The CIM would have been required to state its reasons and specify any adverse effects on the public interest. Powers for subsequent implementation of recommendations would have been very similar to those conferred by the 1965 Act. The CIM would also have had responsibilities concerning the efficiency of public sector undertakings and top salaries in the public enterprises. The bill would also have provided for follow-up investigations of mergers and for advancing warning of company distributions, and increases in prices or charges, claims, settlements, and awards. The introduction of the bill followed a fairly widespread recognition of some overlap in the activities of the MC and the prices and productivity wings of the NBPI.

From 1948 to 1956 restrictive practices were dealt with by the Monopolies Commission, but the basis of the present law is contained in the Restrictive Practices Acts of 1956 and 1968. The 1956 Act defined restrictive practices as agreements under which two or more persons accepted restrictions relating to the price of goods, conditions of supply, quantities or descriptions, processes, or areas and persons supplied. As with monopolies, there were specific exceptions, for example those relating to wages and employment, or authorised by statute. Agreements falling within the scope of the Act were made registrable with the Registrar of Restrictive Practices who was to bring them before the Restrictive Practices Court. This has the status of a High Court and consists of five judges and ten other members appointed for their knowledge and experience of industry, commerce or public affairs. Agreements were presumed contrary to the public interest, and the onus was on the parties to prove the reverse by seeking exemption under one or more of seven escape clauses or 'gateways'. Valid grounds for exemption would be found if it could be shown that the restriction gave protection from injury to the public, or benefits to consumers; was necessary to counteract measures taken by others to prevent competition, or to counterbalance a monopoly or monopsony; avoided local unemployment; promoted exports; or was required to maintain some other restriction which the Court had found to be not contrary to the public interest. If a case had been made out on one or other of these grounds, the Court had then to be further satisfied that, on balance, benefits to the public outweighed detriments. Otherwise, the agreement would be declared void, and continued operation would constitute contempt of court.

---

[1] The 1965 Act also provided that some agreements between firms, not registrable under the 1956 Restrictive Practices Act, and agreements relating solely to exports, might be referred to the Monopolies Commission. The Commission may also be required to make general reports on classes of agreement, a provision originally made in the 1948 Act but withdrawn in 1956.

[2] See also chapter 5, II. 6.

The 1968 Act extended the scope of the legislation to make registrable agreements relating to standards of dimension, quality or design, and agreements under which no restriction is accepted but information is exchanged. It also imposed a time limit for the registration of agreements, and penalties for non-registration. An eighth 'gateway' was introduced—that the restriction does not directly or indirectly restrict or discourage competition to any material degree. And it exempted agreements deemed by the Board of Trade to be in the national interest or intended to hold down prices.

RPM was excluded from the scope of the 1956 *Restrictive Practices Act,* although collective (as distinct from individual) enforcement was proscribed (i.e. agreements between a number of suppliers to withhold goods from a retailer who had cut prices on the goods of one of them). In the late 1950s RPM was voluntarily abandoned in some trades, especially food (where, significantly, developments in supermarkets, etc. have been most pronounced), but it remained common in most consumer durable trades.

Then, in 1964, this decision was reversed with the passing of the Resale Prices Act, which created a general presumption in law that the practice was contrary to the public interest. In form the 1964 Act was very like the 1956 Restrictive Practices Act, with a general prohibition subject to a general exception in the case of 'loss leader' selling, and specific exceptions under five possible escape clauses. These provided for continuation of RPM where the parties could prove that abandonment would result in a loss of quality; a substantial reduction in the number of shops; long-run price increases; a danger to health; or the removal of necessary services. Procedure also closely followed the 1956 pattern, with provision for registration and review by the Restrictive Practices Court; with the onus of proof on the parties; and with a similar, overall 'balancing out' of benefits and disadvantages.

IV.3 The Impact of Policy Measures

Only a small number of single firm monopoly cases have been dealt with by the MC— about a dozen in over twenty years to date.[1] The reports themselves have contained analyses of varying quality, their recommendations have not generally been far-reaching and, perhaps most important, they have not been followed by strong corrective measures by the government.[2] Generally, the Board of Trade has preferred to seek solutions through informal, voluntary assurances of good behaviour from the firms concerned. All in all, the legislation has apparently not made much impact on the dominant firm situation.

In the first five years of merger control about four hundred proposed mergers have been screened by the Board of Trade. Of these only some 3 per cent have been referred to the MC. Three planned mergers have been stopped (though without resorting to statutory powers to do so), and assurances have been sought in eight important cases. If the Board's and the MC's assessment of the public interest and the likely consequences in each case can be relied upon, it would seem that it is only in a small minority of cases that mergers have undesirable effects. However, on the same assumption, that small minority does exist. Meanwhile, the merger boom has continued,[3] at least in terms of the value of assets

---

[1]   See *Monopolies (and Mergers) Act(s) 1948 (and 1965), Annual Reports of The Board of Trade,* HMSO, 1950 onwards.

[2]   See Rowley, *The British Monopolies Commission,* for an account of progress up to 1964.

[3]   In part, perhaps, encouraged by another strand of government policy, the IRC (see p.195). Simultaneous promotion and control of mergers of itself implies no contradiction in different circumstances in which mergers may occur and the different possible motives prompting them. But contradictions clearly could result if policy were uncoordinated, and different criteria were applied in the two strands of policy.

involved, which more than tripled in the years 1965-8, to some £1,653 million. The number of mergers, however, has declined over the same period, from 995 to 598. Clearly, in the latter part of the 1960s the merger boom has been affecting the medium-large and large firm rather than the small and medium-small.

Between the 1956 and 1968 Restrictive Practices Acts about 2,600 cases were registered, mainly price agreements. By the end of this period the Registrar was able to report that virtually no cases of significance remained to be dealt with, the majority having been terminated, others having been varied.[1] Of course not all were heard by the Court. Many were terminated on the results of 'key' cases, as the parties saw the chance of success was slight, and others were terminated by the 'effluxion of time' and were not renewed. Undoubtedly the policy has removed a great mass of overt price-fixing that existed in 1956. But this is not necessarily conclusive testimony of its success. First, both the escape clauses in the 1956 Act and the quality of the Court's reasoning and decisions have been adversely criticised.[2] Thus, it is debatable whether the decisions taken by the Court were the right ones, so far as public welfare is concerned. Secondly, even if the agreements condemned were injurious to the public interest, it is questionable how far their abandonment has improved matters. The thinking underlying the legislation tended to assume that removal of a restriction would result in more competition, and this would automatically ensure benefits to the community (though in unspecified ways). However, one study found a strong tendency for the parties to find alternative ways of producing the same result as under the agreement—notably by information exchange.[3] Moreover, if the practices abandoned were in fairly concentrated, oligopolistic markets, it is quite likely that they merely formalised the mutually accommodating behaviour which would in any case occur. Removal of the agreement would not touch the underlying structural cause of this behaviour.

As outlined earlier, the 1968 Act did deal with the information agreement loophole—and also began to tackle problems of evasion and non-registration—but it did nothing which would reduce the force of the other criticisms.

Since the 1964 Resale Prices Act RPM has been prohibited in a few trades after a Court hearing; substantial lists have been published from time to time prohibiting RPM in trades which had initially sought exemption but had not subsequently attempted to defend the practice; and RPM has also been voluntarily abandoned in many areas without exemption being sought. Altogether, it has ceased to be a common practice in the UK. Price competition between retailers has emerged on some goods (e.g. electrical consumer durables, wines and spirits), but a common reaction has been for manufacturers to substitute, and advertise, recommended prices. Asked to investigate this practice, the MC concluded that it operated with different effects in different industries, not always in a way contrary to the public interest, but that case-by-case review was merited.[4] It is difficult to tell whether or how far the abandonment of RPM has yet contributed towards longer-term developments in retailing methods, etc.[5]

---

[1] See Reports of the Registrar of Restrictive Trading Agreements, Cmnd 1273, 1603, 2246, 3188 and 4303.

[2] See, e.g., Stevens and Yamey, *The Restrictive Practices Court,* chapters 4 and 9.

[3] J. B. Heath, 'Restrictive Practices and After', *MS,* May 1961.

[4] See Monopolies Commission, *Recommended Resale Prices,* HC 100, 1968-9.

[5] The Reddaway Report did find improvements in productivity in retailing, partly due to SET, partly to the abolition of RPM. See *Effects of the Selective Employment Tax: First Report on the Distributive Trades,* HMSO, 1970.

VI.4   An Appraisal of Policy

In view of the uncertainty over the effects of monopolies and mergers, and the fact that
there may be advantages to the community as well as disadvantages, it is appropriate
that the attitude adopted in UK legislation is a 'neutral' or uncommitted one. Thus monopolies and mergers are not made illegal *per se,* but rather are made liable to case-by-case
investigation. Whether there is justification for the more committed line on restrictive
practices and RPM, against which the legislation has created a general presumption of
undesirability, is perhaps questionable. But it is worth noting that this was done (in 1956)
only after the accumulation of some practical experience with such practices,[1] and all
three relevant Acts provide escape clauses, again relating to the effects of the practices.
Moreover, imposing compulsory registration and a general ban, subject to exceptions which
the parties must justify, could be seen as a necessary device to facilitate detection of
restrictive practices and RPM whose existence is less obvious than that of monopolies and
mergers.

The 'second-best' problem—that removal of one monopoly or restrictive agreement out
of many may not improve resource allocation and could even worsen it—has apparently
not concerned the legislators. If taxed with it, however, they might retort that the argument
depends on a particular set of assumptions out of several; that resource allocation is not
the only consideration; and, possibly, that any short-term deterioration must be tolerated
as the price of securing the long-term aim of eliminating or controlling *all* monopolies etc.

The use of a judicial body for the control of restrictive practices has caused some discussion.[2] One main doubt has been whether a court of law is the best place to resolve
complex economic arguments. It has also been argued that the job of balancing advantages
against disadvantages, and of comparing hypothetical with real situations, is quite alien to
usual judicial processes, which are interpretation of the law and finding fact. The suitability of judicial procedures has also been questioned. However, it is difficult to see how the
kind of policy in force at present could work without a judicial body; to change from a
judicial body would probably mean a change to an altogether different type of policy.

Finally, perhaps the most fundamental issue in monopoly and restrictive practices
policy is the underlying presumption in favour of competition. This can be seen at various
points in the legislation and reports. Thus the MC has, in effect, been asked to investigate
the social efficiency of some firms and markets, but only where competition is absent, in
the sense that the one-third rule applied. By implication, markets which are 'competitive'
in this sense do not require investigation. Then, in the reports of the MC there are suggestions that where the Commission has found some competition to exist, it has usually
looked favourably upon the firms concerned and not enquired so deeply into their performance. For instance, the MC seems to have been much less suspicious of high profits
if earned 'in the face of competition'. Thirdly, the general presumption against restrictive
practices is obviously a presumption in favour of competition, since it is competition
which is restricted. Finally, the 1968 Restrictive Practices Act and the 1970 Commission
for Industry and Manpower Bill contained direct statements of preference for competition.
The first introduced the defence for restrictive practices that they do not restrict or dis-

---

[1]   Monopolies Commission, *Collective Discrimination. A Report on Exclusive Dealing, Collective
    Boycotts, Aggregated Rebates and other Discriminatory Trade Practices,* Cmnd 9504, HMSO, 1965.

[2]   See, e.g., Stevens and Yamey, *The Restrictive Practices Court,* Chapters 3, 6 and 7.

courage competition; the second explicitly provided for reference to the future CIM of situations in which two or more firms (with a one third market share) 'inhibit competition'.

It is true that this basic presumption in favour of competition is a qualified one, since it is recognised that monopolies, etc. may not be undesirable in all respects or in all circumstances.[1] But what is meant by competition and exactly how it promotes the public interest is not spelled out, and in practice there is a discernible tendency to regard competition as an end in itself. In fact 'competition' could mean the perfect competition model, the condition that price equals marginal cost, a competitive (atomistic) market structure, or merely some sort of oligopolistic rivalry between firms. None of these can be relied upon with certainty to promote the public interest,[2] especially the last, since this may lead to such forms of competitive behaviour as can produce excessive advertising and unnecessary product proliferation; may result in excess profit; will usually mean price is not equal to marginal cost, etc. Moreover, such evidence as we have suggests that where competition exists in the UK it is usually of this type.[3]

In view of this, the fact that UK legislation has previously not included oligopolistic competition among its targets is a serious omission.[4] The 1970 bill would have done something to make up for this, since many more oligopoly situations would have become liable to investigation. Moreover, the fact that the monopoly and merger problem was, under the 1970 bill, linked up with the problems of large absolute firm size, price restraint, and efficiency in general, does indicate that it was being seen as part of a wider policy area, concerned with the social performance of firms and industries in general.[5] Whether similar policy developments will take place following the change of government in 1970 is uncertain at the time of writing. Even if they do, if the performance of 'competitive' industries cannot be taken for granted, the next logical step would be to drop altogether the remaining bias in their favour, and give, say, a Ministry for Industry a brief for the review and improvement of industrial efficiency, regardless of market structure.

---

[1] The existence of government policies seeking to make good the deficiencies of unaided competition (e.g. through the IRC, the Industrial Expansion Act, finance of R and D, and in individual industries like agriculture, shipbuilding, aircraft and textiles) also indicates acceptance that 'competition' may not automatically achieve all that is desired: but this lies outside the area of legislation considered in the present discussion. See section VII of this chapter.

[2] See also R. M. Cyert and K. D. George, 'Competition, Growth, and Efficiency', *EJ*, March 1969.

[3] In a study using 1951 data, 90 out of 219 trades (41 per cent) were classified as monopolistic or oligopolistic, 69 (32 per cent) were on the borderline of being competitive or oligopolistic and 60 (27 per cent) were classified as competitive. (See R. Evely and I. M. D. Little, *Concentration in British Industry*, Cambridge University Press, 1960). A subsequent study shows that concentration increased in 36 of 63 industries over the period 1951-8, and fell in 16, with two showing no change and nine undetermined. See A. Armstrong and A. Silberston, 'Size of Plant, Size of Enterprise and Concentration in British Manufacturing Industry 1935-58', *JRSS*, Ser. A, 1965.

[4] Oligopoly situations at present fall within the legislation only if one firm has a one-third market share. The arbitrariness of the one-third rule at the margin may be shown by a simple example; an industry where one firm has 34 per cent of the market and three others have 22 per cent each would fall within the UK legal definition of monopoly whereas an industry where four firms have 25 per cent each would not, although behaviour within the two industries might be very similar.

[5] The omission of the IRC in the reorganisation of the MC and NBPI made the tidying up operation incomplete, however.

V   REGIONAL POLICY AND THE LOCATION OF INDUSTRY[1]

V.1   The Regional Problem

The exact nature and extent of the regional problem are hard to define precisely. One recent writer acknowledges that the problem can be seen as any factor which creates a sense of regional grievance.[2] More generally, the regional problem is seen in terms of the 'imbalance' between the various regions of the UK for which statistics are kept[3] in unemployment and activity rates, average income per head, output growth and net emigration. Details of some of these regional disparities are given in chapter 5, III. 2 and table 5.10. Whether these differences between the regions are entirely or mainly due to some regions having an unfortunate industrial structure is a matter of some dispute. But it certainly is true that at least since around the mid-1950s the regional problem has been much affected by the decline of the coal, cotton, textile and shipbuilding industries and by declining agricultural employment.

To keep the regional problem in perspective two points should be borne in mind. One is that by international standards the imbalance between the regions in the UK is rather slight.[4] This probably has much to do with the fact that the UK regions, as defined, are nearly all mixed, urban-rural areas, with a fair spread of activities. Secondly, a successful solution to the regional problem would not necessarily need to eliminate all of the regional disparities noted. For some inter-regional differences would not be valid grounds for a grievance, for example differences in income per head due to regional differences in the skill-mix of the labour force; in productivity (output per man) due to regionally different capital/labour ratios; in activity rates due to differences in the age structure of the population and due to the geographical distribution of the idle rich; and in growth rates which reflect regional differences in natural endowments (provided any social costs, e.g. unemployment, have been taken care of). Moreover, some potential solutions to the regional problem might *increase* some regional disparaties at least in the short run, for example a policy of 'workers to the work' would widen the differences in net emigration rates. The one disparity which probably would need to be eliminated entirely by a successful solution to the regional problem is that in unemployment rates.

V.2   The Objectives of Regional Policy

The original objective of regional policy was to reduce the very high unemployment rates in the regions in the 1930s. The concern with unemployment rates at that time was probably on humanitarian and social justice grounds; it was relatively uncluttered by considerations other than these; and the regional unemployment problem was part of a national unemployment problem.

Concern over regional unemployment is still fundamental to UK regional policy. Doubtless humanity and social justice still help ensure that this is so, but other things have changed. A national unemployment problem no longer exists, and the regional unemploy-

---

[1]   See also A. J. Brown 'Surveys of Applied Economics: Regional Economics, with Special Reference to the United Kingdom', *EJ*, December 1969; G. McCrone, *Regional Policy in Britain*, Allen and Unwin, 1969; and H. Richardson, *Elements of Regional Economics*, Penguin, *1969.*

[2]   Brown, 'Surveys of Applied Economics'.

[3]   The new standard regions for which statistics are given were redefined in 1966 to coincide with the regions used for economic planning. They now are: Northern, Yorkshire and Humberside, E. Midlands, E. Anglia, S. East, S. West, Wales, W. Midlands, N. West, Scotland and N. Ireland.

[4]   Brown, 'Surveys of Applied Economics'.

ment issue has more recently been bound up with other policy objectives. One of these is economic growth and the efficient utilisation of national resources.[1] Thus, one aspect of the regional unemployment issue now much stressed is the loss of potential output which is involved. Absorption of reserves of manpower would permit more rapid growth than was otherwise possible, at least for a time.[2] And although the increased capacity for growth would probably be only temporary, there would be a continuing benefit in so far as, even if the long-run attainable rate of growth were not increased, the once-for-all improvement would mean that future growth took place from a higher base. A second aspect of regional unemployment is the effects on excess demand or supply of labour in the different regions. This is important in connection with government control of the level of economic activity in the country as a whole. The argument is that as momentum gathers in the economy, inflationary pressure is quickly encountered in low-unemployment areas, and this requires restraints to be imposed earlier than would otherwise be the case. Elimination of the existing regional imbalance, it is argued, would permit the economy to be run closer to full capacity for a given degree of inflationary pressure. This particular facet of the regional question was clearly not important in the 1930s. Thirdly, the regional question was set in a wider context in the mid 1960s when it became involved in the more ambitious planning exercises for the economy as a whole which culminated in the publication of the *National Plan*.[3] Finally, it should be added that any regional policy objectives of an economic kind interwine heavily with purely political considerations, especially as the more depressed regions are in general areas of strong Labour Party support.

Underlying all this there are perhaps two basic factors giving rise to a need for a government regional policy. First, persistent regional unemployment indicates a continuing labour market disequilibrium, with excess supply of labour at the existing level of wages in some areas. Manifestly, this has not been self-curing via normal market mechanisms in the past. Presumably this is partly because of the sheer immobility of labour and of firms; it may also be partly due to the downward rigidity of wage rates, etc. such that local unemployment is not reflected in low wage rates that would induce inward migration of firms; or it may be that firms' behaviour, contrary to the profit maximising model, is such that they do not necessarily respond to such inducements. Whatever the reasons for equilibrium not being reached, the need for government intervention to achieve it would be one basic justification of some form of regional policy. The second basic justification would be the

---

[1] See, e.g. *The National Plan*, HMSO, Cmnd 2764, 1965, pp. 11-12; Douglas Jay (then President of the Board of Trade), 'Distribution of Industry Policy and Related Issues', *EJ*, vol. LXXV, no. 300, December 1965; DEA, *The Task Ahead: Economic Assessment to 1972*, HMSO, 1969.

[2] *The National Plan* (p. 37) estimated that if regional unemployment rates could be reduced to the national average level where they are presently higher, an extra 100,000 workers would be added to the total labour force of the UK, while a levelling up of activity rates would add some 360,000. Together these would give an increase in the total labour force of nearly 2 per cent. Total output would not necessarily rise by the same proportion, however, firstly because this depends also on the quantity of capital employed and secondly because a high proportion of the increase in numbers would be women, whose contribution to total output is below the average.

[3] In the event the real impact on regional policy measures was not great. However, the standard regions were redefined in 1966 to coincide with planning areas, and a complex of regional planning machinery was set up. Two types of body were created. *Regional councils,* consisting of around two dozen members drawn from industry, local government and universities, were to advise on broad strategy and assist in the formulation and implementation of regional plans. They were to work in close collaboration with a parallel system of *regional boards,* composed of senior civil servants representing in each region the various Ministries concerned. Authority and responsibility for planning, however, remained with ministers and local authorities. The apparent intention was to ensure that the best use be made of the whole of *every* region's resources in the context of planned or expected national developments. Among these resources pools of unemployed labour would, of course, be counted.

likely divergence of social and private costs and benefits in firms' location decisions. Thus, left to their own devices, firms might well choose locations which permitted minimum cost production—or at least a satisfactorily low level of costs—when only the costs actually entering their accounts are considered. But when the social costs are taken into account (e.g. arising from increased congestion),[1] we might find that the most desirable location was a quite different one. The need to adjust for such discrepancies constitutes the second justification for a regional policy. Of course the two factors are not independent, because the existence of market disequilibrium can itself create social/private divergences of the relevant type. Thus on private grounds a firm might be indifferent as between two locations, but could confer a social benefit by reducing local unemployment in one of them, as against increasing excess demand for labour in choosing the other (assuming this location to be in an area of full employment).

V.3   Regional Policy Measures[2]

Regional policy measures have been taken under a number of Acts, in particular the Special Areas Act, 1934, the Distribution of Industry Acts since 1945, and the Local Employment Acts since 1960, and with modifications in various budgets. The general procedure has been to designate areas or districts with high unemployment rates for special treatment to attract firms to them. Currently these areas are the whole of Scotland (except Edinburgh), the northern region and the Furness peninsular, Merseyside, most of Wales, Cornwall and north Devon, and Northern Ireland.[3]

The forms of special treatment fall into three broad categories. One long-standing measure is government provision of 'advance factory units' for sale or lease to firms at attractive rates. Secondly, various financial inducements have been offered to firms moving to or located in the development areas. Up to 1963 these consisted almost entirely of discretionary loans and grants which were mainly conditional on the creation of sufficient employment (at a capital cost not exceeding certain limits, albeit flexible ones). From 1963 to 1966 these were supplemented by a system of taxation allowances favouring firms in development areas. In January 1966 these tax allowances were replaced by cash grants. For a time these covered 45 per cent of the cost of industrial plant and machinery in the areas compared with 25 per cent elsewhere, but since the end of 1968 the relevant figures have been 40 per cent and 20 per cent. Then, since September 1967, manufacturers in development areas have received a Regional Employment Premium of £1.50 per week for each man employed full time and lower amounts in respect of women, young persons and part-time workers. When the UK devalued in November 1967 firms in development areas gained a further temporary cost advantage (of 37.5p a week in the case of adult male employees) because the withdrawal of the bonus paid to manufacturers in

---

[1]   In general it is not known how large such costs will be. But The Smeed Committee found that the costs incurred by a car or similar vehicle in central London rose from 1.67p per mile at 20 mph to 10p at 12 mph and no less than 30p per mile at 8 mph (a not unrealistic speed for rush-hour periods). See *Road Pricing: The Economic and Technical Possibilities,* HMSO, 1964.

[2]   It seems likely that the new Conservative government will make changes in regional policy measures. It is expected that responsibility for the policy will in future rest with the Board of Trade.

[3]   The 'Special Areas' before the war were S. Wales, N.E. England, W. Cumberland and the Clydeside–N. Lanarkshire area. After the war these were extended and added to to become fairly large development areas. In 1960 these were replaced by some 165 much smaller development districts, based on local labour exchange areas. The idea was to make the system more selective and applicable to 'pockets' of unemployment in more prosperous regions. In the event it gave rise to some uncertainty, since the list of districts was subject to frequent revision. In 1965 sixteen new areas were added making the existing ones (especially in Wales, Scotland and Northern England) more or less continuous and this reversion to broad areas has been continued subsequently.

addition to the SET refund did not apply to them until later. The third main regional policy measure (since 1947), has operated via the issue of Industrial Development Certificates (IDCs), required for factory building or extension. These have always been readily available in development areas and in the 1950s were fairly easily obtained elsewhere. Since then, however, control has been applied strictly in the midlands and the south-east. The total cost of regional policy is estimated at around £260 million per annum.

The previous Labour government had proposed certain modifications to the financial assistance offered under the policy, following the publication of the Hunt Committee Report[1] in 1969. An expected total of up to £20 million per annum assistance was to be given to certain 'grey' or intermediate areas—areas outside the existing development areas, but also suffering from above-average unemployment, etc.[2] This was to be financed by rechanneling some of the assistance going to development areas. Assistance would have taken the form of grants of 25 per cent of factory-building costs, advance factories, and development area training grants and other training assistance.

Alongside these principal regional policy measures there are some other relevant measures. First, in the immediate postwar period the government exercised direct control over available factory space (which happened to be mainly in development areas). Secondly, in the 1960s office development in some areas has been under control, beginning with London (in 1964).[3] Thirdly, government assistance for industrial retraining has an important bearing on regional policy, especially since creating regional employment will usually involve changes in the industrial structure of the regions, and hence changes in the pattern of skills required of the local labour force.[4] Finally, alongside the regional policy has been the New Towns policy under the New Towns Act of 1946 and the Town Development Act of 1952. By this policy around a score of new towns have been established and rather more enlarged. The principal objective here has been to relieve congestion and assist urban renewal in large conurbations. But this policy impinges on regional policy since the new and enlarged towns have by no means all been in development areas, and their creation may have been a counter-attraction to firms which might have moved to development areas.

V.4   Some Issues in Regional Policy

One major criticism of government interference in the location of industry is that this will give rise to an efficiency loss in the form of higher real costs of production.[5] This real cost must be set against the social benefits of regional policy, and might overwhelm them. This argument makes two assumptions. The first is that firms, if left alone, will locate at cost-minimising sites, and the second is that location significantly affects costs.

On the first of these, some recent work suggests that in practice firms do not approach location as a cost-minimising exercise, but more as is predicted by the behavioural theory of the firm.[6] Thus, apparently, firms do not seek an optimum location but rather an

---

[1] *Report of the Committee on Intermediate Areas,* HMSO, Cmnd 3998, 1969.

[2] The areas concerned are the Yorkshire coalfield; N.E. Lancs; parts of Humberside; the Notts-Derby coalfield; limited parts of S.E. Wales; the Plymouth area and Leith.

[3] In February 1969 control of office building ceased to operate in several counties, and the exemption limit in outer London was raised from 3,000 square feet to 10,000 square feet.

[4] See chapter 5. For firms in Development Areas financial assistance towards the cost of training was doubled in 1967.

[5] See e.g., A. C. Hobson, 'The Great Industrial Belt', *EJ,* September 1951.

[6] See B. J. Loasby, 'Making Location Policy Work', *LBR,* January 1967; W. F. Luttrell, *Factory Location and Industrial Movement,* NIESR, London, 1962; and R. M. Cyert and J. G. March, *A Behavioural Theory of the Firm,* Prentice-Hall, 1963, pp. 54-60.

adequate site which satisfies certain minimum requirements (including some which reflect the personal and social desires of the decision-makers). Choice is usually from among a very limited number of alternatives—perhaps no more than two or three. The decision to move is usually stimulated by some problem such as expiry of a lease or a cramped, physically constrained site, rather than by the attractions of alternative locations alone. And search for a new site is 'narrow' in the literal sense of not spreading far from existing operations. Of itself this evidence does not mean that the argument that interference necessarily results in an efficiency loss can be dismissed. For the sites selected might be *lower* cost locations than ones to which government policy directs firms, although not optimal ones. On the other hand they might be *higher* cost locations. Thus, once cost-minimising assumptions are abandoned, it becomes impossible to predict whether (assuming that location significantly affects costs), interference will on balance lead to an efficiency gain or loss.

On the question whether location *does* significantly affect costs, there is some evidence to suggest that it does not, at least for the majority of manufacturing. One study estimated that some 70 per cent of manufacturing is 'footloose', i.e. not critically affected by costs at different locations.[1] Another writer suggests that some two-thirds of manufacturing is probably footloose with respect to transport costs, which are obviously an important consideration in this context and have always received much attention in location theory.[2] A third very comprehensive study found little evidence of continuing excess costs in plants which had moved in relation to the levels in parent or original plants, although it could take five years for initial excess costs to disappear.[3] Thus it is perhaps unlikely that a serious efficiency loss would inevitably result from relocation of at least a good deal of manufacturing industry, though there could obviously be specific exceptions.

A second criticism of UK regional policy has been over its capital bias. Prior to 1967 the various grants loans and tax allowances offered as financial incentives related exclusively to capital expenditures. As a result the policy was especially attractive to firms with capital intensive operations, and this was clearly not helpful to the policy objective of creating new employment. Moreover by lowering the *relative* price of capital inputs, the policy would tend to increase the capital/labour ratio of firms receiving the assistance, perhaps causing this ratio to depart from what it should be for efficient utilisation of resources. Introduction of the REP and SET subventions in recent years—specific subsidies on labour—may have redressed this capital bias in the policy, but it is yet to be shown by how much.

A number of other issues have arisen concerning the nature of the policy instruments used at various times.[4] First, the widening of financial incentives after 1963 to include tax allowances or cash grants for investment, the REP, etc., have been criticised on the ground that a larger and larger proportion of the aid given has become untied to the creation of new jobs: it is available to firms already in development areas as well as to those moving in. As this has happened, it is argued, the cost effectiveness of the policy in creating new jobs must have fallen. However, a profit-maximising firm, with reasonably full information and already situated in a development area, would presumably now find it profitable to expand output and employment and seek to do so, and even satisficing firms with only limited perception would tend to do so insofar as aspiration levels adjust

---

[1]　R. J. Nicholson, 'The Regional Location of Industry', *EJ*, September 1956. But see also Brown, 'Surveys of Applied Economics', on the reliability of this result.

[2]　L. Needleman, 'What Are We to do About the Regional Problem?' *LBR*, January 1965.

[3]　Luttrell, *Factory Location and Industrial Movement*.

[4]　See also T. Wilson, 'Finance for Regional Industrial Development', *TBR*, September 1967.

to what is obtainable and if there is sufficient publicity surrounding the new measures. Secondly, it has been argued that replacement of tax allowances by cash grants meant that assistance is now paid to the inefficient as well as the efficient, since their receipt does not depend, as did the benefits through tax allowances, on profits being earned. Thus present policy may result in propping up ailing firms. On the other hand the arguments in favour of grants carry some force.[1] Broadly these are that grants are more likely to be taken into account in decision-making, since there is evidence that returns on investment are often calculated pre-tax;[2] that grants are more conspicuous and the benefits offered easier to calculate; and that the longish time lag in the 'payment' of tax allowances can be avoided, as can the uncertainty of benefits under the allowance system, since these depend on future, unknown, profitability. Especially if firms' location policy is on behavioural lines, it could well be that a system of grants is necessary for incentives to be effective, even if on other grounds tax allowances might be preferable.[3] Thirdly, it could be argued that the use of IDCs—a negative prohibition—as a policy instrument may be less acceptable than positive financial incentives. For if rigidly applied, IDCs could do harm by choking off investment and expansion altogether in some cases (e.g. in non-footloose trades). Financial incentives on their own would not entail this risk and, moreover, footloose industries would presumably select themselves, thus automatically minimising the real costs of, for example, achieving a given reduction in regional unemployment. This argument is quite strong so long as profit maximisation is assumed. On a behavioural analysis, however, the IDC comes off rather better in some respects. If firms 'satisfice', financial incentives on their own are unlikely to succeed, or will work only sluggishly. For although *higher* profits are made attainable in development areas, the response (especially from existing firms) may well be slight if *adequate* profits can still be earned elsewhere. On the other hand, failure to secure an IDC, like expiry of a lease, is exactly the kind of problem to which firms *are* stimulated to respond, in the behavioural theory, and the obvious response is to move.[4] Thus, like cash grants, the IDCs may be necessary for an *effective* policy, even if there could be other drawbacks. Moreover, on a behavioural analysis, the IDC, or similar controls, may have other merits. Thus, we no longer assume cost-minimising location decisions and, by prompting wider search than would otherwise occur, the IDC *could* increase the chances of lower cost locations being found. And, indeed, it could even be that the IDC is a necessary adjunct to financial incentives because it exercises an attention-focusing role in bringing their existence to the notice of firms.

Finally, let us look at two rather contentious issues in regional policy. One is that offering incentives to individual firms is not an effective way of inducing them to move to areas which are otherwise unattractive to them. More effective would be to create positive, real attractions like new towns or other 'growth points', and by the government undertaking more infrastructural investment in roads, docks, and other items of social

---

[1] The switch to investment grants was, in any case, a *national* rather than a specifically *regional* policy, See *Investment Incentives,* Cmnd 2874, HMSO, 1966.

[2] See NEDC, *Investment Appraisal, HMSO,* 1965.

[3] The preferability of tax allowances is not altogether conclusive, since it is based on equating the earning of private profits with a furtherance of national welfare—a hazardous proposition.

[4] Two pieces of empirical evidence may be cited in this context—Loasby's conclusion that the stimulus to move comes from the 'exporting' area not the 'importing' area (Loasby, 'Making Location Policy Work'), and the belief among the administrators of the policy that, at least up to the mid-1960s, it was the IDC rather than the financial incentives which had most effect.

capital stock.[1] Resolution of these arguments requires a good deal more knowledge than we have at present about firms' motivation, etc.

Secondly, there has been some dispute over the respective merits of the present 'work to the workers' policy and of the alternative solution by encouraging migration ('workers to the work').[2] Against the migration solution are arguments such as that the most mobile workers are probably also the fittest and most skilled, so that the areas they leave become even less attractive to firms; that social overhead capital might be wasted; that congestion in receiving areas would intensify; that the community life and culture in the emptying regions would deteriorate, and so on. However, some limited sorts of migration might avoid these effects (e.g. marginal population movements from large, old, industrial centres to expanding towns outside major conurbations in the prosperous regions). It is very unlikely that a thorough comparison of the costs and benefits of migration and of existing policy would indicate that present policy should be scrapped. But it may be that the two policies are not mutually exclusive and, especially in view of the very small scale of assistance towards migration at present,[3] it could be that some readjustment of the relative weight given to the two policies is desirable.

V.5   The Effectiveness of Regional Policy

A recent study shows that regional policy has had some impact, especially in the 1960s.[4] From 1945-51 about two-thirds of all moves in manufacturing were to development areas. But this was largely because, in this period of postwar reconstruction, the chief factor stimulating moves was availability of factory space, which was under government control and mainly in development areas. Between 1952 and 1959 this government control had disappeared, the shortage eased, financial inducements under regional policy were not yet strong, and IDCs were not too difficult to get outside development areas.[5] As a result, the proportion of moves to development areas fell below 25 per cent. But stricter control over IDCs and larger financial incentives subsequently raised this figure to 50 per cent by the mid-1960s.

However, the acid test of regional policy is its effects on the regional disparities, and here the evidence is somewhat mixed.[6] Up to the end of 1968 there had certainly been no long-run tendency for regional unemployment and activity rates to come more in line with the UK average. None of the depressed regions have apparently acquired rates of output growth significantly faster than the UK average, though regional policy undoubtedly has helped Scotland equal, and occasionally overtake, the overall rate in the 1960s, after a period of very slow relative growth in the second half of the 1950s. Except for Northern

---

[1]   See, e.g., *Report on the Scottish Economy 1960-61* (The Toothill Report), Edinburgh, 1962.

[2]   See H. W. Richardson and E. G. West, 'Must we always take work to the workers', *LBR,* January 1964. The alternative policies may be thought of as eliminating unemployment (excess supply of labour) by shifting the demand curve to the right (work to the workers) and shifting the supply curve to the left (workers to the work). The migration solution, even if successful in eliminating regional unemployment, would not necessarily remove all inter-regional differences. In particular it would, of course, *increase* net emigration from some areas.

[3]   See chapter 5, III.2.

[4]   R. S. Howard, *The Movement of Manufacturing Industry in the UK 1945-65,* Board of Trade, 1968.

[5]   In this period the problem was thought by many to have been solved. But the decline of mining, shipbuilding, textiles and agricultural employment had still largely to come (see section II.2 of this chapter).

[6]   See G. McCrone *Regional Policy In Britain,* Allen and Unwin, 1969, pp. 149-66.

Ireland and the South-West, the 'problem' regions all had higher personal incomes in relation to the UK average in 1954-5 than in the subsequent ten years. Finally, although the drift to the South-East checked in the later 1960s, net emigration from Scotland, the worst affected region in this respect, increased markedly in the 1960s.

Thus, the statistics available at the time of writing show that despite regional policy the regional problem remains. Two qualifying points should be remembered here, however. First, since the analysis of industrial movement shows the policy has had a substantial impact, it appears that the regional imbalance would now be very much more severe in the absence of the policy. Secondly, the longer-term effects, if any, of the latest main extensions of the policy in 1967 have probably yet to be reflected in the statistics.

One doubt about regional policy has always been the damage it might inflict on the non-development areas. The conclusion of the Hunt Committee was that in general this has not been too serious. The policy had diverted expansion from the prosperous South-East and midlands to development areas, without much change in the proportionate share going elsewhere. The measures proposed for a number of intermediate or 'grey' areas are outlined on p. 185.

VI   AGRICULTURAL SUPPORT[1]

VI.1   The Present System

As in almost all other developed countries, UK agricultural production receives government support. For many years now this has been in the form of two main types of assistance to farmers. Firstly, farmers receive 'deficiency payments' on most major products if the ruling market price is lower than a guaranteed price set by the government. This method of support depends on the fact that the UK is a net importer of food and that world food prices are below those of domestic supply. Consumers are allowed to buy at world price levels, but farmers receive the higher guaranteed price, the difference being paid by the Exchequer. Thus total farm revenues are increased (and also shielded from world price fluctuations) and so is domestic supply[2] and, because food prices are reduced below what they would otherwise be, there is likely to be effective redistribution of income in favour of lower-income groups. To set some limit to the Exchequer liability, 'standard quantities' have been in force for most products since about 1963, the guaranteed price falling as these are exceeded.[3]

The second main method of UK agricultural support[4] is via direct grants and subsidies for specific purposes, for example for the use of fertilisers and lime, for farm improvements, to small farmers, on calves, etc. A virtue of providing assistance in this form is that the grants and subsidies can be directed towards specific improvements in the efficiency of the industry. Grants, subsidies and guaranteed prices are reviewed every year in the light of production trends, market requirements, world developments, the cost to the Exchequer, farm incomes and efficiency, trading relations with other countries

---

[1]   See also D. Metcalf, *The Economics of Agriculture,* Penguin, 1969; and G. McCrone, *The Economics of Subsidizing Agriculture,* Allen and Unwin, 1962.

[2]   Assuming supply is not perfectly price inelastic.

[3]   In addition, minimum import prices and quotas have been arranged via bilateral agreements with overseas suppliers. See *Annual Review and Determination of Guarantees,* Cmnd 2315, 1964.

[4]   For certain products there are other special arrangements: thus in the case of milk, market prices are fixed; under the *Horticulture Acts* of 1960 and 1964 horticultural produce is protected by grants and by tariff; and there are arrangements for coordinating the marketing and production of some products, e.g. milk, sugar-beet and potatoes.

(especially the Commonwealth) and the national economic situation. The revisions are published around March every year, in the *Annual Review*.

Thus through the support scheme the government is able to influence unit costs of home production and also determine the effective prices received by UK producers. The total cost to the Exchequer for the year 1970-1 is expected to be £299 million. This compares with an average of around £270 million per annum over the previous three years, and a peak of £343 million in 1961-2.[1] Without this level of support (and assuming other countries continued to support their own industries) it is certain that UK output would be much less than at present. In terms of output, current policy is one of selective expansion, conditional on the maintenance of recent improvements in productivity. Beef, pigmeat, wheat and barley are the production areas where growth of output is currently being encouraged. The need for selective expansion is declared to be to save imports and to reduce the bill if Britain enters the EEC.[2]

The policy of permanently diverting more real resources to agriculture than would otherwise be the case requires justification. The most often quoted justification in recent years is agriculture's alleged import-saving role. It is argued that the extra food produced at home would otherwise have had to be imported; moreover, much of the food supply at present coming from abroad is seen to be technically capable of being produced at home, and so the import-saving argument is advanced in support of an even higher level of assistance. But the real cost of agricultural support—the foregone alternative products of the resources committed—is generally ignored, and in fact the full effect of agricultural support on the balance of payments is a complex matter. The crude figure of imports 'saved' (even after allowing for the cost of extra imports of feed, fertiliser, etc.) is only a starting point. Account must be taken of exports which might have resulted from the use of the same resources elsewhere, net of imports required in these alternative uses. Allowance must also be made for the fact that larger UK food imports might have increased the capacity of overseas food suppliers to buy British exports, and for any difference in terms of trade caused by the smaller scale of UK agriculture. There has been a good deal of dispute over the real balance of payments effect of the existing level of support, and over the external payment effects of enlarging or reducing this level.[3] Certainly the crude import saving argument is not to be accepted without question.

A second reason given for agricultural support is that it raises and stabilises farm incomes. Of course, farmers have no more inherent right to this than any other sector of the community. The case argued for special treatment of agriculture is that because of some particular characteristics of supply, especially the competitive structure of the industry and the immobility of many factors once committed to agricultural use, the industry is unable to adjust to new equilibria following changes in the circumstances it faces, for example technical change. Thus, if totally unaided, the industry has a chronic tendency to disequilibrium, with excess capacity and excess competition, and unduly low returns to farmers. If this analysis is accepted, some form of government intervention is required. However, the remedy applied need not involve holding agricultural output at any particular level. Rather, it might take the form of an attack on the underlying structural characteristics of the industry, countering the various factors operating to prevent equilibrium

---

[1] Figures include grants, price guarantees, administrative cost, and a grant to the Northern Ireland Exchequer of about £10 million per annum.

[2] See *Annual Review and Determination of Guarantees, 1970,* Cmnd 4321, HMSO, 1970. For further details of the selective expansion programme see *National Plan,* Cmnd 2764, HMSO, 1965.

[3] See, e.g., J. M. Slater and D. R. Colman, 'Agriculture's Contribution to the Balance of Payments', *District Bank Review, September 1966,* and references therein.

being reached. Such measures have been taken for other industries, for example under the 1959 *Cotton Industry Act.*[1]

Other arguments in favour of agricultural support include a defence on strategic grounds—a safeguard of food supplies in case of a future war or similar world emergency—and the argument that promoting agriculture helps preserve a valuable national asset, its rural culture and way of life. However, it is questionable whether in modern conditions the UK's ability to produce around one-half of its food is a rational preparation for any future conflict, and the rural culture argument undoubtedly contains a strong emotional content.

In sum, it may well be that there are some benefits to the community from the agricultural support programme. But whether the present form and level of support are the right ones is another matter. The questions of form and level are interdependent. Assuming that the form of support were correct, the test of whether the level of support was correct would be whether or not the net social returns at the margin from agricultural support were not less than would be the marginal return on the resources committed in alternative uses. If this marginal condition does hold at present, it does so by accident, for despite the long history of the policy and the large sums involved, no systematic official appraisal of the costs and benefits involved has ever, apparently, been made.

VI.2   If Britain Joins the Common Market[2]

EEC members are about nine-tenths self-sufficient in food production, and completely so or in surplus for some temperate foods. The Common Agricultural Policy (CAP) provides for both extension of the common market to agriculture and substantial agricultural support. Farmers receive support mainly from high market prices, which are maintained mainly by import levies on imports from non-members, and also by administrative means and support buying. An Agricultural Guidance and Guarantee Fund also provides limited production subsidies, finance for structural reforms, and export subsidies. The total budgetary cost rose from £205 million to £950 million in the three years up to 1968-9, this very large increase being due partly to extended coverage of products and changes in financing arrangements, but also to the emergence of surpluses. When the cost of support via higher prices is also taken into account, it has been estimated that the total cost amounts to about 4 per cent of EEC GNP.[3]

The EEC system has been much criticised.[4] Agricultural support via high market prices tends to produce surpluses, because it simultaneously encourages supply but curbs demand. Moeover, it is regressive, because the burden falls mainly on low income groups, who spend proportionately more on food, and there is no reason to suppose that this is fully offset by the distributional pattern of the out-payments. Then, the EEC system does not permit the same kind of selective encouragement of improved methods, etc. as the UK system of grants and subsidies. (European farming is, on average, much less efficient, in terms of output per man, than British.) Further, the system of uniform prices has been criticised because a price level which stimulates efficiency in one country may well inhibit it in another. Next, the apparent aim of self sufficiency in EEC food supply, together with high food prices, arguably hinders world trade and development. For it reduces exporters' incomes and importing potential in other, food-producing

---

[1]   See above p. 162, footnote 3.

[2]   See also *The Common Agricultural Policy of the EEC*, Cmnd 3274, HMSO May 1967.

[3]   N. Kaldor, 'Europe's Agricultural Disarray', *New Statesman*, 3 April 1970.

[4]   See *ibid.*

countries, and simultaneously, perhaps, reduces the external competitiveness of EEC manufactured goods. Finally, the whole basis of a common market in agriculture has been questioned, since the potential benefits from integrating agriculture between member states are allegedly very minor, compared with those of manufacturing industry.

In joining EEC, assuming CAP remained much the same, Britain would undoubtedly become party to a support policy which is inferior to her present one.[1] The latest estimate is that food prices would rise about 18-26 per cent, and the cost of living, consequently, by 4-5 per cent.[2] Scope for countering the regressive effect of switching from support by taxation to support via consumer prices would be limited by the large amounts Britain would contribute to the community, especially from the levies on Britain's high proportion of food imported from non-members. Farm incomes would probably rise, and agricultural output might be 3-10 per cent above what it otherwise would be. But farmers would lose a good deal of the security and the basis for forward planning permitted by the present UK system. Moreover, the distribution of income would be different, some farmers gaining, some losing. The estimated total cost to Britain, had she been an EEC member in 1970, would have been between £150 million and £670 million *plus* the cost of support via high consumer prices. The estimated effect on EEC entry on Britain's food import bill is between £85 million *less* and £255 million *more* than at present, depending on assumptions made. No recent official estimate of the total balance of payments effect is given, but it is acknowledged that this would be more than the £170-£250 million estimated in 1967.

It is widely accepted that agricultural arrangements are a major difficulty surrounding Britain's entry to EEC.

VII   INDUSTRIAL EFFICIENCY

VII.1   R and D and Technical Progressiveness

The importance of securing technical advances in the form of new products and production methods needs no underlining. Not all stages of innovation, whether product or process, will necessarily require heavy R and D expenditure. In particular many important inventions in the past have been the work of individuals or small firms involving negligible expenditure. But the subsequent stages in the innovation process—development up to the point of commercial application, and actual commercial introduction—typically do involve substantial expenditure. A good recent example here is the hovercraft, a cheap, private, but very important invention which required large-scale government funds for development, etc.

In 1966-7 some 2.7 per cent of GDP was spent on R and D.[3] Of the £883 million total, some £448 million, or 50 per cent, came from government sources (not counting £35 million spent by public corporations). This compares with a total expenditure by private industry of some £352 million. On the other hand, private industry is the largest sector carrying out work (to the value of £561 million in 1966-7), because a large part of the total cost of work done there is met from government funds. In the main these represent government purchases of R and D on defence projects. A breakdown of R and D expendi-

---

[1] Early indications are that the Conservative government will introduce a system of support via higher market prices and import levies in anticipation of (and perhaps regardless of) EEC entry. A system of grants would probably be retained.

[2] *Britain and the European Community: An Economic Assessment,* Cmnd 4289, HMSO, 1970. The other predictions which follow are from this source.

[3] Source: *AAS*

ture by industry shows that the aerospace and electronics industries account for by far the largest shares of the total of work carried out in manufacturing, 26.8 per cent and 18.5 per cent in 1966-7 respectively, followed by the large group of mechanical engineering industries (9.7 per cent) motor vehicles (7.6 per cent) and chemicals and coal products (7.3 per cent). All other industries had less than 4 per cent. Other evidence shows that R and D activity is very much a preserve of large firms in the UK (as in the US). An FBI survey of nearly five thousand firms in 1959 showed that some 350 large firms (employing over two thousand workers) accounted for about 85 per cent of the total R and D expenditure, with medium and small firms contributing only a minor share, and small firms virtually nothing.[1]

This last finding lends support to the hypothesis that large absolute size in firms is a necessary condition for technical progressiveness, because of the large sums required (at least in the later stages of development and for investment in new techniques), etc.[2] Against this, however, there is evidence (both in Britain and in other countries) that large firms are a comparatively minor source of fundamental breakthroughs,[3] and there is something of a suspicion that the R and D resources they commit are devoted mainly to product improvement and modification, perhaps more so than is in the interests of the community.

The question of large absolute size and technical progressiveness intertwines with the argument that market power (large size relative to market supply) is an important facilitating condition.[4] Empirical tests of this hypothesis and its rival—that competition is conducive to technical progress—have so far proved very inconclusive.[5] It is difficult to say why this is. It might be because of practical difficulties in measuring technical progressiveness, of which there is no *direct* measure. Alternatively, the explanation could be that both competition and market power carry with them both advantages and disadvantages from the point of view of securing technical advances, and the balance between them is either roughly equal or varies from case to case. Thirdly, it may be that there are other important factors at work. Some case-study evidence certainly would suggest that there are, the quality of management being a very important one.[6]

---

[1]   See C. Freeman, 'R and D: A Comparison Between British and American Industry', *NIER*, May 1962.

[2]   See J. K. Galbraith, *American Capitalism*, Hamish Hamilton, 1956; and Lord Blackett's evidence to the Select Committee on Science and Technology, *Defence Research*, HC 139-V, 1967-8.

[3]   See, e.g., J. Jewkes, D. Sawer and R. Stillerman, *The Sources of Invention*, Macmillan, 1962.

[4]   See above, p. 176.

[5]   The evidence is mainly for the US. For instance, A. Phillips, 'Concentration, Scale and Technical Change in Selected Manufacturing Industries 1899-1959', *JIE*, 1956, found a significant association between concentration and two partial measures of technical advance, labour productivity and horsepower per employee. D. Hamberg, *Essays in the Economics of R and D*, Random House, 1966, also found a positive relationship between concentration and R and D spending, concentration explaining, at best, some 38 per cent of the inter-industry variance in R and D spending. But non-significant results were obtained, e.g., by N. Terleckyj, in J. W. Kendrick, *Productivity Trends in the US*, NBER, 1961, and by L. Weiss, 'Average Concentration Ratios and Industrial Performance', *JIE*, July 1963. E. Mansfield, 'Size of Firm, Market Structure, and Innovation', *JPE*, 1963, found that the largest four firms had a disproportionately large share of innovations in the petroleum and coal industries, but less than their proportional share in oil and steel. O. E. Williamson, 'Innovation and Market Structure', *JPE*, 1965, using Mansfield's data, found that large firms' relative share of inventions in an industry decreased with monopoly power; one model showed the critical level, where the four largest firms have the same share of inventions as of the market, was when their combined market share was 50 per cent; another put this level as low as 30 per cent.

[6]   C. F. Carter and B. R. Williams, *Industry and Technical Progress*, Oxford University Press, 1957; also *Investment in Innovation*, Oxford University Press, 1958; and *Science in Industry*, Oxford University Press, 1959.

A fairly recent analysis of R and D effort and technical progressiveness in the UK draws attention to the relatively low ratio of high quality personnel to R and D spending; some overinvolvement in fundamental or basic research; and the abnormally large size of some research intensive industries, notably aircraft and electronics (an inheritance from developments in the second world war).[1] The chief constraint on technical progressiveness is diagnosed as a shortage of scientific manpower. The long-term remedy is obviously to increase the supply of engineers and scientists in the education programme, if possible. An interim remedy advocated is the scaling down of basic research and a reduction in size of the aircraft industry.

Previous governments have been well aware of the long-term need for scientific manpower, and have shown some signs of a disposal to limit the aircraft industry's size.[2] Many other public policies have a bearing on R and D and technical progressiveness. The large share of R and D which is government financed has already been mentioned. The benefit to private industry from this work would not be as great as if, for instance, grants of equivalent value were made for firms' own projects. Nevertheless, a substantial overspill of new developments into the firms' other operations does occur, especially in such fields as aircraft, electronics, metallurgy, engines and machine tools. Additionally, the government sponsors work on behalf of industry in its own research establishments; gives grants to cooperative research associations in various industries;[3] and, via the National Research and Development Council (NRDC), finances development of inventions made in government laboratories and universities and by private individuals, where this is in the public interest. A recent Green Paper[4] proposed the establishment of a Government Research and Development Corporation to coordinate the activities of most government R and D establishments and of the NRDC. Thirdly, there have been some very direct and specific measures taken following the establishment of the Ministry of Technology in 1964, notably financial assistance for computer development and advice on their procurement; and a mixture of R and D contracts, government testing, and guarantees for numerically controlled machine tools. Finally, concern to promote technical progressiveness has been one motive of several underlying policies for the structural reform of industries (e.g. via IRC and the Industrial Expansion Act),[5] and another policy which may have had some indirect effects is monopoly and restrictive practices control, though these are very uncertain.

One additional type of policy has been recently advocated which might, *inter alia,* increase firms' efficiency and R and D effort.[6] This is to increase firms' internal growth by fiscal and monetary measures. Drawing on the behavioural theory, the argument is

---

[1]   M. J. Peck, 'Science and Technology', in R. E. Caves (ed.), *Britain's Economic Prospects,* Allen and Unwin/The Brookings Institution, 1968.

[2]   Thus, the Labour government accepted the main implications of the Plowden Committee Report *(Report of the Committee into the Aircraft Industry,* Cmnd 2853, HMSO, 1965) which recommended among other things, that the industry should be made to contract to a size compatible with future demand, and that there should be concentration on projects where development costs were not disproportionate to market prospects.

[3]   These numbered 51 in 1961, and received a quarter of their total income from the government. However the total value of work done by them is very small in relation to that undertaken by private industry as a whole; 1.6 per cent in 1966-7.

[4]   Ministry of Technology, *Industrial R and D in Government Laboratories: A New Organisation for the Seventies,* HMSO, 1970. The future of this proposal is now uncertain.

[5]   See below, p. 195. The underlying argument, presumably, relates to the claimed benefits of large size in R and D work, etc. Structural reform might increase the demand for R and D input, but if the main constraint is on the supply side, the likely advances might be small.

[6]   R. M. Cyert and K. D. George 'Competition, Growth and Efficiency', *EJ,* March 1969.

that this would raise aspiration levels and stimulate more search for ways of reducing cost, and for diversification, etc. than would otherwise occur. Unfortunately, however, the precise policy measures required were not spelled out. Moreover, if the main constraint on technical progressiveness at present is the supply of scientific manpower, this higher level of search activity would have to be achieved via the more efficient use of existing R and D resources, not by increasing the commitment of resources to this activity.

VII.2   Scale, Unit Cost and Structural Reorganisation

There is a widespread view that economies of scale are prevalent, especially in manufacturing, and that they not infrequently fail to be exploited. No doubt this is one reason why the Labour government provided for the structural reorganisation of firms and industries, which usually meant reorganisation into larger units. The two main measures concerned were the creation of the IRC in 1966, and the Industrial Expansion Act, 1968.

The IRC was set up to seek out opportunities for rationalisation in private industry and in these cases initiate and finance mergers which might not otherwise occur.[1] With an initial capital of £150 million, it was empowered to advance both loan and equity capital and also to hold physical assets for sale or lease. Particular attention was to be given to cases where there were prospects for stimulating exports and technical advance, for it was claimed that it was here that many production units were too small and the pace of adjustment through market forces was too slow. The IRC was not given compulsory purchasing powers, nor was it intended to support unviable schemes and so prop up ailing firms and industries. Further, there was no intention that it should acquire a permanent stake in the new enterprises it created, but rather withdraw once the benefits of rationalisation were assured and re-use its capital elsewhere. It was provided that mergers promoted by the IRC would not be subject to review under the 1965 Monopolies and Mergers Act, though monopoly situations created might subsequently be investigated.

In the first year of its existence concrete results of the IRC's work were few. It has subsequently been associated with some spectacular mergers (e.g. Leyland-BMC and GEC-AEI), but the real extent of its initiating and catalytic role is difficult to judge.[2] By end-March 1969 it had invested £13.5 million in ordinary shares and committed some £52.5 million in loans to companies.

The 1968 Industrial Expansion Act was not intended solely to promote structural reorganisation, but one objective was to extend and amplify the work of IRC, and rationalisation schemes were included among those industrial investment schemes or projects for which government financial support was to be given. The Act provided for a maximum £150 million assistance for schemes which would improve efficiency; create, expand or sustain productive capacity; or promote and support technical improvements where these would benefit the economy of the UK, or any area of it, and where these developments would not otherwise take place. The support given could take any form (including loans, grants, government purchase of goods or shares or, by agreement, state purchase of undertakings or parts of them) and the initiative could come from one of several government departments. Where general schemes were involved, covering whole industries or parts of them, there was provision for the establishment of industry boards, to make recommendations to the sponsoring authority and undertake any administrative tasks delegated to it.

---

[1]   See *Industrial Reorganisation Corporation,* Cmnd 2889, HMSO, 1966; and *IRC Act,* 1966.

[2]   For details of industries affected, see *DEA Progress Reports,* no. 40, May 1968, and no. 54, July 1969.

It is worth enquiring what benefits the measures for structural reorganisation are likely to confer, in terms of reduced unit costs of production.[1] To do this we should need to know, first, how great potential scale economies are and, second, the extent to which they are already being exploited. The existence of scale economies can be detected either by observing the physical laws governing inputs and output in production (i.e. estimating production functions), or by direct observation of the behaviour of (long-run average) costs as scale is varied. In general, empirically estimated production functions in both the UK and most other countries have revealed remarkably few results that are inconsistent with a constant returns hypothesis.[2] However, empirical cost functions have tended to show that average costs decline rapidly at first as scale increases, but then fall less and less rapidly as scale is increased further, the cost curve tending to approach the horizontal. Thus, an 'L' shaped long-run average cost curve is observed, indicating substantial scale economies over smaller size ranges; further, but less marked, economies at higher size levels; but no evidence of eventual diseconomies of scale.[3] As one might expect, there is much variation between industries in the magnitude of available scale economies. For instance, according to one set of estimates, a five-fold increase in scale from the smallest size range in the industry leads to a handsome 49 per cent reduction in unit costs in iron-making, compared with only 10 per cent in footwear.[4] However, examination of the major results for UK industries does suggest that one very rough generalisation can be made, namely, that the bulk of scale economies in a trade are likely to have been secured by plants five times as big as the smallest, and, even where economies continue to be enjoyed at larger size levels, they will almost certainly have been exhausted by the time a size ten times that of the smallest plant has been reached.

Combining this tentative conclusion with data on the size distribution of plants in manufacturing enables us to get some rough estimate of existing efficiency loss from expected scale economies. Table 4.6 gives the numbers of plants in manufacturing in various size groups and the proportion of total net output of manufacturing accounted for by each size group. The table clearly shows that the vast majority of UK plants are small; in 1963 some 83.1 per cent employed less than one hundred workers. On the other hand, the tiny proportion of large plants employing over 1,500 workers contributed no less than 31 per cent of total sales. Moreover, over half (54.6 per cent) of total net output was accounted for by plants *at least* five times and *perhaps* ten times the size of the smallest size group (i.e. by those employing more than five hundred), in which we may tentatively assume that the bulk of scale economies can be exploited. Without closer study firm conclusions should not be drawn, but the general drift of the admittedly rough and ready estimates that have been presented would clearly be that the efficiency loss arising from the existence of high cost, 'too-small' plants may be less than is commonly supposed.

---

[1] The subsequent analysis is not intended to reflect in any way on the possible benefits from the speedier reorganisation of industries in response to changed trading conditions than might otherwise occur, or on the possibility of gains via increased technical progressiveness.

[2] See A. A. Walters, 'Production and Cost Functions: An Econometric Survey', *Econometrica*, 1963.

[3] See *ibid.;* also J. Johnston, *Statistical Cost Analysis,* McGraw-Hill, 1960; C. Pratten and R. M. Dean, *The Economies of Large Scale Production in British Industry,* Cambridge University Press, 1965; P. J. D. Wiles, *Price, Cost and Ouput,* Blackwell, 1961. In the present state of knowledge the possibility of eventual diseconomies of scale cannot be ruled out. Investigations so far have failed to reveal them, but there are some features of these investigations which could prevent their being revealed even if they did exist.

[4] Pratten and Dean, *The Economies of Large Scale Production.*

TABLE 4.6

Size Distribution of Establishments in UK Manufacturing, 1963

Number Employed	Establishments Number	(%)	Proportion of Net Output in Manufacturing
1,500 and over	668	(0.8%)	30.9%
1,000-1,499	520	(0.6%)	9.0%
500-999	1,617	(1.9%)	14.7%
100-499	11,440	(13.6%)	28.8%
11-99	69,981	(83.1%)	16.6%

Source: Census of Production, 1963.

VII.3 Productive Efficiency

Most economic analysis proceeds on the assumption that firms are efficient: thus the profit-maximising firm, under any circumstances, produces at minimum cost in the sense that the maximum physical output is derived from whatever resources are used, and also that factor inputs are combined in the most economical way possible, taking their relative prices into account. As a result the main sorts of inefficiency it has been concerned with are 'allocative' ones—the inefficiency of the productive system in promoting consumers' welfare due to the misallocation of resources by monopolies, tariffs, etc. One writer has drawn attention to the fact that such allocative efficiency losses are in practice exceedingly small, frequently no more than one-tenth of 1 per cent of GDP. By contrast, efficiency losses due to simple inefficiency in the everyday sense, i.e. failure to get the most from a given bundle of resources, or in the writer's words, 'X-inefficiency', can amount in many cases to 25 per cent of output and even as much as 80 per cent in some cases.[1] Much of the explanation for X-inefficiency, according to the writer, is motivational, although there is no attempt to link the phenomenon formally to alternative models of firms' behaviour. Doubtless this could be done. Indeed it has already been suggested in this chapter that firms will be inefficient in this sense under at least one of the managerial theories, and the same thing is true, *a fortiori*, of the behavioural theory.[2]

If the relative magnitudes of allocative- and X-efficiency losses are in fact anything like those that have been suggested, there is clearly a need for remedial measures. Two strands of recent UK public policy would be relevant in this context—the family of 'little Neddies' created since 1964, and price control.

Since 1964 some twenty-one Economic Development Committees (EDCs) have been set up in conjunction with NEDC. The original need for such machinery arose from moves towards more comprehensive government planning at the national level. The existing EDCs cover perhaps two-thirds of industry (by employment). Like the NEDC they are composed of representatives of government, trade unions and management, and their original task was twofold. One function has been to serve as a source of information on the performance, prospects and plans of individual industries in the formulation of nation-

---

[1] Harvey Leibenstein, 'Allocative Efficiency vs. X-Efficiency', *AER*, 1966.

[2] See above p. 152. Organisational slack is typically present in both Williamson's managerial model and the behavioural theory. In both cases its extent depends on environmental pressures. Inefficiency also occurs in Marris' model (beyond some point management becomes overstretched in its pursuit of growth, the rate of failure of new products increases and the capital-output ratio also rises). However, revenue maximisers would behave exactly as profit maximisers in this context.

al plans. The other task of the EDCs originally laid down was to report on progress towards achievement of plan targets and to take action on matters likely to prevent their
attainment. The National Plan outlined a number of specific areas where action might be
taken by the EDCs, including import saving and various measures to promote exports;
standardisation of production; rationalisation for greater efficiency; and industrial cooperation by the exchange of information.[1] Subsequent abandonment of the Plan's
growth targets did not by any means render less necessary or desirable fulfilment of this
second function, and, following the publication of *The Task Ahead*,[2] the EDCs now have
a new set of broad national objectives within which to work.

A very wide range of activities has subsequently been undertaken by the EDCs. Several
make regular demand and supply forecasts. Many have sought to probe into factors affecting export performance, sales opportunities in particular markets and import trends. Other
topics which have been variously covered include manpower problems, standardisation,
stockholding procedures, factors affecting investment, R and D, and the effects of decimalisation, taxation and devaluation. The EDCs also appear to perform a useful function
in disseminating information within their industries through their newsletters and reports.
There is also some exchange of information between industries and, in some cases, formal
arrangements for cooperation (e.g. between the chemical and engineering industry EDCs
to avoid problems in the supply of chemical plant), thus making for better coordination
of activities.

Under profit-maximising assumptions the value of all this could be questioned on the
grounds that these are precisely the sorts of things which individual firms and their trade
associations will in any case be doing in their own interests. Thus we might expect a lot
of overlap and duplicated effort. On a behavioural interpretation, on the other hand,
there is much less likelihood of this, and the work of the EDCs might be regarded as
potentially very beneficial, especially insofar as it amounts to enlarged search activity
within the economy. The main reservation would be whether there is much probability
that firms will take action on the basis of new information made available, etc. unless
some sanction is applied (i.e. unless there is a 'problem' to be solved e.g. inability to
maintain satisfactory sales, profits, growth, etc.).

This is precisely where price control comes in. Making firms unable to pass on cost
increases and maintain profit margins via higher prices is exactly the sort of 'problem'
to which firms, according to the behavioural theory, will respond by cutting slack,
widening search for new methods of production and, presumably, taking advantage of
opportunities thrown up by bodies like EDCs.

Recent price control began in April 1965 with the voluntary phase of the policy and
an early warning system for notification of increases.[3] It has subsequently passed through
periods of compulsory control, with a prices 'standstill' and later 'severe restraint', and at
the time of writing has now reverted to an early warning system coupled with government
delaying powers of up to four months, pending report by the NBPI (or CIM if the 1970

---

[1] *National Plan*, p. 46.

[2] Department of Economic Affairs, *The Task Ahead: Economic Assessment to 1972*, HMSO, 1969.
The 1970 election result has now made this a doubtful guide for the future.

[3] For details, see *Prices and Incomes Policy*, Cmnd 2639, HMSO, April 1965; Prices and Incomes
Acts, 1966, 1967 and 1968; *Productivity, Prices and Incomes Policy in 1968 and 1969*, Cmnd
3590, HMSO, April 1968; and *Productivity, Prices and Incomes after 1969*, Cmnd 4237, HMSO,
December 1969.

Bill is passed).[1] Throughout, it has been the duty of the NBPI to determine when price increases (or decreases) should take place, according to a set of prices criteria. These have varied only slightly under the different phases of the policy, and, in general, provided for increases to take place only if they could not be avoided by the firms increasing productivity or, where reasonable to expect it, by accepting a lower return on capital.

Even where the NBPI made no specific recommendations for improved efficiency, the sanction of an application for a price increase being refused could be expected to prod firms into cost-reducing behaviour along lines outlined above. In many cases, however, the NBPI has not only supplied the sanction but has also taken some pains to make specific proposals on how longer-term productivity might be increased to avoid future price increases.[2] For instance, in brewing it urged the use of OR techniques to determine optimal locations for distribution depots and the abandonment of costing conventions which made difficult proper appraisal of the performance of retailing units; the gas industry was recommended to make better estimates of future demand and avoid the use of present, inappropriate methods for determining likely returns on investment; and the coal industry was enjoined to take a more realistic account of the future competitiveness of its product. Proposals have also been made urging the adjustment of working practices to new techniques and changes in payment systems and structures, found by the NBPI to be an impediment to more effective use of men and capital assets. In more general ways, too, the NBPI has sought to modify and improve firms' behaviour, urging greater attention to costs and less preoccupation with the growth of output for its own sake;[3] emphasising to firms that they themselves are often partly responsible for cost increases they regard as beyond their control (e.g. labour costs); and attempting to break down conventions such as the practice of putting up prices on the assumption that cost inflation will continue at the same rate as in recent years.

Once again our assessment of the likely impact of policy depends on our expectations about how firms behave. Under profit maximisation the likelihood of large efficiency gains from the operations of the NBPI is much less than under the behavioural theory. But the very fact that the NBPI has found so much to say by way of specific recommendations for improved efficiency may, perhaps, be taken as evidence of both the existence of large X-inefficiency losses and also of the fact that the behavioural and managerial theories have something useful to say.

REFERENCES AND FURTHER READING

H. A. Simon, 'Theories of Decision-Making in Economics and Behavioural Science', *AER,* June, 1959.
F. Machlup, 'Theories of the Firm: Marginalist, Behavioural, Managerial', *AER,* March, 1967.
R. Turvey (ed), *Public Enterprise,* Penguin Books Ltd., 1968.
First Report from the Select Committee on the Nationalised Industries, *Ministerial Control of the Nationalised Industries,* HC 371-I, II, III.
Nationalised Industries: A Review of Economic and Financial Objectives, Cmnd 3437, HMSO, 1967.

---

[1] See also ch. 5. The future of the NBPI is uncertain. Prior to the 1970 election the Conservatives had promised to abolish it, but retention of some body now seem likely, carrying out at least some of the NBPI's functions.

[2] For useful summaries, see General Reports of the NBPI, Cmnd 3087, 3394, 3715 and 4136.

[3] Thereby, possibly, calling for a change in basic objectives.

A. Hunter, *Monopoly and Competition*, Penguin Books Ltd, 1969.

R. B. Stevens and B. S. Yamey, *The Restrictive Practices Court*, Weidenfeld and Nicolson, 1965.

C. K. Rowley, *The British Monopolies Commission*, George Allen and Unwin, 1966.

C. F. Carter and B. R. Williams, *Industry and Technical Progress*, Oxford University Press, 1957.

R. M. Cyert and K. D. George, 'Competition, Growth and Efficiency', *EJ*, March 1969.

A. J. Brown, 'Surveys of Applied Economics: Regional Economics, with Special Reference to the UK', *EJ*, December 1969.

G. McCrone, *Regional Policy in Britain*, George Allen and Unwin, 1969.

H. W. Richardson, *Elements of Regional Economics*, Penguin Books Ltd, 1969.

D. Metcalf, *The Economics of Agriculture*, Penguin Books Ltd, 1969.

G. McCrone, *The Economics of Subsidizing Agriculture*, George Allen and Unwin, 1962.

J. Johnston, *Statistical Cost Analysis*, McGraw-Hill Book Co., 1960.

C. Pratten and R. M. Dean, *The Economics of Large Scale Production in British Industry*, Cambridge University Press, 1965.

H. Leibenstein, 'Allocative Efficiency vs. 'X'-Efficiency', *AER*, June, 1966.

And for information on current developments in industry and commerce:

National Institute Economic Review (especially the annual survey, February issue each year).

Midland Bank Review, notes on 'Government and Business'.

5

Social and labour problems

I. POPULATION AND LABOUR

I.1 Population and Working Population

Between 1951 and 1968 total home population of the UK increased from 50.3 million to
55.3 million, i.e. by 5.0 million, or 10.4 per cent. The female population increased from
26.1 million to 28.4 million, and the male from 24.2 million to 26.9 million.[1] By 1975 it
is estimated that population will be 57.7 million, and by the end of the century, 70.3
million. In 1967, 23.5 per cent were under 14 years of age, 64.5 per cent between 15 and
64, and 12.5 per cent above 65. The proportion of population below working age increased from 22.4 to 23.5 per cent between 1951 and 1967, and that above 65 from 10.8
per cent to 12.5 per cent.

Between 1951 and 1968 there were net gains of population in England and Wales, and
Northern Ireland, with a small increase in Scotland.[2] Population has also drifted from
northern to southern England. Between 1951 and 1961 the UK death rate per thousand
population dropped from 13.4 to 11.8 for males and from 11.8 to 10.6 for females, whilst
the number of live births per thousand women in the 15–49 year age group has increased
from 62.47 to 77.54. Infant deaths under 1 year of age, per thousand births, dropped
from 31.1 in 1951 to 18.8 in 1967.

The working population is the total number of persons aged 15 and over who work for
pay or gain or register themselves as available for civil employment. The working population may not necessarily grow as population increases since changes in retirement ages,
raising the school-leaving age, increases in the numbers of persons undergoing full-time
educational and training courses, and HM Forces manpower changes, all affect the proportion of the population available for gainful employment. In 1951, this proportion was
47.6 per cent, and it rose to 48.1 per cent in 1966. Between 1951 and 1967, the proportion of the male working population to the total male population fell from 67.4 per cent
to 64.3 per cent, while the female percentage increased from 29.3 per cent to 32.9 per
cent; the absolute increases were 949,000 for males and 1,742,000 for females. Between
1951 and 1963 the working population increased by 0.7 per cent per annum compared to
a 0.6 per cent annual increase in total population. However, total working population fell
by 133,000 to 25.9 million between 1965 and 1967, while the population increased by
632,000. The male share of the working population dropped from 68.4 per cent in 1951
to 64.2 per cent in 1967. An increase in the economically inactive population results in a
proportionately smaller work-force having to support a proportionately larger non-work-
ing population. This has serious implications for future economic growth and for labour-
capital ratios in different sectors of the economy. Recent British population growth is
characterised by increasing proportions of both retired and under working age persons.
It is expected that the growth of working population between 1963 and 1973 will be
only one-third of that of total population growth,[3] and that throughout the 1970s the
working population will grow more slowly, due to the lower birth rates in the 1950s. The
raising of the school leaving age will also adversely affect the working population. No net

---

[1] *AAS* no. 106, Central Statistical Office, 1969.

[2] Population increased by approximately 10 per cent in England and Wales (figures revised for 1966-
9); 9.5 per cent in Northern Ireland and 2 per cent in Scotland.

[3] *EPG*, March 1969, p. 213.

increase in working population is expected up to 1974 since decreases in the under-15 age group will be offset by increases in numbers retired; a net drop of working population to 26.0 million by 1974, followed by a growth to 27.0 million by 1981, is envisaged. In 1967 50.6 per cent of the working population was below 40 years old; by 1981, this proportion is expected to increase to 52.6 per cent.

I.2 Employment[1]

In March 1969,[2] 24.2 million persons were in civil employment, two-thirds being male. 8.7 million or 39.2 per cent of all employed were in manufacturing industry, in which sector engineering and electrical goods (2.3 million or 26.5 per cent of civil employees) and construction (1.4 million or 16.7 per cent) provided the largest employment. 3.3 million persons were employed in finance, professional and scientific services, 2.7 million in distribution trades and 1.5 million in transport and communications.

UK labour market changes since 1951[3] are characterised by:

(a)   absolute and proportional increases in all clerical and allied workers between 1951 and 1961.

(b)   An absolute standstill and a proportional decline in skilled manual workers—around 6.0 million and from 26.3 per cent to 24.9 per cent between 1951 and 1961.

(c)   An increased number and proportion of professional and technical workers from 1.5 to 2.1 million (i.e. 6.6 per cent to 8.9 per cent) between 1951 and 1961.

(d)   An absolute and a proportional decline in semi-skilled manual workers from 6.2 to 6.1 million over the same period;

(e)   Similar reductions for unskilled labour, from 3.9 to 3.8 million between 1951 and 1961.

The total number of clerical, technical and professional workers increased from 28.9 to 34.1 per cent of all employees between 1951 and 1961; their proportion in manufacturing industry increased to 23 per cent of all employees. Total manual employment changed little in absolute terms but proportionately dropped by 5.2 per cent to 65.9 per cent in 1961 in all industries and services and by 5.6 per cent to 77 per cent in manufacturing industry. The long-term increase in white-collar employment is indicated by the continued growth of the proportion of all such employees in manufacturing industry; between 1961 and 1968[4] the proportion of administrative, clerical and technical workers increased from 22.1 per cent to 25.9 per cent. In October 1969, 36.1 per cent of employees in the chemical industry, 31.5 per cent in engineering and 25.5 per cent in printing and publishing were in this category. In the decade after 1951, total white-collar employment grew at the rate of 2.7 per cent per annum in manufacturing industry, slowing down to 1.5 per cent between 1961 and 1964.[5] These trends in employment have important implications for the level, distribution, composition and growth of trade union membership.

The number of managers and directors increased by 250,000 over the period 1951 to 1961. The number of small traders has increased absolutely but declined relatively as

---

[1]   For an analysis of employment and unemployment, see L. C. Hunter and D. J. Robertson, *Economics of Wages and Labour*, Macmillan, 1969.

[2]   *EPG*, January, 1970.

[3]   *EPG*, January, 1968, p.6.

[4]   *AAS*, 1969.

[5]   G. Routh, *Industrial Relations* (ed. B. C. Roberts), Macmillan, 1968.

reorganisation in distribution has taken place, e.g. supermarket development.

The capital-labour ratio and its significance for productivity has substantial repercussions on the size and composition of the labour force in an industry or an economy.
Increases in output obtained through higher productivity, if effected by changes in
capital-labour ratios, may not necessitate increases in the numbers employed. Changes in
production and productivity (output per man or man-hour) are important in the context
of employment. Increases in productivity accompanied by increases in total output may
create jobs of an administrative and clerical nature as well as displace manual workers
from production. Generalisations about the impact of technological changes on employment are difficult to substantiate; such changes do, however, create demands for more
white-collar employees. Table 5.1 indicates the changes in output, productivity and
employment in selected British industries.

TABLE 5.1

Output, Employment and Productivity, 1963-68[1] (UK)

Industry	% Change in Output	% Change in Employment	% Change in Output/head	Absolute Change in Employment[2]
Index of production industries	+19.8	−2.0	+22.2	−91,000
Manufacturing industry	+21.2	−1.2	+22.7	−118,300
Engineering and electrical goods	+30.9	+5.1	+24.5	+93,800
Vehicles	+17.2	−6.3	+25.1	−8,600
Textiles	+19.2	−11.8	+35.1	−90,000
Gas, electricity, water	+28.2	+3.3	+24.1	+9,300
Mining and quarrying	−15.2	−28.5	+18.6	−170,900

[1] *Source:* Derived from indices based on 1963 = 100, *EPG,* January 1970, p.90.

[2] June 1964−June 1968−derived from *EPG,* January, 1970, p.52.

Clearly, in engineering and public utility industries increases in output and productivity
are associated with more job opportunities, while in other sectors productivity increases
relative to output changes appear to have reduced the total labour force.

Employment differences may be qualitative as well as quantitative. New productivity-
increasing technologies demand higher qualified white-collar workers, and, simultaneously,
may render traditional skills redundant. Changing technology, computerisation, office
mechanisation, the growing complexity and size of companies and plants, the greater
demand for services with increasing national income per head, all pose important problems
for the future training and education of suitably qualified manpower. The more rapid the
changes, the more likely it is that existing qualified manpower will become technologically
redundant and so re-training facilities appear imperative if actual redundancy and long-
term unemployment are to be avoided.

Significant changes in female employment have occurred in recent years. The number
of employed females in the UK has increased in both absolute and proportional terms
since 1950. In that year, 6.9 million females were employed and by June 1969, 9.9
million. During the same period the female proportion of the total labour force grew
from 33.7 per cent to 35.5 per cent.

Although female activity rates remained stable between 1961 and 1968 (39.9 per cent
for both years), significant variations by region and age group are to be found. In 1968,
the areas of highest female activity rates were the south-east (43.4 per cent), west midlands
(42.7 per cent), and the north-west (42.1 per cent), while Wales (30.1 per cent) ranked as

the lowest. Between 1965 and 1968 the rate for the 15-24 year age group dropped from 67.9 per cent to 64.3 per cent while that for the 25-44 group rose slightly from 43.3 per cent to 43.8 per cent. The increased number of older females (45-59 age group) was reflected in a higher activity rate—47.2 per cent in 1965 and 50.1 per cent in 1968.

In June 1969, female employment was concentrated in the distributive trades (1.55 million), professional and scientific services (1.93 million), and miscellaneous services (1.01 million). The proportion of females aged over 40 in banking, finance and insurance was low (27 per cent), while in professional and scientific services 54 per cent were over 40 in 1968. In all industries and services, 41 per cent of female employees were over 40.

An increasing proportion of married women have entered employment. In 1950, 40 per cent of all female employees were married; in June 1968, 58 per cent were married; and the proportion is expected to rise to 66 per cent by 1981. In all activities except banking, insurance and finance, shipbuilding, and printing and publishing, married women represented more than one-half of the total female labour force. The lowest proportion of married women to all female employees is in insurance, banking and finance (39 per cent), the highest in metal goods' industries, engineering, bricks, pottery and glass.

An upward age group shift has occurred among female employees. Between 1956 and 1968, the share of the 40-59 years age group grew from 37 per cent to 42 per cent. The earlier family cycle associated with younger marriages frees women for employment in the early middle age span. Evidence[1] indicates that child supervision is an over-riding factor impeding employment of married women.

Significantly, part-time female employment in manufacturing industry has increased from 11.7 per cent of all employed females in May 1956, to 18.9 per cent in September 1969. Domestic commitments make part-time employment attractive to married women, while its casual basis offers employers a degree of labour flexibility.

The highest proportion of part-time female workers to all females employed[2] is found in the food, drink and tobacco industry (32 per cent); other manufacturing industries have 23.6 per cent and textiles 16.5 per cent.

The nature, structure and distribution of female employment has implications for the implementation of equal pay by 1975. While equal pay might resolve sex discrimination by remuneration in employment, some women fear that such equality could lead to their loss of employment if employers preferred to employ men rather than women.

Industries in Great Britain having the highest percentage of female to total employees in June 1968 were clothing (79 per cent), laundries (73 per cent), retail distribution and catering (each 64 per cent) and cotton spinning (54 per cent); the lowest proportions were to be found in chemicals (27 per cent), and engineering and electronics (34 per cent).

I.3   Unemployment

Since the demand for labour is a derived demand, changes in effective demand and government policies to control and shape it are reflected in the degree of unemployment. Between June 1965 and May 1969 the total number of registered unemployed persons in Great Britain increased from 276,142 to 528,283 or from a 1.4 per cent to a 2.4 per cent unemployment rate. In manufacturing industries the numbers unemployed rose from 77,890 to 151,271. Cyclical fluctuations impinge differently upon the demand for the products of different industries. A problem of *structural unemployment* exists where changes in the structure of demand rather than lack of effective demand cause unemploy-

---

[1]   Viola Klein, *Britain's Married Women Workers,* Routledge and Kegan Paul (International Library of Sociology and Social Reconstruction), 1965.

[2]   *EPG,* November 1969, p.1025.

ment. *Technological unemployment* occurs where new production methods displace labour on a significant scale; the process may not necessarily involve redundancies, but may rely on *natural wastage* to reduce the numbers employed in accordance with reduced job opportunities. Where necessary reductions in a labour force do not occur, for example because of trade union rules on manning levels, *underemployment* of labour can result, that is, we have a labour force surplus to technological or product demand requirements.

Certain industries are subject to seasonal variations in demand, for example construction, which can result in *seasonal unemployment*. *Frictional unemployment* arises when there is lack of labour mobility or job information, etc.; such unemployment is usually of short duration. The composition of the labour force influences the level and structure of unemployment: unskilled workers are more likely to become unemployed than white-collar workers. Casual employment, in industries like construction, creates unemployment problems where jobs are filled on a day-to-day basis.

Unemployment represents a waste of a nation's labour resources. It poses labour problems when those who want work cannot obtain it and it raises social problems when it results in reductions of personal and household income and creates undesirable psychological attitudes towards employment. Lack of local job opportunities may induce younger workers to seek employment elsewhere. In 1968, London and the south-east had the highest absolute level of unemployment, a 130,500 monthly average, but the lowest percentage rate at 1.6 per cent. The north-west had the second highest number of unemployed in England, 72,700 or a 2.5 per cent rate; Scotland had the second highest level of the UK at 82,900, but a 3.8 per cent rate. The highest percentage rate, 7.2 per cent in Northern Ireland, represented 37,200 unemployed persons; the second highest rate, 4.0 per cent in Wales, represented a level of unemployment of only 39,200. Clearly, the unemployment rate is a more significant indicator of regional social and labour problems than the actual number unemployed. The turnover rate of unemployed persons on the register was much higher in London and the south-east[1] than elsewhere between 1961 and 1965. Turnover in regional unemployment does not appear to be coincidental with percentage levels of, or changes in, unemployment. The duration of unemployment assumes greater significance when turnover is relatively low: the longer a person is unemployed, the longer he is likely to remain so. Between 1961 and 1965, 6.4 per cent of unemployed persons accounted for 50 per cent of the total number of working days spent on the unemployed register. Between 1961 and 1968, 68 per cent of newly registered unemployed could expect to find employment within four weeks; one-third of the male and half the female unemployed had good employment prospects.

Age is an important factor in securing employment. Men and women under 25 years of age were unemployed for an average period of less than four weeks between 1961 and 1968 compared with a period four to five times greater for men of 55 and over. In February 1969, nearly 45 per cent of unemployed men were 45 and over. In 1964, the age factor was estimated to prejudice the employment of 19.4 per cent of the unemployed (males 23.2 per cent and females 7.9 per cent). Redundancy for men over 40 years of age has profound social consequences—loss of status and income, difficulty of finding similar employment, re-training for other work, and the problem of finding employers prepared to recruit men of over 40 at pay levels acceptable to both parties.

Lack of job opportunity was detrimental to the employment of 18.2 per cent of all unemployed in the UK in 1964; this was particularly important in the case of married women, arising from restrictions on their geographical mobility. Semi-skilled and unskilled unemployed are less likely to move to another area than skilled and qualified persons. A 1967[2] survey indicated that of half the unemployed unwilling to move, 40 per cent gave

---

[1] See *EPG*, August 1968, p.627.

[2] *EPG*, April 1966, p.156, and July 1966, p.385.

family reasons and 25 per cent attachment to their own area. Mobility often raises considerable social problems—disruption of children's education, housing availability and cost, the severing of social and community ties, and uncertainties about new areas. In London and the south-east only 9.1 per cent of the unemployed faced lack of job opportunities in 1968 compared to 29.4 per cent in Northern Ireland, 23.4 per cent in Scotland, 22.9 per cent in Wales and 18.2 per cent in northern England.

Lack of necessary qualifications, experience and skill is claimed to be a less important factor in placing unemployed persons. In 1964, 1.6 per cent of the unemployed in Great Britain possessed qualifications, etc. prejudicial to their finding employment. In Northern Ireland 1.7 per cent, Wales 0.7 per cent, Scotland 2.5 per cent, northern England 1.1 per cent, midlands 2.3 per cent, and London and the south-east 2.1 per cent of the unemployed had unsuitable qualifications.

Government policies have attempted to alleviate some of these problems. Apart from important policies designed to increase regional job opportunities by encouraging the establishment of new industries in development areas,[1] several measures have been implemented. The *Redundancy Payments Act 1965* gives employees statutory rights to minimum periods of notice of termination of contract by employers and tax-free lump-sum compensation payments for dismissal because of redundancy, or for short-time working and lay-offs. The Redundancy Payments Fund is financed by weekly employer contributions of 6.25p for men and 2.75p for women and rights are related to the length of continuous service with the employer. The DEP gives assistance in finding alternative employment before employees become redundant. The DEP has also improved the communication of job opportunities between local employment exchanges. Measures have also been introduced to assist regional mobility. The *Industrial Training Act 1964*[2] aimed at promoting industrial training at all levels of employment, effecting qualitative improvements in training, and spreading the costs involved more equitably over the firms in an industry. The Act provides for industrial and commercial training through industrial training boards established under the guidance of the DEP; by February 1970, twenty-eight boards had been established covering 16 million workers.[3] The financing of training is on a levy-grant basis, the training boards being authorised to introduce and alter levies. Although the Act has brought about improvements in training, it has been criticised on the grounds that it provides no additional training funds, i.e. no funds from outside an industry; that only once-and-for-all training standard improvements are effected; and that the training board system has many aspects, e.g.board decisions replace those of firms, and the present financing arrangements are impediments to better operation of the boards.

I.4   Trades Unionsim

Trades unions are organisations of workpeople, whose main objectives are the protection and improvement of their members' remuneration and conditions of employment. Trades unions register with the Registrar of Friendly Societies to secure legal and other advantages; not all registered unions are affiliated to the Trades Union Congress (TUC), although this organisation represents the major unions in Britain.

---

[1]   See section III.2 of this chapter.

[2]   G. T. Page, *The Industrial Training Act and After,* André Deutsch, 1967.

[3]   D. Lees and B. Chiplin, 'The Economics of Industrial Training', *LBR,* April 1970.

The *Trades Union Congress*, founded in 1868, acts as a voice and coordinator of the British trades union movement;[1] it represents the interests of those unions affiliated to it, and its authority and status are derived from member unions. The TUC has little formal authority; it is governed by and does not govern the affiliated unions, which elect its executive body, the General Council, formulate policies, and take decisions at the Annual Congress. The General Council, acting as the highest body between Congresses, implements Congress decisions, aids member unions attacked on any trades union principles, promotes common action on wages, hours, and conditions of work, and watches and influences legislation affecting labour. The General Council is consulted by government departments and has close consultative contact with corresponding employer organisations. Representing the peak of a decentralised democratic trades union movement, the TUC leaves member unions complete autonomy. The lack of formal powers by the TUC and the decentralised control within the trades union movement have not always been fully understood by the general public; lack of desired TUC action has been interpreted as symptomatic of a dilatory organisation. Since 1965, the TUC has assumed greater responsibilities within the union movement, largely as a result of government policy and proposed legislation. Among the few disciplinary powers possessed by the TUC are those embodied in Rules 12 and 13, as revised in 1969;[2] these relate to intended or actual industrial disputes or stoppages, and inter-union disputes, although the latter have traditionally been resolved by the 'Bridlington Rules', whereby the TUC Disputes Committee hears cases of inter-union disputes and makes recommendations. The General Council may expel an affiliated union, but this is a rare occurrence.

TABLE 5.2

Trades Union Data   UK 1950-68

	Annual % Change in Labour Force	Total Trades' Union Membership (000's)	Annual % Change in Membership	Density %	Number of Unions	Average Size of Unions (000's)	Unions Affiliated to TUC (No.)
1950	+1.3	9,289	−0.3	44.0	732	12.69	186
1951	+0.6	9,535	+2.6	44.9	730	13.66	187
1952	+0.5	9,588	+0.6	45.0	714	13.40	183
1953	+0.4	9,527	−0.6	44.5	712	13.36	184
1954	+1.5	9,566	+0.4	44.0	711	13.45	183
1955	+1.3	9,738	+1.8	44.3	702	13.37	186
1956	+1.1	9,776	+0.4	44.0	683	14.31	185
1957	+0.7	9,827	+0.5	43.9	683	14.38	185
1958	−0.2	9,636	−1.9	43.1	673	14.31	186
1959	+0.3	9,621	−0.2	42.9	666	14.44	184
1960	+1.6	9,832	+2.2	43.2	662	14.85	183
1961	†1.2	9,893	+0.6	42.9	643	15.38	182
1962	+1.4	9,883	−0.1	42.3	622	15.88	182
1963	+0.5	9,934	+0.5	42.3	602	16.49	175
1964	+0.6	10,079	+1.4	42.6(1)	598	17.03	172
1965	+0.6	10,181	+0.9	42.6	583	17.39	170
1966	+0.6	10,111	−0.7	42.6	574	17.50	169
1967	−1.1	9,967	−1.4	42.5	555	17.95	158
1968	−0.6	10,048	+0.8	42.8	534	18.82	156

Sources: DEP; AAS; TUC Annual Reports

Note: Computation of DEP employment figures was altered for 1964 and after; figures not strictly comparable with pre-1964 years.

[1] A Scottish TUC also exists, and in Northern Ireland unions have connections with the Irish Congress of Unions, Dublin.

[2] See section II.7 of this chapter.

Table 5.2 indicates (a) the long-term reduction in the number of unions, (b) slow membership growth, (c) membership reduction in economically less favourable periods, e.g. 1958-9, (d) the decline in density of organisation, i.e. the proportion of actual to potential trade union membership from 44 per cent to 42.8 per cent, and for TUC unions from 38.2 per cent to 37.1 per cent. The average size of unions has increased from 12,690 to 18,820 members between 1950 and 1968. Distinctions must be made between the total number of unions, the number of registered unions and the number of TUC affiliated unions; in 1968 these numbered 555, 345, and 157 respectively. Over the period 1958-68 the total number of unions fell by about 20 per cent, and TUC affiliated unions by 16 per cent. The membership of trades unions increased by 8.6 per cent between 1950 and 1968, a growth rate less than that of the labour force. Overall membership growth masks important developments within different sections of the labour force. Between 1950 and 1964 manual worker membership increased by only 2.5 per cent, actually declining by 0.6 per cent from 1955 to 1964. Thus only one-quarter of the 11 per cent increase in TUC membership is attributable to manual workers over the period; this section of the labour force remained static. But there have been substantial increases in the membership of white-collar unions;[1] more than three-quarters of TUC membership growth between 1948 and 1964 is associated with white-collar organisations and membership of these as a proportion of TUC membership increased from 8.2 per cent to 13.3 per cent between 1948 and 1964.[2]

The British trades union movement is characterised by the predominance of horizontally organised unions, i.e. unions whose membership is drawn from and distributed over a range of different and unrelated industries. Few unions exist which are organised vertically, with membership drawn from and confined to one industry. Examples of horizontal unions are the craft and general unions, the Amalgamated Union of Engineering and Foundry Workers (AEF) and the Transport and General Workers Union (TGWU); and among vertically organised unions (industrial unions) are the National Union of Mineworkers (NUM) and the National Union of Railwaymen (NUR).

Although organised unions like the AEF or TGWU can offset membership losses in one industry, sector or labour force by widening their membership bases or devoting more resources to membership recruitment in other sectors, industrial unions have little scope for compensating membership losses associated with manpower reductions in their industries. Turner has modified the traditional union classifications of craft, general and industrial, by distinguishing between 'open' and 'closed' unions;[3] Hughes conceives of sectoral or sectoral general unions.[4] Employers' attitudes may promote or impede unionisation of their labour forces: some employers have 100 per cent membership agreements with unions, when union membership becomes a condition of employment, and some operate subscription check-off systems, when union dues are deducted from pay packets.

The *distribution of membership* between unions is lopsided in Britain. In 1968, 222 unions, 41.6 per cent of all unions, had less than 500 members each and represented 0.4 per cent of all members; 9 unions (1.7 per cent), had more than 250,000 members each and represented 54.7 per cent of all union members. The largest 19 unions (3.6 per cent), each with membership of over 100,000, represented 7.0 million or 70 per cent of all union members, while 358 unions of less than 2,500 members each represented 2.1 per cent or 204,000 members. 28.6 per cent of TUC affiliated membership in 1968 was

---

[1] G. S. Bain, 'Growth of White Collar Unionism', *BJIR*, November 1966.

[2] *Ibid.*

[3] H. A. Turner, *Trade Union Growth, Structure and Policy*, Parts III and VI, Allen and Unwin, 1962.

[4] John Hughes, *Trade Union Structure and Government*, Research Paper 5 (Part 1), Royal Commission (Donovan), 1967.

represented by two unions, the Amalgamated Engineering and Foundry Workers Union, 1.1 million, and the Transport and General Workers Union, 1.5 million; inclusion of the General and Municipal Workers Union, 0.8 million, accords these three unions (1.9 per cent of affiliated unions) 3.4 million members, or 38 per cent of TUC membership. The largest 15 unions contained three-quarters of all members. The membership concentration in TUC unions causes problems for that organisation; it gives a few unions a disproportionate influence within the TUC. A more even distribution of membership is alleged to be conducive[1] to increasing the credibility of the TUC as a body representative of trade union opinion, if only by reducing the political influence of large unions.[2]

Organisation density in 1960 was high in local government (84 per cent), national government (83 per cent) and insurance, banking and finance (31 per cent); the density in all these sectors increased very considerably between 1948 and 1960. In spite of considerable absolute and percentage increases, overall white collar density has barely kept pace with the rapid expansion of the white collar labour force since 1948; in 1948 overall density was 28.8 per cent, in 1964 29.0 per cent. Over the same period, manual-worker density dropped from 53.1 per cent to 51.0 per cent. White-collar gains have been insufficient to offset the decline in manual worker organisation. Total female trade union membership increased from 20.7 per cent to 23 per cent of all union members between 1950 and 1968, and from approximately 23 per cent to 25.7 per cent of the total female labour force. Density of female manual workers increased from 25.3 per cent to 28 per cent between 1948 and 1964. Failure to organise a higher proportion of the expanding white-collar and female labour forces, and stagnation or decline in the manual worker labour force, resulting in a falling proportion of manual union members, characterise important membership trends in the British trades union movement.

Membership changes and the degree of organisation are influenced by the level of employment, by changes in industrial structure, the changing composition of the labour force, the size of establishments, and the effectiveness of union recruitment drives. Different work groups have different propensities to join unions: e.g. females and white-collar workers are traditionally difficult to organise. The type of union and work status affect the level, composition and growth possibilities for union membership; craft union members who have served apprenticeships must retain their membership to secure craft employment, while non-craft workers need not necessarily join a union or retain membership, except where a 100 per cent membership arrangement is operative or union stewards are otherwise active.

The TUC has long recognised the problems posed by trade union structure. Membership concentration is not peculiar to the British movement; the predominance of horizontally organised unions is, however, a major cause of union and industrial relations problems. In 1924, 1946 and 1964,[3] the TUC examined the possibilities of restructuring the movement on the basis of industrial unionism, but recognised the practical difficulties. Instead, TUC policy has concentrated on reducing the number of unions by *amalgamations*,[4] encouraging *joint working arrangements* and *closer unity* policies, and operating the *Bridlington principles* (1939) for resolving inter-union membership disputes. Amalgamations of unions need not necessarily lead to a particular structural form; indeed where they result in the growth of larger horizontal unions, they may exacerbate rather than ease structural problems.

---

[1] H. A. Turner, 'British Trade Union Structure: a new approach', *BJIR*, vol. II, no. 2, 1964.

[2] E.g. the open opposition of the AEF and TGWU to the Labour government's incomes policy.

[3] See TUC Annual Report, 1964, or *Trade Unionism*, TUC Evidence to the Donovan Committee, 1966.

[4] The Trades Union (Amalgamation) Act 1963 considerably eased the legal position regarding amalgamations.

Shop Stewards[1] : At workplace level union members elect spokesmen to represent them.
These are known as shop stewards, although various titles are used, e.g. corresponding
member, father of the chapel; and they are a voluntary workplace official of their union.
Their term of office is usually specified, and they are subject to re-election. Although
formally subject to union jurisdiction, few unions' rules adequately describe the actual
functions of stewards. The formal functions vary between unions, the informal between
industry, plant and workshop.

In 1968, there were an estimated 175,000[2] shop stewards, a 14 per cent increase
since 1958. Approximately 45 per cent of all stewards were in metal-handling industries,
13 per cent in other manufacturing industries, and 36 per cent in non-manufacturing
industries. 24 per cent of all stewards were in the engineering and 11 per cent in the
vehicles industry; Marsh and Coker[3] estimated a 50 per cent increase in engineering
stewards between 1947 and 1961. In 1968 80 per cent of AEU, 34 per cent of TGWU,[4]
29 per cent of NUGMW, and 39 per cent of ETU stewards were in the metal-handling
industries. Over 40 per cent of general unions stewards were in non-manufacturing industries. Little uniformity exists in shop steward constituency size; this varies according to
industry, plant and workshop size, type of worker and union. The average[4] was estimated
to be 327 in 1961, but it ranged from 46 for skilled worker unions to 563 for general
unions.

In 1968, the average number of members per steward was 60; AEF stewards represented 45, TGWU 75, and NUGMW 65 members. In metal handling industries 45 per cent
of all stewards represented 25 per cent of all union members; in other manufacturing
industries 22 per cent of all members were represented by 13 per cent of stewards; and
in non-manufacturing 36 per cent of all stewards represented 49 per cent of union membership. All this indicates an average constituency size of approximately 32, 96 and 41
respectively.

Full employment has altered the status and functions of shop stewards. Their credibility depends upon member support, and the degree to which they reflect shop floor
attitudes. Although influential in shaping shop floor opinion and action, stewards are subject to collective regulation by their members. Stewards cannot effect strikes against
members' wishes, nor can they always succeed in preventing strike action by a determined membership. A sample survey[5] has shown that higher management and union members
consider stewards less militant, i.e. less keen to take action, than their membership, while
union officials consider stewards more militant than members. Management also regards
stewards as receptive to policies and instructions. In engineering, agreements exist conferri▮
recognition on shop stewards, but in most industries recognition has developed informal-
ly; most personnel managers would prefer to deal direct with stewards.[6,7] Recognition
has, however, created union and management problems in a collective bargaining system
which has relied upon industry-wide agreements and dispute procedures. Many industries
have a senior steward system; a *convenor* of stewards is elected by the stewards in the
plant and may represent one or several unions' stewards. In many plants, convenors are

---

1   See Royal Commission (Donovan) *Research Papers* no. 1 and no. 10, 1968.

2   Donovan Commission, *Research Paper* no. 10.

3   A. Marsh and E. E. Coker 'Shop Stewards and the British Engineering Industry', *BJIR, June 1963.*

4   H. A. Clegg, A. J. Killick and R. Adams, *Trade Union Officers,* Blackwell, 1962.

5   Donovan Commission, *Research Paper* no. 10

6   A. Marsh, *Managers and Shop Stewards,* Institute of Personnel Management, London 1963.

7   A. J. Allan, *Management and Men,* Hallam Press, 1967.

occupied full time on labour and union business with management. Negotiations with management and discussions with constituents appear to be the stewards' major activities. The range of bargaining covers wages, working conditions, hours of work, discipline and employment issues. The most common arguments used by stewards to increase members' earnings are comparisons with other workers in the same or other workplaces, abnormal conditions of work, and changes in the nature of the job. Stewards consider abnormal conditions and management comparability as the most convincing arguments.

The shop steward-union administrative relationship has tended to be ambiguous. As voluntary workplace officials, stewards fulfil an indispensable role for the union; that organised stewards could form 'unions within unions' has been a possibility viewed with suspicion by many union leaderships whose status and credibility would be threatened by such developments. Multi-union representation at plant level, frequently ineffective official approaches to shop floor problems, and increasing *de facto* recognition by management of shop stewards' bargaining powers are among the factors promoting the growth of unofficial *joint shop steward committees,* membership of which tends to absolve stewards from compliance with their own union's official policies and instructions. In some industries, e.g. vehicles, linking of unofficial plant committees to form either temporary or permanent *combine committees*[1] of stewards has occurred. Such committees usually link up different plants of the same company but may also link plants of different companies in the same industry. They have created problems for union officials and management, by acting as a union within the union, i.e. a body more effective than the official union machinery, and have secured some degree of formal recognition by unions and management, albeit slowly and reluctantly. Because the committees coordinate labour policy in the face of management's attempts at differential wage and other measures in its different plants, their existence and effectiveness are difficult to overlook.

I.5   Employer Organisations

Employers have both trade and collective bargaining interests, and separate organisations usually cater for each of these. In some countries, e.g. West Germany, a clear organisational distinction is made; in Britain, while examples of both types of organisation exist, there are many which fulfil both trade and collective bargaining functions simultaneously. Trade interests are represented by employer organisations, collective bargaining interests by employer associations. The structure of organised employer bodies is complex and diverse; this arises in part from historical and industrial factors, e.g. concentration of an industry in a particular area. The 39 organisations in the Engineering Employers Federation vary in both size and geographical distribution: 13 organisations are located in Lancashire and Cheshire, while one covers the West of England.[2] The proportion of 'federated firms', i.e.

---

[1]   Shirley W. Lerner and John Bescoby, 'Shop Stewards' Combine Committees in the British Engineering Industry', *BJIR,* July 1966.

[2]   A. Marsh, *Industrial Relations in Engineering,* Pergamon Press (The Commonwealth and International Library), 1965, p. 62.

firms belonging to their appropriate association or organisation, is usually high where trade union organisation is high. In major industries federated firms are estimated to employ 80 per cent or more of the total labour force in those industries. Employer associa tion services to their members include advice, information and representation; protection and support in industrial disputes; and the opportunity for members to influence associa tion policies, e.g. on wages, conditions of employment, etc. Associations are financed by subscriptions based on total wage bills; trade and collective bargaining organisations by contributions based on plant employed, production or similar factors. The basic pay and conditions determined through negotiation are considered to be those within the econo mic capabilities of the least efficient firm. Membership of an organisation usually has less appeal to very small firms where personal relationships between employer and employed are close, and very large firms able to negotiate either plant or company agreements with trade unions. Labour market pressures, and internal wage arrangements, e.g. incentive payment schemes, can cause employee remuneration to exceed the basic minimum laid down in agreements.

The many local employer associations and trade organisations combine to make indus try level federations and associations; these, in turn, combine nationally in the Confeder ation of British Industry formed in 1965 from a merger of the British Employers' Federa tion (a collective bargaining organisation), the Federation of British Industries (a trade organisation) and the British Manufacturers' Association (a federation of small employ ers). Nationalised industries and local transport undertakings also belong to the Confeder ation.

In the context of collective bargaining the traditionally defensive and conservative policies and attitudes of employer associations have not been conducive to those altera tions in the system necessitated by changing industrial and labour market conditions. Some companies have found it necessary to resign from their associations in order to effect some change in collective bargaining, e.g. Esso withdrew from associations prior to concluding the Fawley Productivity Agreement in 1960.

II   COLLECTIVE BARGAINING

II.1   The System

The British collective bargaining system is characterised by a two-tier structure of formal national-level bargaining between trade unions and employer organisations and of informal plant or enterprise-level bargaining between shop stewards and management. There are, however, industries in which formal local bargaining between trades unions and employers still determines the changes in conditions of employees e.g. the cotton and textile trades. The formal industry-wide system operates either through *ad hoc* arrangements, as in engin eering, or through the National Joint Industrial Councils system established in 1916 as a result of the recommendation of the Whitley Committee Report of that year. Joint indus trial councils vary in structure, size, scope of activity and authority, and may be supple mented by similar councils at district level. There are currently about two hundred joint industrial councils, which normally deal with wages, working conditions, and disputes pro cedures. In the Civil Service, National Whitley Councils exist to perform similar functions.

For industries in which trades union organisation is insufficient to promote voluntary collective bargaining, wages councils may be established, composed of trades union and employer representatives and independent members. The proposals agreed to by the council are submitted to the Secretary of State for Employment and Productivity, who cannot over-rule the proposals, but only recommend modifications. Once authorised by the Secretary, wages council wage rates, holidays and holiday pay, are legally binding on employers. An inspectorate exists for the purpose of examining employers' wage records, and acting on behalf of the employee where the employer is in default. Between 1945 and 1967 the number of wages councils increased from 45 to 57, covering three and a half million workpeople, an increase regarded by some as prejudicial to the growth of trades union organisation in these industries e.g. catering, clothing.

National agreements establish minimum wage rates throughout an industry, although in recent years some have established minimum earnings levels. Provision may be made for local variations in terms and conditions and/or for the negotiation of district or works agreements and the fixing of piece-work rates. Bonus-scheme rates are often based on minimum hourly rates. Employee remuneration increases as a result of national increases, bonus increases, overtime, and over-minimum payments negotiated by employers and shop stewards. Prolonged full employment has promoted the development of informal plant or shop-floor wage bargaining in some major industries e.g. engineering, and has led to wage drift, i.e. the tendency over time for actual earnings to diverge from negotiated wage rates.[1]

Several systems of wage payments exist. The most common is a fixed time rate or fixed weekly or monthly wage salary. Many employers, however, prefer to incorporate motivational wage payment arrangements which offer employees higher pay for higher effort. Several forms of payment by result exist: some give rewards for actual units of output produced as straight piecework, others for time saved per unit of output below time allowed with different systems effecting different allocations of time saved between employee and management. One-third of all employed persons is currently recorded as receiving payment by results. Between 1938 and 1961, the proportion of male workers affected by such schemes increased from 18 per cent to 30 per cent, while the proportion of females dropped from 46 per cent to 42 per cent.[2] In 1961, 42 per cent of all employees in manufacturing industry were paid by results, ranging from 67 per cent in shipbuilding to 21 per cent in chemicals. Evidence suggests, however, that many payment-by-results schemes have long since ceased to provide a suitable basis for the effort-reward relationship. Less directly related remuneration arrangements have gained ground in recent years: *measured day work* provides guaranteed remuneration for a guaranteed level of employee effort; *profit sharing schemes* relate the employee's additional income to the prosperity of the firm, or company.

Changing systems of reward reflect changing employer and labour attitudes towards the motivational elements in pay arrangements. Technological changes may invalidate the use of direct incentive payment schemes if the intensity of employee effort ceases to be a major determinant of output.

Wage differential structures have been based on skill differentials, i.e. pay rewards based on the man. A wage structure may be based on an *analytical job evaluation* scheme,[3] which relates other factors in addition to skill on a points basis. The pay is based on job performed, not employee status. Job evaluation may be better suited to new technological conditions in an industry or service; it need not, however, replace payment by results schemes.

---

[1]   There are several definitions of wage drift. See S. W. Lerner, J. R. Cable and S. Gupta, *Workshop Wage Determination*, Pergamon Press, 1969, p. 17-22.

[2]   *Payments by Results*, Report No. 65, p. 76, *NBPI* 1968.

[3]   *Job Evaluation*, Report No. 83, *NBPI, Cmnd 3772, 1968.*

II.2   Wage Differentials[1]

Between 1962 and 1969 average weekly earnings of male manual workers increased from
£15.59 to £23.90, or by approximately 54 per cent; female earnings increased from
£7.88 to £11.75 (50 per cent). The manual male-female earnings differential has widened
by £4.45 over the period. Earnings of male administrative, technical and chemical workers
increased from £21.13 to £29.77 (40 per cent) between 1962 and 1969; female earnings
rose from £11.80 to £15.76 (33 per cent). The sex differential widened by £4.68. The
male inter-occupational (manual-white collar) cash differential remained fairly constant,
only changing from £5.49 to £5.87; larger percentage increases for manual workers have
prevented this differential from widening. Between 1967 and 1969, however, manual
workers' earnings have grown more rapidly than average salaried earnings.

The three industries paying the highest average weekly earnings to male manual
employees in April 1969 were vehicles, £28.30, printing and publishing, £27.75, and
metal manufacture, £25.16; and to females, transport and communication, £15.85, vehicles
£14.32, and engineering, £12.40. The lowest paying industries for males were public administration, £18.45, miscellaneous services, £20.45, and clothing and footwear, £20.60,
and for females, miscellaneous services £10.05 and leather goods and fur £10.45.

For male clerical, administrative and technical workers the top paying industries in
1969 were chemicals, £33.83, printing £31.82, and other manufacturing industries,
£30.38; and for females the public utilities sector, gas, water and electricity, £14.09,
public administration, £17.75, and mining and quarrying, £14.17. The lowest paying
industries for male clerical workers were shipbuilding, bricks, glass and pottery, mining
and quarrying, and gas, water and electricity, all ranging between £28.1 and £28.6 per
week; and for women, shipbuilding, textiles, bricks, glass and pottery, timber and furniture, and metal goods were all in the range £11.4 to £11.8.

Differences in the number of hours worked and paid for and differences in average
hourly earnings must be considered when comparing differentials in pay. For example, in
October 1968 the below average weekly hours worked in vehicle production (43.9) were
compensated by the highest average hourly earnings, £0.60; in mining and quarrying the
highest average hours worked (51.1) were associated with the lowest hourly earnings
rate paid, £0.44. Similar considerations apply to inter-area pay differentials. In October
1968,[2] highest weekly average earnings for male manual workers in manufacturing
industry were received in the west midlands, £24.91, the south-east, £24.77, and Wales,
£20.0; hours worked in the west midlands and Wales were below average and among the
lowest (44.7 and 44.6 respectively), and the hourly earnings rates the highest, at £0.55
and £0.53 respectively. Average weekly earnings, £20.40, average hourly earnings, £0.4,
and average hours worked (44.6) were lowest in Northern Ireland.

II.3   The Legal Framework

Employers in Britain are under no legal obligation to recognise and negotiate with trades
unions, except in parts of the public sector, e.g. nationalised industries. Trades unions
have generally secured recognition through industrial action, and belief in this method is
deep rooted in trades union tradition.

Under the terms of the 1871 *Trades Union Act*, agreements concluded between trades
unions and employer organisations cannot be made collectively and directly binding.

---

[1]   *DEP* data.

[2]   *Regional Abstract of Statistics*, 1969, table 54.

Collective agreements are therefore not legally binding contracts; nor can either party mount court proceedings to have agreement terms implemented.

The terms of collective agreements form part of the contract of employment between employer and employee, and this contract is legally binding. A Court, in judging an individual case, may take the terms of a collective agreement as strong evidence of implied terms in contracts, thereby imparting indirect support to the agreement.

Section 8 of the *Terms and Conditions of Employment Act 1959*, accords trades unions and employers the right to invoke the adjudication of the Industrial Court where an employer fails to comply with the terms of a current collective agreement in that industry.

In addition to indirect legal support to voluntary collective bargaining, statutory provisions exist (a) for direct support to industries in which union organisation is insufficient to support effective collective bargaining, (b) for compliance with prevailing wage rates by employers undertaking government contracts. Agricultural workers are covered by the Agricultural Wages Act (1948) and a similar Act for Scotland. In other industries, the *Wages Councils Act 1959* consolidates legislation facilitating the establishment of wages councils whose functions are the determination of minimum wage rates, holidays and holiday pay. The Department of Employment and Productivity has statutory powers to inspect wage needs, to act on behalf of employees to recover minimum wages unpaid by employers, and to prosecute employers for breach of wages council terms.

The *1946 Fair Wage Resolution* places an obligation on contractors undertaking government work to pay wages and apply conditions no less favourable than those established under collective agreements. The contractor must recognise the right of employees to be trades union members and is responsible for compliance by subcontractors with the Resolution.

Labour's ultimate sanction in the bargaining process is strike action. Legislation does not confer a legal right to strike as in other countries; nor can collective agreements impose legal restrictions against collective strike action.

The *1871 Conspiracy and Protection of Property Act* legalised peacful picketing, and established that no act undertaken in combination was punishable, except in the event that the act would itself be criminal if undertaken by an individual acting alone. The Act also made it an offence for Gas and Water Industry employees to undertake collective or individual action prejudicial to public health and safety. The *Electricity Supply Act 1919* imposed similar constraints on employees in electricity concerns. The *Conspiracy and Protection of Property Act 1875*, eliminated the crime of conspiracy from trade disputes. The *Trade Disputes Act 1906* defines a 'trade dispute' very broadly, effectively making no distinction between official, unofficial, or unconstitutional strikes and according immunity against legal proceedings for most forms of strike action. The Act protects work people involved in industrial action from the tort of conspiracy, providing that the action is within the definition of a trade dispute as given in the Act.

The legal significance of strike action is, however, different for individual contracts of employment. Withdrawal of labour without the required period of notice breaches the employment contract, permitting the employer to terminate the contract and sue the employee for damages.

The *1963 Contract of Employment Act* stipulates one week as the minimum period of notice which an employee must give if terminating his contract; one week has become the minimum period of notice for strike action. Certain occupations, however, involve much longer periods of notice, e.g. a term for teaching staffs. It is generally acknowledged that strikes suspend and do not terminate contracts of service; this is important since employee benefits under the *Redundancy Payment Act 1964*, as well as the period of notice to which he is entitled under the *Contract of Employment Act*, are based on the length of continuous service.

Employers bear responsibility for initiating legal action resulting from the breach of contracts by employees involved in strikes without notice, often called wildcat strikes. However, it is a legal right rarely exercised by employers. This has important implications for the effectiveness of proposed legal sanctions relating to unofficial and unconstitutional strikes.

Collective bargaining often results in a failure to agree on terms, and necessitates further machinery for resolving the issues in dispute. Some industries have their own established procedures for reaching agreement. The state also assists by providing three methods for settling disputes—conciliation, arbitration and investigation by a formal enquiry—its powers being embodied in the *Conciliation Act 1896* and the *Industrial Courts Act 1919*.

Conciliation is the adjustment of differences by mutual agreement between employers and employees. The DEP has statutory powers to effect action which is deemed likely to promote settlement of a dispute. Industrial relations officers of the DEP maintain touch with employer and employed, but do not formally intervene in a dispute until requested to do so, and then only when an industry's own machinery has been exhausted without agreement being reached.

The *Industrial Courts Act* provides for the establishment of the Industrial Court to act as arbitrator in disputes referred to it by both sides. The scope of the Court has been extended by further Acts since 1919. Decisions of the Court are not legally binding on the disputants, although both sides usually undertake to abide by the arbitration decision. Decisions do acquire legal status where they form part of individual contracts of service.

In addition to the Industrial Court, a dispute may be referred by the DEP to a single arbitrator or board of arbitrators, members being nominated by unions and employers with an independent chairman. The *Industrial Courts Act* also provides for the establishment of Courts of Enquiry as a means of informing Parliament and the public of the facts and causes of a dispute. Courts are appointed when no dispute settlement seems possible. The DEP may also refer issues to the Commission on Industrial Relations,[1] which will investigate and recommend courses of action.

The *Conciliation Act* also empowers the DEP to appoint a Committee of Investigation into the causes of a dispute, although no report is submitted to Parliament.

II.4   Problems of the System

The increase of shop-floor power due to prolonged full employment has resulted in the emergence of shop steward authority in the work-place bargaining system. The growth of shop-floor bargaining has arisen from management's inclination to pay higher wages when labour is scarce, and the capitalisation of this by the shop stewards. Many national agreements formally provide for local bargaining to establish terms and conditions suitable to local circumstances; however, informal bargaining has also occurred, on an unregulated basis, with the result that in many sectors take home pay is considerably in excess of national agreement rates. Successive governments have expressed concern at the excessive growth of earnings in relation to productivity, asserting that the failure to secure productivity increases commensurate to pay rises results in wage-price inflation. Take home pay may lie above agreed minima as the result of (1) management's upward manipulation of pay scales and earning expectations to recruit or retain labour, (2) abuses of incentive payments schemes by both management and employees, (3) frequency of shop-floor negotiations on wage adjustments, e.g. over piecework rates, (4) factory wage structures providing more differentials than are specified in national agreements.

---

[1]   See section II.5 of this chapter.

Overtime payments have become an important component of an employee's take home pay in many industries. Ostensibly used to increase the supply of man hours in response to production requirements, overtime has become an institutional arrangement, under which an employer may offer and pay guaranteed overtime ('policy overtime'), with little regard to production conditions. Overtime may be paid, for example, when employees are on holiday, and many employers offer guaranteed overtime in recruiting labour. Both management and trades unions have been unable to resolve the problems arising from overtime working within the framework of the traditional collective bargaining system. Management has been reluctant to eliminate overtime or to exercise greater control to secure higher labour efficiency at shop-floor level; union officials could not realistically advocate that their members abstain from practices and methods of creating overtime when this resulted in reductions of weekly take home pay. Not suprisingly, negotiated reductions in the *standard working hours* have not been accompanied by commensurate reductions in total hours worked. In 1951, the average normal weekly hours for manual workers were 44.6, and actual hours worked 46.3; in 1968, normal working hours had dropped to 40.5, while actual hours worked were 44.5, i.e. a 9.4 per cent decrease in standard hours was accompanied by a 3.3 per cent reduction in actual hours worked. In May 1961, 29.3 per cent of operative labour (excluding maintenance workers) averaged 7½ hours overtime per week; in January 1969, 35.7 per cent of workers averaged 8½ hours overtime. Due to premium payments, e.g. double time on Sundays, hours of work paid for will exceed hours worked.

Many trades union members have vigorously applied union rules to protect security of income and employment; historically, employers themselves encouraged craft demarcation in several industries. Technological changes can outdate traditional craft arrangements and may result in inter-union *demarcation disputes*. Union rules may be applied against the employer only, e.g. insistence on traditional manning arrangements on new plant, resulting in underutilisation of labour and sometimes of capital equipment, and reducing productivity. The traditional collective bargaining system in some industries has been unable to resolve such matters in an acceptable and permanent manner.

In many firms and industries, the collective negotiating system has failed to establish effective and rapid *grievance handling procedures*. In some sectors none at all exist, especially for industrial white-collar employees, and in others those devised have become increasingly inadequate to accommodate the changing power relationships in industry. Frustration with such procedural arrangements has precipitated direct strike action in breach of procedure. The speed with which such strikes achieve their objectives has convinced industrial shop-floor workers of their effectiveness.

Strikes occurring with union authorisation are termed *official*, without authorisation *unofficial*; strikes in breach of a grievance handling procedure are termed *unconstitutional* and strikes in support of other workers involved in a dispute *sympathetic*. Unconstitutional strikes are invariably unofficial although many unions have provisions for making official strikes which are initially unofficial. Unofficial strikers forfeit strike pay and supplementary social security benefits are payable to the striker's family but not the striker. The law effectively makes little distinction between these different forms of strikes; proposals to reform industrial relations and collective bargaining have, however, emphasised the introduction of legislation with respect to strikes. Preoccupation with the incidence and character of strikes has overshadowed the relatively favourable international position of Britain in this area, as well as diverted attention away from underlying causes. Absence of strikes is not necessarily symptomatic of a good industrial relations situation; preventing strikes may not resolve the deeper causes of a dispute. There are other forms of industrial action more damaging to an employer than strikes, for example, a go-slow or work-to-rule.[1]

---

[1]   Note that a work-to rule means exact compliance with job instructions and regulations and is therefore a precise fulfilment of individual contracts of employment; a go-slow could involve breaches in contract due to poor or ineffective workmanship.

Between 1957-61 and 1967-8 the number of strike days per striker dropped from 6 to 3, total strike-days lost fell from 4.6 to 3.8 million; the number of strikes fell from 2,630 to 2,240, while the number of strikers per strike increased from 320 to 670. 1969 was however a peak year for industrial disputes, there being 3,021 recorded strikes in all.

Between 1968 and 1969, more than half the number of working days lost occurred in the engineering, shipbuilding and vehicles industries, with mining and quarrying as the second most important. Between 1964 and 1966, 190 working days were lost per 1,000 employees through strikes, compared to 870 in the United States, 40 in Sweden, 1,620 in Ireland and 400 in Australia. An average 340 work people were involved per stoppage in the UK, compared to 470 in the United States and 570 in Sweden. The average duration of strikes in Britain was 3.4 days, in the United States 14.2, in Sweden 15.4 and in Germany 3.6. Although different definitions of strikes prevent the strict comparability of international data, strikes in Britain appear to have a different pattern from elsewhere, having both a shorter duration and involving comparatively fewer workers than in other countries. Global measures, however, mask significant changes in the industrial distribution of strikes. Between 1957 and 1967, the number of stoppages in the coal mining industry, traditionally highly strike-prone, decreased considerably from 2,224 to 341, while an increase from 635 to 1,694 occurred in the rest of the economy. Of 2,272 stoppages during 1964-6, 96 per cent were *unofficial,* involving 86 per cent of all workers involved in stoppages and representing 67 per cent of all working days lost.[1]

Inadequate disputes procedures, multi-unionism and maintenance of wage differentials, and new power relationships in industry have contributed to the growth of unofficial strikes. Such strikes are usually the result of accumulated frustrations and grievances at shop-floor level; one issue can then precipitate strike action. Such strikes may, however, have disproportionate effects within and across firms and industries and they can embarrass a trades union administration. The Donovan Report rightly asserted that legislative action to make such strikes unlawful will be ineffective and, more importantly, will not cure the underlying causes of discontent. Wage issues are the most important causes of strikes; certain wage systems and technologies appear conducive to higher strike incidence, e.g. payment by results in parts of the motor industry.

II.5   The Donovan Commission Report

In July 1968 the *Royal Commission on Trades Unions and Employer Associations (Donovan Commission)* submitted its Report after three years' work.[2] The Commision's recommendations related to the system of industrial relations, the reform and extension of collective bargaining, and the efficient use of manpower; strikes and other industrial action; the enforcement of collective agreements and changes in the law; safeguards for employees against unfair dismissal, and safeguards for individuals in relation to trades unions; labour tribunals; the organisation and role of trades unions and employer associations; and works participation.

The Commission confirmed situations well known to informed observers. It classified as 'good' those aspects of the industrial relations system which were formal, written and codified, and 'bad' the informal, unwritten and uncodified elements of the system. The Report's findings were strongly influenced by industrial relations in a few industries,

---

[1]   Donovan *Report,* 1967, p.96.

[2]   Cmnd 3623, HMSO, London, 1968.

namely docks, engineering and the motor industry; generalisations derived from the experiences of such industries are questionable. The Report favoured greater formalism in our industrial relations system than hitherto, and was mainly concerned to remedy causes of current shortcomings in the system rather than the symptoms produced by it. It favoured substantial institutional and legal changes, although continued reliance on the parties involved was foreseen.

The perceived disorder in factory and shop-floor relations and pay structures was attributed by the Commission to the simultaneous existence of a formal and informal system of industrial relations, the former embodied in official labour and employer institutions, the latter arising from the actual behaviour of these institutions and their members. The Commission recommended that industry-wide agreements be limited to issues that can be effectively regulated; and that greater emphasis be placed on the conclusion of factory or company agreements facilitating regulation of particular plant-level industrial-relations problems and arrangements. Acceptance of greater responsibilities by boards of directors and management, and 'substantial increases' in the number of union officials were foreseen as necessary concomitants of formalised plant bargaining. The Commission claimed that factory agreements, if properly formulated, would be conducive to higher productivity and efficiency and the promotion of factory agreements was seen by the Commission as a major function of employer associations. The Commission made a number of proposals to this end. It recommended the passing of an *Industrial Relations Act* compelling companies over a minimum size (initially 5,000 employees) to register their collective agreement with the DEP. It also recommended the establishment of an *Industrial Relations Commission* (CIR) its functions to include investigations, reporting and recommending on industrial relations issues referred to it by the DEP, in particular matters arising out of the registration of company or plant collective agreements, union recognition, promotion of efficient use of manpower, and legal aspects of industrial relations. The CIR was established in 1969. The Commission recommended that boards of directors ought to review their industrial relations with a view to developing comprehensive and authoritative collective bargaining machinery at plant or company level, the establishment of rapid and equitable grievance handling procedures, the conclusion of agreements regulating the position and functions of shop stewards and redundancy, effective rules and procedures for disciplinary matters, and regular joint discussion of measures to promote safety at work.

To promote the extension and reform of collective bargaining the Commission recommended that contractual clauses prohibiting employee union membership be void, that the procedure for the abolition of wages councils be simplified, that Clause 8 of the Terms and Conditions of Employment Act 1959[1] be amended to cover wages council industries, and that unilateral compulsory arbitration by the Industrial Court be restored.[2] The Commission rejected the idea of legal enforcement of collective agreements because such a measure would break the voluntary principle of British industrial relations and would be contrary to the wishes of both employers and employees; the legal enforcement of inadequate procedure agreements was considered undesirable, and likely to impede resolution of the real causes of industrial disputes. The Commission considered the application of legal sanctions against individuals and trades unions in breach of procedure as impractical, but did not exclude the future use of *ad hoc* sanctions for irresponsibility and ill-will in the presence of adequate procedural arrangements. The Commission's recommendations on strikes reflected its conviction that permanent improvements in industrial relations will be more effectively realised by reforms in the collective bargaining system and its institu-

[1] See section II.3 of this chapter.

[2] Trades unions favour re-establishment of this form of arbitration, which was abolished in 1959.

tions rather than by the application of legal sanctions within the present system. The suggestions of compulsory strike ballots, a 60-day cooling-off period and new procedures for dealing with strikes of national significance were rejected by the Commission. Instead, the value of DEP, CIR and other inquiries in identifying the causes of particular strikes was stressed by the Commission and provision of more resources for these activities was support The Commission rejected the establishment of inquiry agencies to investigate unofficial strikes, but recommended investigation by a DEP manpower advisor or the CIR. Reliance on removing the causes of such strikes and improving the formal machinery for their avoidance characterised the Commission's approach. Improvements in the present machinery for the judicial determination of disputes arising out of employer-employee contractual relation ships was recommended; present industrial tribunals should have new scope, should be extended to include such disputes, and ought to be renamed labour tribunals. The tribunals should have exclusive jurisdiction where statutory rights were concerned, and have a primary duty to promote settlement of disputes by conciliation.

The encouragement of union mergers and closer working arrangements, the establishment of factory union branches, the replacement of the present unconstitutional shop steward combined committees by constitutionally recognised bodies, and the revision of union rules in relation to shop stewards, were recommended by the Commission as necessary and conducive to the reform of the trades unions. Responsibility for these changes rests with the unions and the Commission advocated intensified TUC[1] efforts to promote the reforms. Participation by the CIR was also envisaged. The Report proposed that employer associations ought in future to assist the development of orderly and efficient systems of industrial relations in members' undertakings; that rules obstructing effective collective bargaining be amended; that employer associations encourage more favourable attitudes and policies towards white-collar unions; that amalgamations of smaller associations be encouraged; and that cognisance be taken of the advantages of organisations combining employers' trade and collective bargaining interests. In addition it was suggested that the engineering employers' federation establish a national division to which multiplant companies could affiliate directly, and that the CBI widen its scope to include companies at present excluded from membership.

The Commission recommended legal changes to clarify[2] and tidy existing law and confine some legal privileges to trades unions and employer associations only. Codification of labour law was considered urgent, and it was recommended that the legal definition of a trades union be restricted to employee organisations only.[3] Trades unions and employer associations ought to have corporate personality, and should register with the Registrar of Friendly Societies within a stated period. Support was given to making expressly applicable to trades unions the immunities from criminal and civil prosecutions accorded by various laws to acts committed by any persons in contemplation and furtherance of a trade dispute The Commission recommended that Section 3 of the Trades Disputes Act 1906 and the 1965 Trades Dispute Act should no longer apply to persons or combinations other than trades unions and employer associations, and a majority of the Commission advocated the repeal of Section 4 of the 1871 Trades Union Act;[4] This would place trades union agreements with their members on the same footing as any other contractual relationship. Peaceful picketing of an employer's customers ought to be clarified as lawful, and it was recommended that the protection at present accorded inducement to breach a contract of

---

[1]   *Report*, paras 723-727.

[2]   *Ibid.*, paras 751-993.

[3]   Under the 1871 Trades Union Act employer and employee organisations are defined as trades unions.

[4]   *Ibid.*, para. 815.

employment be extended to cover inducement to breach any contract by trades unions and employer associations only. Changes were recommended in the 1965 National Insurance Act to the effect that a claimant for benefit should not be regarded as financing a trade dispute because he is a member of a union involved in the dispute, nor must the claimant have to prove that he/she is not a participant or interested party in a trade dispute.

II.6 Innovations in the System

Productivity Bargaining: A significant development in the British collective bargaining system occurred with the conclusion of the Fawley Agreement[1] in 1960. This agreement marked the beginning of the era of *productivity bargaining*. A productivity agreement is a 'settlement in which workers agree to make changes in working practices which themselves lead to more economical function of a plant, company or industry—and in return the employer agrees to increase pay, improve fringe benefits, raise workers' status, increase their leisure time or to make a combination of these improvements'.[2]

Traditional collective bargaining usually produced wage settlements resulting in higher pay for employees and a higher wage bill for employers, without commensurate increases in productivity, efficiency or even agreement on large-scale changes in working arrangements. The traditional system proved unable to resolve the problems of inefficient use of labour and capital, restrictive practices, overtime working, resistance to new working methods or techniques, inter-union demarcation, and security of employment. A wage increase was no guarantee of industrial peace to an employer, since disputes could arise out of the issues listed above.

Productivity bargaining has provided a potentially more effective method of resolving these problems, as well as improving the utilisation of labour and capital, and lowering unit labour costs. Productivity agreements have powerful economic advantages for managements. They can secure improved efficiency and check rising labour costs in a labour market situation conducive to rapid and necessary increases in pay. The rising cost of labour and the changed balance of power in favour of shop-floor employees have encouraged managements to devise new methods of relating wage payment to labour effort and supply. Productivity bargaining offers a method of buying higher manpower and capital utilisation at an acceptable cost and presupposes and necessitates changes in managerial attitudes towards their own and labour's problems. Employees are concerned about their security of employment and maintenance of income, and have devised and practised arrangements to protect these. A productivity agreement guarantees an agreed income level and creates the environment in which changes in labour practice are more likely to be accepted by unions and their members. Productivity agreements usually secure labour cooperation by increasing manpower utilisation through inter-craft flexibility arrangements, widening the range of jobs to be performed, devising new manning scales, eliminating or reducing overtime working, establishing a new pattern of working hours; they can also secure changes in wage structures, acceptance of new working methods, machines, processes, etc. removal of labour-imposed restrictions on output, reduced working hours, the introduction of work measurement techniques, and a mechanism facilitating management's manipulation of its labour resources in response to improving technology and labour and product market pressures. Increased manpower utilisation usually involves a reduction of the labour force normally achieved through natural wastage; voluntary redundancy, with higher redundancy payments, may also be used.

---

[1] A. Flanders, *Fawley Productivity Agreement,* Faber & Faber, 1964.

[2] *Report* no.36, NBPI, June 1967.

Labour gains from productivity agreements may include higher and/or guaranteed take home pay, improved fringe benefits often associated with higher status, shorter working hours and greater job interest. Some work people may, however, suffer loss of earnings, social inconvenience of new work patterns, and loss of status; trades unions may fear reduced future membership resulting from reduced job opportunities and loss of control over jobs, e.g. craft unions.

Productivity agreements can be concluded at any level. Plant agreements have been the most common and have involved an average of 1,000 work people, e.g. petrochemical firms. Company-wide agreements, (e.g. BOAC) have covered several thousand employees and the industry-wide agreement in the Electricity Supply Industry involved 155,000 workers in 1964. Agreements have tended to be concluded in capital- rather than labour-intensive industries. Implementation of agreements has invariably necessitated bargaining at plant or shop-floor level; only at this level can many restrictive practices be defined and changes in working methods and labour utilisation be negotiated and agreed. Trades union officials, shop stewards and management expend considerable effort in securing the gains from productivity agreements.

Productivity bargaining was reinforced by the provisions of the national incomes policy, and the establishment of the NBPI in 1965. Proven increases in productivity, resulting from changes in working practice by labour, constituted a major determinant of authorised pay increases between 1966 and 1969.

Incomes Policy: Dissatisfaction with incomes and price developments, the shortcomings of the collective bargaining system in relating wage increases to increases in productivity, and difficulties with the balance of payments have engendered growing 'pressure from above'[1] by successive British Governments. Four attempts to establish a voluntary system of incomes restraint have been attempted in the postwar period. The objectives ascribed to British incomes policy have been the maintenance of price stability by keeping the rate of growth of incomes in line with the growth in productivity; as a complement to monetary and fiscal policy to contain demand in emergency situations, e.g. balance of payments crises; as a means of redistributing national income in favour of low-income sections of the community, a method known to be less effective than social security and welfare arrangemants;[2] the achievement of a faster growth in real living standards, and a more rational relation between incomes of different groups.[3]

In 1948, the Labour government, with the support of the trades unions, attempted to restrain wage increases. While national minimum wage rates remained fairly steady, actual earnings rose faster, i.e. wage drifting occurred, and the price rises in 1950-1 associated with the Korean War and the devaluation of 1949 caused trades union leaders to abandon attempts to restrain wage growth. In 1956 and 1961 Conservative governments introduced voluntary and temporary 'wage pauses', but lacking trades union support such attempts fell short of their objectives. In 1962 the National Incomes Commission was established with the function of examining and reporting upon specific wage agreements referred to it; the trades unions, however, did not support it. In 1964, the Labour government secured a declaration of intent from trades unions and employer associations to support a voluntary policy on incomes, prices and productivity. A National Board for Prices and Incomes was established by the government in 1965.

---

[1] A. Flanders, *Collective Bargaining; What's wrong with the System?,* Blackwell, 1967.

[2] S. W. Lerner, J. Cable and S. Gupta, *Workshop Wage Determination,* Pergamon Press, 1969.

[3] Cmnd 4237, para 11.

The NBPI was to review proposed or agreed pay and price increases[1] referred to it by the government in the light of criteria contained in a *White Paper* of April 1965.[2] An incomes norm for pay increases of 3-3½ per cent was set, which could, however, be exceeded if essential to secure manpower redistribution, to raise income of work groups whose pay was widely recognised as having fallen seriously out of line with that for similar work, whose current pay levels were insufficient to support a reasonable standard of living, or where employees contributed directly to increased productivity by undertaking changes in their working practices. In November 1965, a 'voluntary' early warning[3] system was established; this compelled the TUC and Employer Associations to refer pending price or wage increases to the government for possible examination before their implementation. A TUC wage vetting committee was established, to which affiliated unions were expected to refer proposed pay claims and from which they were to await approval. Persistent balance of payments difficulties, failure to reduce domestic demand, and associated foreign pressures culminated in the government introducing strong deflationary measures, which included a price and wage standstill,[4] in July 1966, supported by statutory powers of enforcement under the Prices and Incomes Act of August 1966. The Act gave the NBPI a statutory basis, making the early warning system compulsory; provided a means of delaying implementation of a settlement; empowered appropriate ministers to prohibit a wage or price increase or reverse such increases implemented since 20 July 1966; provided legal protection for employers withholding pay increases in compliance with government instruction; established a system of fining trades unions or employers in contravention of the Act's provisions; and granted deferment for the implementation of wages council awards. The Act and the subsequent Acts which followed it were each to run for twelve months, and the government intended that the Acts' provisions be used only if needed, reliance being placed on a 'voluntary' incomes policy.

The compulsory elements in the government's incomes policy largely prevented wage increases from July 1966 to January 1967. A zero norm for pay increases was laid down in a *White Paper* in November 1966[5] except when increased efficiency, a need to improve low-paid workers' living standards, or problems of acute labour shortage, could be proven. Pay increases scheduled for implementation during the first half of 1967 were deferred until 1 July 1967. In March 1967 a further *White Paper*[6] outlined plans for a return to a voluntary incomes policy after June of that year. The NBPI wage norm would be zero, and while stating that Part IV of the 1966 Act would lapse in August 1967, the government indicated its intention to activate Part II of the Act (compulsory early warning obligation) prior to the lapsing of Part IV. This intention was realised in the Prices and Incomes Act, August 1967. This Act gave the government statutory power to delay a proposed pay (or price) increase for up to seven months, subject to reference to the NBPI; a wage increase could be delayed but not prevented from taking place. Provisions were made in the Act for employers who granted an unauthorised increase to be fined; fine provisions were also applicable to trades unions or persons precipitating strike action to compel an employer to implement an unauthorised settlement.

A 3½ per cent annual ceiling on wage increases and the reintroduction of a twelve-month lapse between successive increases laid down in another *White Paper* represented

---

[1]   *Machinery of Prices and Incomes Policy,* Cmnd 2577.

[2]   *Prices and Incomes Policy,* Cmnd 2639.

[3]   *Prices and Incomes Policy: An Early Warning System,* Cmnd 2808

[4]   *Prices and Incomes Standstill,* 1966, Cmnd 3073.

[5]   *Prices and Incomes Standstill,* Cmnd 3150, HMSO, 1966.

[6]   *Prices and Incomes Policy after June 1967,* Cmnd 3235, HMSO, 1967.

the important parameters of incomes policy for 1968 and 1969. In December 1969 a White Paper on *Price, Productivity and Incomes Policy after 1969* stated that the delaying powers of the 1967 and 1968 Acts would lapse, but Part II of the 1966 Act would continue from January 1970.

The statutory power of intervention in the operation of the voluntary collective bargaining system accorded the government by the Prices and Incomes Act represents a major, if resented, innovation in peacetime. Unlike earlier attempts at wage restraint, provisions of recent policies impinged on shop-floor as well as higher levels of the bargaining system. Wage increases for more than 100 workers were referable to the DEP, which in turn decided whether to refer to the NBPI or not. Wage increases for less than 100 workers were also referable if they involved a significant section of a labour force. Some of the traditional criteria for justifying wage increases were rejected by the NBPI. Cost of living increases could not be used to support a pay rise.[1] Increases could not be justified by labour shortage problems,[2] employers being urged to improve the utilisation of existing labour. Inter-industry comparability[3] formally ceased to be an acceptable basis for pay increases by the NBPI, although such comparability was used in assessing the pay of government employees. The major justifications for pay increases acceptable to the NBPI were those based on proven productivity increases,[4] and such criteria were established as guidelines for productivity agreements; modifications followed in August 1969 as a result of further examination of productivity agreements. Incomes policy assisted the growth of productivity bargaining; productivity agreements were claimed by the NBPI to result in more efficient firms, more effective management, more paid leisure and security for employees, more union authority at work-place level, and stable or lower prices for consumers.

Government claims for the success of the policy are based on the data in table 5.3 below.

TABLE 5.3

Percentage Increases (at Annual Rates) of Wages UK 1965-69

Period	Hourly Wage Rates	Earnings (seasonally adjusted)	Retail Prices	Wages and Salaries per unit of output
April 1965–January 1966	7.4	7.6	5.1	7.0
July 1966–June 1967	2.8	1.7	2.5	0.3
July 1967–March 1968	4.2	8.8	2.8	4.3
April 1968–December 1968	4.5	7.9	5.5	1.9
Jan. 1969–September 1969	4.3	6.6	5.1	n.a.

Source: Productivity, Prices and Incomes Policy after 1969. Cmnd 4237, HMSO, December 1969, p. 6.

[1]   Cmnd 2839, para. 28.

[2]   *Report* no. 42, *Second General Report,* Cmnd 3394, HMSO, 1967.

[3]   Cmnd 3087, para. 62.

[4]   NBPI *Report* no. 23. See also Reports nos. 36 and 123.

II.7   Reforming the System

Proposals for improving the collective bargaining system rely to varying degrees upon modifying the present legal framework, attempting reforms in trades union structure, and augmenting the powers of the government to intervene in the system. Evaluation of the proposals of each group ought to consider the antipathy of the trades union movement towards legislation in industrial relations; the impracticability of trades unions attempting to take or support disciplinary or legal actions against their own members; the reliance on and general reluctance of employers to initiate legal actions against their employees; the previous use of legal sanctions in tackling collective bargaining problems; trades unions' reliance on industrial action to secure their goals, e.g. recognition, protection against dismissal, etc.; and the resentment of unions and their members towards 'outside' interference in their internal affairs.

In January 1969, a White Paper[1] presented the Labour government's proposals for changes in the industrial relations sytem with emphasis on improving the collective bargaining system by effecting reforms in traditional arrangements, extending the scope of collective agreements and by providing new aids for the parties involved. The government's justifications for its proposals were that they would help contain industrial conflict and promote desired changes in the industrial relations system; and that the efforts of employers, employees and unions to effect the reforms needed the active support and intervention of the government.

The White Paper, like the Donovan Report, placed major responsibilities for reform on management, particularly at board level. Major reforms were foreseen in the negotation of formal and comprehensive agreements at plant or company level where industry-wide agreements were ineffective; in widening the contents of collective agreements to provide links between pay and productivity increases, to contain effective disputes procedures, to provide quick recourse to arbitration in the event of deadlocks in negotiations, and to offer the means of raising important issues with the highest levels of management. Collective agreements could be legally binding when both parties wished. Agreements as to the functions and facilities accorded shop stewards were recommended. The government measures for promoting reforms included the registration of collective agreements with the DEP and the improvement and extension of that Department's conciliation and arbitration services; by further legislation relating to unfair dismissals, disclosure of information by management, and revision of the Contracts of Employment Act 1963 to give greater protection to employees, and by the establishment of a Commission on Industrial Relations (CIR) with the primary function of reforming the collective bargaining system. This body was established in March 1969. Proposals for improving collective bargaining by strengthening both sides of industry included making union recognition legally binding on an employer; authorising the CIR to conduct inquiries into recognition and other union problems and empowering the DEP to enforce CIR recommendations; facilitating trades union reorganisation to achieve 'one union for one grade of work within a factory'; establishing a trades union development scheme under which the CIR would administer financial aids for union reorganisation; and reforming the structure, organisation and functions of employer associations.

The most controversial proposals were those relating to strikes, under which the Secretary of State for the DEP would be given discretionary powers to impose a 28-day conciliation pause (cooling-off period) in unconstitutional strikes and other strikes of major importance, and also cause unions to hold secret ballots of their members where a major official strike threatened. Financial penalties were proposed for individual workers who failed to comply with the conciliation pause. The Donovan Commission recom-

---

[1]   *In Place of Strife*, Cmnd 3883, HMSO, 1969.

mended against such measures, the TUC considered them impractical and undesirable and the CBI that they did not go far enough towards containing the strike problem. A new Industrial Board was proposed to deal with certain types of cases against employers, unions, and employees. The above, and other proposals, were to be included in an Industrial Relations Bill.[1] At the time of writing this Bill has been introduced but not yet passed: if it is, it is unlikely to contain those proposals regarding strikes and interference in union affairs to which the trades union movement objected.

Trades union opposition to the White Paper proposals prompted the TUC General Council to formulate its own proposals contained in a *Programme for Action*[2] and convene a Special Congress to discuss the issues involved in June 1969. The Congress endorsed the General Council's proposals, the essence of which gave the government assurances that the TUC, through agreed revisions of Congress Rules 11, 12 and 13, would assume greater influence in actual or intended official or unconstitutional strikes involving affiliated unions. The TUC believes its measures to be potentially more effective than those involving increased government interference in such issues as strikes.

The Conservative Party, while supporting the view that 'no government action can, of itself, create good industrial relations', proposes[3] that government action through legislation and other means could be effective in alleviating the problems of industrial disputes, restrictive labour practices, abuse of authority by organisations and pressure groups, and the misuse of economic power for the furtherance of sectional objectives. Three forms of government action are proposed: first, the introduction of an Industrial Relations Act; second, the creation of a Productivity Board responsible for promoting better manpower utilisation and the removal of restrictive practices; and third, new powers for the DEP. The present legal framework is considered unjust and anomalous. The legal changes proposed include narrowing the definition of a trade dispute (1906 Trades Dispute Act) and amending other legislation to exclude from immunity sympathic strikes, inter-union disputes, strikes to enforce a closed or union shop or prevent or enforce employment of particular individuals, blacking of goods and services; secondly, repeal of the 1965 Trades Dispute Act to deter individuals from threatening strike action; thirdly, amending the 1871 Trades Union Act to make collective agreements legally binding, giving them similar status to other contracts; breaches of agreements would be processed in a new Industrial Court, upper limits specified for damages, and immunities granted to unions and employers proven to have done everything possible to avoid the breach.

It is proposed that a new Registrar of Trades Unions and Employer Associations be established with more powers than at present; that a legal obligation be placed on employers to recognise and negotiate with representative trades unions; that individuals would have a legal right of appeal against unfair dismissal; and that the Productivity Board be used to promote desired changes in the institution and the machinery of the collective bargaining system. A Code of Practice for management, unions and employees is proposed as a Schedule to the Industrial Relations Act, laying down basic standards and guidelines for the desired behaviour of the parties. The extended powers proposed for the DEP are the exercise of its conciliation functions at its own discretion, a proposal similar to that of the present government; power to refer to the Industrial Court for arbitration disputes threatening the national interest; power to apply to the Industrial Court for an injunction to delay or stop a strike (cooling-off period) for a specified period—a minimum of 60 days; and power to effect a secret ballot among work people involved in a dispute, the ballot being organised not by the union(s) involved, but by the DEP or another outside body. The last three powers could only be exercised after a report from a Board of Enquiry.

---

[1]   The Bill lapsed with the dissolution of Parliament in May 1970.

[2]   *Programme for Action*, Trades Union Congress 1969. See also TUC Annual Report, 1969, p. 229.

[3]   *Fair Deal at Work*, Conservative Political Centre, February 1970.

Although differences and similarities exist between proposals for reform, in the last analysis the effectiveness of the proposals depends to a large extent upon the cooperation and attitudes of both trades unions and their members and employers. The TUC and the Donovan Commission place greater emphasis upon voluntary non-legislative reforms, whilst the Labour government and the Conservative Party envisage legal changes and extensions of the powers of the DEP as measures aimed at reforming the collective bargaining and industrial relations systems.

III   WEALTH AND POVERTY

III.1   Relative Wealth and Poverty

The unequal distribution of income before and after tax may be seen in table 5.4. Calculations of the income distribution profile in 1967 show that 93.3 per cent of all income tax units received less than £2,000 per annum, or 78.26 per cent of pre-tax income and 81.6 per cent of income after tax. 4.7 per cent of tax units received between £2,000 and £3,000 per year, corresponding to 10.86 per cent of pre-tax income and 10.56 per cent of income after tax. 2.0 per cent of tax units had incomes of more than £3,000 a year, or 10.85 per cent of income before tax and 7.85 per cent after. Compared to 1965, a change in the income distribution profile has occurred. In 1965, 1.65 per cent of tax units recorded more than £3,000 a year, or 10.6 per cent of total pre-tax income and 17.29 per cent of income after tax.

In 1965, 53.81 per cent of tax units had incomes below £800; in 1967, the proportion had dropped to 46.8 per cent. The number of tax units in £800-£1,500 income groups increased from 35.4 per cent in 1965 to 36.5 per cent in 1967.

Table 5.4

Distribution of Personal Income UK 1967

Income Range		Number of Incomes (000s)	Income Before Tax (£ million)	Income Tax and Surtax at Current Rates (£ million)	Income After Tax (£ million)
£	£				
50–	250	2,338	493	–	493
250–	300	940	256	–	256
300–	400	1,912	662	8	654
400–	500	2,104	940	32	908
500–	600	2,068	1,131	45	1,086
600–	700	1,904	1,232	77	1,155
700–	800	1,729	1,292	104	1,188
800–	1,000	3,435	3,071	297	2,774
1,000–	1,500	6,741	8,251	946	7,305
1,500–	2,000	2,769	4,721	676	4,045
2,000–	3,000	1,298	3,061	490	2,571
3,000–	5,000	370	1,369	377	992
5,000–10,000		150	1,000	361	639
10,000–20,000		35	467	245	222
20,000 and over		7	233	176	57
Total		27,800	28,179	3,834	24,345
Income not included	..		5,386	..	..
Total personal income	..		33,565	..	..

Source: *NIBB*, 1969, table 23, page 28.

TABLE 5.5

Variations in Taxes and Benefits for all Households by Original Income Range, UK, 1961, 1965, 1968

Original Income Range (£)	(1)			(2)			(3)			(4)			(5)		
	1961	1965	1968	1961	1965	1968	1961	1965	1968	1961	1965	1968	1961	1965	1968
260–	145	157	209	23	23	23	16	18	18	52	55	72	169	190	251
365–	114	141	182	29	23	25	21	17	18	40	49	67	143	166	221
382–	111	135	158	27	28	27	18	20	19	36	51	59	133	167	193
460–	102	110	132	27	31	27	17	21	19	29	39	48	121	138	160
559–	94	109	119	28	30	30	17	18	20	23	38	44	112	131	146
676–	91	95	102	29	31	32	18	19	21	21	27	34	110	115	128
816–	88	91	95	28	33	34	16	18	20	17	24	29	105	111	117
988–	85	85	88	28	32	35	16	18	20	14	18	23	101	103	109
196–	82	83	83	29	32	36	17	18	20	12	15	20	98	100	103
1,448–	80	81	79	30	32	35	17	17	20	10	13	16	95	97	98
1,752–	78	77	77	30	34	36	16	19	20	8	11	13	92	94	95
2,122–	76	74	75	30	36	36	15	20	19	6	10	12	89	91	92
2,566–	74	73	73	31	34	37	15	17	19	5	8	10	87	88	89
3,104–	70	72	71	34	34	36	13	14	17	3	6	8	90	84	86
Average over all income ranges	87	86	84	29	32	35	16	18	19	17	19	20	103	103	103

NOTES:

Column (1) = Income after all taxes and benefits as percentage of original income (table 4(I) p. xxxvi)

Column (2) = Total taxes as percentage of original income plus cash benefits (table 4(III), p. xxxviii)

Column (3) = Indirect taxes as per cent of income after direct taxes and benefits (table 4(V), p. xi)

Column (4) = Total benefits as percentage of original income plus cash benefits (table 4(IV), p.xxxix)

Column (5) = Income after direct taxes and benefits as per cent of original income

Source: *ET*, February 1970, tables as specified below

Redistribution of income is effected through the system of public expenditure, including social security, and taxation. The estimated incidence of taxes and social security benefits on different sized families and income groups is given for specific years in *Economic Trends,*[1] using information from *'The Family Expenditure Survey'.*[2]

The taxes and benefits included in the estimates are: (1) direct taxes; (2) direct benefits, (a) cash benefits, e.g. national insurance and pensions, (b) benefits in kind—welfare benefits, education etc.; (3) indirect benefits, e.g. housing subsidies; (4) indirect taxes on final consumer goods and services, e.g. customs & excise duties, local rates, purchase tax, motor taxation; (5) indirect taxation on intermediate products: payments by business in respect of local rates, vehicles licences, duties on oil.

The relative changes in final income, 1961-8, between income groups can be evaluated from table 5.5. Final income is influenced by the relative impact of taxes and benefits on original income levels. Table 5.5, column (1) indicates that the break-even point between tax deductions and benefit additions has moved to higher income groups over the 1961-8 period. The observed changes in final income as a proportion of original income indicate (a) that the ratio of final to original income was less the higher the level of income in a given year; (b) that the final income of lower income groups was an increasing proportion of original income over the 1961-8 period; (c) that final incomes in higher income groups have slightly diminished as a proportion of original income since 1961. The proportion of total taxation to original income plus cash benefits (column 2) has not varied much between income groups in a given year, and has increased over the 1961-8 period more for the middle and higher income groups than for the lower ones. The proportion of indirect taxation to income after direct taxes and benefits was inversely related to the level of income in 1961 and 1965, was invariant to income in 1968, and over the 1961-8 period increased slightly for most income groups (column 3). The incidence of different types of indirect taxation shows considerable variation. Purchase tax appears to be neutral, local rates and tobacco duties are regressive, taxes on beer and intermediate products are mildly regressive, and taxation of alcohol is not clearly progressive or regressive.

Column 4 shows that total benefits have formed a higher proportion of the original income of lower than of higher income groups in all years; this discrepancy has become more marked over the years and therefore progressive direct taxes and benefits combined reduced the final incomes of higher groups and substantially increased those of lower income groups (column 5). Table 5.5 indicates that these are due more to higher benefits than lower taxation of the lower income groups. Although there has been a movement out of the three lowest income groups since 1961, resulting income gains may be more apparent than real, as the higher taxation and lower benefits at higher income levels erode away the advantages of higher original incomes.

Within each income group, taxes and benefits combined have favoured larger families. Table 5.6 indicates that in 1968 total taxation did not differ greatly between income groups for given family sizes, but marginally favoured larger families within given income groups (column 2). Indirect taxation was a higher proportion of income for lower income families than for higher income ones (column 3). Only local rates and taxes on drink formed a smaller proportion of income for larger than smaller families.

Total benefits were a higher percentage of original income plus cash benefits for larger families in each group, and decreased with income for any given family size (column 4). Since 1961 larger sized lower income families have received substantially greater increases in total benefits compared to higher income families of the same size.

---

[1] See *ET,* February 1970, p. xvi. For criticism of CSO data see A. Peacock and R. Shannon, 'The Welfare State and the Redistribution of Income', *Westminster Bank Review,* August 1968.

[2] Published annually by the Department of Employment and Productivity.

TABLE 5.6

Variations in Taxes and Benefits by Family Size and Income Level, UK, 1968

	(1)				(2)				
	2A	2A/1C	2A/2C	2A/3C	2A	2A/1C	2A/2C	2A/3C	2A
Original Income Range (£)									
560–	119	–	–	–	30	–	–	–	21
676–	95	97	116	–	34	36	29	–	23
816–	86	89	100	111	35	35	32	33	22
988–	74	82	93	105	37	35	32	31	22
1,196–	69	78	85	100	39	35	34	33	23
1,448–	68	75	84	93	38	35	33	31	22
1,752–	67	75	82	90	37	35	33	32	21
2,122–	67	72	81	90	36	36	31	30	18
2,566–	65	73	79	86	37	33	33	29	20
Average over All income ranges	76	79	85	94	36	34	33	32	20

NOTES A =.Adult   C = Children

Column (1) = Final income after all taxes and benefits as a percentage of original income (table A, p. xvii)

Column (2) = Total taxes as a percentage of original income plus cash benefits (table C, p. xix)

Column (3) = Indirect taxes as a percentage of income after direct taxes and benefits (table E, p. xxi)

Column (4) = Total benefits as a percentage of original income plus cash benefits (table D, p. xx)

Column (5) = Final income after direct taxes and benefits as a percentage of original income (table B, p. x

Source: *ET*, February 1970.

Whether income distribution in the UK is becoming more or less egalitarian depends on the way income is computed.[1] A common means of measuring the inequality of income distribution is to express the area between the diagonal and the curve in the Lorenz diagram (Figure 5.1) as a proportion of the area of half the box. The percentages of income and income units are plotted cumulatively along the axes XY and OX, the dotted line representing a typical situation. The measure of inequality is (A/A + B). 100. If all units had identical incomes then the line would follow the 45° line and the proportion be 0 per cent, i.e. perfect equality.

In the case of one unit holding all income the cumulative distribution line would follow the perimeter of the box (OXY) and the proportion be 100 per cent, i.e. perfect inequality. Thus inequality can be measured as rising from 0 per cent to 100 per cent. A line, for example, to the right of the dotted one would represent greater inequality, i.e. a greater proportion of income being held by the top income groups. This measure is known as the Gini Concentration Ratio. Table 5.7 reproduces the Gini concentration ratios for the data given in the Inland Revenue's annual Reports.[2]

There is a clear trend towards greater equality. However, this may be a misleading result. First, the Inland Revenue data, unlike the NIBB and ET data, exclude all incomes

---

[1] A study of these problems was made by Dr T. Stark (New University of Ulster) in *A Survey of the Distribution of Income in the U.K. since World War II* (Ph.D. thesis, University of Manchester). The remainder of this section is an extract from an appendix specially prepared by Dr Stark for this chapter.

[2] See, e.g., 108th *Report*.

(3)			(4)				(5)			
2A/1C	2A/2C	2A/3C	2A	2A/1C	2A/2C	2A/3C	2A	2A/1C	2A/2C	2A/3C
1	1	–	43	–	–	–	151	–	–	–
23	19	–	30	33	42	–	121	126	142	134
22	19	18	23	25	32	43	108	111	123	127
21	19	18	14	18	25	35	94	102	114	120
20	20	18	9	14	20	33	88	97	105	113
19	18	18	7	10	17	25	86	92	102	108
20	18	17	5	10	15	22	84	92	99	105
18	15	14	4	8	12	20	82	88	96	97
17	15	12	3	7	12	15	81	88	93	94
19	18	18	14	13	13	27	95	96	102	114

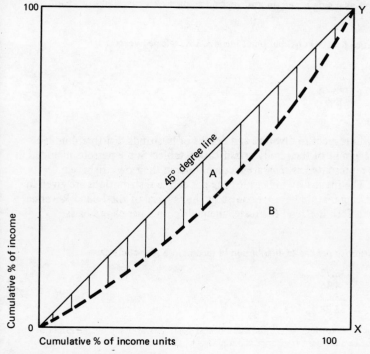

Figure 5.1   The Lorenz Diagram

TABLE 5.7

Gini Concentration Ratios for Inland Revenue distribution of income, UK, selected years

1949	35.31
1954	33.89
1959	33.66
1963	32.24

These results are for the Inland Revenue distributions adjusted to a calendar year basis.

Source: T. Stark, 'A Survey of the Distribution of Income in the UK since World War II', unpublished Ph.D. thesis, Manchester University Library.

below the effective exemption limit[1] and several types of non-taxable incomes above
these limits. Secondly, the income unit concept can hide basic changes in the social
structure of incomes, e.g. an increase in the number of married persons can lead to a
movement of incomes to higher income ranges without any necessary increase in per
capita income.

The first criticism can be partially overcome by an analysis of the CSO distributions
of income, published in *NIBB;* these extend Inland Revenue surveys to include
most State benefit and National Insurance incomes, e.g. national assistance, unemployment, maternity, sickness grants, educational scholarships and some incomes in kind.[2]
The overall coverage for these distributions is approximately 85 per cent of total Personal
Income. Table 5.8 suggests that the CSO distributions do not point to any general trend
towards greater inequality.

Both the first problem and the second (the income unit definition) can be overcome by
readjusting the CSO distributions to a per capita basis,[3] by linking up the total numbers
of units, the total numbers of persons and the family size classification of units. This
latter information is provided for most income units in the Inland Revenue surveys. In
undertaking this adjustment attention must be paid to the extensive double-counting of
persons in the CSO distributions, e.g. new marriages cause double-counting, as the wife
is counted twice, first as a single person and second as part of a married unit. Similar

TABLE 5.8

Gini Concentration Ratios for CSO distribution of income, UK, selected years

1949	38.72
1954	39.26
1959	39.25
1963	38.67

Source: T. Stark, *ibid.*

phenomena occur with respect to divorces and deaths of husbands. Further double-
counting occurs on account of the family classification tables. Some persons included in
these tables are also represented as separate income units in their own right, e.g.
dependent relatives. The inequality indices for the per capita distributions are given in
table 5.9. The interesting feature here, of course, is the reversal of the Inland Revenue
trends. There is now a definite trend to greater inequality on a per capita basis.

TABLE 5.9

Gini Concentration Ratios for per capita distribution of income, UK, selected years

1949[1]	33.72
1954	34.45
1959	35.62
1963	35.78

[1]   Only half of the double-countings were eliminated in this year. However the overall effect on the
      Gini ratio would not be sufficient to change the rankings of the four years.

Source: T. Stark, *ibid.*

There are also further problems not touched on here, concerning the definition and measurement of inequality.[4] Evidence suggests that there is no marked decrease in the number of
poor persons which, of course is another means of judging the extent of income inequality.

[1]   The effective exemption limits for 1949, 1954, 1959 and 1963 were £135, £155, £180 and £275
      respectively.
[2]   The definitions are outlined in, e.g. *NIBB*, 1965, p. 97.
[3]   See A. R. Prest and T. Stark, 'Some Aspects of Income Distribution in the UK since World War
      II', *MS*, September 1967.
[4]   E.g. if the data are transformed to an equivalent adult basis, there is then some movement towards
      greater equality over the period.

III.2   Regional Profile

The various regions of the UK may be separated into rich and poor in accordance with the data in table 5.10. The ranking order varies according to the criterion used. Clearly, some regions rank rich on one basis and poor on another, e.g. Wales. These shifts arise from the relative inter-regional differences in various socio-economic factors. An adequate explanation must consider:

(1)   Levels of employment and unemployment;
(2)   Industrial structure and changes therein;
(3)   Prevailing wages paid by industry, by region, by occupation;
(4)   Activity rates, for men and women, by region;
(5)   Number of persons per household and number employed and unoccupied.

Table 5.10 shows that richer regions are characterised by below-average unemployment rates; poorer by rates well above national average. Actual numbers unemployed are less significant than the rate of unemployment as an indicator of social and economic well-being. The activity rate, the number of employees in an age/sex group as a percentage of the age/sex group in the population, indicates the participation rate of population in employment. Both richer and poorer regions have much higher rates for males than for females; the richer, however, have higher male rates than the poorer, and also tend to have higher female rates, indicating the greater proportion of women at work. This latter manifests itself in a higher-than-average number of persons working per household in the richer regions than the poorer, and this in turn creates higher average income per head and per household. Clearly, any given criteria for evaluating relative regional wealth and poverty must be related to other socio-economic factors. For example, Wales ranks high by average hourly and weekly earnings, but income per person per household is below the national average; those employed are well paid but a high unemployment rate, below-average activity rate for men, and the lowest rate for women in the UK place Wales among the poorest regions in terms of income per head per household per week. Some regions, however, rank persistently rich or poor; for example, London and the south-east on the one hand and Northern Ireland on the other, characterise the extremes of the regional spectrum.

Regional socio-economic problems are aggravated by demographic factors: population density, migration, age structure and skills and aptitudes of working population. Population movement is either inter- or intra-regional; outward migration tends to leave behind a population of low intra-regional mobility, a factor important to regional industrial structures. There is evidence of a persistent southward population drift, regional immigration being higher the further south the region is situated.[1] Inter-regional mobility has been greatest into London and the south-east, where population is about three times greater than that of any other region. Population immigration may cause urban congestion and can render the existing stock of social capital inadequate; regional population emigration can create other undesirable social and economic conditions, particularly when an increasing proportion of the remaining population is in older age groups, less inclined to move to new employment and often possessing skills and aptitudes inappropriate to newer industries.

Population movement is influenced by received and expected income, occupation, industrial structure changes, family size, marital status, age, educational qualifications, job opportunities inside and outside the region, and social and psychological factors related to family cohesion. Industrial structure has important implications for regional

---

[1]   D. Friedlander and R. J. Rostner, 'Internal Migration in England and Wales', *Journal of Population Studies,* Vol. 20, 1967.

TABLE 5.10

UK Regional Profile

	(1)	(2)	(3)	(4)	(5)	(6)	(7)
	£	%	£	%	£	£	£
UK	23.62	100	0.517	100	26.717	8.917	7.440
Northern	22.967	97.2	0.504	97.6	23.810	7.844	6.633
Yorkshire/Humberside	20.004	93.3	0.470	91.4	25.562	8.796	6.954
East Midlands	22.742	96.3	0.467	96.6	25.487	8.492	6.680
West Midlands	24.913	105.5	0.473	108.0	28.494	9.35	7.562
East Anglia	21.69	91.8	0.467	90.2	24.135	8.410	7.179
London/south-east	24.73	104.7	0.535	103.8	29.725	10.175	8.440
South-west	22.87	96.6	0.496	96.1	25.258	8.556	6.962
North-west	22.95	97.2	0.498	96.4	25.473	8.440	7.271
Wales	24.09	102.0	0.542	104.8	23.954	8.154	6.937
Scotland	22.95	97.2	0.500	96.8	25.654	7.95	6.942
Northern Ireland	20.40	86.4	0.458	88.6	21.967	6.019	5.717

Sources: (a)   *Regional Abstract of Statistics*, no. 5, 1969
           (b)   Column (9), P. Devine, *MS*, June 1969 (As these data relate to the old standard Regions, they do not conform fully with the other columns)

NOTES: *Key to Table 5.10*

Column (1) Average weekly earnings in manufacturing industry, October 1968.
Column (2) Average weekly earnings in manufacturing industry, October 1968 as per cent of UK average.
Column (3) Average hourly earnings in manufacturing industry, October 1968.
Column (4) Average hourly earnings in manufacturing industry, October 1968 as per cent of UK average.
Column (5) Average income per household per week, 1965-7.
Column (6) Average income per person per week, 1965-7.
Column (7) Average weekly expenditure per person, 1965-7.
Column (8) Average gross annual earnings in civil employment for men, 18-64 age group, 1967-8.
Column (9) Gini concentration ratios of regional income, 1964-5.
Column (10) Average number of persons per household, 1965-7.
Column (11) Average number of working persons per household, 1965-7.
Column (12) Per cent unemployment rate, 1968.
Column (13) Number of employees in employment, June 1968.
Column (14) Population mid-1968 (home resident population).
Column (15) Per cent activity rates (male and female), 1968.

wealth and poverty, insofar as some regions have relied heavily on industries whose market significance has declined. Inter-area wage differentials have not promoted that degree of labour mobility necessary to ease the regional unemployment problem, although younger age groups have tended to move to areas of better job opportunities. Successive governments have introduced measures aimed at eliminating the regional disparities of unemployment by encouraging new industrial development in development areas, and by various schemes for promoting labour mobility.[1]

The Industrial Development Act 1966 established new development areas for the purposes of assistance. In 1967, a *Regional Employment Premium* was introduced, aimed at reducing labour costs in manufacturing in development areas by a subsidy of £1.50 per head per week.[2] *Government Training Centres* and the establishment of *Industrial*

---

[1]   *The Intermediate Areas*, chapter 7, Cmnd 3998, HMSQ, 1969; and chapter 4. V.

[2]   *Regional Employment Premium*, Cmnd 3310, 1967. SET concessions were made in 1968 for employees in hotels situated in rural parts of development areas.

(8)	(9)	(10)	(11)	(12)	(13)	(14)	(15) %	
£		No.	No.	%	000s.	000s.	M	F
1249	32.85	2.99	1.34	2.6	23,125	55.282	74.1	39.8
1158	30.0	3.04	1.25	4.7	1,255 ,	3,341	74.9	34.8
1159	31.82	2.91	1.31	2.6	2,002	4,804	74.7	38.8
1171	30.5	3.00	1.35	1.9	1,398	3,322	74.1	39.8
1252	N.A.	3.05	1.48	2.2	2,271	5,084	78.4	42.6
1128	31.45	2.88	1.25	2.0	607	1,637	64.6	33.1
1355	36.21	2.91	1.34	1.6	7,856	17,230	77.9	43.4
1155	32.52	2.95	1.22	2.5	1,312	3,700	63.5	32.2
1219	31.25	3.02	1.39	2.5	2,899	6,755	75.9	42.1
1189	29.64	2.94	1.18	4.0	950	2,720	65.6	30.1
1163	32.73	3.23	1.43	3.8	2,086	5,188	74.5	40.4
1057	32.65	3.67	1.29	7.2	480	1,502	64.0	35.5

Training Boards have assisted in training work people in new skills and jobs. In 1969, there were forty-two government training centres; five new centres were established in development areas in 1968-9. A *Resettlement Transfer Scheme* benefits those unemployed workers who have no early prospect of employment in their area and move to another beyond daily travelling distance. The *Key Workers Scheme* benefits employees required to move to a development area to set up a new industrial project. The *Nuclear Labour Force Scheme* assists work people recruited in high unemployment areas to be transferred to a parent factory for a period of training before commencing permanent employment. Some industrial undertakings have their own schemes for encouraging labour mobility, e.g. the National Coal Board. Variations in persistent unemployment levels are reflected in regional incomes. Table 5.10 indicates the several measures of income. The difference between highest and lowest gross annual earnings in 1967-8 per man was about £300; inter-regional average expenditure per person in 1965-7 varied from £5.70 to £8.40 per week; average income per person in 1965-7 ranged from £6 in Northern Ireland to £10.20 in London and the south-east.

A recent study[1] shows that between 1949 and 1964, the degree of inter-regional income inequality has declined; the percentage difference between the Gini concentration ratios of the most equal and most unequal areas fell from 29.92 per cent to 20 per cent. In 1965 income in Greater London was 11.67 per cent above the UK national average and in Wales 12.11 per cent below. However, little correlation was shown to exist between the degree of inequality and average income. Between 1949 and 1965 Gini ratios indicate a trend towards greater equality, although regional differences in the speed of this process are apparent, being, in general, more rapid between 1949-50 and 1954-5, than in the 1955-65 period.

---

[1] P . J. Devine 'Inter-regional variations in the degree of inequality of income distribution: UK 1949-65' *MS*, June 1969.

III.3   Low Pay

In October 1968, average weekly earnings of manual male workers in manufacturing industry were £23.60 and in all industries and services £23; non-manual male workers earned £29.90 and £29.75 respectively. However, 59 per cent of manual and 36.1 per cent of non-manual male employees earned less than £24 per week in all industries and services, while 99 per cent of manual female and 88.8 per cent non-manual female employees earned less than this amount. Some employed persons earn much less than the national average. In 1969-70 persons earning less than £15 per week or £0.375 per hour were considered low paid, although the Prices and Incomes Board considers 'that anyone whose pay is scarcely above the level of national assistance is low paid.'[1] Wages councils are intended to protect poorly organised workers by establishing a statutory minimum wage. Marquand (1967)[2] found that of twenty manufacturing industries with low paid workers, fourteen industries were covered by wages council arrangements; workers in these industries, although receiving legal minimum wages, were still earning less than their supplementary benefit level. The low paid are women, juveniles, sick and disabled, and employees in high unemployment areas. Low pay is associated with industries employing a high proportion of women and older men; industries with contracting labour forces; shrinking manufacturing industries; industries having wages council arrangments: and industries where payment systems offer little opportunity of bonus earnings or overtime working, e.g. local authorities. Low paid workers may also be found in industries not ranked as low paying, e.g. shipbuilding. Weak trades union bargaining strength and organisation, pressures from higher paid union members to maintain wage differentials, labour market pressures, discrimination by age, sex and occupation all contribute to the low pay problem.

Sample survey results for September 1968[3] show that nearly 10 per cent of male manual and 86.2 per cent of female manual workers earned less than £15 per week in all industries and services; in manufacturing industry 4.6 per cent of male and 83.6 per cent female workers earned below £15. Particular industries had high proportions of low earning employees, especially coal mining, distributive trades, clothing and footwear and insurance and banking services (see table 5.11).

The labour force age structure may aggravate the low pay problem. Male earnings increase rapidly between 21 and 34, reaching a peak in the late 40s, thereafter falling while females' earnings are absolutely lower throughout and also decline after reaching a peak in the late 20s. A high proportion of female employees is above 35-40 years old.

In 1968[4] 3.2 per cent of male and 80.6 per cent of female skilled labour, 6.2 per cent of male and 83.3 per cent of female semi-skilled workers, and 19.2 per cent of male unskilled and 92.0 per cent of female unskilled workers earned less than £15 per week. Sex differentials appear to outweigh the degree of skill in the determination of pay. The extent of low pay will be influenced by hourly rates of pay, hours worked, possibilities of extra earnings, and by regional industrial and employment structures and changes therein. The industrial distribution of employment, and inter-area and inter-industry wage differentials, influence the scale and level of low pay, particularly where high earnings industries employ less than the national average proportion of workers. Evidence suggests, however,[5] that

---

[1]   NBPI *Second General Report*, Cmnd 3394, 1967.

[2]   J. Marquand, 'Which are the Low Paid Workers?', *BJIR*, vol. 5, no. 3, November 1967.

[3]   *EPG*, May 1969, p. 400.

[4]   *EPG*, May 1969, p. 407, table 4 and table 5.

[5]   *EPG*, March 1969, p. 232.

TABLE 5.11

Earnings Distribution: Percentage of Employees Earning less than £15 Per Week, UK, September 1968

	Male		Female	
	Manual	*Non-Manual*	*Manual*	*Non-Manual*
All Industries and Services	9.4	4.6	86.2	55.5
All manufacturing industries	4.6	2.6	83.6	70.0
All non-manufacturing industries	13.4	5.8	88.8	51.3
Selected Individual Industries				
Food, drink and tobacco	5.9	3.8	88.7	69.0
Coal mining	11.0	5.1	–	–
Engineering	4.8	2.1	84.8	55.7
Textiles	8.1	3.0	81.5	72.3
Clothing	10.4	–	84.6	–
Distributive trades	19.4	6.2	94.5	74.9
Retail distribution	23.3	6.1	94.5	76.7
Insurance/Banking	28.7	6.4	–	63.1
Public administration	21.3	4.9	75.8	38.5
Catering, etc.	47.5	–	92.4	–

Source: *EPG,* June 1969, p. 518, tables 15-18.

inter-regional differences in employment structures only marginally determine regional weekly earnings differentials, but are more significant for differences in average hourly earnings. Low pay may be viewed as either a social or a labour problem. A social problem exists where the absolute amount earned is insufficient to support the wage earner's family; a labour problem exists when earnings are low compared to those in other industries. The NBPI considered: 'By and large, however, the concept of the low paid is a relative rather than an absolute one; the most that can be said . . . is that pay is too low, or alternatively too high, in comparison to somebody else's.'[1]

Solutions to the problem of low paid families include appropriate changes in the social security system, e.g. higher family allowances; reforms in the taxation system favouring low earning families; strengthening the bargaining position of the low paid workers, e.g. stronger trades unionism; creating a statutory national minimum wage, and improvements in the educational and training opportunities of low paid families.

III.4 Social Security and Superannuation

The cost of providing social services in Britain increased during the 1960-9 period: housing from £426 million to £1,094 million; education from £917 to £2,292 million; health and welfare from £830 to £1,770 million; child care from £24 million to £63 million; and social security from £1,416 million to £2,292 million. These increases arose from a number of demographic and social changes. Between 1960 and 1969 the number of retired persons increased from 7.7 to 8.5 million; increases also occurred in the number below working age. The upward movement in living standards has necessitated increasing pension, health, educational and other standards. The social services may be financed through general taxation, contributions from employers and employees, charges for the use of services, or by transferring the cost from the public to the private sector, e.g. private health and superannuation schemes, or increases in house ownership.

The social security system since the second world war has been based on equality of benefit for equality of contributions. The National Insurance scheme provides basic flat-

---

[1] *NBPI, Second General Report.*

rate benefits during sickness, unemployment, widowhood and retirement in exchange for weekly flat-rate contributions. There are some small elements of graduation in contributions and benefits arising from legislation in 1961 and 1966. National Insurance contributions also include a payment to the National Health Service. Inequalities remain, however, when all recipients of benefits receive similar cash amounts regardless of their personal circumstances. Although Supplementary Benefits[1] are payable to those in proven need, the present National Insurance arrangements have been unselective, i.e. those in greater need have not received greater benefits from the scheme. In spite of the increased costs of operating the system, poverty and social distress continue to exist. Attempts to benefit the poorer sections of the population have resulted in global increases for all sections, an apparently expensive and ineffective method of coping with poverty. Adverse demographic changes, the payment of full retirement pensions to all, the necessity to maintain their real value by successive universal increases, and the payment of supplementary benefit as a rule rather than an exception, characterise the social security arrangements for the retired population. The present system involves considerable administrative overlap and cost. In January 1969 a government White Paper[2] declared the present scheme inadequate to cope with the social and economic problems of the country.

Problems arise from disparities between previous earned income levels of retired persons and the level of retirement benefits, flat-rate payments (e.g. family allowances) to large low-income families whose income needs are manifestly greater than high income families, and discrimination in supplementary benefit payments between different sections of beneficiaries. In April 1970, National Insurance unemployment and sick pay was £8.10 per week for a married man; the retirement pension was £5 per single person and £8.10 for a married couple.

A new *earnings-related scheme* was presented by the Labour government in January 1969[3] to replace the existing scheme in April 1972. The present flat-rate contributions would be replaced by graduated payments of 6.75 per cent of earnings for employees up to a limit of 1½ times national average earnings (£1,900 in April 1969); employers would contribute 7 per cent of the total earnings of all employees with no upper limit.[4] Separate National Superannuation and Social Insurance Funds would be established.[5] The National Insurance card would be abolished and payment effected through the PAYE system used for tax collection. Employees earning below the PAYE exemption limit would not be required to contribute under the scheme, though they could contribute voluntarily. In 1969, 1½ million persons earning less than £5.25 weekly would have been exempt.

The full pension benefits, payable from 1992, would be based on an average of the ratios of actual and national average earnings over an individual's working life, this average ratio then being applied to national average earnings in the year of retirement. On April 1969 figures, the main retirement pension would have consisted of 60 per cent of the first £630 of an individual's 'life average' earnings, plus 25 per cent of any earnings between

---

[1] Additional benefits paid to persons not in full time employment whose weekly income is below a certain level; supplementary pensions are payable to retired persons and supplementary allowances for those over 16 years of age, but below retirement age, whose income is below a certain minimum standard.

[2] *National Superannuation and Social Insurance*, Cmnd 3883, HMSO, 1969.

[3] *Ibid.*

[4] *Explanatory Memorandum on the National Superannuation and Social Insurance Bill 1969*, Cmnd 4222, HMSO, December 1969.

[5] National Superannuation and Social Insurance Bill 1969, *Report by the Government Actuary on the Financial Provisions of the Bill*, Cmnd 4223, HMSO, 1969.

£630 (half national average earnings) and £1,900 (one and half times national average earnings). Adjustments in the cash figures would be made as earnings rise, and pension rate adjustments in accordance with price changes would take place every two years of retirement. An individual earning half national average earnings in April 1969 would have received £7.20 per week under the new scheme compared to £5.10 per week at present. Table 5.12 indicates the contribution scales (including graduated payments with the old scheme) under the old and the new schemes for men and women not contracted out. (Provision was made for employees covered by an approved occupational pension scheme to contract out of part of the personal retirement pension of the new scheme.)[1]

TABLE 5.12

Employee Weekly Contributions (Present and Proposed National Insurance Schemes) (£)

Annual Earnings	Present Scheme Contributions (1)	Contributions under the New Scheme (2)	Change in Contributions (±) (3)
MEN			
450	0.88	0.58	−0.30
630	1.04	0.82	−0.22
1,000	1.36	1.30	−0.06
1,250	1.52	1.62	+0.10
1,500	1.65	1.95	+0.30
1,900	1.70	2.47	+0.77
WOMEN			
450	0.75	0.58	−0.17
630	0.90	0.82	−0.08
1,000	1.22	1.30	+0.08
1,250	1.34	1.62	+0.18
1,500	1.52	1.95	+0.43
1,900	1.57	2.47	+0.90

Source: Cmnd 4222, appendix B. Present scheme figures are end-1969.

Sickness benefit, at present payable indefinitely after 156 contributions, would have been payable for up to 28 weeks under the new scheme. Thereafter, an *invalidity pension* would be paid, calculated in the same way as the proposed earnings related retirement pension; most of those likely to receive such a pension would be in the 50-60 year-old age groups. Unemployment benefit would be paid for the same maximum period as at present, 52 weeks. The unemployment and sickness benefits would continue to use the two-part basis for the present scheme, a flat-rate personal benefit of £5 per week and an earnings related component based on one-third of weekly earnings between £8.33 and the earnings ceiling (£36 per week in April 1969 figures). The earnings related supplement would be payable for a maximum of 26 weeks. In 1973-4, the additional costs of the new scheme over the present one were estimated at £10 million for unemployment benefit, £48 million for short-term sickness benefit, and £8 million for invalidity pension. The total extra cost of Social Insurance benefit was estimated as £85 million in 1973-4, rising steadily to £247 million by 2002-3.[2]

The proposed scheme represented a depature from the principles of equality of contribution and benefit found in the present system. It has been criticised on the grounds

---

[1]   Cmnd 4222, paras 67-76.

[2]   Cmnd 4223, table 2.

that private occupational schemes would give individuals greater benefits than the proposed scheme for a given outlay, and that the new scheme would need a higher revenue from which to pay proposed benefits than that likely from the new contributions. The principle that benefits must be earned by contributions does not represent a significantly different approach to the problems of poverty; lower income contributors will receive lower benefits than higher income groups, but not proportionately so. But there is a built-in system of redistribution in the new scheme due to the pensions formula.[1,2]

Reverse Income Tax: An alternative to the present and proposed social security arrangements is based upon a reverse income tax or negative income tax concept, i.e. a form of income supplementation based on a system where the amount of government out-payment is greater the lower the individual's income. Such a system could give greater selectivity than present arrangements with minimum social ignominy since necessary means testing could be effected through the Inland Revenue Department to which taxpayers at present make annual returns of income and details of personal circumstances. An RIT would not discriminate between categories of poorer persons, e.g. the sick, the unemployed, the employed (but low paid) in determining necessary income levels. Many of the numerous benefits paid at present could be abolished under an RIT scheme.

Two main forms of RIT are available: the *Social Dividend Plan* and the *Poverty Gap Plan;* both rely upon some standard of income determined as reasonably adequate. Under social dividend schemes, all families or persons would receive a state payment of a prescribed maximum income, regardless of their own private incomes. Taxation of private income, i.e. excluding the state payment, would then reduce the net cash benefit derived from the state payment as family income increased. Poor families would derive a net surplus from the state payment, while for high income families tax paid would exceed the state payment. Under poverty-gap schemes state payments would be made to give a minimum guaranteed income by covering the difference between actual family or personal income and a prescribed standard income. Some schemes, e.g. the type proposed by Milton Friedman, would compensate for only a part of the poverty gap. Both plans involve a break-even level of income at which tax liability equals the income benefits of state payments. The net cost per annum of two proposed social dividend schemes in Britain is estimated at £3,697 million and £1,881 million, while a poverty-gap scheme would cost £925 million per annum and a Friedman-type scheme £463 million.[3] Schemes for alleviating poverty must consider their possible effects upon the incentive to work. Negative income tax not only increases the total disposable income attainable from employment; it also reduces both the potential income gain from increased work effort and potential loss of income from reduced work effort. These leisure-inducing effects may apply not only to unemployed but also to employed persons. One view[4] is that RIT measures for alleviating poverty amongst low paid households would have no more disincentive effect than present Supplementary Benefit arrangements, and that RIT measures would ensure that state payments and their associated disincentive effects would be concentrated on persons in households below the poverty line minimum income.[5] If a scheme

---

[1]   See A. R. Prest 'Some Redistributional Aspects of the National Superannuation Fund', *TBR*, June 1970.

[2]   The Bill lapsed with the dissolution of Parliament in May 1970.

[3]   *Policy for Poverty*, Research Monograph 20, pp. 38 ff. *Institute of Economic Affairs*, 1970.

[4]   *Ibid*, pp. 70-7.

[5]   E.g. £349 per annum for a single householder, £731 for a married couple with two children (Department of Health and Social Security figures). See *ibid.*, pp. 30-31.

could be designed to preserve the incentive to work it would potentially solve the problem of poverty without distorting the market price mechanism.

The selectivity exercised under social security arrangements has important implications for the solution of poverty problems. The principal opposition to increased selectivity arises from objections to 'means testing', a method of determining a family's or person's needs considered to be humiliating and likely to deter applications for benefits, e.g. from old age pensioners. Proponents of increased selectivity are critical of a system of equal social benefits for all as a means of eliminating poverty, and argue that greater selectivity between rich and poor would more effectively alleviate poverty at an acceptable cost.

III.5   A National Minimum Wage

Evidence indicates that many families with two or more children receive income less than supplementary benefit allowances, and that some employed male workers earn even less than supplementary benefit level of income.[1] This situation has stimulated proposals for a national minimum wage to eliminate poverty among wage earners. £15 per week has been proposed by trades unions, or as an equivalent £0.375 per hour; government sources have declined to stipulate an amount, but have emphasised guaranteed hourly pay as a suitable basis. The shortcomings of the wages council[2] system have encouraged the proponents of a national minimum wage. However, the failure of existing arrangements has implications for a permanent solution to the low pay problem.

The purposes of a national minimum wage[3] would be to protect the weakly organised low paid worker; to effect a redistribution of income favourable to low income wage earners; to alleviate poverty among the employed; and to encourage improved manpower utilisation by raising the price of labour. The main beneficiaries of a national minimum wage would be women; younger workers between 18 and 24; elderly workers; workers in development areas; and those in high paying industries who receive less than average earnings and less than £15 per week. However, a national minimum wage appears potentially less effective in relieving poverty than selective social security payments and fiscal measures which allow for differences in the personal circumstances of low paid workers; non-employed income groups would derive no benefit from a national minimum wage and two-thirds of 4.1 million households in 1966 receiving less than £15 per week contained no employed person. A national minimum wage would also have to be established at such a level that it would not invoke consequential claims by higher paid workers, resulting in substantial additions to the national wages-salary bill.

The national minimum wage inquiry examined the estimated additional costs of various hourly rates of pay, using three classifications:

(1) No repercussions—where direct costs were estimated on the basis that pay increases were confined to those where earnings were below the given minima.

(2) Limited repercussions—where the extra costs of wage adjustments for workers slightly above the minima were estimated.

(3) Extensive repercussions—allowing for extra costs of comprehensive adjustments resulting from the minima.

Relevant data for a £0.375 per hour minimum are given in table 5.13 below.

---

[1]   See Ministry of Social Security, *Report of Circumstances of Families,* 1966.

[2]   See section II.1 and section III.3 of this chapter.

[3]   See *National Minimum Wage: An Inquiry,* DEP, HMSO, 1969.

TABLE 5.13

Estimates of Costs and Number of Employees affected by a National Minimum Wage, UK

	No Repercussions			Limited Repercussions			Extensive Repercussions		
	I £m	II %	III Nos(m.)	I £m	II %	III Nos(m.)	I £m	II %	III Nos(m.)
Men and youths	363	1.7	2.3	495	2.3	5.5	1578	7.4	All
Women and girls	1065	5.0	5.0	1099	5.1	5.8	1539	7.2	All

I = £ million per annum additional cost
II = Percentage of national wage and salary bill
III = Estimated number (millions) affected by £0.375 per hour minimum

Source: National Minimum Wage.

The inferior wage position of nearly two-thirds of the employed female labour force is clear from table 5.13. Clearly the impact of a national minimum wage would depend upon its level, the differences of existing pay and employment situations within and between industries, and the extent and effectiveness of differential wage adjustments by higher paid workpeople. A minimum of £0.375 per hour for men and £0.25 per hour for women would cost an extra £2,800 million per annum, while equal payment to females would increase total costs by £3,800 million, approximately one-sixth of the total wage and salary bill.

Employers could react to increased labour costs by endeavouring to increase labour productivity, or reducing the size of their labour forces, or accepting reductions in profits, or raising prices. Reductions in labour forces would be particularly significant in industries in less prosperous areas and in those employing high proportions of female labour. For special groups of work people a national minimum wage might raise employment problems. Of the 650,000 registered disabled employees in 1969, a large proportion is in low paid jobs; a national minimum wage would create problems for this work group. Strong precedents exist against applying a national minimum wage to younger workers, i.e. males under 21, females under 18. Some countries apply a percentage system to minimum pay for younger workers. The lowering of the age of majority to 18,[1] with commensurate payment of adult rates, is estimated to add £100 million per year to the national wage and salary bill.

Price increases would be inevitable in certain service industries (and in parts of the public sector) where product prices are sensitive to earnings changes, where productivity increases are difficult in the short-term, and where little margin for profit-squeezing exists. Such price increases could negate any real income gains to lower paid workers. Under the tax and social security arrangements operative in October 1968,[2] allowing £2 per week for rent and £30 per year for rates, a minimum earnings level of £15 per week would give a net disposable income of £12.525 per week to a married couple with no children (half the national average level of earnings), £15.125 to a two child family,[3] and £18.75 to a four child family.[4] While notions of social justice may underlie a national minimum earn-

---

[1] See *Age of Majority*, Cmnd 3342, HMSO, 1969.

[2] See *National Minimum Wage, op.cit.*, appendix III, p.68.

[3] Including £1.72 in allowances, e.g. school meals etc.

[4] Including £4.88 in allowances.

ings level, resultant net incomes may not effectively alleviate poverty, particularly when real income is eroded by subsequent price increases.

Experience in the United States and France indicates that a national minimum wage has only a short-term compressive effect on the national wage structure, occupational differentials restoring themselves in the longer term.

IV   HOUSING

IV.1   Housing Problems

Housing problems arise when the number of households requiring dwellings exceeds the number available; this causes sharing of accommodation and overcrowding. In 1966, 3 per cent of all dwellings in England and Wales were shared, i.e. 422,350; in five major conurbations (excluding Greater London) 25 per cent of dwellings were shared.[1] The age structure and movement of population create demands for different types of accommodation, and raises distributional problems of dwellings. The geographical distribution of dwellings may be unsuitable for the existing demand, and family cycles tend to render housing facilities unsuitable for long periods, with e.g. overcrowding followed by surplus accommodation capacity as children leave home. Housing problems are influenced by demographic, social, economic and occupational factors, such as changes in marriage and birth rates, changes in the level and distribution of personal incomes, changes in interest rates and budgetary policy, changes in public taste in relation to acceptable and desired housing standards. Greater difficulties in securing housing requirements are faced by low income unskilled households, by immigrants to an area, by small households of young and old and by large low-income families. The cost of accommodation, both private and public, and the methods of acquiring it create problems, and have important implications for the housing market. Private housing raises problems of securing mortgages for certain age groups, income groups and occupations, while long waiting periods on public housing lists, the cost of new housing and its geographical location raise financial and social problems for most age groups, especially the young married family and those households accustomed to paying low rents in older property. Slum clearance rehousing can remove households to peripheral urban areas far removed from places of employment, involving higher rents and transport costs.

The determination of housing shortage is not simple. The difference between the existing housing stock and the number of households as a measure of present and future housing shortage overlooks possible qualitative changes in acceptable housing standards which may make the existing housing stock socially and physically obsolescent. Changes in the rate of household formation and their size (whether due to changes in economic or other conditions) or shifts in social attitudes and personal income have important implications for both the demand and supply of housing facilities. For example, changes in the pattern of family life and leisure may arise from variations in the number and pattern of hours worked.

The distribution of housing between the public and the private sector raises economic and political problems. Government policies affect the public sector directly, e.g. through housing subsidies; and they affect the private sector through budgetary policy, interest

---

[1] *Royal Commission on Local Government in England,* 1969, vol. III, Research Appendix p. 61, Cmnd 4040-II, HMSO, 1969.

rates, etc. Increasing the proportion of owner-occupiers shifts the costs from the public to the private purse. Particular problems arise for owner-occupiers in properties situated in slum clearance areas due to discrepancies between market and site values of dwellings, and the fact that households may have invested life savings in their home.

Measures for improving and maintaining housing standards give rise to problems where the costs involved may not be recoverable from permitted increases in rents, due to rent restriction. Clearly, there is not one but a series of housing problems.

IV.2 Housing—Quantitative and Qualitative Aspects

Housing programmes must provide for the replacement of dwellings demolished under slum clearance schemes, make good the present housing shortage, and provide for future increases in the number and size of households. The upward trend in slum clearance over the past two decades seems likely to continue in the 1970s. Between 1960 and 1969 643,040 dwellings[1] were demolished or closed, and some 4.5 million pre-1880 dwellings will have to be replaced over the next decade. The present housing shortage is estimated at 700,000,[2] and between 1968 and 1981 an expected 1.6 million[3] increase in the number of households will add to housing demand. The target figure of 500,000 new houses per annum by 1970 laid down in the government's 1965-70 housing programme seems unlikely to be realised;[4] in 1969, for instance, only 378,324 new dwellings were completed in Great Britain. Table 5.14 indicates the numbers of private and public sector dwellings completed in the UK during the 1960-9 period. In 1959 private sector house-building in the UK exceeded that in the public sector for the first time during the postwar period. Depressed market demand resulting from financial constraints caused private sector house-building to fall below public sector building in 1967 and 1969 (see table 5.14).

The capacity of the construction industry is a major limitation on the rate of house-building. Between 1959 and 1968, annual output averaged 343,500 houses; in 1968 426,000 houses were built, an all-time record; industrialised methods, i.e. factory-built units, have helped to increase the provision of dwellings. The total number of such completed dwellings in England and Wales increased from 14.4 per cent to an estimated 37 per cent of all dwellings between 1964 and 1969; the cost per square foot of industrialised housing in England and Wales increased from £3.59 to £3.90 compared with a corresponding rise from £3.27 to £3.91 in traditionally built dwellings. Provisions also exist for improving older dwellings up to certain standards; for instance, 109,978 dwellings had improvement grants approved in 1969.[5] Grants are made for improvements in domestic amenities (e.g. baths and hot water supply) for dwellings providing at least ten years' further habitation.

Various standards for evaluating the suitability of dwellings for habitation have been devised in terms of physical structure, and/or amenities and/or living space. But several

---

[1] MHLG *Housing Statistics*, no. 16, February 1970, table 34.

[2] H. W. Richardson and Joan Vipond, *Housing in the 1970s, LBR*, April 1970.

[3] MHLG, table A, p.74.

[4] 'Current Trends in Housing Progress', *ET*, May 1968.

[5] See table 5.14.

TABLE 5.14

Housing Data, UK, 1960-9

	(1) No.	(2) No.	(3) No.	(4) No.	(5) No.	(6) £ million	(7) No.
1960	132,850	171,405	304,255	56,561	2889	73	48,013
1961	122,434	180,727	303,161	61,969	3795	76	47,945
1962	135,432	178,211	313,643	62,431	4404	78	41,768
1963	129,927	177,787	307,714	61,445	3673	80	42,701
1964	161,928	221,264	383,192	61,215	3817	83	45,050
1965	174,072	217,162	391,234	60,666	3590	93	40,100
1966	187,362	208,647	396,009	66,792	4906	98	39,960
1967	211,247	204,208	415,455	71,152	4867	110	46,606
1968	199,767	226,068	425,835	71,586	9979	129	46,178
1969	192,408	185,916	378,324	69,233	N.A.	N.A.	49,384

	(8) No.	(9) No.	(10) £	(11) £ million	(12) £ million	(13) £ million	(14) No.
1960	82,819	130,832	N.A.	558	78	N.A.	9,385
1961	79,831	127,776	N.A.	544	107	N.A.	4,676
1962	68,732	110,550	N.A.	618	94	118	3,524
1963	77,278	119,979	3195	852	119	107	3,806
1964	76,635	121,685	3433	1052	195	132	3,094
1965	82,893	122,993	3768	965	244	163	2,129
1966	67,760	107,720	4030	1245	134	147	1,678
1967	66,536	113,142	4283	1477	168	124	1,234
1968	68,038	114,216	4499	1587	108	168	657
1969	60,594	109,978	4819	1544	N.A.	181	N.A.

Sources: (1) MHLG, *Housing Statistics*, February 1970.
           (2) *N.I.B.B.* 1969.

Key

Column (1) = Permanent dwellings completed, UK Public Sector
Column (2) = Permanent dwellings completed, UK Private Sector
Column (3) = Permanent dwellings completed, UK Total
Column (4) = Total number of houses demolished or closed under slum clearance schemes, England
                  and Wales
Column (5) = Sales of local authority dwellings in England and Wales
Column (6) = Central government housing subsidies to local authorities (England and Wales)
Column (7) = Number of dwellings for which discretionary grants approved (England and Wales)
Column (8) = Number of dwellings for which standard grants approved (England and Wales)
Column (9) = Total number of dwellings for which improvements grants made ((7) plus (8))
Column (10) = Average price of new dwellings mortgaged by private owners (Great Britain)
Column (11) = Advances for house purchase made by building societies (UK)
Column (12) = Advances for house purchase made by local authorities (UK)
Column (13) = Advances for house purchase made by insurance companies (UK)
Column (14) = Building Society guarantees by local authorities in England and Wales

housing standards have been implemented by local authorities with little uniformity, and this has resulted in unsatisfactory evaluation of housing conditions. A government sample survey in 1966 indicated that qualitative housing problems were worse and that poor housing was geographically a more dispersed problem than previously thought. The 1957 Housing Act placed emphasis on the physical condition of a dwelling; and housing below the necessary standard of repair was to be considered unfit. The Act provides local authorities with little guidance on dwellings 'not reasonably suitable for occupation' and makes relative assessment difficult. Dwellings may be declared fit even though they have inadequate heating and sanitary arrangements. The *Standard Grant* standards, which are above Housing Act standards, are concerned with domestic facilities; thus grants are made for improvements in sanitary facilities. The *Housing (Financial Provisions)* Act 1958 laid down a twelve point standard, under which discretionary grants are given for improvement of dwellings having not less than thirty years' useful life. The Housing Act *Overcrowding* standard uses the maximum number of persons per square foot of living area as a criterion; the Census *Room* standard uses habitable rooms as a standard of fitness; while the Social Survey *Bedroom* standard attempts a more accurate evaluation of the density of occupation using a given number of bedrooms for each type of household. The Parker-Morris *Space* standard[1] defines fitness of a dwelling according to minimum floor areas per person (150 sq. ft. in houses, 320 sq. ft. in flats), and the availability of a garage. Qualitative improvements have occurred over the past twenty years. In 1951,[2] 52 per cent of households in Great Britain had exclusive use of basic domestic amenities; by 1966 the proportion had risen to 72.9 per cent. Over the same period, the estimated number of households without fixed baths decreased from 37 per cent to 15.4 per cent, and without water closets from 8 per cent to 1.8 per cent. Between 1961 and 1966 there was a drop in the number of households in shared dwellings up to six rooms.[2] Between 1961 and 1969, the number of new two-bedroom houses completed fell from 29.7 per cent to 19.2 per cent of total new housing, the number of three-bedroom houses completed increased from 62.6 per cent to 69.4 per cent; and the number of six-roomed dwellings occupied by householders increased from 15.8 per cent to 31.8 per cent. Nonetheless, quantitative and qualitative housing problems persist. Between 1961 and 1966 the number of households in shared dwellings increased from 2.3 million to 3.1 million; overcrowding problems are also much worse within underdeveloped regions than average figures suggest.

IV.3   Housing—Financial aspects

Financial aspects of housing relate to the cost of supplying new and improved older dwellings, the methods of financing both supply and demand, and the influence of government policies on the housing sector both directly, e.g. through legislated rent controls, or less directly through general economic policy, e.g. manipulation of Bank rate. The distribution of housing between rent-paying tenants and owner-occupiers poses immediate and future financial problems.

In 1966, of 15.3 million households, an estimated 47 per cent owned their own accommodation, 25 per cent rented accommodation from local authorities, and 23 per cent from private persons or companies.[3] It is expected that the trend to increased owner-occupation will continue; and sales of local authority dwellings increased during the 1960s (see table 5.14, Column 5). Between 1964 and 1967 the average cost of constructing three-bedroom houses for local authorities increased from £2,303 to £2,951 in England and Wales. Local authority building is heavily subsidised from both Central and local sources. Central govern-

---

[1]   *Homes for To-day and Tomorrow,* Parker-Morris Report, HMSO, 1964.

[2]   *Sample Census 1966,* Housing tables, Part I, HMSO, 1968.

[3]   *Ibid,* table 2.

ment housing subsidies increased throughout the 1960s (table 5.14, Column 6) and local authority subsidies increased from £31 million to £85 million per annum over the 1960-9 period. Discrepancies in the amount and distribution of government subsidies between local authorities arise because the various housing Acts have provided different subsidies for dwellings built at different periods, e.g. authorities not building new houses continue to receive subsidies for older dwellings built at a fraction of present day costs.[1] Local authorities administer funds for improvements in older dwellings under the *Housing Act 1969*. Discretionary Grants of half the estimated total costs of improvement up to a limit of £1,000 per dwelling are available to house owners to improve domestic amenities up to Twelve Point Standard or to convert old dwellings into more modern housing. Standard Grants, available as of right, award half the improvement costs actually incurred up to a limit. Special Grants available at the discretion of local authorities were introduced in England and Wales in 1969 for improving amenities in houses in multiple occupation. Table 5.14, columns 7-9, gives data for the 1960-9 period. The *1969 Housing Act* is intended to promote greater flexibility in dealing with housing improvements. The *Rent Act 1968* and Part II of the *Housing Act 1964* give local authorities powers to enforce improvements on defaulting landlords. Improvement in amenities is a criterion for granting rent increases to landlords. Table 5.14, column 10, indicates the rapid rise in the average price of new private sector dwellings in Great Britain—51 per cent between 1963 and 1969. Columns 11-13 show that the major source of finance for house purchasing is the building societies; in 1968, building societies lent 83 per cent of all advances for house purchase. Money loaned for house purchasing, i.e. a mortgage, is on the security of the property; the building society holds the title deeds until the mortgage is repaid, usually over a 20-25 year period. In 1968, 20.8 per cent of mortgages were repayable over 20 years, 54.7 per cent over 25 years. The cost of a mortgage is influenced by money market conditions since building societies compete with other financial institutions to secure loans; increases in general interest rates raise the charges to mortgagees.[2] Mortgages may be straight loans or may be combined with an endowment insurance policy; the latter method is likely to prove a less expensive one, since changing house does not always involve taking a complete new mortgage on which the higher interest charges of the early years of the loan have to be paid. Under the *Housing (Financial Provisions) Act 1958*, the local authorities in England and Wales may guarantee mortgage repayments to a building society; the number of such guarantees has dropped during the 1960s (table 5.14, column 14). The *House Purchase and Housing Act 1959* empowers local authorities to make up to 100 per cent mortgage advances to private persons. The *Housing Subsidies Act 1957* introduced an option mortgage scheme whereby the interest rate is 2 per cent below that on a normal mortgage, subject to a minimum rate of 4 per cent; mortgagees do not, however, benefit from the income tax deductions for interest payments allowed on normal mortgages. In the fourth quarter of 1969, 11.5 per cent of local authority loans were option mortgages. Difficulties in securing mortgages arise from the proportion of the house price for which advances are granted and the incomes of prospective mortgagees. In 1968, the average mortgage advanced was 75.5 per cent of the average house price for new dwellings and 71.1 per cent for old dwellings; the average recorded income of borrowers increased from £1,469 to £1,618 between 1966 and 1968. Building societies impose their own limits, related to borrowers' incomes, on sums advanced; borrowers must find the difference between the amount advanced and the dwelling price themselves. Housing associations also finance private house purchases; and advances received from local authorities increased

---

[1]   A. S. Merrett and A. Sykes, *Housing Finance and Development,* Longman Green & Co., 1965.

[2]   See chapter 1 p. 15 and chapter 2 p. 70.

from £1.34 million to £11.3 million between 1960 and 1969. Housing associations are particularly used by local authorities in slum clearance schemes.

The Rent Act 1968 consolidated previous legislation on rent controls in respect of e.g. house improvement rent adjustments. A fair rent for a privately rented unfurnished dwelling is determined with respect to its age, character, locality and state of repair. Rateable values of dwellings, assessed by the Inland Revenue Valuation Office, are determined by the rent a dwelling could have reasonably commanded in 1963. Fair rents are registered by the Rent Officer on application of landlord or tenant, or both; Rent Assessment Committees determine a fair rent in disputed cases.[1]

Rent control is related to the type of tenancy and changes in circumstances affecting a dwelling. A protected tenancy is one where a dwelling house is let as a separate dwelling unless its rateable value exceeds £400 in Greater London and £200 elsewhere. A tenancy is not protected if the rent is less than two-thirds of the rateable value on 23 March 1965 or if full board is included in the rent.[2] A controlled tenancy is one under which the rent payable is not less than two-thirds of the 1939 rateable value.[3] A regulated tenancy is a protected tenancy which is not a controlled tenancy (the Act also defines other types of tenancy to which rent control applies). For registered rents the limit is the rent so regulated; where not registered, the rent limit is that of the last previous tenant for the last rented period, or the rent payable under the agreement creating the tenancy.

Rent increases are possible when changes in rates occur, when the costs of services provided by the landlord have increased, or where improvements in amenities have been made.[4] For improvements effected after 5 July 1957, the rent limit under a controlled tenancy can be increased by a given percentage per annum of the amount spent on the improvements. Improvements effected before 24 March 1961 justify an 8 per cent increase, and after that date a 12 per cent rent increase. Where improvements grants are made, the actual amount spent on improvements minus the grant made, whether claimed or not, equals the amount on which rent increases are based. Street work improvements are admissible as improvement costs.

Between January 1966 and September 1969, 31 per cent of registered rents decreased, 9 per cent remained the same and 60 per cent increased.[5] Rent controls often deter private landlords, especially small scale private owners, from undertaking improvements since increased chargeable rent may offer insufficient compensation.

Average local authority weekly rents in England and Wales in 1968-9 were £1.72 for dwellings built before 1945, £2.06 for 1945-64 built dwellings and £2.49 for post-1964 built dwellings. Council tenants may apply for rent rebates under schemes operated by local authorities. No statutory obligation rests on local authorities but most have established schemes based on government guidelines.[6] Rent rebates are determined by the level of standard rent and the gross income of households applying. Standard rent is calculated by allocating the total required rent income over all an authority's dwellings with respect to their size, age, location and amenities; it averaged £2.25 per week in 1969.

---

[1] For data see MHLG, *Housing Statistics,* February 1970, table 57.

[2] Rent Act 1968, Part I, para. 2.

[3] *Ibid.*

[4] *Ibid.,* Part I, para 7(3).

[5] *Ibid.,* Part II, para. 21.

[6] *Rent Rebate Scheme,* Circular 46/67, MHLG, 1965.

Gross value may also be used as one basis. The tenant's assessed gross income from all sources before tax and benefits is then taken into account.

Under the *General Rating Act 1967*, all households not receiving supplementary benefit for rates are eligible for a local authority rebate if their gross income is less than £9 for single persons or £11 per week for a married couple, £2 allowance being made for each child. The rebate is normally two-thirds of the amount by which the rate bill exceeds £7.50 per annum. Consideration is also given to the number of related adult persons in a dwelling, reductions in rates being geared to the number of occupants. In 1968-9 rebates were received by 5.1 per cent of domestic hereditaments in England and Wales; the average rebate was £15.75 in 1967-8. Rate rebate schemes are a statutory obligation on local authorities, rent rebate schemes voluntary. An attempt has been made to extend the rent rebate schemes to privately owned rented dwellings. Insofar as rebates are related to rateable value, regions like Greater London will tend to give higher rebates than poorer regions. The level of household incomes by region will also determine the variations in amounts paid and the number of households eligible for rebate. Clearly housing market conditions and the level of personal incomes are likely to produce relative disparities between local authority areas.

REFERENCES AND FURTHER READING

D. J. Robertson and L. C. Hunter, *Economics of Wages and Labour*, Macmillan, London, 1969. Evidence given to the *Royal Commission on Trades Unions and Employers Associations* by

    (1) Professor E. H. Phelps Brown. Minutes of Evidence No. 38.
    (2) Professor D. J. Robertson. Minutes of Evidence No. 46.
    (3) Professor B. C. Roberts. Minutes of Evidence No. 33.
    (4) Professor K. W. Wedderburn. Minutes of Evidence No. 31.
    (5) Motor Industry Employers. Minutes of Evidence No. 23.
    (6) Professor Cyril Grunfeld. Minutes of Evidence No. 12.
    (7) Mobil Oil Company. Minutes of Evidence No. 49.
    (8) Esso Petroleum Company. Minutes of Evidence No. 48.
    (9) Institute of Personnel Management. Minutes of Evidence No. 40.

Post-Donovan Conferences, *Trades Union Congress*, London, 1968 and 1969.

ECE *Incomes in Post-war Europe; A Study of Policies, Growth and Distribution*, UN, 1967.

A. Flanders, *Collective Bargaining: Prescription for Change*, Faber and Faber, 1967.

O. Kahn-Freund 'Industrial Relations and the Law', *BJIR*, vol. VII., no. 3, November 1969.

B. J. McCormick and E. O. Smith (eds), *The Labour Market*, Penguin Books Ltd, 1968.

D. T. B. North and G. L. Buckingham, *Productivity Agreements and Wage Systems*, Gower Press, London, 1969.

Tony Cliff, *The Employers' Offensive; Productivity Deals and How to Fight Them*, Pluto Press, London, 1970.

Amelia Harris and Rosemary Clauson, *Labour Mobility in Britain 1953-63*, Government Social Survey, 1966.

M. Bosanquet, *Pay, Prices and Labour in Power*, Young Fabian Pamphlet No. 20, November 1969.

Arthur Seldon and Hamish Gray, *Universal or Selective Social Benefits*, Institute of Economic Affairs, Research Monograph No. 8.

H. A. Turner and H. Zoeteweij, *Prices, Wages and Incomes Policies in Industrialised Market Economies*, International Labour Office, 1966.

L. Needleman, *Economics of Housing*, Staples Press, 1965.

TABLE A-1

UK De Facto or Home Population[1] 1954-69 (Thousands)

Year	United Kingdom			England and Wales			Wales	Scotland			Northern Ireland		
	Total	Males	Females	Total	Males	Females	Total	Total	Males	Females	Total	Males	Females
Census Figures													
1951	50,225	24,118	26,107	43,758	21,016	22,742	2,599	5,096	2,434	2,662	1,371	668	703
1961	52,709	25,481	27,228	46,105	22,204	23,801	2,644	5,179	2,483	2,697	1,425	694	731
Sample Census													
1966	53,788	26,044	27,745	47,136	22,841	24,295	2,663	5,168	2,479	2,689	1,485	724	761
Mid-year Estimates													
1954	50,765	24,401	26,364	44,274	21,288	22,986	2,601	5,104	2,436	2,667	1,387	676	711
1955	50,946	24,509	26,437	44,441	21,389	23,052	2,603	5,111	2,441	2,670	1,394	679	715
1956	51,184	24,644	26,540	44,667	21,517	23,150	2,608	5,120	2,446	2,674	1,397	681	716
1957	51,430	24,777	26,653	44,907	21,648	23,259	2,611	5,125	2,448	2,677	1,398	681	717
1958	51,652	24,887	26,766	45,109	21,744	23,365	2,615	5,141	2,459	2,682	1,402	684	719
1959	51,957	25,043	26,913	45,386	21,885	23,501	2,622	5,163	2,472	2,690	1,408	686	722
1960	52,373	25,271	27,102	45,775	22,097	23,678	2,629	5,178	2,482	2,696	1,420	692	728
1961	52,816	25,534	27,282	46,205	22,353	23,852	2,635	5,184	2,485	2,699	1,427	696	732
1962	53,341	25,854	27,487	46,709	22,660	24,049	2,653	5,197	2,495	2,702	1,435	700	736
1963	53,678	26,038	27,640	47,028	22,834	24,194	2,663	5,205	2,499	2,705	1,446	705	741
1964	54,066	26,254	27,811	47,401	23,044	24,358	2,676	5,206	2,500	2,707	1,458	711	747
1965	54,435	26,440	27,995	47,763	23,227	24,536	2,693	5,204	2,497	2,707	1,469	716	753
1966	54,654	26,505	28,149	47,985	23,295	24,690	2,704	5,191	2,490	2,701	1,478	720	758
1967	54,978	26,681	28,298	48,301	23,465	24,836	2,713	5,187	2,489	2,698	1,491	727	764
1968	55,283	26,852	28,431	48,593	23,630	24,963	2,720	5,187	2,489	2,698	1,502	733	769
1969	55,534	26,984	28,550	48,827	23,752	25,075	n.a.	5,195	2,494	2,701	1,512	738	775

Source: A.A.S. No. 106; M.D.S. No. 285 (Sept., 1969); No. 290 (Feb. 1970).

Note: [1]   The de facto or home population relates to people actually in the country (excluding members of H. M. forces serving overseas, while including Commonwealth and foreign forces in the UK).

TABLE A-2

UK Gross Domestic Product, Expenditure (at 1963 prices) 1954-69 (£ million)

Year	Consumers' expenditure Durable goods	Consumers' expenditure Non-durable goods & services	Public authorities Current expenditure	Gross domestic capital formation excluding dwellings	Gross domestic capital formation dwellings	Value of physical increase in stocks and work in progress	Exports of goods and services	Total final expenditure at market prices	Adjustment to factor cost[1]	Imports of goods and services at factor cost	Gross domestic product at factor cost
1954	875[2]	14,597	4,952	2,382	810[2]	60	4,393	28,069	2,516	4,151	21,402
1955	965[2]	15,138	4,801	2,614	758[2]	346	4,664	29,285	2,617	4,569	22,099
1956	849[2]	15,387	4,761	2,811	715[2]	270	4,868	29,661	2,605	4,582	22,474
1957	952[2]	15,629	4,687	3,031	683[2]	277	4,992	30,251	2,664	4,697	22,890
1958	1,113	15,895	4,572	3,093	644	107	4,911	30,335	2,881	4,753	22,701
1959	1,328	16,408	4,668	3,283	742	186	5,045	31,660	3,122	5,062	23,476
1960	1,370	17,048	4,770	3,584	834	632	5,329	33,567	3,285	5,669	24,613
1961	1,334	17,512	4,945	3,952	895	337	5,487	34,462	3,342	5,628	25,492
1962	1,411	17,847	5,100	3,905	924	80	5,578	34,845	3,346	5,736	25,763
1963	1,703	18,422	5,184	3,972	944	219	5,815	36,259	3,487	5,946	26,826
1964	1,865	18,954	5,272	4,542	1,175	642	6,027	38,477	3,752	6,501	28,224
1965	1,842	19,335	5,420	4,751	1,198	400	6,315	39,261	3,755	6,545	28,961
1966	1,821	19,809	5,561	4,899	1,206	241	6,555	40,092	3,871	6,697	29,524
1967	1,908	20,166	5,853	5,204	1,304	169	6,560	41,164	4,026	7,098	30,040
1968	1,977	20,564	5,873	5,472	1,363	155	7,356	42,760	4,217	7,602	30,941
1969	1,818	20,802	5,815	5,387	1,235	311	7,968	43,336	4,245	7,767	31,324

Sources: NIBB various; *Preliminary Estimates of National Income and Balance of Payments, 1964-69,* Cmnd 4328; April 1970.

Notes: 1   This represents taxes on expenditure, less subsidies, valued at 1963 prices.

2   These figures were not available at 1963 prices and were calculated from 1958 price data.

TABLE A-3

UK Personal Income, Expenditure and Saving 1954-69

PERSONAL INCOME BEFORE TAX

Year	Wages and Salaries £m	Forces[1] pay £m	Employers[1] contribu- tions £m	Current grants from public author- ities[1] £m	Other personal income[2] £m	Total £m	Transfers (net) and taxes paid abroad £m	UK taxes on income (pay- ments) £m
1954	9,310	363	611	1,021	3,038	14,343	−4	1,236
1955	10,210	356	678	1,115	3,212	15,571	9	1,330
1956	11,120	396	746	1,193	3,283	16,738	26	1,452
1957	11,770	392	806	1,252	3,432	17,652	28	1,602
1958	12,135	395	940	1,407	3,647	18,524	7	1,696
1959	12,725	389	993	1,555	3,968	19,630	11	1,776
1960	13,735	393	1,046	1,569	4,415	21,158	9	1,991
1961	14,855	385	1,167	1,712	4,765	22,884	7	2,249
1962	15,640	401	1,266	1,885	4,933	24,125	14	2,458
1963	16,390	419	1,382	2,133	5,279	25,603	33	2,510
1964	17,750	450	1,503	2,257	5,712	27,672	42	2,801
1965	19,085	467	1,709	2,604	6,214	30,079	52	3,344
1966	20,325	523	1,893	2,834	6,485	32,060	71	3,733
1967	21,055	524	2,042	3,199	6,872	33,692	83	4,109
1968	22,480	542	2,282	3,685	7,208	36,197	102	4,624
1969	24,135	543	2,431	3,938	7,444	38,491	109	5,173

Sources: *NIBB*, 1969; *Preliminary Estimates of National Income and Balance of Payments*, 1964-69, Cmnd 4328; April 1970; *E.T.*, April 1970.

Notes: [1]   Figures since 1958 revised to exclude the net cost to public authorities of school milk and welfare foods provided free or at subsidised prices. This is now included in public authorities' current expenditure on goods and services.

[2]   Before providing for depreciation and stock appreciation.

[3]   Before providing for additions to tax reserves.

National insurance and health contributions £m	Total personal disposable income £m	CONSUMERS' EXPENDITURE				PERSONAL SAVINGS[3]		
		Durable goods		Other	Total			
		Amount £m	As % of P.D.I.	Amount £m	£m	£m	As % of P.D.I.	Year
532	12,579	837	6.65	11,327	12,164	415	3.25	1954
594	13,638	934	6.85	12,179	13,113	525	3.86	1955
642	14,618	884	6.05	12,945	13,829	789	5.40	1956
657	15,365	1,005	6.54	13,594	14,599	766	4.99	1957
859	15,962	1,175	7.36	14,121	15,296	666	4.17	1958
897	16,946	1,379	8.13	14,727	16,106	840	4.96	1959
913	18,245	1,420	7.78	15,489	16,909	1,336	7.32	1960
1,072	19,556	1,388	7.10	16,422	17,810	1,746	8.92	1961
1,197	20,456	1,476	7.22	17,430	18,906	1,550	7.57	1962
1,303	21,757	1,703	7.83	18,422	20,125	1,632	7.50	1963
1,444	23,385	1,883	8.05	19,610	21,493	1,892	8.09	1964
1,685	24,998	1,894	7.58	20,971	22,865	2,133	8.53	1965
1,804	26,452	1,894	7.16	22,389	24,238	2,214	8.37	1966
1,909	27,591	2,025	7.34	23,332	25,357	2,234	8.10	1967
2,167	29,304	2,196	7.56	24,874	27,070	2,234	7.62	1968
2,249	30,960	2,098	6.78	26,492	28,590	2,370	7.66	1969

TABLE A-4

Great Britain, Working Population, Unemployment etc. 1954-69 (Thousands)

Year	Total working population[1]	Total in civil employment	Estimated number of employees[2]	H.M. Forces and Women's Services	Registered unemployed	Wholly unemployed excluding school leavers[3]	Unfilled vacancies	Unemployment rate[4] (PER CENT)
	(AT JUNE IN EACH YEAR)				(MONTHLY AVERAGES)			
1954	23,725	22,662	21,190	845	285	266	329	1.3
1955	23,969	22,990	21,460	809	232	209	405	1.1
1956	24,156	23,200	21,700	767	257	226	357	1.2
1957	24,246	23,291	21,850	708	313	289	276	1.4
1958	24,117	23,129	21,820	620	457	402	198	2.1
1959	24,196	23,242	21,944	569	475	433	223	2.2
1960	24,526	23,711	22,326	518	360	337	314	1.6
1961	24,773	24,044	22,628	474	341	305	320	1.5
1962	25,046	24,232	22,944	442	463	419	214	2.0
1963	25,138	24,250	28,064	427	573	502	196	2.5
1964	25,268	24,527	23,209	424	381	362	317	1.6
1965	25,463	24,770	23,417	423	329	308	384	1.4
1966	25,583	24,913	23,554	417	360	323	371	1.5
1967	25,391	24,509	23,294	417	560	512	250	2.4
1968	25,233	24,326	23,151	400	564	541	271	2.4
1969[5]	25,144	24,281	23,083	380	559	535	285	2.4

Sources: *MDS* No. 287, (November 1969); No. 291 (March 1970): *EPG* November 1969, February 1970.

Notes:

1 The total working population represents the total number of persons aged 15 and over who work for pay or gain or who register themselves as available for such work. Part-time workers are treated as equivalent to whole-time workers. Most, if not all, persons registered as temporarily unemployed are on the payrolls of employers and are included in the number in civil employment. To avoid duplication, therefore, the total working population is obtained by adding together the figures for H.M. Forces and Women's Services, men and women on release leave, the total in civil employment and registered wholly unemployed; registered temporarily stopped are omitted from the addition.

2 The figures relate to the total number of employees insurable under the National Insurance scheme. They represent the number of employed persons aged 15 and over who work for pay or gain or register themselves available for such work. Part-time workers are counted as equivalent to whole-time workers. In 1965 the Ministry of Labour reverted to the pre-1959 method of estimation. The figures for 1959-64 have been recalculated on the old basis.

3 As these figures are monthly averages they cannot be simply compared with series taken at June each year.

4 The unemployment rate is the number of registered unemployed expressed as a percentage of the estimated number of employees.

5 Figures of . . .

TABLE A-5A

UK Currency Circulation, Clearing Bank Deposits and Consols Yield 1954-69

Year	Estimated currency in circulation with public (average) £m	London clearing banks' gross deposits (average of monthly figures) £m	2½% Consols–Gross flat yield % (Average of working days)
1954	1,551	6,495	3.75
1955	1,657	6,454	4.17
1956	1,765	6,288	4.73
1957	1,842	6,432	4.98
1958	1,905	6,636	4.98
1959	1,969	6,935	4.82
1960	2,062	7,236	5.42
1961	2,151	7,395[1]	6.20
1962	2,161	7,611	5.98
1963	2,210	7,971	5.58
1964	2,332	8,550	6.03
1965	2,483	8,989	6.42
1966	2,637	9,376[2]	6.80
1967	2,700	9,772	6.69
1968	2,838	10,431	7.39
1969	2,914	10,610	8.88

Sources: FS, November, 1969 and March, 1970.

Notes: [1] Excluding the business of Lloyds Bank Eastern branches after December, 1960
[2] Excluding the Irish business of the National Bank after March, 1966

TABLE A-5B

UK Bank Rate Changes 1954-69

Date of change	New rate %	Date of change	New rate %
1954 May 13	3	1962 March 8	5½
1955 Jan. 27	3½	1962 March 22	5
1955 Feb. 24	4½	1962 Apr. 26	4½
1956 Feb. 16	5½	1963 Jan. 3	4
1957 Feb. 7	5	1964 Feb. 27	5
1957 Sept. 19	7	1964 Nov. 23	7
1958 Mar. 20	6	1965 June 3	6
1958 May 22	5½	1966 July 14	7
1958 June 19	5	1967 Jan. 26	6½
1958 Aug. 14	4½	1967 Mar. 16	6
1958 Nov. 20	4	1967 May 4	5½
1960 Jan. 21	5	1967 Oct. 19	6
1960 June 23	6	1967 Nov. 9	6½
1960 Oct. 27	5½	1967 Nov. 19	8
1960 Dec. 8	5	1968 Mar. 21	7½
1961 July 26	7	1968 Sept. 19	7
1961 Oct. 5	6½	1969 Feb. 27	8
1961 Nov. 2	6	1970 Mar. 5	7½

Sources: FS, November, 1969 and March, 1970

TABLE A-6

UK Public Sector: Current Account 1954-68 (£ million)

Year	1954	1955	1956	1957	1958
RECEIPTS					
TAXES ON INCOME	2,110	2,287	2,334	2,570	2,704
TAXES ON EXPENDITURE					
Central government	2,041	2,177	2,271	2,351	2,390
Local authorities[1]	460	475	556	615	650
NATIONAL INSURANCE AND HEALTH CONTRIBUTIONS	532	594	642	657	859
GROSS TRADING INCOME					
Central government & local authorities	108	112	122	128	155
Public corporations	354	315	345	323	340
GROSS RENTAL INCOME	244	261	297	330	365
INTEREST AND DIVIDENDS etc.					
Central government	51	73	81	68	77
Local authorities	17	19	22	26	28
Public corporations	23	31	32	38	35
GRANTS FROM ABROAD	50	46	26	21	3
TOTAL	5,990	6,390	6,728	7,127	7,606
EXPENDITURE					
Current Expenditure on Goods and Services[2]	3,113	3,171	3,428	3,585	3,750
Subsidies	422	350	359	407	385
Current Grants to Persons	1,021	1,115	1,193	1,252	1,407
Current Grants Paid Abroad	65	70	73	75	77
TOTAL CURRENT EXPENDITURE EXCLUDING DEBT INTEREST	4,621	4,706	5,053	5,319	5,619
Debt Interest:					
Central government	637	708	723	705	780
Local authorities	54	62	79	101	117
Public corporations	127	137	126	144	149
TOTAL CURRENT EXPENDITURE	5,439	5,613	5,981	6,269	6,665
CURRENT SURPLUS[3]	551	777	747	858	941
TOTAL	5,990	6,390	6,728	7,127	7,606

Sources: *NIBB* 1965 and 1969

Notes: [1]   Rates

      [2]   Excluding current expenditure on goods and services on operating account of public corporations and other public enterprises.

      [3]   Before providing for depreciation and stock appreciation and additions to tax and interest reserves.

1959	1960	1961	1962	1963	1964	1965	1966	1967	1968
2,747	2,713	3,066	3,447	3,379	3,522	4,021	4,419	5,083	5,632
2,486	2,620	2,812	2,980	3,033	3,359	3,758	4,237	4,529	5,392
714	771	831	916	1,014	1,096	1,228	1,374	1,473	1,568
897	913	1,072	1,197	1,303	1,444	1,685	1,804	1,909	2,167
164	179	96	71	78	91	96	87	92	111
391	539	645	751	846	931	995	1,049	1,139	1,352
398	437	485	521	549	597	670	745	804	886
94	78	95	121	97	100	124	134	133	118
34	37	40	48	52	59	70	84	89	93
38	46	50	51	37	41	50	56	58	61
–	–	–	–	–	–	–	–	–	–
7,963	8,333	9,192	10,103	10,388	11,240	12,697	13,989	15,309	17,380
4,001	4,248	4,589	4,920	5,184	5,512	6,043	6,572	7,246	7,702
369	487	586	600	560	510	564	556	791	886
1,555	1,569	1,712	1,885	2,133	2,257	2,604	2,834	3,202	3,687
82	94	118	121	132	163	177	180	188	178
6,007	6,398	7,005	7,526	8,009	8,442	9,388	10,142	11,427	12,453
774	861	897	878	934	942	973	1,043	1,113	1,249
139	164	211	240	269	320	380	429	468	543
159	154	162	170	94	105	119	107	155	123
7,079	7,577	8,275	8,814	9,306	9,809	10,680	11,721	13,163	14,368
884	756	917	1,289	1,082	1,431	1,837	2,268	2,146	3,012
7,963	8,333	9,192	10,103	10,388	11,240	12,697	13,989	15,309	17,380

TABLE A-7

UK Balance of Payments, 1954-69   (£ million)

| | CURRENT ACCOUNT | | | | | | | LONG TERM CAPITAL ACCOUNT[1] | | | | | | | |
| | Visible Trade | | Visible balance[2,3] | Invisible Trade | | | Current balance | Official Capital (net) | Private Investment (net) | | | Balance of long term capital | Balance of current and long-term capital transactions | Balancing item | Balance of Monetary movements[1,4] |
Year	Imports[3] (f.o.b.)	Exports and re-exports[2] (f.o.b.)		Government military	other	Private			Abroad	In the UK	Total				
1954	2,989	2,785	−204	−60	−71	+452	+117	−28	−238	+75	−163	−191	−74	+57	+17
1955	3,386	3,073	−313	−67	−71	+296	−155	−62	−182	+122	−60	−122	−277	+121	+156
1956	3,324	3,377	+53	−101	−74	+330	+208	−68	−258	+139	−119	−187	+21	+42	−63
1957	3,538	3,509	−29	−61	−83	+406	+233	+66	−298	+126	−172	−106	+127	+80	−207
1958	3,377	3,406	+29	−126	−93	+534	+344	−50	−310	+164	−146	−196	+148	+67	−215
1959	3,639	3,522	−117	−129	−98	+487	+143	−124	−303	+172	−131	−255	−112	−22	+134
1960	4,138	3,732	−406	−172	−110	+423	−265	−103	−322	+233	−89	−192	−457	+299	+158
1961	4,043	3,891	−152	−198	−134	+480	−4	−45	−313	+426	+113	+68	+64	−25	−39
1962	4,095	3,993	−102	−224	−136	+574	+112	−104	−242	+248	+6	−98	+14	+75	−89
1963	4,362	4,282	−80	−237	−145	+576	+114	−105	−320	+276	−44	−149	−35	−72	+107
1964	5,005	4,486	−519	−268	−164	+558	−393	−116	−399	+161	−238	−354	−747	−15	+762
1965	5,054	4,817	−237	−268	−179	+603	−81	−85	−354	+242	−112	−197	−278	+31	+247
1966	5,255	5,182	−73	−282	−188	+583	+40	−80	−304	+277	−27	−107	−67	−37	+104
1967	5,674	5,122	−552	−267	−197	+694	−322	−57	−463	+381	−82	−139	−461	+227	+234
1968	6,916	6,273	−643	−267	−195	+796	−309	+21	−732	+622	−110	−89	−398	−145	+543
1969	7,214	7,056	−158	−266	−191	+981	+366	−95	−593	+709	+116	+21	+387	+182	−569

Sources: UK Balance of Payments 1969; Preliminary Estimates of National Income and Balance of Payments, 1964-69, Cmnd. 4328; April, 1970; ET March, 1970.

Notes: Assets: − increase/+ decrease.   Liabilities: + increase/− decrease.

1   Assets: − increase/+ decrease.   Liabilities: + increase/− decrease.
2   Including allowance for net under-recording of exports.
3   Including payments for US military aircraft and missiles.
4   Excluding certain adjustments made as a consequence of devaluation.

TABLE A-8

UK Reserves, Net Liabilities and Overseas Holdings in Sterling 1954-69 (End of period) £ million

External Liabilities (net) and/or overseas holdings in sterling[1]

Year	Gold and convertible currency reserves	Total		International organisations		Sterling area countries		Non-sterling countries	
		External liabilities in sterling (net)	Overseas sterling holdings	Excluding International Monetary Fund	I.M.F.	External liabilities in sterling (net)	Overseas sterlings holdings	External liabilities in sterling (net)[2]	Overseas sterling holdings
1954	986	—	4,179	96	380	—	2,822	—	881
1955	757	—	4,045	89	380	—	2,764	—	812
1956	799	—	4,091	87	582	—	2,730	—	692
1957	812	—	3,918	62	583	—	2,608	—	665
1958	1,096	—	3,976	49	574	—	2,519	—	834
1959	977	—	4,212	32	673	—	2,704	—	803
1960	1,154	—	4,432	27	522	—	2,478	—	1,405
1961	1,185	—	4,504	62	896	—	2,631	—	915
1962	1,002	3,769	4,106	89	517	2,430	2,675	733	826
1963	949	3,889	—	105	522	2,592	—	670	—
1964	827	4,296	—	110	881	2,591	—	714	—
1965	1,073	4,849	—	104	1,377	2,593	—	775	—
1966	1,107	5,135	—	117	1,538	2,595	—	885	—
1967	1,123	5,324	—	101	1,439[2]	2,448	—	1,336	—
1968	1,009	6,019	—	117	1,965[2]	2,311	—	1,626	—
1969	1,053	5,415	—	173	1,950[2]	2,526	—	766	—

Sources: *ET*, March, 1970; *UK Balance of Payments*, 1969.

Notes: 1 At the end of 1962 the series 'UK external liabilities and claims in sterling replaced the series' overseas sterling holdings'.

2 Includes increase in liabilities resulting from revaluation payments at the time of devaluation.

TABLE A-9

UK External Trade[1]   1954-69

| | Value of the external trade of the UK (£m.)[2] | | | | | Volume Index Numbers 1961 = 100[2] | | | | Unit value index numbers 1961 = 100[2] | | | | |
| | Imports (c.i.f.)[3] | | Exports (f.o.b.)[4] | | | Imports | | Exports | | Imports | | Exports | | |
Year	Total	Manufactures	Total	Manufactures	Re-exports (f.o.b.)	Total (weight = 1000)	Manufactures (weight = 337)	Total (weight = 1000)	Manufactures (weight = 843)	Total (weight = 1000)	Manufactures (weight = 337)	Total (weight = 1000)	Manufactures (weight = 843)	Terms of Trade[5]
1954	3,359	679	2,650	2,107	98	73	50	82	79	104	98	91	89	87
1955	3,936	971	2,957	2,392	116	80	62	87	85	108	106	92	90	86
1956	3,944	984	3,226	2,638	143	80	62	91	91	110	107	95	93	87
1957	4,139	1,012	3,374	2,776	130	83	66	93	93	111	100	100	96	89
1958	3,834	978	3,250	2,714	142	84	67	89	89	103	96	99	97	96
1959	4,087	1,127	3,422	2,876	131	90	76	93	92	102	98	98	97	96
1960	4,655	1,523	3,648	3,059	142	101	100	97	97	102	101	100	99	97
1961	4,547	1,531	3,796	3,199	158	100	100	100	100	100	100	100	100	100
1962	4,627	1,556	3,905	3,270	157	103	103	102	101	99	99	101	102	102
1963	4,984	1,702	4,211	3,499	154	107	112	108	107	103	101	104	104	101
1964	5,696	2,160	4,411	3,695	154	119	136	111	111	107	105	106	106	99
1965	5,752	2,254	4,728	3,997	173	120	137	116	117	107	109	109	109	102
1966	5,947	2,471	5,047	4,278	194	122	146	121	121	109	114	113	114	104
1967	6,434	2,844	5,029	4,274	185	132	168	119	119	109	116	114	116	105
1968	7,890	3,772	6,182	5,285	220	146	195	136	136	121	135	123	126	102
1969	8,323	4,136	7,039	6,092	259	149	207	153	138	126	142	127	130	101

Sources: *R.O.T.* October 1969, *Board of Trade Journal*, No. 3805, 18th February 1970.

Notes:

1   This table is based on revised figures first appearing in *ROT* March 1966. These differ from earlier figures because of (a) revised estimates for parcel post and (b) the inclusion of figures for trade in precious stones and pearls.

2   Excludes imports and re-exports of spares for foreign registered and owned aircraft on international air services from January 1968. It is estimated that in 1967 imports were £14m and re-exports £9m.

3   The import figures differ from those in Table A-7 because of the inclusion of charges for insurance and freight. Apart from this both series will differ because of certain adjustments made for valuation and coverage. A further explanation is to be seen in the 1967 *UK Balance of Payments*.

4   Including repayment of lend-lease silver to the USA valued at £22.4m for 1956 and £7.1m for 1957.

5   Export unit value index

TABLE A-10

Productivity in UK 1954-69: Index numbers 1963 = 100

| Year | Output per person employed | | Output per man hour worked |
	Gross domestic Product	Total industrial production	Manufacturing
1954[1]	84	83	78
1955[1]	86	84	82
1956[1]	86	84	81
1957[1]	88	86	83
1958[1]	89	86	84
1959	92	90	88
1960	95	94	92
1961	96	94	92
1962	97	96	95
1963	100	100	100
1964	105	107	105
1965	106	108	110
1966	108	110	113
1967	111	114	117
1968	116	122	125
1969	119[2]	126	129

Sources: *NIER* Feb, 1970 and May, 1970.

Notes: [1]   Figures for these years were not directly available on the basis of 1963 = 100 and have been calculated from 1958 = 100 data.

[2]   Provisional.

TABLE A-11

UK Prices 1954-69 Index numbers 1963 = 100

Year	Retail prices	Consumer goods and services							
		Total	Food	Drink tobacco	Housing (incl. rent and rates)	Durable goods	Clothing	All other goods	Services
1954[1]	76.3	78.2	81.0	82.3	61.0	95.7	88.8	77.1	71.5
1955[1]	79.8	81.0	85.9	82.8	63.0	96.9	89.1	80.1	74.3
1956[1]	83.8	84.7	89.5	85.6	65.2	104.1	91.1	85.0	79.4
1957[1]	86.9	87.5	91.5	87.8	69.5	105.6	92.6	88.6	83.0
1958	89.5	89.9	92.8	89.6	77.4	105.6	93.4	90.7	85.9
1959	90.1	90.8	94.0	87.8	81.6	103.8	92.9	90.8	87.7
1960	91.0	91.8	93.6	89.2	84.0	103.7	94.1	91.4	91.6
1961	94.0	94.5	95.0	93.3	87.9	104.1	95.7	94.9	95.1
1962	98.0	98.2	98.3	98.7	93.6	104.6	98.5	98.4	97.5
1963	100.0	100.0	100.0	100.0	100.0	100.0	100.0	100.0	100.0
1964	103.3	103.3	102.7	105.4	106.7	101.0	101.5	102.9	102.9
1965	108.2	108.0	106.3	115.8	113.7	102.8	103.7	107.1	107.4
1966	112.4	112.1	109.6	119.3	121.0	104.0	106.4	110.8	112.9
1967	115.2	114.9	111.8	120.8	125.2	106.1	107.9	113.2	117.8
1968	120.7	120.1	115.2	125.5	129.9	111.1	109.6	121.1	124.9
1969	127.2	126.4	121.5	135.2	136.9	115.4	113.9	126.6	130.9

Source: NIER Feb, 1970 and May, 1970.

Note: [1] Figures for these years were not available at 1963 prices and were calculated from 1958 price data.

TABLE A-12

Wages Rates, Earnings and Salaries in UK 1954-69.   1955 = 100

Year	All manual workers[1]			
	Weekly rates of wages	Hourly rates of wages	Average weekly earnings	Average salary earnings[2]
1954	93.7	93.6	91.5	–
1955	100.0	100.0	100.0	100.0
1956	107.9	108.0	108.0	107.3
1957	113.4	113.6	113.0	114.8
1958	117.5	117.9	116.9	118.5
1959	120.6	121.1	122.2	126.3
1960	123.7	126.3	130.1	133.4
1961	128.8	134.3	138.0	139.9
1962	133.6	140.5	142.9	147.7
1963	138.4	145.7	148.9	155.8
1964	144.9	153.2	161.8	164.5
1965	151.2	162.9	174.8	178.4
1966	158.3	173.7	185.0	186.1
1967	164.2	180.8	192.3	194.7
1968	175.1	193.1	208.1	206.9
1969	184.3	203.5	224.4	222.9

Source: EPG March, 1970

Notes: [1]   The indices of rates of wages refer to manual workers in all industries and services but those for average weekly earnings cover only those included in the Department of Employment and Productivity half yearly earnings enquiries.

[2]   October in each year.

Index

Index